Shepherds and Demons

Knut Holter
General Editor

Vol. 6

PETER LANG
New York • Washington, D.C./Baltimore • Bern
Frankfurt am Main • Berlin • Brussels • Vienna • Oxford

Hans Austnaberg

Shepherds and Demons

A Study of Exorcism as Practised by and Understood by Shepherds in the Malagasy Lutheran Church

PETER LANG
New York • Washington, D.C./Baltimore • Bern
Frankfurt am Main • Berlin • Brussels • Vienna • Oxford

Library of Congress Cataloging-in-Publication Data

Austnaberg, Hans.
Shepherds and demons: a study of exorcism as practised by
and understood by shepherds in the Malagasy Lutheran Church / Hans Austnaberg.
p. cm. — (Bible and theology in Africa; v. 6)
Includes bibliographical references and index.
1. Exorcism—Madagascar. 2. Fiangonana Loterana Malagasy.
3. Madagascar—Religious life and customs. I. Title.
BX8063.M28A97   264'.041099409691—dc22   2007000751
ISBN 978-0-8204-9717-4
ISSN 1525-9846

Bibliographic information published by **Die Deutsche Bibliothek**.
ie Deutsche Bibliothek lists this publication in the "Deutsche
Nationalbibliografie"; detailed bibliographic data is available
on the Internet at http://dnb.ddb.de/.

The paper in this book meets the guidelines for permanence and durability
of the Committee on Production Guidelines for Book Longevity
of the Council of Library Resources.

© 2008 Peter Lang Publishing, Inc., New York
29 Broadway, 18th floor, New York, NY 10006
www.peterlang.com

All rights reserved.
Reprint or reproduction, even partially, in all forms such as microfilm,
xerography, microfiche, microcard, and offset strictly prohibited.

Printed in Germany

To Liv Helga
    for her patience and support

Table of contents

List of Figures and Tables xiii

Acknowledgments xv

List of Acronyms and Abbreviations xvii

1	Introduction 1
1.1	Problem and delimitation 1
1.2	Background and motivation 9
1.3	Sources and methodology 13
	1.3.1 Research population and field material 14
	1.3.1.1 Qualitative methods 14
	1.3.1.2 Research population and production of field material 16
	1.3.1.3 Clarification of the field material 23
	1.3.2 Written sources and previous research 25
	1.3.3 Interpretation and writing 29
	1.3.3.1 Hermeneutics 29
	1.3.3.2 Levels and contexts of interpretation 31
	1.3.3.3 Comments on the text of the book 36
1.4	Outline of the book 37

2	The setting of exorcism: Historical roots and essential characteristics of the *Fifohazana* 41
2.1	A brief sketch of the historical roots of the *Fifohazana* 41
	2.1.1 The historical development...42
	2.1.2 Handling differences: "Unity in spite of diversity" 46
	2.1.3 *Mama* Nenilava..49
	2.1.3.1 Childhood, calling and instruction for ministry 49
	2.1.3.2 Extension of the Nenilava-movement 53

2.2	**Essential characteristics of the *Fifohazana***		**55**
2.2.1	The movement as a whole		55
2.2.2	Calling, instruction and consecration of shepherds		58
	2.2.2.1	Calling	58
	2.2.2.2	Instruction	61
	2.2.2.3	Consecration	64
2.2.3	The shepherds' life and conduct		68
2.2.4	Shepherds and pastors		72
2.2.5	Elements in the shepherds' view of demons		76
2.2.6	Shepherds and traditional healers		84
2.2.7	The shepherds' terminology related to demons and exorcism		87
2.3	**Summary**		**94**
3	**Elements in a healing service**		**97**
3.1	**Prayer, singing and preaching**		**100**
3.1.1	Prayer		100
3.1.2	Singing		103
3.1.3	Preaching		106
	3.1.3.1	Repentance to faith	109
	3.1.3.2	The devil and Jesus	109
	3.1.3.3	The Christian life	110
3.2	**Expulsion of demons**		**111**
3.2.1	Preparation		112
	3.2.1.1	The congregation's preparation and organisation of people in need of exorcism	112
	3.2.1.2	The shepherds' preparation	114
3.2.2	Scripture reading		115
3.2.3	Expelling demons		118
	3.2.3.1	Dress and equipment during exorcism	118
	3.2.3.2	Initial casting out of demons	119
	3.2.3.3	The shepherds' concentration on the patients at the front of the church	120
	3.2.3.4	The shepherds' movements	121
	3.2.3.5	The shepherds' words	123
	3.2.3.6	Dialogue with evil spirits	126
	3.2.3.7	The atmosphere	127
	3.2.3.8	Observable reactions	128
	3.2.3.9	Shepherds and pastors on the first bench	132
	3.2.3.10	Duration and organisation	133

3.3		**Prayer with the laying on of hands/"strengthening"**	**135**
	3.3.1	Who are prayed for?	135
	3.3.2	How is the "strengthening" organised?	137
	3.3.3	The content of the "strengthening"	138
	3.3.4	Specific traits and importance of this session	140
	3.3.5	The closing of the healing service	141
3.4		**Summary**	**142**
4		**The shepherds' understanding of their practice**	**145**
4.1		**The wider contexts of exorcism: traditional Malagasy culture and biblical message**	**145**
	4.1.1	Traditional Malagasy culture	147
	4.1.1.1	Traditional Malagasy universe of spirits and forces	149
	4.1.1.2	The relation between humans and spirits/forces	153
	4.1.1.3	Traditional Malagasy conception of sickness and healing	164
	4.1.2	Biblical message	172
	4.1.2.1	The concept of God	175
	4.1.2.2	Rebellion against God	176
	4.1.2.3	Cosmic battle	178
	4.1.2.4	Battleground	183
	4.1.2.5	The cross of Jesus	187
	4.1.3	Summary	189
4.2		**The closer context of exorcism: Christian teaching and God's word**	**191**
	4.2.1	Exorcism in the framework of Christian teaching	191
	4.2.1.1	Public teaching	191
	4.2.1.2	Consultations	193
	4.2.1.3	Training of shepherds	195
	4.2.1.4	The purpose of exorcism	196
	4.2.2	The use of the Bible in the shepherds' practice	199
	4.2.2.1	Frequently used biblical passages	200
	4.2.2.2	Biblical basis	201
	4.2.2.3	The shepherds' use of biblical passages	202
	4.2.3	Summary	204
4.3		**People in need of exorcism**	**205**
	4.3.1	Identifying the "assaulted by demons"	205
	4.3.1.1	Reported signs of demonic oppression: classification and numbers	206
	4.3.1.2	The shepherds' understanding of signs	213
	4.3.1.3	Other means of identification	220

4.3.2		What causes people to be in need of exorcism?	227
	4.3.2.1	Idol worship	229
	4.3.2.2	Other causes	234
	4.3.2.3	"God's program"	239
4.3.3		Exorcism of Christians	241
	4.3.3.1	Terminology	242
	4.3.3.2	Committed Christians may become "assaulted by demons"	242
	4.3.3.3	Jesus has power to protect his children	244
	4.3.3.4	How do shepherds explain exorcism of Christians?	245
4.3.4		Distribution of gender related to exorcism	246
4.3.5		Summary	250
4.4		**Expelling demons and related issues**	**251**
4.4.1		Addressing the demons in general and casting out of individuals	251
4.4.2		The shepherds' movements and their loud voices	256
4.4.3		What do the shepherds expel?	259
	4.4.3.1	Naming human conditions/attitudes	259
	4.4.3.2	The shepherds' reasons for expelling undesirable human conditions/attitudes	261
	4.4.3.3	Relationship between human conditions/attitudes and evil spirits	263
4.4.4		Understanding of the dress	264
4.4.5		Use of water while expelling demons: a controversial issue	267
4.4.6		Summary	270
4.5		**Exorcism as healing**	**271**
4.5.1		Sickness and exorcism	271
	4.5.1.1	Bodily, mental and spiritual sickness: terminological considerations	272
	4.5.1.2	The understanding of sickness	274
	4.5.1.3	Treatment	281
4.5.2		The healing process in the shepherds' overarching theological perspective	291
	4.5.2.1	Testimonies, reports and signs of healing	292
	4.5.2.2	The shepherds' basic concern is faith in Jesus	300
	4.5.2.3	Renouncing of all other powers—burning of charms	304
	4.5.2.4	A communal understanding of healing	307
	4.5.2.5	The climax of healing	317
4.5.3		Summary	328

4.6 Crucial issues: An attempt at interpreting the understanding......330
    4.6.1   All spirits in traditional worship are demonic..............................333
        4.6.1.1   The consistent "either-or"-principle..336
    4.6.2   The shepherds' comprehensive use of exorcism........................339
        4.6.2.1   Frequency..341
        4.6.2.2   The structure of exorcism...342
        4.6.2.3   The wide range of people treated with exorcism....................345
        4.6.2.4   A variety of evils are expelled..347
        4.6.2.5   Exorcism understood as a fight between God and the devil...349
    4.6.3   The shepherds' conception of healing as primarily
               faith in Jesus 351
        4.6.3.1   A living faith in Jesus is more important than healing
                        from observable sicknesses 353
        4.6.3.2   Is faith in Jesus a prerequisite for healing of
                        observable sicknesses?...355
    4.6.4   Summary..359

5   Concluding summary and emerging questions....................................363
5.1   Concluding summary...363
5.2   Emerging questions..368
    5.2.1   Demonology and demonic involvement in human life...............368
    5.2.2   If it is not God, it is a demon 369
    5.2.3   The appropriateness of exorcism for people with a wide
               range of problems 370
    5.2.4   Expulsion of sickness, sin and a variety of evils........................371
    5.2.5   The position of shepherds..371
    5.2.6   Exorcism—faith—salvation: closing remarks............................372

Appendices...375
Appendix 1: Questionnaire shepherds...375
Appendix 2: Questionnaire non-shepherds...376
Appendix 3: Observation of healing services...377
Appendix 4: Interview guide case histories..377

Glossary..381

Field material 383

Bibliography..393

Index of Authors...403

Index of Biblical References...407

Figures and Tables

Figure 1: Hiebert's Tribal View of Spiritual Encounters 147
Figure 2: Hiebert's Biblical View of Spiritual Warfare 173

Table 1: Signs violating common conduct 208
Table 2: Bodily signs 209
Table 3: Supernatural signs 210
Table 4: Theological signs 211
Table 5: Causes for people to be in need of exorcism 229
Table 6: Signs of healing 298

Acknowledgments

The present book is a revised edition of my PhD dissertation. It did not originate as a well-prepared doctoral research study. Rather it started in practical life with a curiosity to discover more about the Malagasy shepherds' life and practice, and it has come into being little by little. When my wife and I came to Madagascar in 1983, I had the opportunity to work in the Malagasy Lutheran Church both as an evangelist and a theological lecturer for nine years. During the last two years of our stay I started systematic fieldwork.

Without the support and encouragement of other people my fieldwork material probably would have stayed untouched. It was Professor Torstein Jørgensen at the School of Mission and Theology (MHS), Stavanger, who first encouraged me to make use of this material for a doctoral dissertation and several people gave me valuable comments and suggestions in the early phases of the project. I want to express my gratitude to Professor Øyvind Dahl and Professor Antonio Barbosa da Silva at MHS and Associate Professor Sigmund Harbo and other former collegues at Stavanger College, now the University of Stavanger, where I worked as a lecturer from 1996 to 2000. Dr. Rakotojoelinandrasana Daniel and Dr. Rasolondraibe Péri accepted to be part of a doctoral study committee for this project in 1996, but due to changes in the progress of study, I have not been able to follow up their willingness to contribute.

I am indebted to Professor Raherisoanjato Daniel at the Institut des Civilisations, Université d'Antananarivo, who granted me permission to do necessary fieldwork for my dissertation. The basis and backbone of the study, however, rest in all my informants' willingness to share their knowledge and their experience with me. I am deeply indebted to and thankful for their generosity and co-operation. I especially mention students at the regional theological seminary Atsimoniavoko who inspired me with their interest in the project and volunteered to be my field assistants.

Acknowledgments

Since 2001 I have been a participant in the doctoral program at the Norwegian Lutheran School of Theology (MF), Oslo, with Professor Jan-Martin Berentsen (MHS) as my supervisor and Professor Tormod Engelsviken as co-supervisor. I wish to thank this institution, fellow postgraduate students and professors at the section of church history, especially Professor Oskar Skarsaune, for valuable insights and comments to my project. From February 2005 I have been participating in the doctoral program at MHS and I appreciate this institution's readiness to receive me into their program.

It is not too much to say that it is because of my supervisor, Professor Jan-Martin Berentsen's thorough reading and carefully formulated questions that this project has been brought to a conclusion. He has patiently motivated and encouraged me all the way since 1997 and I am deeply grateful for his support.

When all this is said, however, I would like to emphasise that deficiencies and shortcomings in this work are on my own account and that the choices made are my responsibility.

Most of the time I have been working with the project in addition to full time employment as a lecturer and later as a parish pastor. I want to express my gratitude for study leaves and funding to the following institutions: the diocese of Stavanger in the Church of Norway, the Norwegian Missionary Society, the Norwegian Research Council and the School of Mission and Theology. Special thanks to Cheryl Hogarth who proofread the manuscript. I also want to express my gratitude to Dr. Paul G. Hiebert who generously permitted me to use any of the material he has written on Spiritual Warfare and to the Norwegian Research Council for a grant that covers the printing subsidies of the book.

The book is dedicated to my wife Liv Helga who never tired of motivating and encouraging me to continue the work. Without her patience and support, I would not have been able to complete the project.

Hans Austnaberg
Stavanger, June 2007

Acronyms and Abbreviations

AIC	African Initiated Churches
FFPM	Fiombonan'ny Fiangonana Protestanta eto Madagasikara (the Union of Protestant Churches in Madagascar)
FJKM	Fiangonan'i Jesoa Kristy eto Madagasikara (Church of Jesus Christ in Madagascar)
FLM	Fiangonana Loterana Malagasy (The Malagasy Lutheran Church)
Log 238, 67 Ha	The house in Antananarivo where *Mama* Nenilava used to live and where there were healing services regularly. Log 238, 67 Ha refers to the apartment number (Logement 238) and the section in the city (67 Hectares).
Mal	Malagasy
MF	Det Teologiske Menighetsfakultet (The Norwegian Lutheran School of Theology), Oslo
MHS	Misjonshøgskolen (School of Mission and Theology), Stavanger
NMS	The Norwegian Missionary Society
NT	The New Testament
OT	The Old Testament
RSV	Holy Bible, Revised Standard Version
STPL	Seminery Teolojikam-Paritany Loterana (Lutheran theological regional seminary)

Abbreviations in footnotes referring to my field material

CHIN + digit	Case history interview with non-shepherd

CHINA + digit	Case history from interview by non-shepherd field assistant
CHIS + digit	Case history interview with shepherd
CHISA + digit	Case history from interview by shepherd field assistant
CHQ + digit	Case history from the questionnaires
IA + digit	Interview by field assistant
IG + digit	Group interview
IN + digit	Interview with non-shepherd
IS + digit	Interview with shepherd
L + digit	Information in letter
O + digit	Observation material
QN + digit	Questionnaire from non-shepherd
QS + digit	Questionnaire from shepherd

1 Introduction

In this book we meet a church with a history of more than 150 years, throughout the great island Madagascar and with approximately 2 million members, the Malagasy Lutheran Church. Within this church we find the so-called revival movement (*Fifohazana*) with shepherds (*mpiandry*) who form a special ministry. Shepherds are lay, not salaried, consecrated church workers. They have followed a two-year part-time training program and their main task is to preach the Gospel and cast out demons.[1]

In this chapter I present the problem, the study design and the necessary delimitations of the book. Then follows some background information for my choice of subject and in a third subchapter I present my underlying sources and methodology. Finally, I give a brief outline of the book.

1.1 Problem and delimitation

I have called the subject matter *Shepherds and Demons*. From a range of possible study areas involving *Fifohazana*,[2] the shepherds' dealing with the spirit world crystallised itself as the most interesting to me.[3] Reasons

---

[1] To the historical roots and essential characteristics of the revival movement, see chapter 2.

[2] *Fifohazana* literally means revival/awakening but when I describe this movement, I use *Fifohazana*, revival and revival movement interchangeably. This is in line with the common usage in English. Rasolondraibe 1989, Ramambason 1999, Randrianarivelo 2000. The revival comprises both a renewal of Christians and non-Christians converting to this faith.

[3] Inter alia, the following could have been interesting themes of study: A historical presentation of one part of the movement from the beginning in 1894 till now. A study of the shepherds' preaching of the Gospel, which they say is their primary

for this choice are that this area is especially unfamiliar to a Westerner and thus somewhat obscure, it causes controversy among the shepherds and within the church and when ordinary people talk about shepherds, they normally mention the shepherds' exorcism as the most distinguished feature in the movement. The shepherds themselves, moreover, emphasise the fight with demons as a significant part of their work.[4]

My research task is to provide new knowledge about one aspect in one sector of the Malagasy revival movement, i.e. the shepherds' practice and understanding of exorcism, within the context where this practice belongs. Exorcism in the Malagasy revival movement is a practice consisting of two main parts, which always go together. The shepherds' most common way to designate this practice is *asa sy fampaherezana* (work and strengthening). "Work" points to part one with expulsion of demons and "strengthening" is the second part, the subsequent individual prayer with the laying on of hands.[5] The terminology is not fixed and some shepherds use *famoahana demonia* (expulsion of demons) to denote both parts of the practice while others use *fampaherezana* (strengthening) with this comprehensive meaning.[6]

This study does not enter into a discussion about the phenomenon of exorcism *per se*. The aim is to work with and arrange my material in a way, which may help the reader to grasp how the shepherds understand their own practice of exorcism. Due to this perspective, I do not find it relevant to discuss problems arising when a Western worldview encounters the shepherds' exorcism. Rather, in order to help the reader

---

task. An investigation into the role of shepherds in the rapidly increasing number of Christians in the Lutheran church in Madagascar.

[4] It should be emphasised, however, that according to the shepherds' self-understanding, their task is more comprehensive. The joint statutes say: "They preach the Gospel to all the people, take care of the insane and the poor." "They preach the Gospel and cast out demons (*mamoaka demonia*) ...." Fifohazana FFPM 1980: no 2, 23.

[5] In the initial phase of the project my interest was concentrated especially on the expulsion-part of exorcism. I soon realised, however, how important the shepherds considered the immediate context with preaching, singing and prayer in order to perform exorcism. The unity of expulsion of demons and prayer with the laying on of hands has become increasingly clear as of utmost importance to the shepherds as I have been working with the field material. In the shepherds' conception, it seems as it is the subsequent prayer with the laying on of hands that constitutes the climax and enlightens the entire liturgy.

[6] When the shepherds use the words "work, to work, those who are worked with" (*asa, miasa, iasana*) the casting out of demons is primarily in mind.

grasp the shepherds' understanding of exorcism I will point to what I deem to be the shepherds' horizons of understanding, i.e. influence from the traditional Malagasy culture and the biblical message. When this practice is viewed within its proper contexts it is my conviction that the shepherds' understanding of exorcism will be more understandable to the reader.

In my investigation I call the shepherds' practice exorcism but I emphasise that exorcism in my usage covers an actual Malagasy reality. I am aware of problems connected with my usage: The word exorcism may recall a historical practice with incantations and abuse of power and uneasy feelings may be associated with the word by Western readers. Such sentiments are not congenial with the Malagasy practice and my usage of the term and all preconceptions should be set aside in order to obtain a proper understanding of the shepherds' exorcism. I have chosen to keep the word exorcism, in spite of possible objections, after having rejected other possible alternatives. The lack of consistency in the shepherds' way of labelling their practice has given me a reason to be pragmatic and use a word that the shepherds do not use.[7] Other Western researchers also seem to use exorcism/"exorcisme" about the shepherds' practice.[8] I underline strongly, however, that the word exorcism in my study is used with a special content to cover the Malagasy reality.[9]

The central problem of the study, indicated in the subtitle, is: How do the shepherds practise exorcism and what is their understanding of this practice? Consequently, the main research questions can be formulated in the following way: A. What are the basic characteristics of exorcism as practised by shepherds in the Malagasy Lutheran Church? B. What is the shepherds' understanding of people in need of exorcism and how do they understand the casting out of demons and the healing process?

With the words "as practised and understood" in the subtitle I want to signal primarily an emic interest.[10] The Malagasy actors are in the centre of this study and I wish to let them be heard as far as possible.

---

[7] It would have been a possibility to use e.g. demon-expulsion (*famoahana demonia*) to designate the whole practice but this would easily have been confused with the first part of exorcism.

[8] See Sharp, Estrade, Althabe, Dubourdieu-Jaquiers.

[9] I never use the verb "exorcise" to denote my informants' practice. This word is only used with reference to other researchers' terminology.

[10] With "emic interest" I mean an inquiry from the inside. Cf. 1.3.3, footnote 94.

CH. 1: INTRODUCTION

Themes of special interest for them will be focussed and given the most space. The study design is exploratory and descriptive because the field of study to current date has been insufficiently covered and my goal is—as far as possible—to reach the shepherds' own understanding of their practice.[11] With this orientation I join a research tradition, which primarily will describe and understand. A. Walls underlines that

> It will be one of the tasks of African academic theology to explore and articulate the forms and formulations of Christianity already made in thousands of congregations over several generations.[12]

But, is it possible for me, a Western researcher, to give such a presentation? The research project originated in my thinking and logic, the questions I posed to my informants, the categories I used, my methods of selection and ways of understanding have been influenced by my person and my culture. I had a certain pre-understanding of the topic and a set of prejudgements even before I started my fieldwork. I freely admit all this. The quality of my presentation then depends on my ability to put this into parenthesis while I am observing, exploring and describing the phenomenon. I am empathetically striving to take the actors' points of view and understand them on their own premises. On the other hand, the quality of the description also depends on my ability to reflect on my pre-understanding. It is the awareness of my own pre-understanding, which enables me to distinguish between this and the essential features of my study matter. This awareness helps me understand the phenomenon from the perspective of those experiencing it. When all this is said, I am aware that any understanding is partial and that the researcher always filters the actors' points of view. The text of

---

[11] Hummelvoll and Barbosa da Silva 1998:455–456.

[12] Walls 1996:14. J. S. Pobee and G. Ositelu II writes with regard to the study of the African Initiated Churches (AIC): "we plead for an *emic* approach—one which reads the story of AICs through the actors and participants in the particular tradition". Pobee and Ositelu II 1998:3 (italics in original). The Norwegian professor of history, J. Simensen, also strongly emphasises that the research interest in African religion should concentrate on what Africans see as most important. He recommends that the African actors should be in focus and that they should be interpreted within their own contexts. He especially asks for a description of the syntheses between African tradition and Christian standards. Simensen 1996.

the book is my interpretation of the shepherds' understanding,[13] and my limited perspective[14] can only be an indication and not a totality of the shepherds' understanding.[15] Nevertheless, I strive to be attentive to the shepherds in order for my presentation to be as close to their practice and understanding as possible.[16]

My research is situated within the field of missiology.[17] One of the main tasks of this discipline is to analyse critically the encounter between biblical message and different cultural contexts. This informs my choice of theoretical perspective. My basic assumption is that some sort of synthesis between biblical message and traditional Malagasy culture has resulted in the shepherds' actual practice of exorcism. The purpose of the present project then is to show what this synthesis looks like. I do so primarily by furnishing a basic description[18] of exorcism as practised and

---

[13] Throughout the book the words "understanding" and "interpretation" are used consistently to denote the distinction between the shepherds' understanding and researchers' (including my own) interpretation (of this understanding).

[14] With a limited perspective I think primarily of my research population compared to the thousands of shepherds in the Lutheran church.

[15] Spradley 1979:204, Østberg 1998:30, Haus 2000:13.

[16] As will be accounted for in 1.3.3.2 I will also make use of an etic perspective in addition to the emic and these two perspectives supplement each other. Krogseth 1991:6, Simensen 1996:163–164.

[17] There has been much discussion as to define what missiology is, not least because of diverging opinions about what mission fundamentally is. In my thinking mission is the sending of the church to the world, founded in the Great Commission in Mt 28:18–20. The plurality of approaches to missiology may be seen as complementing and supplementing each other, according to Scherer 1987:513–514. Missiology has interdisciplinary aspects: historical, systematic and practical theological but it also stands in correspondence with non-theological research traditions such as the social sciences. Berentsen, Engelsviken and Jørgensen 1994:17. My project is situated in the interplay between systematic theological and practical aspects, with an extensive use of methods from the social sciences to describe the encounter of worldviews present in the shepherds' exorcism. To grasp a sector of reality is a complicated task and my opinion is that different research traditions may give complemantary maps of this reality, provided they are grounded on the same epistemology. Hiebert 1994:25.

[18] With "basic description" I mean an investigation, which is exploratory and has as its purpose a rather wide presentation of the field. Scholarly investigation of the shepherds' exorcism is to present date lacking and my "basic description" consists in a presentation of the shepherds' practice and understanding of exorcism, supported by available written guidelines.

understood by the shepherds. This means a rather wide presentation of exorcism as situated within the two contexts and constitutes the main bulk of the book. I attempt, however, also to interpret a few main themes in the shepherds' understanding in light of the contexts.[19] My findings seem to show that shepherds primarily emphasise the biblical background of exorcism and have difficulty discovering traditional cultural factors, while Western researchers seem to think that exorcism primarily should be explained on the basis of traditional Malagasy culture. My presentation aims to take both contexts into consideration and to be sensitive to how they both have contributed to a new synthesis in the shepherds' exorcism.

Several delimitations are necessary.

- Exorcism in a Christian context is complex and raises many questions. My own training is theological with special interest in missiological issues and when I planned this project, I worked as a seminary teacher in Madagascar, mostly occupied with the New Testament. In the initial phase of the project I planned to study some of the theological implications of the shepherds' practice, evaluated from a biblical, systematic-theological and a practical theological angle.[20] These could have been interesting areas of research, but when I examined available literature about the Malagasy shepherds' exorcism I found it too scanty and insufficient to carry out the original plan. This caused me to redefine the project. I was convinced that I had to furnish a basic description of the shepherds' exorcism and only afterwards could I turn to the question of specific theological implications. As the work continued, however, I realised that to accomplish both tasks would exceed the limits of this investigation and my own resources. I therefore decided on attempting a description of how the shepherds themselves practise and understand exorcism.

---

[19] This is done in 4.6. See further 1.3.3 to the methodology of how I will accomplish this.

[20] Questions like the following especially stirred my interest: Is this practice a valid contextualisation of the Gospel? What would a comparison between expulsion of evil spirits in traditional Malagasy religion and exorcism in the church be like, or a comparison between exorcism as practised and understood in the AICs and in the Malagasy revival movement? Is exorcism only a cultural expression of certain needs or does it reflect a transcendent reality?

PROBLEM AND DELIMITATION

- Since I am presenting such a description I have chosen to focus on the official practice, i.e. the practice as presented by leaders in the revival and supported by handbooks and written guidelines. This prevents me from studying possible discrepancies between the official version and how mainly uneducated shepherds or people treated with exorcism understand the practice. I still find my choice most relevant in view of the present situation, however, since basic descriptions of the practice on a scholarly level to present date are lacking.
- My choice of presenting an official version of the practice has guided the selection of informants. I have consciously selected people with a certain level of theoretical education, shepherd leaders and educators of novices.[21] This group of informants is not a majority among the shepherds but they influence many others. The revival movement is comprehensive and includes a whole range of people from theological doctors to illiterates. Methodologically it would have been difficult to include all these people in one study. When a basic description of the official version is available, however, it will be an interesting and important task for other researchers to investigate other groups of informants, perhaps holding differing or opposing opinions.
- My study is delimited to the Malagasy Lutheran Church (Fiangonana Loterana Malagasy, FLM). Pentecostals have churches spread over most of the island and independent churches are increasingly being established, especially in the Antananarivo-area. Many of these churches expel demons but I have not studied their practice. Neither do I include in my project the practice of the independent revival movement *(Fifohazana tsy miankina)*, which seceded from the Lutheran church in 1954 and now has its own church organisation.[22] The *Fifohazana* is mainly found in the Protestant churches and I have chosen to concentrate on the Lutheran church partly because the revival has had its strongest impact in this church, partly because I served in the Lutheran church myself and partly because of the need to have a project of a manageable size.
- Shepherds practice exorcism all over the island. Some may argue that people's reactions to the shepherds' exorcism are more frequent and more spectacular in the coastal areas, where the Christian faith

---

[21] See a more detailed description in 1.3.1.2 below.
[22] Barrett 1968:214–215 and Hovland Undated.

has had less impact than in the high plateaux. Originally, I planned to cover both the high plateaux and the coasts with my study and the first part of fieldwork included both areas. In this study, however, I have only used data from the high plateaux and it is mainly delimited to the Farihimena- and Ankaramalaza-branches of the revival.[23] I have thus delimited the scope of the project to mainly one area: the southern part of Imerina, especially Antsirabe and its surroundings.[24] My point is not to generalise from my material to what happens everywhere in the Malagasy Lutheran Church but rather to present the practice as leaders in the revival conceive it. The research population is therefore more important than the geographical area. My choice of area is partly guided by availability, since I was working near Antsirabe when I undertook my fieldwork, partly by the fact that many key people in the revival movement live in the high plateaux and partly because of the need to limit my material to a manageable size. I have to admit, however, that the practice of exorcism is difficult to delimit according to geography and I cannot rule out that part of my field material may reflect experiences and practices outside the chosen area because of great mobility among the shepherds and influence from the different branches of the movement.

- Exorcism is occasionally performed in private homes and most local churches have healing services on a regular basis. My study is mainly delimited to exorcism in healing services in a *toby* (revival centre), but these services were always open to people from outside not living in the *toby* campus.[25]

---

[23] Cf. 2.1.1.

[24] The list of the field material shows that there are scattered references to sources from Antananarivo and a few from Fianarantsoa.

[25] According to Dubourdieu-Jacquier 1996:609 the word *toby* is borrowed from the military vocabulary of the Merina armies from the 19th century and signifies a camp where the army settled in order to conquer the coastal kingdoms. A *toby* is a place where shepherds take care of ill people through preaching of God's word, exorcism and caring. As a general rule people with the most abnormal behaviour are sent to a *toby* for intensive and lasting treatment. My observation material consists of both these people and people from the near-by area coming to the *toby* only to attend the healing services. The justification for treating these two groups together is that the shepherds' exorcism, which is the focus of my project, is applied to both groups in the same manner and according to the same liturgy.

1.2 Background and motivation

A Malagasy named *Dada* Rainisoalambo initiated the Malagasy revival movement[26] in 1894 and to a great extent it has been led by Malagasy Christians from the very beginning. The rise of the movement was spontaneous and their teaching and practice have been especially relevant in the Malagasy cultural setting. Throughout Madagascar the revival today has a profound impact on church life, not only in the Lutheran church where I served, but also in other Protestant churches and even to some extent in the Roman Catholic Church. The movement is ecumenical, but rests—with one major exception[27]—faithful to its mother churches and operates as a revival movement within the historical churches. Approximately 25.000 people altogether—men and women—have a special consecration as shepherds and each year 500–700 more shepherds are consecrated.[28]

Although the Malagasy revival differs in many aspects from the African Initiated Churches (AIC), these churches seem to be the closest parallel to the Malagasy revival movement.[29] The AICs represent a Christian response to spiritual forces by taking seriously the African worldview.[30] Spiritual healing, often including expulsion of demons, is a principal focus of worship and liturgical practices in most of the AICs.[31] Demon-expulsion, usually called exorcism by the authors, has been

---

[26] D.B. Barrett defines a revival movement as "any orthodox renewal or awakening of Christian faith within the mission churches, characterized by enthusiasm and a large following…". He identifies the Malagasy *Fifohazana* within a great movement of independence, taking place in various countries in the African continent, some as latent independence and other as manifest independence and he maintains that movements inside and outside the churches are organically related. Barrett 1968:47, 180–183, 212–215. Barrett's link between the Malagasy revival and independence has been criticised by Ramambason 1999:74–75.

[27] I refer to the great schism in the Soatanana-branch of the movement in 1955. Barrett 1968:212–217. Cf. however, tensions within the revival movement as a result of a new practice in the Reformed church from the late 1990's. See 2.1.2.

[28] The numbers refer to all four branches of the revival and are my estimation (2002) based on statistics from leaders in the revival movement in 1996. The general secretary of the FLM, visiting Norway in August 2001, admitted that statistics are scanty and that they do not know the exact number of shepherds. See further 2.1.1.

[29] There are also some similarities with the East African revival movement, which has stayed within the historical churches, especially its strong emphasis on atonement. Pretorius 1987:137.

[30] Igenoza 1985:179–193, Oosthuizen 1988:414–433.

[31] Pobee and Ositelu II 1998:71.

discussed and different opinions have been voiced. B.G.M. Sundkler maintained that healers were a threat to the progress of the African,[32] while A. Shorter suggests that the practice encourages dualistic attitudes, causes fear of demons and makes people demonise their experience of suffering. People may be diverted from prayer and sacraments and exorcism may degenerate into a power-phenomenon and not a prayer-phenomenon.[33] A.O. Igenoza sees possible objections to exorcism: failures in healing, it may cause disorder and it may be said to be unscientific. On the other hand, its success in healing is widely recognised, it counters the danger of superficial Christianity and it allows the possibility to construct a Christian worldview to meet the religious aspirations of African Christians.[34] M.L. Daneel emphasises a real and lasting healing resulting from the practice and says that exorcisms attack the roots of witchcraft and results in freedom from fear. But he also sees a danger of magical interpretation and he fears a stigmatisation and enslavement of the victims.[35]

According to my experience, contact between the AICs and the Malagasy shepherds plays no important role and this has caused me not to include material from mainland Africa as a significant part of my study. Occasionally, when of particular interest, some material from mainland Africa will be referred to in footnotes but my project does not intend to compare the Malagasy revival with the AICs.[36]

One of my first encounters with *Fifohazana* was a rather shocking experience.

> I had just started to work as an evangelist in the Antalaha-area on the North-East coast. One Sunday I was asked to hold a service in a newly founded congregation in the countryside and since I had a large car, the local pastor

---

[32] Sundkler 1961:237.
[33] Shorter 1985:196–199.
[34] Igenoza 1985:187.
[35] Daneel 1990:241–246. See also Daneel 1987, Oosthuizen 1988, Ejizu 1991, Kitshoff 1997.
[36] Since the aim of this study is to describe exorcism as practised and understood by Malagasy shepherds, interpreted within their own horizons of understanding, I do not allow any space for the Western debate on spiritual encounters. See McAlpine 1991, literature overview in Stieglitz 1991:10–17 and Moreau: Spiritual Conflict in Missiological Perspective. A Selected Bibliography, http://www.lausanne.org/dufe/bibliogr.html, 26.01.2000.

BACKGROUND AND MOTIVATION 11

advised me to bring some shepherds from where I was living. It is an exhausting experience to hold a three hour long service, standing on a podium only one meter below a burning hot tin roof and I was rather tired when the service ended. Then the shepherds approached me together with a couple of people from the village and asked me to perform an urgent baptism. An old lady who would die soon wanted to be a Christian but she was not yet baptised.

I tried to excuse myself by saying that I could send a local pastor the next day but they seemed to doubt that she would live that long, so I did not have much choice. For the first time I performed the baptism liturgy in the Malagasy language, without any prior practice and I am sure the old lady did not understand much. But with some help from her close family she nodded "yes" to my questions and was baptised. It was what happened next that shocked me. During the hymn after the baptism the shepherds started to put on their long white dresses. They sang a new hymn: "Come, ô Holy Spirit …", which always precedes exorcism, they prayed, read some passages from the Bible and one of them said with a strong voice: "In the name of Jesus of Nazareth, the powerful, I command the work of the darkness and all the evil spirits: Get out in Jesus' name." The other shepherds joined in with him, all shouting the same words and the volume of their voices was enormous. Perhaps it was felt even more overwhelming in the little house with only one room of approximately 3 x 4 metres, crowded with people. Only the old lady was seated on the floor, the rest of us had to stand. Soon the old lady, who was almost unable to move her lips during baptism, started to move the upper part of her body rhythmically. The shaking increased in intensity and her whole body was thrown back and forth so that the shepherds had to seize her to prevent her from being injured. She seemed to jump on the floor while sitting.

I was scared. This was so different from everything I had experienced earlier and I was sure that the old lady would die as a result of the treatment. I could not even stay inside until the end of the liturgy. After some time the sound level decreased, the singing of hymns started again and the shepherds came out of the house with smiling faces.

Surely, this lady was "assaulted by demons" but now she is calm, they said. They had cast out demons, prayed for her with laying on of hands and promised her forgiveness of sins and the Holy Spirit.[37]

This incident did not take place in my area of research but the main components in the shepherds' practice of exorcism are the same. For some reason the person was considered in need of exorcism, the shepherds performed the fixed liturgy with singing, prayer, expulsion of demons and prayer with the laying on of hands and they considered their action a means of God's forgiveness and the Holy Spirit to flow to the

---

[37] Cf. 1.3.3.3.

person. These components will be investigated in more detail in the book.

The person mentioned showed severe reactions to exorcism but this is not observable in most of the cases where exorcism takes place. My own understanding of what people the shepherds treat with exorcism changed during the work with the project. Initially, I had in mind only severely ill people who normally would be labelled as demoniacs by the shepherds.[38] As time went on, however, I have observed a wide range of people treated with exorcism and I came to know that the shepherds would only label a few of them as demoniacs. This comprehensiveness made me even more curious to investigate the shepherds' arguments for their practice.

During my work as an evangelist I came to know several shepherds and I experienced their eagerness in evangelism, their ethical sincerity and their willingness to take care of disabled and sick people. When I served as an evangelist in the North-East part of the island I realised that most of the people who had converted to Christianity as adults, had been convinced because of the shepherds' work. I also realised, however, that the existence of shepherds in a church might cause problems. My colleagues, both shepherds and non-shepherds, told me about incidents of strife within congregations between shepherds and other church-workers, controversies about elements in the shepherds' practice and several asked for a better training of shepherds, indicating anxiety for an unintended development in the future. Foreign missionaries also discussed the shepherds' practice and their views differed according to personal experiences with shepherds.

All this stirred my interest in knowing more about the shepherds and their work. The fact that the revival was initiated by a Malagasy in the 1890's and to a great extent has been led by Malagasy Christians from the beginning suggested to me that this is a significant example of a Malagasy contextualised theology. After working in Madagascar for some years and having a greater understanding of traditional cultural thinking, I found several seemingly parallels between the shepherds' practice and that of traditional healers. This increased my eagerness to investigate this area more profoundly.

African Christians have criticised the Western missionary enterprise for lack of interest and even unattentiveness to the Christian view of

---

[38] Cf. 2.2.7.

spirits and powers.[39] With my study I hope to bring back impulses from the Malagasy experience concerning these elements in the Christian message. From one point of view, this study can be seen as a repayment of debt to the churches in Africa by letting the Malagasy shepherds' understanding of a more than 100-year-old practice be the focus of interest.

Another motivating factor to write this book is a lack of scientific study covering this interesting field. Until now scholarly knowledge of exorcism in the Malagasy revival movement is to a large extent lacking and I wish to contribute to remedy this situation. My hope is that this work will stir the interest of other researchers since many aspects of the exorcism practice need a more thorough analysis than can be given in one study alone.

1.3 Sources and methodology

The frame of discourse in this project is theology. My own training is theological and the theological framework shapes my presuppositions. An underlying and fundamental assumption for the theological research tradition is a transcendent dimension of reality: God has revealed himself to humans. God's special revelation is found in the Bible and any movement that defines itself as Christian sees the Bible as its most important document.

This assumption is in line with the shepherds' understanding and this congeniality with the informants' assumptions will be a strength in obtaining a valid understanding of the phenomenon to be studied. The subject of study is a phenomenon within a movement, which both defines itself and is defined by the church as Christian. The result of this project: the presentation of the shepherds' practice and understanding will be an example of local Christian theology in Madagascar. My project then may provide a basis for further theological follow-up research on the *Fifohazana*.

In the search for appropriate material enabling me to accomplish my research task I found only a few written contributions which could be of value. I soon realised that I had to establish my own sources for the most part. This is the reason for the outline of the following presentation, where my research population and methodological considerations concerning this material is presented before I turn to the written sources

---

[39] Igenoza 1986, Abijole 1988.

at my disposal. In the third part of this subchapter I reflect on the interpretation and the writing process.

1.3.1 Research population and field material

Before describing my detailed procedures in choosing informants and making them my sources, I will briefly present the methodology behind my reflections at this point.

1.3.1.1 Qualitative methods

As missiology is interdisciplinary it is a valid procedure for me as a theologian to make use of methods from the social sciences. This is in line with the South African Reformed Church theologian and social anthropologist M. L. Daneel when he says:

> To my mind it is a task for theologians and more specifically missiologists, to create facilities for empirical research in the field and to collect for themselves—by means of scientific sociological and anthropological fieldwork techniques—the data necessary for on-going reflection.[40]

The production of empirical material by using methods from the social sciences is relevant to the purpose of my theological project, i.e. to furnish a basic description in order to provide a starting point for later systematic theological and practical theological reflection. The theological context of my project, i.e. a research deeply rooted within the setting of church, theology and missiology, also legitimises this production of empirical material by means of sociological methods for theological research.[41]

Since little precise knowledge existed about this sector of the shepherds' ministry, I sought to learn from my informants. I consciously went to the field with only some broad themes discovered from my earlier experiences with shepherds. I wanted to learn what was essential from

---

[40] Daneel 1987:249–250.

[41] Brunstad 1998:6. Limitation of space does not allow me to enter into the debate about the relation between social sciences and theological research. See Brunstad 1998:7, footnote 3 and Hegstad 2002.

the actors' points of view.[42] I sought closeness to the reality I wanted to investigate and through qualitative methods including in-depth qualitative research interviews with a limited number of people I aimed at describing qualitative variations, structures and relations. My goal with the investigation has been to come to a more proper understanding of the shepherds' practice and understanding of exorcism, not to prove a pre-set thesis.[43]

There are several limitations and weak points with qualitative methods. Since I have chosen my informants in order to highlight the official teaching of the revival movement, I cannot claim that their opinions are representative for all shepherds. Statistical generalisation has not been aimed at but insights gained through this study contribute to our understanding of how a certain layer of shepherds perceives of their exorcism. The openness of a qualitative research design and the flexibility according to new insights during the production of data is a strength but can also be considered a weakness. It may complicate a comparison of data from the interviewees and the contexts of understanding during interviews may change as the investigation proceeds. The most obvious problem with qualitative methods is, however, that the researcher himself is part of the situation he is studying and subjective interests and interpretation may colour the description too heavily. It is recognised that the results are coloured by the personal relationship and interaction between interviewer and interviewee but this is unavoidable in the process.[44] This problem has been reduced, as far as possible, by accounting for the premises and procedures of research and by a constant checking and questioning of material and conclusions

---

[42] This includes both questions and answers, according to Spradley 1979:4, 84.

[43] Holme and Solvang 1991:75–76. Alasuutari 1996:145. Quantitative and qualitative methods are two different approaches within the social sciences. According to Holme and Solvang 1991:74 the basic difference between the two consists in the following: In a quantitative approach data is transformed to numbers and quantities, which is open to later statistical analysis. In qualitative methods, a collective term for a set of different methodological approaches, it is the understanding and interpretation of information, which is of paramount weight, e.g. a researcher's interpretation of frames of references, motives, social processes or relations. A common denominator is that this cannot or should not be rendered in numbers or analysed statistically.

[44] Cf. "change" as one of 12 aspects representing the main features of the qualitative research interview, i.e. an interviewee will in a second interview use his or her insights gained from the first interview and thus another scholar may not get the same results. Hummelvoll and Barbosa da Silva 1998:464.

through 'triangulation', use of multiple sources and by using different methods for data-production.[45]

1.3.1.2 Research population and production of field material[46]

The subtitle of the book already points out the group of people I have studied: shepherds in the FLM. The field material stemming from these shepherds constitutes the most important sources for the presentation.[47] Since I have delimited my work to a basic description, I have chosen to focus on the official practice and the selection of informants has taken place according to this focus. I deliberately looked for informants with a certain level of formal education and ability of abstract thinking and informants with leadership-positions in the church and revival movement.

As I was a seminary teacher when I started the investigation, I naturally turned to my students.[48] They were easily accessible and provided the possibility of being able to follow-up on obscure elements in the material. I also thought that students would be co-operative to a large extent. Shepherds and non-shepherds were almost evenly distributed among the students and thus I would be able to trace differences in viewpoints. The formal level of education was uneven among them but they all had managed the entrance exam to the seminary. Some were in the first year of theological studies while others were close to finshing the fourth and last year of study. Students from three sets are found in the

---

[45] Holme and Solvang 1991:76–78. Brunstad :41–42. Dahl 1993:194. "Triangulation" is a method of comparison. It may be applied to different sources, different methods and different investigators.

[46] I use the word research population to denote the selected group of people I have studied. van der Ven 1993:140.

[47] My field material also includes non-shepherds and I call this "reference material". The purpose of the reference material is to enlighten the main subject of the study, i.e. the shepherds' practice and understanding of exorcism and thus this material will be of subordinated importance.

[48] The researcher may have several roles in the research situation. Fossåskaret, Fuglestad and Aase 1997:27–34 shows that this depends on a negotiation and not all roles are equally relevant. I insisted on an apprentice role concerning the shepherds' exorcism and this gave me access to valuable material but I am fully aware that some of the informants attributed (mostly implicitly) other roles to me as well: Lutheran missionary, Seminary teacher, Westerner etc. Cf. Haus 2000:10–11.

material, mostly men.[49] The majority came from the countryside, from various parts of the selected area.

In order to get an overview of the field, I made a questionnaire with open-ended questions, which I distributed to those who were shepherds among the students. The reply percentage was high.[50] The open-ended questions resemble a more structured interview and I have made no effort to systematise the answers by quantification.[51] 44 questionnaires from shepherds are used in the description. 26 different questionnaires from non-shepherds play a role as reference material.[52]

All the students knew me personally and this may have coloured their answers, both in positive and in negative direction. I did not teach any subjects concerning the revival movement, however, so the students did not know my personal opinions.[53] I made it very clear that I undertook this research with an open mind eager to learn more. The questionnaire asked for name and place of birth but I informed the students when I presented the research that to fill in this information was facultative. Only one student did not fill in his/her name. I interpret this as openness to the investigation and a wish to inform me about this area of life, which for them is so important.[54]

---

[49] This is because the vast majority of students at the seminary were men. To the fact that my field material consists of mostly men, see reflection below and footnote 63.

[50] 83 % in the oldest set, 97 % in the middle and 100 % in the youngest set of male students. In the women's class the reply percentage was 40 %. I did not make a follow-up of the relative low percentage in the women's class, especially when I realised that at least some of their answers resembled much their husbands' answers. In general, the women had less formal education than the men.

[51] Occasionally, I have counted findings in my material and drawn some preliminary conclusions but I consider this as making use of "Ad Hoc meaning generation". See Kvale 1996:203–204, who sees no problem in joining aspects both from quantitative and qualitative methods in the same project.

[52] See the original questionnaires and the English translation in Appendix 1 and 2. I have not summed up the reply percentage among non-shepherds.

[53] In the seminary curriculum only Church History touched on the subject of the revival movement, mostly its historical development.

[54] It is of course possible to see the filling in of names as negative, because this may have prevented the students from revealing what they really meant about the subjects under investigation. A wide variety of opinions in the answers, also critical to the movement, seem to indicate that the students were not afraid of this. They were also aware of the anonymity in the handling of their answers.

In order to avoid a distortion of the cultural interpretation J.P. Spradley suggests that observation of actors in a natural setting has to supplement interviewing.[55] During the years as a missionary in Madagascar, I attended many healing services, where exorcism is a vital part. I decided, however, to make accurate observation of healing services a part of the project. I regularly attended healing services at the Ambohimahazo *toby*, situated 3 km east of Antsirabe. This *toby* was selected because of accessibility, its good reputation in the area and because it has functioned since about 1950. It is now affiliated with the Farihimena-branch of the movement. When I first arrived there, I was introduced to the shepherds and attendants of the healing service. My role as a seminary teacher with a desire to learn more about the shepherds' exorcism was made clear and it was agreed that I would observe the services. Occasionally I was invited to give a testimony during the preaching part of the service, which I normally accepted, but I never took part in exorcism. I sat among the attendants observing and making notes as accurately as possible. The other *toby* where I made some of my observations was in the capital, called Log 238, 67 Ha,[56] the first *toby* established in the high plateaux by the Ankaramalaza-branch of the movement. The practice there differed slightly from that in Ambohimahazo, which I will account for in chapter 3. I have also included a few other healing services in my selected material, which counts a total of 27.[57] In addition, I have some other observation material, obtained through informal conversation and sudden experiences relating to the theme of my project. This material may be of value because it would not have been easily obtainable by formal fieldwork methods.

It is possible that my presence made the shepherds more observant about how they acted, or that they acted differently because of the observer. My observation of healing services in different places showed similarity to a great extent, however, because the shepherds follow a rather fixed liturgy. I had a personal relation with several of the shepherds[58] and they got used to me staying at the healing services. All this may have counter-acted this danger.

---

[55] Spradley 1979:33.

[56] This points to the address where this *toby* is situated: Logement (habitation) no 238 in the city district called 67 Hectares (The size of the district is 67 hectares, which has become its name).

[57] See List of field material and Appendix 3.

[58] The personal relationship and the familiarity with me staying there was especially the case in the Ambohimahazo *toby*.

SOURCES AND METHODOLOGY

With the questionnaires and the observation of healing services in mind, I made qualitative research interviews with 25 people. Some of these were selected because I thought they may hold valuable information about my subject but as the interviewing proceeded, the interviewees also suggested other people, whom I ought to talk with.

The phenomenological perspective, also called the inside perspective, is a vital part of the qualitative research interview (QRI) and I have attempted to reach the subject's point of view. This required a "bracketing" of my own presuppositions and a conscious effort to distinguish between these and the essence of the phenomenon to be studied. The goal has been to describe the phenomenon as correctly and objectively as possible.[59] I was conscious not to interrupt the flow of thinking from my informants and this gave me information about themes that I probably would have missed if I had pursued the main subject more narrowly. The interviews focussed on the shepherds' exorcism and in the interview setting I was able to clarify somewhat obscure sayings from the interviewees. Sometimes the informants discovered new facets of their practice as they were explaining it.[60]

6 of the interviewees are shepherd leaders or leaders of churches at a *toby*. 12 people have gone through the consecration into the shepherd ministry, 2 of them were consecrated after their ordination as pastors. A majority of the interviewees are pastors and they are all treated as shepherds in the study, although 13 of them practise exorcism on the basis of their ordination without having any shepherd-consecration. This is in full concordance with the joint statutes of the revival movement, which allows any pastor the authority to practise exorcism because of his ordination.[61] Some of the pastors in my material take part in exorcism regularly but most of them respect the division of work and allow the shepherds to take care of exorcism. All of them define themselves as positive to exorcism, however and may practise when the situation urges them to do so.[62] I have several reasons for my choice: Pastors in general

---

[59] Hummelvoll and Barbosa da Silva 1998:455–456, 461. The phenomenological method, where we find the term phenomenological perspective, is used to "describe existential experiences".

[60] I have applied S. Kvale's 12 aspects of QRI as these are essential elements in the method. Hummelvoll and Barbosa da Silva 1998:462–465.

[61] Fifohazana FFPM 1980: no 19.

[62] My presentation of pastors counted among the shepherds may seem somewhat confusing but this reflects the status of pastors in relation to the *Fifohazana*. Pastors and shepherds have two distinct ministries in the church and their "entrances" into

are influential in the revival movement, because they normally are in charge of the formation of novices to become shepherds, at least when there is no *toby* nearby to take care of the formation. I have also chosen these pastors because of their level of education, both formally and theologically, because I thought they may have an ability to discover and voice problematic aspects with the practice and because they have much experience and great knowledge of the subject.

All of the interviewees are men and this is an obvious weakness with the investigation, since women are in the majority among shepherds. My research population partly reflects the state of leadership in the revival movement in the FLM, however and it is also due to my conscious choice of interviewing primarily theological students and pastors. The FLM does not allow ordination of women to become pastors. Some of the students at the theological seminary are female shepherds, however, a fact reflected in other parts of the field material.[63]

---

the ministries are different. In this study I distinguish between the shepherd's consecration and the pastor's ordination for the purpose of clarity. In Malagasy, the word *fanokanana* (separation) may be used to denote both of them but the Malagasy variant of the French "ordination" *ordinasiona* is normally only used about pastors. The shepherds are not allowed to administer the sacraments but the pastor, on the other hand, is allowed to perform all the shepherds' work. This is so because the pastor's ordination is considered to include also the shepherd's consecration (cf. the joint statutes above). Randrianarivelo 2000:41 argues that pastors are already shepherds by referring to the fact that the shepherds' work only constitutes one part of the pastoral work and by saying that the shepherds' two years of instruction is included in the seminary program for pastors. In practical life, however, not all pastors sympathise with the shepherds and thus they exclude themselves from their rights to perform shepherds' work. Pastors can thus be divided into two groups with fluid limits: those who co-operate closely with the shepherds and practise exorcism when necessary and those who do not consider themselves included in the shepherds' practice but choose to stay at a distance. In my experience, very few pastors oppose the shepherds. Naturally, my choice of pastors is from the first group and I do not hesitate to treat them as shepherds in my material. For a closer description of the relation between shepherds and pastors, see 2.2.4.

[63] See list of field material. If my study had not focussed on the official version of exorcism in the movement, it would have been an even more obvious weakness not to interview female shepherds. Many women find in the revival movement an open arena for their spirituality, which is not granted them in other parts of the church. At the leadership-level, however, female shepherds are still very few and this has caused the overweight of men in this study. I invite other researchers to remedy this situation and design a study with female shepherds in focus. The gender of the people treated with exorcism is briefly dealt with in 4.3.4.

Most of the interviews lasted from 1 to 1½ hours and were recorded on tape.[64] Three group interviews and some shorter interviews with non-shepherds are included in the material. The latter functions as reference material to my main purpose.

The fieldwork with regard to the production of case histories followed three steps:

One of the questions in the questionnaire to the shepherds was: "If you have seen a person seriously "assaulted by demons", then report in detail about him/her".[65] Out of 44 people selected according to the criteria, I was amazed that as much as 16 of the shepherds said they had not seen such a person. Some said that they had seen people seriously "assaulted by demons" but since they did not know their story in detail, they refrained from reporting.[66] This material consists of 28 stories told from memory and amazingly detailed.

The second step was when some of the students at the seminary became very interested in the project and volunteered as field assistants. I gave them a brief introduction in fieldwork methodology[67] and made an interview guide.[68] Their task was to interview or make a report of a person "assaulted by demons" from their own district. This meant that they knew the interviewee and the network in which he/she lived. They were advised to search for stories of people actually treated by the shepherds' exorcism. I have 9 detailed stories in this category.

The third step in the production of case histories was when I made 5 in-depth interviews with people who had been "assaulted by demons" but had recovered or with the close family of those who were still in treatment.

---

[64] IS 76, IS 325 and IS 326 are shorter and not taped.

[65] "Assaulted by demons" is my rendering of the common Malagasy expression to denote a person afflicted by demons: *voan'ny demonia*. I use quotation marks since it is a translation. Cf. 2.2.7.

[66] The Malagasy rendering of the question: *voan'ny demonia mahatsiravina* points to a severe case. It is possible that my question made my informants cautious as to what story to choose and consequently, has to be complemented with other observed stories. I count the shepherds' reserve in telling stories as a pointer to the reliability of the stories that actually were told.

[67] I asserted especially that they should only report what they observed to be going on and if they wanted to comment on the history, to mention this clearly when they did so.

[68] See Appendix 4.

Both the questionnaires and the material produced by my field assistants are valuable, because the life-stories are mediated through the shepherds and consequently reflect their views. It consists of what the shepherds themselves have observed and how they understand their observations and thus this material relates to the main task of the project.[69] It can be argued that the above material is even more relevant than my own interviewing, since I am a Westerner, influenced by my observations and categories of understanding. In fact, the field data will supplement each other and more than one investigator augments the validity of the material.[70]

I have to be especially attentive to problems arising because of my selection of informants. They are people with a certain level of formal education who are able to describe the official practice and since several of them are leaders in the movement, they may be tempted to describe an ideal situation rather than the actual state. Their level of education and position in the Lutheran church and the revival movement may indicate that some of them are aware of part of the discussion going on concerning exorcism and this may colour their answers. Since the researcher is a Westerner, a missionary and a seminary teacher, they may have given, perhaps without intending to do so, a picture of exorcism that they supposed would please me. The fact that I already knew many of the informants and had a personal relation to some of them may intensify the tendency to give answers they thought I would like. Would they have used different words if they were talking to their co-shepherds?

My personal acquaintance with some of the informants also had positive aspects.[71] They seemed to be relaxed during the interview

---

[69] Two of my field assistants were non-shepherds but I have included their case histories in this material. One of them interviewed the parents of the sick who tell much of the story. In addition the field assistant refers much to what shepherds said and how they understood the sickness. The other story is about a very close relative of the field assistant and thus he knows it well. See List of field material.

[70] Cf. Yin 1994:92, who cites Patton, M.Q.: investigator triangulation.

[71] Fossåskaret, Fuglestad and Aase 1997:34 says that the quality of the interview depends on the quality of the interaction between researcher and informant. According to Hummelvoll and Barbosa da Silva 1998:458, 464 empathetic capacity is an important factor in the qualitative research interview and the reciprocal influence between interviewer and interviewee in the interview situation is counted as a strong point.

situation, much humour was used and because of my knowledge of Malagasy the informants could all talk in their mother language in order to express nuances in meaning. Several of them also told me their opinions on subjects that they not yet had revealed officially, normally because they supposed this would cause problems in the co-operation with other shepherds. I take this as an indication of confidence. In addition, my personal relation to some of the informants enabled me to interpret their answers in a wider context, which was not unfamiliar to me. Sources of error are always a possibility but I have kept the possible sources of error in mind when analysing the material. Methodologically, I have counteracted sources of error by asking the same questions to several people (methodological triangulation), having theological students, leaders in the movement, healing services etc. as my sources (multiple sources) and by using questionnaires, interviews, observation etc. (different methods) for data-production. I have tried to follow the advice that data never should be taken at face value.[72]

1.3.1.3 Clarification of the field material

Most of the individual interviews were taped and all the interviews from my first fieldwork period (1992–1994) were transcribed, except my 5 interviews referred to as case histories. I had Malagasy research assistants doing this work and this should secure a high level of textual understanding since they transcribed both from and to their mother tongue.[73] Afterwards I have checked the transcripts for possible errors by listening to the tapes. Transcribing interviews involves interpretation and transcripts may be called "decontextualized conversations".[74] In order to preserve the original context I have listened to the interviews repeatedly during the writing process, which has recalled gestures, laughing and other circumstances accompanying the words. The interviewee's voice tells a lot about what he/she means and this can only be part of the interpretation if the audio tapes are listened to.[75]

---

[72] Hammersley and Atkinson 1995:232.
[73] By mistake I had two different research assistants transcribing the same tape and their transcripts are almost completely identical.
[74] Kvale 1996:165.
[75] Hammersley and Atkinson 1995:218 says that "there must be constant recourse to the material one is analysing".

The interviews from the second fieldwork period (1998) were only partially transcribed , with weight on the parts with special relevance to the purpose of my investigation. I have made expanded accounts of all the interviews, in order to be able to retrace the content.[76]

I have clarified the material and made it amenable for analysis, distinguishing between essential and non-essential, marking out superfluous material and I have developed meanings in the material, mostly by condensation of meaning and ad hoc methods.

Condensation of meaning consists of reading through the material several times, determining natural meaning units and then formulating the central message (theme) in these units. This procedure is followed in the case histories,[77] while other material is partially treated in this way. Ad hoc methods are what Kvale calls a set of different approaches and techniques for meaning generation. It consists in a free interplay of methods such as noting patterns and themes, making contrasts and comparisons, counting etc.[78] My general approach in selecting methods of analysis has been a pragmatic one, guided by two principles: the methods which has facilitated the continuing unfolding of the meaning generation and those which have led to the maximum understanding of the phenomenon in its context.[79]

It could have been possible to arrange my research population in groups, e.g. theological students, shepherd leaders, pastors with and without the shepherd consecration, but I found no specific differences in the material along these lines, so I have assimilated all the field data together.[80]

---

[76] According to Kvale 1996:170–173 and Spradley 1979:75 it is not necessary that transcripts are done word by word. With "expanded account" Spradley means a comprehensive report without transcribing the whole interview. The purpose is to facilitate the work with the content.

[77] This is why the case histories are not transcribed word for word, cf. above.

[78] Kvale 1996:193–194, 203–204.

[79] Dahl 1993:30.

[80] Some differences in opinion seem to follow level of education but this does not mark one group in the field material from the other. Rather, my informants sometimes refer to uneducated shepherds as distinct from themselves and with diverging opinions.

1.3.2 Written sources and previous research

In this subchapter I start with introducing statutes of the revival movement, internal instruction material and testimonies. Then I present other written sources relating to exorcism in the revival movement. This material is mainly found in articles and parts of works dealing with other themes, the sources are few and their scholarly level varies. When I refer to these sources, I will keep this diversity in mind. In the end of this subchapter I list some of my sources not directly relating to exorcism. The following is a brief presentation.

The joint statutes agreed by the four branches of the revival movement—Fifohazana FFPM 1980—constitutes the basis of the movement,[81] and a pamphlet with internal statutes including a sketch of the training program for novices to become shepherds—Fifohazana miray ao amin'ny FFPM 2000—has been issued lately.[82]

The need of guidance in the instruction of novices has resulted in some written documentation. Of special importance is Tobilehibe 1997, which I refer to as the handbook. Its most interesting part is a description of exorcism (*asa sy fampaherezana*) with special weight on biblical legitimisation. The book is written in the name of the Ankaramalaza-*toby* and pretends to be the teaching of the Ankaramalaza-branch but the book has also gained reputation and use in other branches of the movement.[83] I occasionally refer to other written material used in the instruction of novices. Rasolondraibe 1994 is a sketch of key words for the instruction, Ankaramalaza 1997 is questions and answers about some issues in the shepherds' daily work and A.M.M.T. 1999A; A.M.M.T. 1999S are two articles presented as the biblical teaching about Satan and demons.[84] I

---

[81] According to L 322 these statutes need revision but in May 2000 the appropriate bodies (Fifohazana FFPM and Komity Protestanta) had not yet done this.

[82] L 322 admits that there are some minor divergencies between the two mentioned statutes, due to lacking revision of the oldest. Every *toby* and church synod normally has statutes for the shepherds' work and I have consulted two of these: Fikambanana Toby Lehibe Ankaramalaza 1990, Unidentified Undated.

[83] The handwritten manuscript from the pastor in charge of the Ambohimahazo *toby*, Randriatsarafara 1998, is clearly dependent on the first, much shorter version of the handbook. Unidentified undated. Both IS 201 and IS 325 refer to the handbook and IS 325 asserts that it is generally accepted but some parts cause discussion among shepherds.

[84] A.M.M.T. refers to the author of the articles. As it now stands, it may refer to the initials of his/her name or it may be a pseudonym.

have no reports of how widespread the use of these works are in the movement.

Several leaders in the Protestant churches and in the revival movement present their testimonies in the second part of Ankaramalaza undated. The book was issued on the 50th Anniversary of the Ankaramalaza-branch and the focus of the testimonies is on the impact *Mama* Nenilava has made in these leaders' lives. I also have a report from a shepherd gathering in Antsirabe, Tobilehibe 1995, where several challenges for the movement in the new era were discussed. All these sources are written in the Malagasy language.[85]

With regard to other sources relating to exorcism in the revival movement, some are written by people who are shepherds themselves—Rasolondraibe 1989, Rakotondrasoa 1996, Pitaka 1999—others by pastors or missionaries in the Lutheran church—Syvertsen 1983, Gonia 1993, Randrianarivelo 2000. This material is basically positive to the shepherds' practice, the resemblance between the shepherds' practice and biblical accounts are especially underlined but also the cultural background and relevance of the shepherds' practice. The positive attitude does not exclude a critique of some of the aspects in the practice, however, especially found in Syvertsen and Randrianarivelo. Dahl mentions the revival in his doctoral dissertation on Intercultural Communication, and says that the shepherds "preach the Christian belief within the framework of the old world view, without questioning its animistic set up".[86] This assertion calls for a more thorough analysis: Do the shepherds merely accept the traditional Malagasy worldview or do they also alter it by their preaching and exorcism? In what ways are elements from two worldviews combined in their practice?

I have been able to find only one larger work dealing with exorcism in the revival movement as its main theme. It is a Master thesis, composed in Norwegian by a former missionary in the Lutheran church: Haus 2000. G. Haus' aim is to show how the shepherds interpret and reformulate the culturally shaped phenomena "possession" and "exorcism" and put them into a Christian context. The most important contribution may be her presentation of part of the shepherds' theology, which she, from her contextualisation-perspective, finds is heavily

---

[85] As a reference material I have statutes, teaching and instruction of novices in the Reformed church, in FJKM 1997.

[86] Dahl 1999:35–36, 168. This is in accordance with Aano 1984:187.

dependent on elements in traditional Malagasy religion. The conclusions in Haus' thesis and my project are not directly comparable and there are several reasons for this: While my research population has a certain level of theoretical education, most of her informants seem to be ordinary shepherds working in different *toby*. Normally, these shepherds have little theoretical education. Her informants seem profoundly influenced by traditional religion while the shepherds in my material show little knowledge of this field.[87] In my opinion, her choice of informants from several different places in the coasts and the high plateaux—with great differences in cultural background and degree of Christian influence—is a methodological weakness and throughout the thesis she is very much present with her own interpretation of her informants. I have seldom observed severe manifestations in connection with exorcism, while it seems as the opposite is the case with Haus' informants. I do not find it relevant to use "possessed" to describe the phenomenon treated with exorcism by the shepherds, while Haus constantly uses this word.[88]

Other works are written by researchers outside the Lutheran church, mostly non-Malagasy. Althabe 1984 only touches on the shepherds' exorcism in passing but he interprets the revival movement as such as an imaginary escape from difficult living conditions. Estrade 1985 mentions the Protestant shepherds briefly by characterising them in a negative way, in his comprehensive study of *tromba* throughout the island. Rajaonarison and Rakotomalala 1987, in an article on medical anthropology and development in Madagascar, is also critical to the shepherds' practice and consider it destructive to both Malagasy culture and development, especially since the shepherds so strongly oppose traditional medicine. The cultural anthropologist L.A. Sharp has devoted a chapter to the Protestant shepherds in her doctoral dissertation on possession in Ambanja—Sharp 1993. In an article on the shepherds, whom she calls exorcists, in North-Western Madagascar she concludes by saying that exorcisms performed by the shepherds are a threat to the Malagasy culture—Sharp 1994. It is a puzzling conclusion, since she has shown convincingly that the shepherds are successful in their curing of sickness caused by spirit-possession and her informants themselves have

---

[87] See 2.2.6.

[88] Norwegian: "besatt". The main reason for my reserve concerning this word is the connotations connected to the word "possessed", which differ from the Malagasy *voan'ny demonia* (assaulted by demons), normally used by the shepherds. See further 2.2.7.

described their condition as a suffering from which they wanted to be cured.[89] Sharp's analysis of the Malagasy shepherds and their exorcisms is certainly interesting, but also displays a lack of historical knowledge of the movement. She seldom investigates the shepherds' explanations for their actions and the overall theological frame of reference, which is so important for the shepherds, is lacking in her analysis.[90]

In addition to material relating directly to exorcism, different kinds of sources are used in each chapter and the literature will be referred to in footnotes as the study is evolving. These works will only be listed here without further commentaries, since I presume they are known from previous research on Madagascar and since they only serve to elucidate the background and contexts for the topic of this study.

Historical presentations of the rise and development of the movement will mostly be referred to in chapter 2. In addition to some of the works above, Chapus and Bøthun 1951, Rajoelisoa 1977–80, Dubourdieu-Jacquier 1996, 1999, Ramambason 1999 could be mentioned.[91]

The ethnography and history of the people in Vakinankaratra is well documented and there is a large number of studies in existence.[92] I have found the following especially interesting in dealing with traditional

---

[89] Sharp also shows the inefficiency of psychiatric cure as practised in an asylum in Madagascar, due to a Western reductionistic approach which did not take the patients' cultural categories into account. Sharp 1994:535–540.

[90] Ambanja is the geographical area of Sharp's project and it seems as the shepherds referred to are working in the FJKM church (Sharp only talks about the Protestant church and does not distinguish between the Reformed and the Lutheran). Their practice may differ from the practice in the high plateaux but Sharp has not made any delimitations in this respect.

[91] Several pamphlets are composed in Malagasy and published in a limited number of copies. These especially concern the biographies of the founders and the historical development—Tsivoery 1972/1991, Ramampiandra 1986, Rakotomamonjy 1993 among others. A huge book with more than 500 pages about the crowning of *Mama Nenilava* in 1983 was issued in 1999 in a limited number. Rabarihoela 1999.

Some theses (most of them rather brief) about various issues in the revival movement have been composed at Norwegian theological faculties (MHS, MF)—see databases at the faculties and Austnaberg 1996:143. Theological faculties in Madagascar (FLM, FJKM) also increasingly have found interest in studying the revival movement and this has resulted in a number of theses. References to FJKM-theses can be found in Ramambason 1999:201–208.

[92] Dahl 1999:23.

Malagasy culture and religion in chapter 4: Bloch 1971, Cabanes 1972, Estrade 1985, Bloch 1986, Raison-Jourde 1991, Skeie 1994.

In order to describe, in chapter 4.1.2, the biblical message in the church context into which the shepherds have been socialised, I have chosen to follow a close-to-the-text interpretation as given by scholars in the tradition of a conservative biblical theology.[93] In addition to several articles from The Anchor Bible Dictionary, the following works have been helpful: Ladd 1975, Dunn and Twelftree 1980, Ferguson 1984, Abijole 1988.

My investigation is placed within the field of missiology and several works have played a role in my work with this project, without necessarily being cited in the text. Some concern missiology in general with weight on contextualisation: Hiebert 1985, 1994, 1999, 2000, Scherer 1987, Berentsen, Engelsviken and Jørgensen 1994, Kraft 1996, Hwa 2000. Others are missiological works with special emphasis on Africa/Madagascar: Barrett 1968, Appiah-Kubi 1981, Igenoza 1985, 1999, Daneel 1987, 1990, Rasolondraibe 1994, Ramambason 1999.

1.3.3 Interpretation and writing

With the purpose of furnishing a basic presentation of the shepherds' practice and understanding of exorcism, this study is primarily descriptive and I have used a hermeneutic-phenomenological methodology.[94]

1.3.3.1 Hermeneutics

Hermeneutics is the art of interpretation and understanding and the aim of hermeneutics as a specific method is to come to a better understanding

---

[93] See 1.3.3.2 and 4.1 p. 145–146 for argumentation of my choice.

[94] A hermeneutic-phenomenological method means the phenomenological method combined with hermeneutics and is used to describe people's lived experiences or phenomena, according to Hummelvoll and Barbosa da Silva 1998:462. This methodology corresponds roughly with Pike's distinction between emic and etic perspectives. The emic approach means an inquiry from the inside, where the subjects' point of view and their categories and understanding are observed and described as objectively as possible. The etic approach, on the other hand, is an inquiry from the outside, which uses experience-distant concepts with the purpose of comparing and interpreting the subject's point of view with a broader material in a theoretical perspective. Dahl 1993:13.

of a phenomenon and to understand the deep, existential meaning of experience. Characteristic of the hermeneutic approach is the back and forth process between part and whole, as pictured in the spiral image. This will enable me to view the different actors in exorcism and their actions in the light of the greater context, namely the traditional Malagasy culture and the biblical message and the circularity between part and whole implies a possibility of a deepened understanding of the practice. Another characteristic is that the hermeneutic method presupposes a preunderstanding/prejudgement on the part of the interpreter. I am both a Westerner brought up in a culture where the unseen part of reality is given very little weight and have been living in the Malagasy culture for years and have knowledge of the revival movement and its pratices on a general level.[95] This background and knowledge of the subject has influenced my understanding but in a hermeneutic approach the foreknowledge is a plus to research, when taken into account and made explicit as far as possible. I am conscious of the fact that my inferences are made on the basis of both a phenomenological description and my foreknowledge of the subject. The central element in a hermeneutic method is constantly to question and be critical to one's interpretations.[96]

---

[95] I am brought up in a Norwegian, Lutheran, conservative church tradition and I have served in the Malagasy Lutheran Church (FLM) from 1983–1994 as an evangelist and a seminary teacher. I speak Malagasy fluently, know the Malagasy culture and history, I have lived in different local communities close to the Malagasy and I know many key persons in the Malagasy Lutheran Church and the revival movement. These are qualifications of great importance for conducting a study of this kind.

[96] Hummelvoll and Barbosa da Silva 1998:458–462. As for reservations with regard to the methods and the problems of using phenomenology and hermeneutics, which stem from different philosophical traditions, together, see Kvale 1992:188–189.

1.3.3.2 Levels and contexts of interpretation[97]

In line with S. Kvale's grouping I have tried to distinguish between three levels of interpretation in my work with the material: the informants' self-understanding,[98] a critical common-sense understanding and a theoretical understanding. This distinction creates an awareness of the different interpretational levels, points to an analytical progression and serves to make the questions posed to the material explicit.[99]

Alasuutary says that local explanation is the most important aspect of all in qualitative research.[100] At the level of self-understanding I attempt to formulate the informant's viewpoints and his/her intended meaning with the statements as objectively as possible. The validation was done in the interview situation, where the meaning of unclear statements was sent back to the interviewee for further clarification. It is practically impossible to do so with all parts of an interview and thus the interviewees' viewpoints can only be presented as the researcher understood them. When giving citations and condensed summaries from my field material in the book, I am at the level of self-understanding.

At the level of critical common-sense understanding I have included a wider frame of reference. The different shepherds' self-understanding about a subject is put together, which brings other perspectives on the same theme, sometimes disagreement and differing experiences. In addition, I have—in footnotes—when my material mentions this, presented the understanding of non-shepherds to the same subject and occasionally I have enriched the presentation with secondary literature, when such literature is available. Sometimes this is in consensus with the

---

[97] For the sake of clarity, I use the expression "levels of interpretation" to refer to S. Kvale's distinction between self-understanding, a critical common-sense understanding and a theoretical understanding (see below). Kvale himself uses both level and context to denote this but in his rendering of Kvale's views, Brunstad 1998:44–45 consequently seems to use the word "level". I reserve the expression "contexts of interpretation" to traditional Malagasy culture and biblical message, which I in 1.1 have introduced as the horizons of understanding and contexts of interpretation for the shepherds' exorcism.

[98] Kvale uses this expression to mean the informants' own opinions on the subject in question.

[99] Kvale 1996:214–216.

[100] With "local explanation" he understands how the interviewees themselves explain their situation. Alasuutari 1996:152, 165.

shepherds' understanding and sometimes there are disagreements. The process is primarily focussed on content and not on the person, i.e. the individual shepherd's self-understanding is structured in themes, which emerges from an evaluation of all my material. This means that individual statements are placed both within a new totality and in a new sequence, compared to the original interview. Validity here depends on "whether the documentation and the argumentation are convincing to members of the general public" and whether the presentation is "reasonably documented and logically coherent".[101] The majority of the presentation in the book belongs to this level. My primary aim is exploratory and descriptive and my purpose is to let the actors and participants be heard as far as possible.[102] I am aware, however, that the writing of the book is already an interpretation, through my selection, grouping of statements, thematic organisation, accentuation etc.[103]

The theoretical level of understanding is an attempt to interpret the material in an etic perspective. The results of the interpretation will vary according to choice of theoretical perspective. I assert that some sort of synthesis between biblical message and traditional Malagasy culture is at work and can be observed in the shepherds' practice and understanding of exorcism,[104] and I have chosen to use elements from worldview theory, especially the knowledge that implicit worldview assumptions to a large degree guide human understanding and practice, as a means of interpreting a few main lines in the material.

Each culture is an integrated entity and can be analysed at different levels. The surface level of a culture can be observed in the explicit explanations people give when they are asked about how things function, or about what they are doing. Underlying these explicit explanations and practices are basic assumptions. The basic assumptions are to a great degree implicit, but the study of worldview is constantly looking for occasions where these implicit assumptions are made explicit. The

---

[101] Kvale 1996:217.

[102] Cf. 1.1.

[103] Kvale understands the three levels as abstractions from a continuum of levels and my presentation mainly relates to the areas of self-understanding and critical common-sense understanding. Kvale 1992:182.

[104] These are the contexts within which the shepherds have grown up and have been socialised into but which seem to be unarticulated by them to a great degree.

American professor of mission anthropology P.G. Hiebert says that these basic assumptions of a culture "are sometimes called a worldview".[105]

When I interview the shepherds they can tell me a lot of shared cultural knowledge. This is useful information in the process of analysing the shepherds' understanding of exorcism. I have to be aware, however, that underlying all this explicit knowledge are implicit assumptions at a deep level, which serve as the foundation upon which the shepherds build their beliefs and understanding. It will be an important task to search for some of these core traits of the culture, i.e. elements in the shepherds' worldview and give examples of how these basic assumptions seem to mould the shepherds' practice and understanding of exorcism.

Such a search for implicit worldview assumptions is prompted by three observations in my material: A. discovery of controversies among the shepherds, B. elements in their practice and understanding that seem obscure to me and C. the fact that some elements are emphasised more than others. I want to show that these controversies, obscure elements and differences in emphasis in my material can be more properly understood by using elements from worldview theory as a means of interpretation.

In order to establish my perspective I have to furnish a presentation of the two contexts, both of which have influenced the shepherds. With traditional Malagasy culture as one of the contexts I am trying to show some of the underlying traits of the culture, which I assert are still

---

[105] "Taken together, the basic assumptions about reality which lie behind the beliefs and behavior of a culture are sometimes called a worldview .... Because these assumptions are taken for granted, they are generally unexamined and therefore largely implicit". Hiebert 1985:45. Hiebert has written several books and articles on the subject of culture, worldview and gospel, he has much experience both as a foreign missionary and as a missionary trainer and few has been working more with the subject of spirit encounter in a missionary context than him. His special interest has been to investigate the point of contact between the biblical message and different cultural contexts and how this encounter has caused changes in the worldview assumptions of the believers. He became increasingly aware of how worldview assumptions at the deepest level of a culture guide all thinking, emotional reactions and evaluative decisions in a comprehensive way. Nishioka 1998. My assertion is that the shepherds' exorcism constitutes such a point of contact between the biblical message and the traditional Malagasy culture and thus Hiebert's theories seem to be fruitful in my project.

underlying Malagasy thinking today.[106] Significant traits in the traditional Malagasy culture will be described as far as they have relevance to exorcism and thus I am not pretending to include all aspects. My sources for this description are not the shepherds themselves but works of Malagasy and non-Malagasy researchers from the fields of religious studies, cultural anthropology and theology.

Concerning the biblical message as the second context, I have chosen to present a close-to-the-text description in the tradition of biblical theology because of my conviction that this biblical theology has influenced my informants.[107] I will not make a broad description including all theological perspectives but delimit the presentation to selected elements in the biblical material with relevance to exorcism. I also maintain that a conservative understanding of the biblical message has been most prominent in the Malagasy Lutheran Church.[108] The

---

[106] I am saying "traditional Malagasy culture" and not only "Malagasy culture". If the word "traditional" is omitted, the expression would be too indefinite to use as a tool in my analysis. This would mean the culture as it persists in Madagascar today and the Malagasy culture today shows obvious signs of Christian and Western influence, especially in the geographical area covered by this work. Dahl 1999:33.

[107] According to B.S. Childs, the focus of biblical theology is to relate the diverse biblical witnesses to the unity of the one Word of God. In exploring the nature of the Bible's witness and in analysing the inner coherence within the biblical texts, the discipline tries to uncover the early roots of the doctrine. Childs 1992:369–371. Biblical theology focuses upon what the texts meant to the first readers who were living in a "pre-critical" world, which will be the case also for many Malagasy readers, most of the shepherds included. It is probable, however, that my informants, with their level of education, are more influenced by Western thinking than shepherds in the countryside with little or no formal training.

It is interesting to notice that the preachers in healing services often comment on the text from the perspective of the time it was written before relating it to the present situation. I understand this both as an underlining of the text itself and as an awareness that the text was initially written in another context. See 3.1.3.

It may be objected to my approach at this point that no biblical theology is a neutral interpretation of the text but somehow conveys the views of the author. Even though the author tries to describe the meaning of the texts to the first readers, it is impossible to avoid an element of interpretation in writing biblical theology. It has to be admitted that all writing includes an element of interpretation and so this critique will also concern the description of the traditional Malagasy culture. At least, biblical theology is a descriptive theological field and the aim of the authors is to keep as close to the writing situation as possible.

[108] It was missionaries from the Norwegian Missionary Society (NMS) who came to Madagascar in 1867 and later founded the Malagasy Lutheran Church (FLM). Lutheran Christians in the US were contacted and the first missionaries came in

SOURCES AND METHODOLOGY 35

sources of my description of biblical message will then be scholars in a conservative theological tradition, both Western and non-Western.[109] I do not say that my description of the biblical message is more correct than others or that all the members in the Malagasy Lutheran Church understand the Bible in this way. It is likely, however, that a description of the biblical message as I have chosen to present it in chapter 4.1.2 is close to a message, which has been preached in the Lutheran church and

---

1888. Aano 1984:37. The American Lutheran Church (ALC), whose theological basis was not far from the NMS', sent these missionaries. Missionaries of rather conservative traditions have been influencing the Malagasy Christians until the present through parish work, Bible schools and theological seminaries.

Another indication of the dominant theological course in the FLM can be documented by examining theological literature available in the Malagasy language. The main bulk consists of books written by Norwegian (and some American) theologians and translated into Malagasy. I mention some of the authors related to the study of the NT: Olaf Moe (introduction to the NT), Sigurd Odland (Mt), Hans Kvalbein (Lk), C.R. Johnson (Jn), Erling Danboldt (1 Cor), Per Undheim (Gal), O. P. Stavaas (Heb, Jas, 1 Pet). TPFLM 1998:307. This literature has been used to a great extent at Bible schools and seminaries but also as study books for Christians in general.

[109] I have been struggling to find the most relevant methodological tool for analysing the shepherds' biblical worldview and what I have chosen is not without problems. I have investigated other possible solutions in order to establish alternative methodological tools to analyse the Christian influence in the shepherds' understanding of exorcism but I have decided not to use any of them.

Initially, I intended only to present the shepherds' own biblical understanding but I realised that this would not be feasible as a tool of analysis. To be able to analyse their actual understanding I have to establish a tool outside the shepherds themselves, as I have done in describing the traditional Malagasy culture.

A second possibility, was to search for an African way of understanding the biblical message and compare this with the shepherds' actual understanding. This would have established a tool outside the shepherds but other problems occurred: Africa is a vast continent and what biblical understanding should be chosen? How can I establish that an African biblical understanding is more congenial with the shepherds' than e.g. a conservative Western understanding? A comparison between the shepherds and similar movements in Africa would have been a possibility but I have delimited my work not to include such a comparison. The main argument against this possibility is the seemingly lack of a direct link between an African understanding and the shepherds' environment.

A third possibility was to establish the "biblical message" on the basis of available theological literature in the Malagasy language. This literature is too scanty to cover this theme, however and a selection of only written literature in the Malagasy language might also underestimate the passing on of oral teaching on this theme through foreign missionaries and Malagasy Christians.

thus has influenced the listeners, included the shepherds. My intention is not to use the description as a tool to evaluate or criticise the shepherds' understanding of the Bible. My treatment is descriptive and the biblical message as a context of understanding will only be used to highlight the shepherds' own understanding and emphases.

The purpose of the presentation of both contexts is to draw some lines in the material, which presumably have influenced the shepherds. I emphasise, however, that traditional Malagasy culture and biblical message only furnish horizons of understanding and tools of interpretation with the aim of interpreting more properly the shepherds' practice and understanding of exorcism and thus the contexts are not my focus of interest.[110]

The validity of the interpretation at this level depends on whether the chosen elements from worldview theory are valid for analysing the shepherds' implicit assumptions leading to their exorcism practice and whether the interpretations follow logically from the theory. Other researchers will be the validating community.[111] Because the purpose of this study is to furnish a basic description of a scholarly unexplored area, the theoretical interpretation as such will be granted only a limited number of pages at the end of chapter 4.[112] The missiological perspective, however, i.e. the phenomenon of exorcism as a synthesis of biblical message and traditional Malagasy culture in the shepherds' thinking, is the backbone throughout the book.

1.3.3.3 *Comments on the text of the book*

In parts of the book where I refer to shepherds and non-shepherds I have reserved the text solely to the shepherds' understanding, i.e. where I refer to field material from non-shepherds, this is always done in footnotes. In the following when I use "informant" in the text referring to my field material, this always means material from shepherds. This is done with the purpose of clarification and variation.[113] In some parts of the book, this causes somewhat comprehensive footnotes but it is a conscious

---

[110] See the presentation of both contexts in 4.1.
[111] Kvale 1996:217–218.
[112] See 4.6.
[113] The word "informant" is a general term and would normally be used to cover all the people in my field material, regardless of whether they are shepherds or not. My usage is special.

choice facilitating the reading of the text with reference to the shepherds' practice and understanding running through the main text of the whole book.

Indentation with reduced characters is used to present longer citations and more extensive summaries of both my field material and published sources.

I use italics to indicate Malagasy words except personal names and place names. The first use of a Malagasy word, a brief translation will appear in the text.[114] It is often an intrigueing and difficult task to translate Malagasy words to English and in order to give people competent in the Malagasy language access to the original wording, in relevant cases I render the Malagasy expression.

Quotation marks are also used when I translate Malagasy words to English.[115]

References to literature are given in footnotes with author, year of publication and reference to pages.

Acronyms are printed in full the first time they appear in the text.[116]

The numbers in cross-references point to chapters and subchapters and refer to the Table of contents. When the cross-reference is found in an unnumbered title in a subchapter, I list the concerned title in paranthesis in the reference.

1.4 Outline of the book

After having presented in this first chapter the problem, background and motivation of the present work, together with a presentation and reflection on the methodological questions concerning production and interpretation of data, the rest of the book consists of three main chapters.

The setting of exorcism is the theme in chapter 2. Firstly, I give a brief historical sketch of the movement from the calling of the founder *Dada* Rainisoalambo in 1894 to the death of *Mama* Nenilava in 1998, the

---

[114] See further Glossary.

[115] E.g. "strengthening" is used with quotation marks whenever it refers to the second part of exorcism, because it is a direct translation of the Malagasy word *fampaherezana*. The first part of exorcism, casting out of demons, has no quotation marks, however, because it is no direct translation of the Malagasy wording. The shepherds usually say *asa*, which is translated "work" to denote this first part.

[116] See Acronymns and abbreviations.

last of the great founders of the four main branches. The fragility of the shepherds' oneness is exemplified. Secondly, essential characteristics of the *Fifohazana* are presented: calling, instruction and consecration of shepherds, their life and conduct and their relation to pastors and traditional healers. I also present elements of the shepherds' view of demons and their terminology related to demons and exorcism. My purpose with this short overview is to enable the reader to see exorcism within the framework of the revival movement as a whole.

Chapters 3 and 4 constitute the main part of the book. In chapter 3 I describe the elements in a healing service where exorcism takes place. I have focused on elements, which could be observed, registered and described. What? and How? are the main questions. Prayer, singing and preaching are necessary elements to be included, but the main focus of my presentation is exorcism. I describe how shepherds and the congregation prepare themselves, Scripture reading, important elements in the casting out of demons (*asa*) and the organisation and the content of the following "strengthening" (*fampaherezana*).

Chapter 4 is the most comprehensive and the shepherds' understanding of exorcism is arranged thematically according to central themes emerging from the preceding description of a healing service. In line with my missiological perspective, the shepherds' understanding is interpreted within the two wider contexts: traditional Malagasy culture and biblical message, which are briefly presented in the beginning of this chapter. I briefly describe the shepherds' understanding of the relation between exorcism and Christian teaching/God's word. I then concentrate on the shepherds' understanding of people in need of exorcism, how to identify these and what causes this need. The shepherds' understanding of the two parts of exorcism is then dealt with: expulsion of demons and related issues and the healing process, which also includes a subchapter on sickness and exorcism. At the end of chapter 4 I have attempted to interpret a few main themes in the shepherds' practice and understanding, called crucial issues, in light of my theoretical perspective. I have done so by making explicit as far as possible some of the shepherds' underlying assumptions and the purpose is to further enlighten the shepherds' understanding of exorcism.

Chapter 5 is a concluding summary to the research questions presented in the Introduction. In an outlook at the end, I list some important theological questions emerging from my presentation without trying to discuss them within the scope of this project. In this way, however, I announce the pressing need for further theological work with the subject.

2 The setting of exorcism: Historical roots and essential characteristics of the *Fifohazana*

In the first part of this chapter I will give a brief sketch of the historical roots of the *Fifohazana*. The purpose is to furnish a broader picture of the movement, of which exorcism is a part. The second part ranges from characteristics of the movement as a whole to the narrower picture with special relevance to my project. The shepherds are the focus; their way to consecration, characteristics of their living, their view of demons and their terminology characterising my subject. I use both written sources and my field material in the description.

2.1 A brief sketch of the historical roots of the *Fifohazana*

The experiences of the founders are important to the shepherds and the founders' teaching has great authority when it comes to practice and understanding today. This historical orientation makes it necessary to recapitulate some of the *Fifohazana* history. In the following I will present the founders through a brief historical sketch and give some lines in the subsequent development of the *Fifohazana*, including an example of the fragility of the shepherds' oneness.

2.1.1 The historical development

The *Fifohazana* originated in Soatanana in the Fianarantsoa-district, initiated by *Dada* Rainisoalambo, in 1894.[117] Several years earlier he had been baptised by English missionaries but had turned back to the practice of traditional medicines and he was a respected person because of his skills of divination and healing. During a period of trouble and illness, where *Dada* Rainisoalambo himself turned severely ill, he sought his charms and idols to rescue him. All of that failed but one night he had a vision of a person dressed in white who told him to throw away all his charms. He was convinced that the person was Jesus, he obeyed Jesus' order, his sickness vanished and he became a committed Christian. At once he shared this experience with his family and close friends. The revival spread quickly and *Dada* Rainisoalambo organised his followers, called disciples of the Lord (*mpianatry ny Tompo*) or apostles (*apostoly*) and set them a severe discipline of hard work, purity, prayer and reading of the Bible. He gave them a proper instruction and sent them as messengers (*iraka*) to different parts of the isle. They walked from village to village, from house to house proclaiming the good news of forgiveness of sins. *Dada* Rainisoalambo ordered them not to model the preachers in the churches, who preached the power of Jesus Christ but did not dare to cast out sicknesses and demons. They should never separate preaching and signs. *Dada* Rainisoalambo's revival originated within the area of the Lutheran church, by then led by Norwegian missionaries and *Dada* Rainisoalambo instructed his followers always to stay within the church. In 1954, however, a great schism appeared and 90 % of the Soatanana-branch seceded from the Lutheran church and formed a "non-dependent church" (*Fifohazana tsi-miankina*).[118]

The *Fifohazana* originating with *Neny* Ravelonjanahary in Manolotrony, near Ambalavao in the Finarantsoa district is the only branch, which came into being outside the area of the Lutheran church.

---

[117] People use parental terms to refer to the founders. *Dada* means "dad", *neny* means "mum", *mama* means "mama" and *datatoa* means "uncle" (see names below). Ramambason L.W. maintains that the four gifted founders have generated four "families" of "children" and that community life can be compared to Malagasy extended family life. Ramambason 1999:62 (quotation marks found in Ramambason).

[118] Since the *Fifohazana* originating with *Dada* Rainisoalambo is the first of the great revivals in Madagascar, it is fairly well documented. See, among others, Thunem and Rasamoela 1972, Rajoelisoa 1977–80, Rabehatonina 1991, Dubourdieu-Jacquier 1996, Dubourdieu-Jacquier 1999.

A BRIEF SKETCH OF THE HISTORICAL ROOTS OF THE *FIFOHAZANA* 43

Neny Ravelonjanahary was brought up in an environment of traditional religion and her grandfather was a recognised traditional healer. The revival started around 1900 and the characteristics of her ministry were her preaching of repentance and her healing activity. Exorcism was an integrated part of her work.[119]

By 1938 revival had come to the South-Eastern coast of the isle. It started in the Vangaindrano district, where a local king and traditional healer (*ombiasa*) converted to Christianity. While he was still a non-Christian, he became severely ill and people supposed him to be mad. But the next day he summoned the people to come to church and told that Jesus had appeared to him through a vision.[120] This happened not far from the area where another of the revival founders, *Mama* Nenilava lived and her husband, Mosesy Tsirefo, had also been in contact with the revival people (*mpifoha*) and had experienced spiritual renewal. I will give a more detailed picture of this third branch of the *Fifohazana*, the Ankaramalaza movement initiated by *Mama* Nenilava, in the subsection below.

The Farihimena-revival is the fourth of the great branches of the *Fifohazana* in Madagascar. It is closely knit to the young Lutheran pastor Rakotozandry Daniel and his pastoral ministry in the tiny village of Farihimena, not far from Antsirabe, from May 1946 to his death in November 1947, aged 28. He was often sick from infancy. At the age of 8 he was taken to shepherds who cast out demons and prayed for him. The 25th of August 1946 the Lord spoke to him during his sickness and ordered him to rise up and prepare to meet a delegation of Christians visiting him. He did so and he preached God's word of repentance in a way that touched the listeners to tears. They spent the following night in prayer and the 26th of August a large number of people repented from their sins. This date has since then been the commemoration day of this branch of the revival movement. In the months that followed, the powerful preaching of *Dadatoa* Rakotozandry touched thousands of people. Repenting sinners brought their charms and amulets to Farihimena, people were healed from sicknesses and demoniacs were set free. Love of the Bible and confession of sins are characteristics of this

---

[119] See Aano 1984 and Rabehatonina 1991.
[120] Randrianarivony 1942.

branch of the revival movement, which mostly took place among members of the Lutheran church.[121]

According to Ramambason, the status and function of shepherds took definite shape in the 1950's. He refers to a couple of lectures about the *Fifohazana* at a Malagasy conference in 1953, where the shepherds' practice and the results of their work are commented.

> Shepherds practise counselling in private homes, they lay hands on people for exorcism, healing and strengthening and their ministry has born visible results. Many churches have been started through their work, they have brought renewal to established churches and church attendance has increased. The shepherds are described as people of prayer, they are simple, patient and enthusiastic and they work in close co-operation with local pastors and leaders.[122]

While the *Fifohazana* originated as a revival, prompted by the Holy Spirit, according to the shepherds' understanding, it is also institutionalised as departments within the Protestant churches. In the Lutheran church, to which my project is delimited, the *Fifohazana* is called a *sampam-pikambanana* in the church, i.e. a "branch where people gather" or a department of the church.[123] The *Fifohazana* has committees on every level, from the local church, to the parish, in the synod and in a committee covering the whole church. It is under the jurisdiction of the church and its purpose is to help the church fulfil its mandate.[124]

This double obligation, both to the founders of the *Fifohazana* and to the church organisation, has not been without problems. In addition, it has been a challenge to settle the differences between the branches. When shepherds from all four branches co-operate in the same church, problems easily emerge, especially connected to differences concerning dress and practice. Each of the branches tends to emphasise their way of doing things as the true one and they all refer to their founders. The pastors in the church are expected to solve these disagreements, since the

---

[121] See, among others, Chapus and Bøthun 1951, Rajoelisoa 1977–80, Rabehatonina 1991.

[122] This is a brief summary of Ramambason 1999:67–68. He refers mainly to the reports from the Soatanana- and Farihimena-branches but this could also be said about the Ankaramalaza-branch of the *Fifohazana*.

[123] Other departments at the same level are e.g. Sunday school work, women and men's work and the evangelism department.

[124] Fiangonana Loterana Malagasy 1984:55–56.

A BRIEF SKETCH OF THE HISTORICAL ROOTS OF THE *FIFOHAZANA* 45

shepherds are under the pastors' jurisdiction and this sometimes causes trouble in the relation between shepherds and pastors.[125]

In 1965 the four main branches of the revival movement were officially united in the *Fifohazana FFPM*, without erasing the characteristics of each branch. This is a joint committee, reflecting the ecumenical orientation of the *Fifohazana* within the Protestant churches in Madagascar. One of the purposes was to create a common ground for the branches to discuss dissimilarities and to work for joint statutes for the movement. The joint statutes became a reality, discussed again in 1980 and given a partial renewal in 2000.[126]

---

[125] The shepherds' double obligation is illustrated by a question in the pamphlet with questions and answers, issued by the Ankaramalaza-*toby*: Who is the appropriate authority to reinstate a shepherd who has been taken out of service? The answer refers to the procedures in the Lutheran church and underlines that the shepherd is a church worker, even if he/she is not salaried. Thus, the parish has authority both to take the shepherd out of service and to reinstate the shepherd if it is clear that he/she has repented and turned away from his/her wrongdoing. This removal/reinstatement may also be done in all the *toby* having the right to consecrate shepherds. When a *toby* reinstates a shepherd, they should always report this to the district pastor (*mpitondra fileovana*), because he stamps the shepherds' legitimisation cards annually. Ankaramalaza 1997:34.

[126] Fifohazana FFPM 1980, Fifohazana miray ao amin'ny FFPM 2000. According to Rabehatonina 1991:100–104 there were lots of problems between the *Fifohazana* FFPM and the church administration because the shepherds followed their own statutes and not the regulations in the churches. To remedy this situation the general meeting of the Protestant churches organised the Lutheran and the Reformed *Fifohazana* in the *Fiombonan'ny Fifohazana Protestanta*—FFP (the union of the Protestant *Fifohazana*) in 1989. It was then emphasised that the *Fifohazana* belongs to the church and is subject to the organisation and statutes of the churches and that the *Fifohazana* has been given gifts of grace to lay hands on people, expel demons, heal the sick and instruct the Christians to love prayer. To my knowledge the FFP has not played any major role in the organisation of the *Fifohazana*.

Rabehatonina belongs to the Reformed church (FJKM) and to me, it seems as the problems between the *Fifohazana* and the leaders of the church have been more visible there than in the Lutheran church. Cf. the new orientation of the Reformed church towards the *Fifohazana* described in 2.1.2 below, which seems to be an effort both to reinforce the confessional bonds between the *Fifohazana* and the church and to modernise the shepherds' practices. I will not describe and discuss challenges connected to the structure of the *Fifohazana* in the present project. This could be the theme of a separate study.

2.1.2 Handling differences: "Unity in spite of diversity"

The shepherds acknowledge a basic unity although they accept differences in practices and customs.[127] Each *toby* is attached to one of the main branches of the revival movement and all the shepherds working in a *toby* follow its practice, irrespective of their personal *toby*-affiliation.[128] The shepherds' oneness is rooted in the fact that they are all assigned by the Lord to one specific service.[129]

When some of my informants characterise the different branches of the revival movement, they normally talk of Farihimena and Ankaramalaza as having many similar points: strong sentiments, people cry, the shepherds cast out demons with loud voices and there are manifestations of demonic oppression. In the Soatanana-branch, on the contrary, the healing services are calmer, with prayer as the emphasised element in "work and strengthening".[130]

> What caused the practices were the different gifts of grace to the founders in the beginning. God works in many ways but this does not exclude unity. The Farihimena revival put great stress on God's word within the person, according to Jesus' saying: "If you abide in me, and my words abide in you, ask whatever you will, and it shall be done for you," (Jn 15:7) and this led to the custom of pressing the Bible to the chest during expulsion of demons. The custom in Farihimena is to walk around and command the demons loudly to depart, just as Jesus rebuked (*niteny mafy*) the demons. ... Dadatoa Rakotozandry cast out demons with a loud voice, the raised hand gesticulating in the air stems from Ankaramalaza and the way of laying hands on people comes from Soatanana.[131]

---

[127] IS 210. The heading is a citation from this informant.

[128] O 343. The shepherds use their own dresses, however, which are slightly different from branch to branch. As mentioned, it is the pastors in the local churches who are expected to regulate the choise of one practice but it is also possible to follow different practices by rotation, as it is done in Ambositra, according to IS 322.

[129] Tobilehibe 1997:87. This unity has been preserved, since the beginning of the movement, by shepherds in different church families (the Lutheran, the Reformed and even the Roman Catholic Church), a fact, which indicates that the unity does not stem from a theological consensus in all matters but from the shepherds' one specific service. It is a standing challenge that the shepherds both belong to the revival movement and that they, at the same time, are members of different historical church families.

[130] IS 318, O 343. IS 205 says, however, that the Farihimena-practice is quiet (*mangina*) while they make noise (*mitabataba*) in Ankaramalaza.

[131] IS 210. Rajoelisoa A.'s way of describing the gifts of grace seems to imply that each branch's gift (note singular) from the Holy Spirit includes a whole array of

It is not to be denied, however, that sometimes the differences in practice cause division between the shepherds, especially in the towns where shepherds from all the branches co-operate.[132] This calls for a more profound teaching, according to one informant, because if the shepherds are sufficiently trained, different working methods do not constitute any problem. "The wisdom from above is easily put in order (*mora alahatra*)," he says.[133]

> The four branches of the revival movement can be compared to the four Gospels but if the training of shepherds is insufficient, they tend to exaggerate visible customs and practices on how to cast out devils and how to lay hands on people. Then they are unable to see the basic meaning of the revival and they forget the Bible.[134]

Recently, the unity acknowledged by the four main branches of the revival movement is under threat. This is due to an effort from the Reformed church (FJKM) to introduce only one practice of exorcism in all its churches. This started in 1997, according to one of my informants.[135]

---

different actions. He says that in Soatanana the spiritual gift (note singular) consists of preaching the Gospel, forgive sins, heal the sick, laying on of hands, cast out demons and apply the great law of love for God and neighbours. In Farihimena the gift (note singular) consists of repentance, which leads to conversion and healing and the following witnessing of what God has done. In Ankaramalaza the gift (note singular) works through the word of God, which through a direct message leads the people to know Jesus as saviour and Lord and thus to be converted. Rajoelisoa 1977–80:141. Even if it is not mentioned specifically it is implied that exorcism is part of the treatment in all the branches.

[132] A non-shepherd accuses some shepherds for listening more to the founder of the *toby* than to Jesus and he says that the branches' different practices also cause divisions in the church, which he compares to the situation in Corinth. "The shepherds seem to believe that human customs enable them to cast out demons and not the power and words of Jesus," he says and he draws this conclusion since the shepherds from each *toby* stick so firmly to their own practices. QN 136.

[133] IS 322.

[134] IS 210. Rajoelisoa 1977–80:147 admits that sometimes two branches of the revival movement in the same town have their separate services and they may accuse each other to be wrong and only think of themselves as right. These are exceptions but nevertheless they exist. "On the other hand," he says, "the revival has accelerated the movement of oneness in the country" (p. 153).

[135] IS 323. IS 210 said in 1998 that the FJKM-custom of casting out demons was less than 5 years old, i.e. it was more common after 1993.

My informants see several reasons for this new orientation: The most important biblical basis for FJKM-shepherds when casting out demons is that "this kind cannot be driven out by anything but prayer" (Mk 9:29). Therefore they emphasise that it is by prayer the demons shall be expelled.[136] According to one informant, 70 % of the *toby* dependant on the Soatanana-branch are found within the Reformed church.[137] Thus the Soatanana-custom may furnish most of the background for their new practice. Soatanana-shepherds use low voices when casting out demons, almost whispering and they base this on 1 Kings 19:11–13: "The Lord was not in the strong wind, neither in the earthquake, nor in the fire but in a still small voice." Some informants also see a reaction against the Lutheran church (FLM) in the new FJKM-practice. Three of the four main *toby* originated in the area of the Lutheran church and the FJKM originally made a supplication to become a 5th main *toby*: *toby* FJKM. Later on they decided to drop this idea preferring to create their own practice by putting together elements from all four *toby* to one.[138]

The FJKM maintains that since God is one, there should only be one custom of e.g. expelling demons.[139] My informants think that the FJKM-church wants to adapt to modern times but they question the breaking off from the four main *toby*, because this has cut the ties to the historical foundation.[140] This breaking off from the four main *toby* and the inherited practice of the shepherds has also caused problems within the FJKM-church itself. My informants told about 50 FJKM-churches in the Fenerive Est-area who had announced transfer to the FLM-church because the shepherds there were not allowed by the FJKM-leaders to

---

[136] IS 210. "In my opinion, however," this informant says, "I think there are kinds of demons, which need to hear voices commanding them in the name of Jesus in order to leave."

[137] IS 322.

[138] IS 210. The Protestant revival committee (*Fifohazana FFPM*) did not agree to the supplication, according to this informant because people cannot just decide to inaugurate a *toby*. A *toby* only comes into being by God's work in a special place and this does not depend on human decision. IS 315 says that the FJKM-shepherds do not bring their sick to the FLM-*toby* any more but treat them in their churches if there is not a FJKM-*toby* near-by, since they want to take responsibility for the healing process themselves and do not want to be dependent on the FLM. Some of the reaction is also said to concern what they understand as exaggerated movements and level of voices in the *toby* dependent on the FLM. Cf. 4.4.2.

[139] IS 210.

[140] IS 210, IS 323.

use the traditional Soatanana-practice of exorcism.[141] I heard this in 1998 and in 2001 I was informed that shepherds who had been trained by FLM-leaders are not allowed to "work" in the FJKM-churches and the FJKM arranges their own consecration of shepherds, independent of the four main *toby*.[142]

2.1.3 *Mama* Nenilava

Due to limitation of space, I concentrate on one of the revival leaders in the following presentation. The purpose is to furnish a picture of the revival movement through the example of one of its branches. I choose *Mama* Nenilava and the movement she initiated. She was still alive influencing the movement when I did my fieldwork, I have personally met her, many of the shepherds and one of the *toby* in my material are affiliated to the Ankaramalaza-branch and this branch of the movement has been the most vital until the present. *Mama* Nenilava has always considered herself as part of the Lutheran church and Ramambason L.W. says that her "extraordinary physical and mystical stature has overshadowed the revival fathers and mothers in *Fifohazana* history".[143]

2.1.3.1 *Childhood, calling and instruction for ministry*

The story of *Mama* Nenilava's childhood, calling and subsequent instruction for the ministry is fairly standardised in the literature subsequent to Pastor Zakaria Tsivoery's book, written in 1970 and published in 1972.[144] It is an insider's story, a biography resembling a

---

[141] IS 210. IS 322 mentioned 120 churches in this area about to leave the FJKM-church. I have not been able to verify this piece of information.

[142] L 337. I emphasise that almost all my information about the controversy between FJKM and FLM stems from shepherd leaders in the FLM, except for one Reformed pastor/shepherd. Thus I am not pretending to give a balanced historical picture of the situation but I use it in order to show the fragility of oneness in the movement. A thorough study of this new orientation of the FJKM-church regarding the shepherds' practice is an interesting theme for further research but it lies outside the scope of the present work.

[143] Ramambason 1999:68.

[144] Tsivoery 1972/1991. In the preface Tsivoery emphasises that it was not his intention to write a book about Nenilava until she had visited Fort Dauphin in 1963. After some time he asked Nenilava for permission to do so, which she granted him because of its worth for the many Christians who would read it. An article in the

hagiography, which is not written according to scholarly standards. I will firstly present this Malagasy hagiographic version and afterwards I briefly present elements of the same story from a Western viewpoint.

Mrs Volahavana Germaine from the Antaisaka tribe was born around 1920 in the Vohipeno district on the South-East coast. Her name from birth was Baolava. Germaine was a name taken at baptism in the near-by Lutheran church. Jesus used the name Volahavana when he talked to her and Nenilava was a nickname given by her adversaries. She is mostly known by Nenilava, which means "tall mother". Her father was a local king and a traditional healer (*ombiasa*) but *Mama* Nenilava never appreciated his skills. She was timid as a child, some sort of a loner and she had an eager desire to see the living God. At the age of 10, she heard the Lord's calling through dreams, voices and visions. Jesus called her by name when she was 12 but she thought it to be her father. Her parents feared she had become mad. Jesus' calling continued as she grew older, sometimes through voices, sometimes through dreams or visions. In 1937 her parents arranged her marriage with the old widower, Mosesy Tsirefo. His wife had died, leaving him with many children. Mosesy was a Christian, even a church worker (*katekista*) and he arranged for his young wife to be baptised after only a few weeks of instruction. She was married until Mosesy died in 1949 and has never been married since. She has not given birth to any children.[145] Only after baptism she realised that it was Jesus who had called her by name and revealed himself to her. Jesus repeatedly ordered her to preach the Gospel and cast out demons but she felt too young and in addition she did not know to read and write.

In May 1941 *Mama* Nenilava had a vision of visiting heaven together with two other women mentioned by name. They were shown

---

church magazine *Ny Mpamangy* and a book written by a retired pastor (may it be Rajosefa undated?) is mentioned as being issued prior to Tsivoery's book.

Tsivoery's book is written in Malagasy, as are also several theses (Randriamalala 1998, Pitaka 1999) and pamphlets (e.g. Botofotsy undated, Ramampiandra 1986) to this story. Two theses present Nenilava's story in French (Rajoelisoa 1977–80) and English (Randrianarivelo 2000) respectively. All the mentioned are written by Malagasys.

[145] The marriage with the old Mosesy (more than 60 years old at the time of marriage) is considered a way God prepared *Mama* Nenilava for her ministry. Randriamalala 1998:7 says that Jesus let her marry Mosesy to keep her conduct from being polluted, that she stayed a virgin and that the couple never slept in the same bed, because in the night Nenilava always slept together with some of Mosesy's children.

A BRIEF SKETCH OF THE HISTORICAL ROOTS OF THE *FIFOHAZANA* 51

the beauty of heaven and many chairs prepared for people on earth, but also some chairs that were turned over. A voice told them to return to earth and speak about the vision. *Mama* Nenilava insisted to stay in heaven but when Jesus showed them the fires of hell, she agreed to go back if Jesus would reveal to her what to do and say.

The 1st and 2nd of August of that year is seen as the starting point of her ministry. One of her stepdaughters had become severely ill. She was diagnosed to have demons and Mosesy had sent for another church worker, Petera, who was a shepherd. He tried to heal the girl by casting out demons but did not succeed. The next day, the 1st of August, he continued his work with the sick girl and *Mama* Nenilava sat by the fire watching. Suddenly she heard a voice from behind. A tall, strong man ordered her to stand up and work. It was Jesus standing behind her and almost pushed her to the bed where the sick stepdaughter lay. She felt a power within her and she cast out demons. When the devils left, they said: "We leave because the one who is stronger than us has come."[146] The stepdaughter recovered immediately and her mind was healed. The following night *Mama* Nenilava again heard the Lord's calling: "Stand up, preach the Gospel everywhere and cast out demons." This day, the 2nd of August is celebrated as the commemoration day of the Nenilava-movement and a great gathering is held every year in the Ankaramalaza *toby* as a remembrance of the calling of *Mama* Nenilava to the ministry.

Jesus took care of the following instruction of *Mama* Nenilava. During three months he taught her to speak in different tongues and when he revealed himself to her, he used these languages. Seven times Jesus took her to heaven to teach her the Holy Scriptures and to read the Bible. Jesus informed her beforehand when she would be taken away and for 2–3 days she lay as if she was dead. Her friends thought she had passed away; they sang hymns, prayed and mourned over her but suddenly she woke up and preached the Gospel with power. She told that Jesus had explained chapters and verses from both the Old and the New Testaments to her and she was able to ask him when she did not understand. In order to train her to fight with the demons, Jesus once led her to a forest place where she had to fight with the dragon, the devil himself. The struggle was fierce for three days and afterwards she

---

[146] This may point to Jesus as stronger than the demons but it may, as well, be understood as pointing to *Mama* Nenilava and the power inhabiting her. The second interpretation may be reflected in the followers' strong focus on *Mama* Nenilava's person and in the miracles happening wherever she went.

needed a whole month to recover. Her training also included abstinence from some sort of food, especially rice, which is most appreciated in the country.

Mama Nenilava's way of working was prayer, preaching of God's word, counselling, a calling to repentance, expulsion of demons and prayer with the laying on of hands. In the church in Madagascar she is considered as both a priestess with the Old Testament High Priest as a model and as a prophetess. She loved Jesus more than anything and she was always obedient to his orders.

The Norwegian missionary, G. A. Meling, who knew *Mama* Nenilava personally for about 30 years and co-operated with her almost on a daily basis for 10 years, has given a short biography in a Norwegian book intended to support the missionary activity.[147] It is not written according to scholarly standards but his presentation has a somewhat different character, compared to the above and therefore I recount part of the story. Meling's version goes as follows:

> He first met the tall, young and uneducated woman in 1938. In 1941 one of Mosesy's daughters fell ill and nearly died. Then the young Nenilava kneeled at the child's bed, laid the hands on her head and asked God to show his power. The healing was visible for everybody and the rumour spread in the area. The happening shocked Nenilava, she was a person of few words and it was difficult for her to be in the centre of people's conversation and longing to meet her. She never used to say anything in open gatherings until once a female missionary challenged her to say some words as a closing of a women's meeting. Then she was filled with the power of the Holy Spirit, she felt a deep peace and she preached with conviction. The audience was startled. This was God speaking to them. The result was crying and confession of sins among the audience. Nenilava was still afraid, however. She felt ignorant and could not even read the Scriptures. One day she disappeared and for 2–3 months she lived in the forest. Meling admits that it is a riddle how she could find food and keep alive during this period. The rumour said that she had fasted all the time. She did not remember much from the period, except for the spiritual experiences she had, which she kept in her heart. Sometimes she told part of this story and Meling says that this has made people invent the most incredible stories about her, like journeys to heaven and other miracles.[148] He refers to a pastor from the high plateaux who has written an entire book about

---

[147] Meling 1972.

[148] The Norwegian text reads: "… noe som igjen har gitt næring til folkefantasien som lager de forunderligste historier om hennes bortrykkelse til himmelen og andre varianter av underhistorier." Meling 1972:55.

all the supernatural happenings around Nenilava.[149] Most of this is "hardly more than overwrought and uncritical verbosity",[150] according to Meling. Nenilava herself was little fond of all the talk around her. She has told him, however, that once her soul was caught up to heaven where she learnt what to do and where she recognised Jesus' nail-marked hands. Everywhere she came, renewal followed her. Meling describes her as extremely quiet, resembling Jesus and always willing to serve others. Jesus told her not to be afraid and promised always to tell her what to say and do. People crowded at her door and God has given her the ability to see what is hidden. She knew people's heart and when she pointed out a number from the hymnbook and a verse from the Bible, people were astonished because it fit exactly their situation.

The differences between the two stories are worth noticing. The Malagasy pastor emphasises the supernatural aspects of the story and underlines the fight with demons, healing and miracles from the very beginning, without setting aside *Mama* Nenilava's extraordinary abilities as a preacher and her love for Jesus. The Norwegian missionary, on the other hand, tends to underline the preaching of the Gospel and her devotedness to Jesus. He seems critical of miracle stories and mentions exorcism only in passing.

2.1.3.2 *Extension of the Nenilava-movement*

Mama Nenilava's ministry was not recognised by the Lutheran church until 1953. That year she started her visits in the Antsirabe district in the high plateaux and since then she has journeyed a lot in the entire country and also abroad. People have crowded to her meetings and they have brought their sick and people afflicted by demons. When she had still not finished the preaching of God's word of repentance, demoniacs showed observable reactions (*mihetsika*) and exorcism was performed.[151]

The rural area where *Mama* Nenilava and her husband Mosesy Tsirefo lived was called Ankaramalaza. The extraordinary experience of

---

[149] I suppose he refers to Rajosefa undated.

[150] Meling 1972:56 (my translation).

[151] The Norwegian missionary B. Bruknapp says that four pastors followed her and "worked". She uses quotation marks on "arbeidet" ("worked"), which most probably indicates that she renders the Malagasy word *miasa*. In connection with the shepherds' activities, this is used about the first part of exorcism (*asa*). It can also be used about exorcism as such (both casting out of demons and laying on of hands) and I suppose that this is the meaning here. Note that *Mama* Nenilava from the beginning used pastors to help her. Bruknapp 1979:2.

August 2nd 1941 took place there and this place constituted the centre for the further activities. When Mosesy died, *Mama* Nenilava inherited the place and in 1953 Ankaramalaza was recognised as *toby lehibe*, i.e. as one of the four main centres of *Fifohazana*. It is situated about 20 kilometres North-West of the city Vohipeno on the eastern coast. Marginalised people, physically or mentally sick, came to seek healing and deliverance in *Mama* Nenilava's house. Many of the healed decided to live there and new houses were built. From being a tiny village, it has now grown to about 200 houses with 800 people, a primary and secondary school, a hospital and a concrete church.[152]. People in need of long-term care, who *Mama* Nenilava met on her travels, could not all be sent to the Ankaramalaza *toby*. Then the idea of building small *toby*, affiliated to the main *toby*, was born and in the Ankaramalaza-branch alone there are today 39 such centres spread throughout the country.[153]

Mama Nenilava always respected the other branches of the revival movement and she, as often as possible, visited the other main *toby* at the commemoration days. She told her followers to obey the church organisation and its leaders, i.e. the pastors, because they all come from God.[154] She worked as an evangelist within the Lutheran church and she did not consider herself above the head-office of the church. Her primary activity was to lead people to Jesus and she often told people to hold on to Jesus.[155]

Mama Nenilava died the 22nd of January 1998 in Ankaramalaza and was buried there the 30th of January. A multitude of people were present at her burial, including a delegation from the President of the country. The Prime minister decorated her with a medal of honour (Commandeur de l'Ordre National) at this moment.[156] In a press conference held by leaders of the movement at the occasion of her burial, the question of the future of the *Fifohazana* Ankaramalaza after *Mama* Nenilava's death

---

[152] The numbers are taken from Ramambason 1999:69 and goes back to about 1990.

[153] The number is found in Randrianarivelo 2000:55. A majority of my observation reports refer to the Ambohimahazo *toby*, which is affiliated to the Farihimena-branch of the revival movement. To the history of this *toby*, see Randriakoto 1982. Another *toby* in my material, where I have observed the shepherds' work, Log 238, 67 Ha, is affiliated to the Ankaramalaza-branch. See Ankaramalaza undated:81–83, 166–167.

[154] Randrianarivelo 2000:57.

[155] Rabenandrasana 1998:15.

[156] She had earlier been awarded the Norwegian St. Olavs order.

was commented on. It was emphasised that Jesus is the Lord of the movement and Jesus is going to guide and continue the work:

> But if the future work will be grounded on miracles and different visions, it will be demolished. To all of us who continue her work: We should not be filled with worries ... but be strong and have faith. *Mama* said: "If you want to call me *Mama*, love Jesus."[157]

2.2 Essential characteristics of the *Fifohazana*

2.2.1 The movement as a whole

According to the shepherds' own thinking, expressed in the handbook, the *Fifohazana* is defined as God's work through the Holy Spirit.[158]

> The reason for its existence is to proclaim and "perform" (*manatanteraka*) the Scriptures, by preaching and by performing signs. Four decisive points are singled out in "Jesus' founding" of the *Fifohazana* and the shepherds' work, firstly, God's word and the teachings given by Jesus to the founders.[159] The basis of everything God does is his word and it is the basis from which the revival emerges. Since the teachings of the founders are grounded in God's word, their teachings, too, are considered a basis, upon which the revival is built.[160] Secondly, the *Fifohazana* maintains its unity with the church. The shepherds belong to the *Fifohazana* and should take care of this calling but the shepherds belong to the church as well and they should co-operate closely with the pastors. The unity of the revival movement with the church is grounded in the history of the founders, because God gave the revival movement to the church and made the founders co-operate closely with pastors and other church-workers. It is also grounded in Jesus' care for the church, which he calls his own body.

---

[157] Rabenandrasana 1998:16 (translation and italics mine). Leaders in the Ankaramalaza-branch led the press conference: Andreas Richard, Rakoto Endor Modeste and Rabarioelina Bruno.

[158] The following description is summarised from Tobilehibe 1997:15–29.

[159] The founders are called *raiamandrenim-pifohazana* (the revival fathers and mothers). Cf. 2.1.1.

[160] The handbook criticises those who overlook the significance of the founders. In traditional Malagasy thinking a notion of shame is connected to ignorance about the forefathers and foremothers.

This means that the unity with the church ultimately is built upon God's word.[161] The third decisive point is the unity within the revival movement.[162] It is said that the different branches of the revival movement have the same basis,[163] the lives of the founders are examples of the unity between them and the practical organisation of the shepherd life expresses this unity.[164] The fourth point mentioned is the unity in the emphasis of the *toby*-institution and in the consecration of shepherds. It is maintained that Jesus has established the *toby* and the four main centres are called *tobilehibe* (great *toby*).[165] A *toby* affiliated to the main centre is called *zanatoby* (a toby-child) or only *toby*. God's intervention, not only in the coming into being of the *tobilehibe* but also in founding new *toby*, is emphasised. The model of *toby*-life is Jesus' parable of the Good Samaritan and there is an indispensable link between the shepherds and the *toby*.[166]

In the first part of the joint statutes, called definitions, the task of the *Fifohazana* is stated: "To preach the Gospel to all people, take care of the mentally sick and the poor."[167] This task is accomplished through the revival movement's preparing and teaching of shepherds and *iraka* (itinerant shepherds) to do this.[168] Another paragraph summarises the task

---

[161] The handbook opposes the opinion that the revival movement is independent of the church. This misunderstanding may be held both by shepherds and by church officials.

[162] This does not exclude differences among the shepherds, which is compared to children in the same family who do not look exactly like each other and do different things, but they still belong to the same family.

[163] This includes the Bible, certain common characteristics (Jesus' name, repentance and faith, the Holy Spirit's work, the unity with the church, the teachings of the founders, the work of shepherds, the *toby*, the service of all people and the whole human) and a common upbringing: repentance and faith.

[164] e.g. the shepherds are free to choose the *toby* where they will be consecrated, regardless of where their instruction has been and all of them carry the same name: *zanaky ny Fifohazana* (children of the revival).

[165] *Toby* Soatanana (1894), *Toby* Manolotrony (1927), *Toby* Ankaramalaza (1941), *Toby* Farihimena (1946). These four constitute what I call the four branches of the revival movement.

[166] The calling of shepherds, their instruction and consecration will be treated in a separate subsection below.

[167] Mal: *Mitory ny Filazantsara amin'ny olombelona rehetra, mikarakara ny marary saina sy ny mahantra koa izy*. Fifohazana FFPM 1980:no 2. To the issue of sickness and exorcism, see 4.5.1.

[168] Itinerant shepherds, called *iraka* (those who are sent), are mentioned together with shepherds. An *iraka* has been given additional instruction, after having practised as a shepherd for some time and he/she is sent on mission to poorly evangelised areas.

ESSENTIAL CHARACTERISTICS OF THE *FIFOHAZANA*

even more by saying that the work of the shepherds is to "preach the Gospel and cast out demons...".[169] I choose to interpret the two paragraphs as complementing each other, pointing to the shepherds' threefold work: preaching, caring and exorcism. Exorcism does not exclude the loving care of sick and poor people, a fact exemplified by the shepherds' care of the sick and disabled in the *toby*.[170]

When Rajoelisoa A. characterises the revival movement, he mentions firstly the essential indigenous aspect and that the different movements originated in distinct, localised areas of the island.[171] Secondly, he attributes the movement to a direct calling of the founders by God. Thirdly, he describes the indisputable and important role of the Bible, which leads the shepherds' actions and serves as a reference for all they do. Fourthly, the fruits of the revival are mentioned: repentance from sin, healing from sickness and demonic oppression and spiritual growth in the church. The shepherds' effort to improve the social conditions for people is also underlined, giving shelter and food to the poor. In the Ankaramalaza *toby* there is an elementary school and a dispensary for medical aid.[172] Ramambason L.W. cites a report from 1953, telling about the main results of the *Fifohazana* and he believes that these practices and results are the same today: Many Christians have forsaken their idols, healing has happened and revival has appeared in the church. Ramambason interprets the *Fifohazana* as a reaction to the powerlessness of the ministry of pastors to respond meaningfully to some of the problems facing church members and he points out three areas where pastors were able only to contribute a little, but where shepherds have contributed more. In addition to seeing *Fifohazana* as (1) an anti-idol movement and (2) successful in healing and deliverance

---

The actual number of *iraka* in the area of my investigation seems to be low. I only recall to have met one person.

[169] Fifohazana FFPM 1980:no 23. Mal: *Mitory ny Filazantsara sy mamoaka demonia...*

[170] In an overview article, I have presented the task of *Fifohazana* to be threefold: to preach the Gospel to all people, to take care of the sick and poor and to perform exorcism. Austnaberg 1996:133.

[171] See 2.1.1. He makes a point of the fact that none of the founders operated in the Merina tribe, which historically has been dominant over the others and he calls this a turning upside down (French: "renversement") of what happened in the political scene.

[172] Rajoelisoa 1977–80:126–139.

mentioned above, he also emphasises (3) the economic self-support as remarkable.[173]

2.2.2 Calling, instruction and consecration of shepherds

To become a shepherd is considered a special call from God. As a response to God's calling, a person enters into a training program, which after two years culminates in consecration.[174]

2.2.2.1 Calling

It is believed that the *Fifohazana* from the very beginning came into being through a direct intervention by God. Ramambason L.W. says that *Fifohazana* insiders think that God in person revived *Dada* Rainisoalambo through sickness and miraculous healing. The Holy Spirit is seen as the core cause of the emergence of the revival leaders and the shepherds. Ramambason notices that this insider explanation has not been challenged so far. To the contrary, it seems to be reinforced by the fact that efforts to make revival happen elsewhere have failed.[175] This belief may have contributed to the shepherds' thinking that without a true calling from God, a person should not practise as a shepherd. The handbook makes the point crystal clear when it says that "there is nobody who becomes a shepherd if he/she is not appointed by God to this service".[176] The rest of the handbook's teaching on this matter can be summarised as follows:

---

[173] Ramambason 1999:68, 78. As early as 1914 the Norwegian missionary Johnson defined four characteristics of *Fifohazana*: Firstly, its resemblance with the traditional religion, which he sees in the power-aspect and the casting out of demons. Secondly, the ethical preaching of repentance, including a life of love and humility. Thirdly, the personal experience of God: his intimacy and the power of prayer. Fourthly, the inter-confessional attitude of *Fifohazana*. Johnson 1914:143–146. I only refer to Johnson among the missionaries who commented on the *Fifohazana*, because he did so fairly early in its history and his characteristic is interesting from my point of view.

[174] The three basic elements in Jesus' founding of the shepherd institution (*ny nanorenan'i Jesosy ny maha-mpiandry*), according to the handbook, is a true calling, learning and instruction and consecration. Tobilehibe 1997:29.

[175] Ramambason 1999:76.

[176] Mal: *Tsy misy na iza na iza tonga mpiandry raha tsy voatendrin'Andriamanitra ho amin'izany izy*. The handbook refers to some people's teaching that all believers are

ESSENTIAL CHARACTERISTICS OF THE *FIFOHAZANA*

> A true calling comes from the true God and it is based on God's word, not on the person's zeal, or other people's advice, or problems in life, or dreams and visions. God's call to salvation is distinguished from his call to a special service in the church.[177] The calling of Isaiah is set as a model, when God asked the prophet: "Whom shall I send, and who will go for us?" (Is 6:8) There are many ministries in the church and when God calls a person, it is important to become aware of which kind of service his calling concerns. It is emphasised that the shepherd work and other services in the church supplement each other.[178]

According to Randrianarivelo J., the calling may come through visions or dreams, through trials and troubles in a person's life, or through an experience of healing of the person or someone in his/her close family.[179] B.S. Lie has noticed that most of the people volunteering to become shepherds are ordinary Christians who want a more profound knowledge of their Saviour and assistance to find a way to serve the Lord. He says that many formerly sick and possessed[180] people who have been healed through the shepherds' work are attracted to this service.[181]

Let me insert a calling story from my field material. In the questionnaires to shepherds I asked them to describe briefly why they had become shepherds.

> Before I became a shepherd I was a member of the University Bible Groups.[182] Some people there performed exorcism without being shepherds allowed to perform the shepherd work, with reference to Mk 16:17–18. These people are not given a proper instruction, they are not consecrated and they may not even be called by God to do this work. According to *Mama* Nenilava, these people will soon be tired and abandon their service, because they are not firmly grounded or empowered (*tsy niorina na voafafy hery*). They resemble people going to war without bringing their weapons. Tobilehibe 1997:29.

[177] This distinction is also part of the instruction of shepherds, according to Rasolondraibe 1994:4.
[178] Tobilehibe 1997:29–31.
[179] Randrianarivelo 2000:40.
[180] Norwegian: "besatt".
[181] Lie 1981:8. Most of the shepherds in the area where Lie worked were from the lower classes, in the towns a considerable number came from the middle class and a few from the higher social strata. It should be noticed that Lie has most of his experience in the coastal areas of Madagascar, but his findings do not seem to differ largely from my own impression of the distribution on social strata in my research area.
[182] Groupes Bibliques Universitaires (GBU).

but I saw no real healing and many of them experienced their work as tiresome. At that time, I did not like the shepherd work at all. Some time later my brother's wife fell ill with *ambalavelona*, which is a demoniac and some people took us to a *toby* for treatment. Many shepherds worked with her and they also imposed their hands on my wife and me. My sister-in-law was healed. During this time I heard the words of a shepherd praying for me, saying: "Jesus is calling you to serve him and this is the meaning of what is happening." I did not agree at once but sought the advice of another *Fifohazana* elder, who confirmed to me that Jesus wanted me to become a shepherd. From then I was convinced and I started with the instruction.[183]

This story shows that sickness was a decisive factor in becoming a shepherd. It also shows that other shepherds encourage people who are healed or their relatives to become shepherds. According to the handbook, it seems to be a problem that some shepherds equal troubles in a person's life to be God's calling of this person to become a shepherd. Some may even promise that if the person becomes a shepherd, he/she will be free from trouble. The handbook opposes this tendency, saying that it is immature thinking because the basis of God's calling is always his love and it is never an act of making mutual business.[184]

The idea of testing the people who wish to become shepherds is important. The handbook refers to 1 Jn 4:1 and says that a new Christian should not be taken into the training program (1 Tim 3:6). He/she will not be capable of carrying the heavy burdens of other people and cast out fierce demons.[185] The following criteria should be fulfilled in order to receive a person as novice (*mpiomana*), the name people obtain when preparing to become shepherds:[186] To be a communicant, to be able to read, to have a letter of recommendation from the church/parish/synod, to be at least 25 years old at the consecration,[187] not smoke, not use snuff or drink alcohol. If the person is married, the marriage has to be

---

[183] QS 117. This is a summary of a part of the informant's answer.

[184] Tobilehibe 1997:31. Another problem seems to be that some shepherds separate themselves too much on the basis of their calling and have an attitude which excludes non-shepherds. IS 310.

[185] Tobilehibe 1997:30–31.

[186] *Mpiomana* literally means "one who is preparing".

[187] Ankaramalaza 1997:38 says, however, that the lowest age to enter the training program is 18 years and nobody less than 20 years should be consecrated. The leaders (*raiamandreny*) who make decisions about access to consecration have the last word in this respect and may decide that the novices should wait another year.

authorised according to the state and the church. The person cannot have a physical handicap making him/her unable to perform the shepherd work.[188] The people in charge of the instruction program, which often is the pastor, elders or leaders of the *toby*, discuss and make decisions on whom to accept to become novices.[189]

2.2.2.2 *Instruction*

It is of vital importance for the revival movement to secure a good knowledge of God's word and keep the doctrines clean, according to the handbook.

> *Mama* Nenilava's example shows this, because she never stopped seeking the will of God and held the Bible in high esteem. The basis for the need of instruction is Jesus' words in Jn 8:31: "If you continue in my word, you are truly my disciples." A continuing instruction secures a proper performance of the shepherds' work and keeps them from heresies. Paul is referred to as an example. He did not think that he knew everything (Phil 3:13). The goal of the instruction is a change of life and not outward conformity to certain customs.[190]

The training program for novices is agreed by the four branches of the revival movement, as expressed in the joint statutes.

> The training normally takes place in the local churches and lasts for two years with not less than four days of instruction each month, with another two weeks of intensive training in the *toby* where the person is to be consecrated.[191] The

---

[188] Fifohazana miray ao amin'ny FFPM 2000:7–8, 20.

[189] Tobilehibe 1997:32.

[190] Tobilehibe 1997:32–33.

[191] In the joint statutes of 1980 (Fifohazana FFPM 1980:no 11,4) one and a half years of the training is supposed to be in the home church, while the last 6 months should be at a *toby*. This is in accord with Lie 1981:6. The current program has reduced the period of training at a *toby* very much. As an exception, some novices are consecrated after only one year of instruction, if there is a special reason for doing so, but they have to follow the second year of training after their consecration. Ankaramalaza 1997:37. In 2001 the General Secretary of the FLM said that the training program now should last 3 years but I am not aware of what the application of this means. L 337. I have not had this confirmed by other sources, although already in 1995 a shepherd conference proposed the training period to last for 3 years, with a continuing training for shepherds also after the consecration. Tobilehibe 1995:30.

instruction is divided into five main topics. In the first year 1) teaching of faith, 2) ethics and 3) church history should be taught and in the second year 4) the shepherds' work[192] and 5) laws and regulations.[193]

The statutes further briefly describe the content of each of these topics.

> The teaching of faith includes an overview of the books in the Bible, main themes in dogmatics, the ecumenical creeds and the creeds of the Lutheran and the Reformed churches respectively. Ethics is divided into individual and social ethics, with a separate paragraph on the conduct required by the *Fifohazana*. A brief sketch of the church history from A.D. 30 to the present is given and secondly, the history of the Malagasy *Fifohazana*. The shepherds' work includes preaching, evangelism, exorcism, home visits and prayer fellowship. Laws and regulations are about the church constitutions,[194] the laws of the ecumenical organisations in Madagascar and the regulations of each of the four branches of the *Fifohazana* (the *tobilehibe*).[195]

In an instruction manual written by Rasolondraibe P. the above program is covered in more detail. His book is a guide for the teachers of novices and he includes key words to each theme.[196] In addition to Rasolondraibe the handbook is also used in the instruction of novices, but the outline of this book does not follow the topics prescribed in the joint statutes. It gives more background on the basics of the *Fifohazana* and concentrates on exorcism as its main part.[197]

According to the Ankaramalaza-movement, the organisation of the instruction should be as follows:

> Every church where there is a pastor has the right to start a class of novices. They should only send a letter to the central committee of the *Fifohazana* for

---

[192] Mal: *Ny Asa fanompoana*.

[193] Fifohazana miray ao amin'ny FFPM 2000:8, 19. Randrianarivelo 2000:42 asserts that "only pastors have charge to teach these subjects", which in the context seems to point to the basic doctrines of the Lutheran church. It is not clear what his source for this is and I have not had it confirmed by others.

[194] The Lutheran, the Reformed, the Roman Catholic and the Anglican churches.

[195] Fifohazana miray ao amin'ny FFPM 2000:15–19.

[196] Rasolondraibe 1994. The book has 43 pages and does not contain the 5th topic above: laws and regulations.

[197] Tobilehibe 1997. The reformed church has also issued an instruction manual for their training of novices: FJKM 1997. It has 90 pages and includes the regulations for the revival movement within this church. It could have been interesting to give a critical evaluation of the instruction program according to available written manuals but it would lead too far and exceed the limits of this project.

information. The teachers could be the pastor, the leader of the local *toby*, people appointed by *Mama* Nenilava, elders appointed by the pastor to co-operate with him and people appointed by the committee of teachers of novices in the local church.[198] An examination decides whether the novices are allowed to move from the first to the second year of training. People who do not fulfil the requirements, repeat the first year's course. People who have followed the training program are not automatically given the right to be consecrated if there are still demands that are not fulfilled. Before being accepted for consecration, the novices should have a spiritual conversation (*dinika*) with the teachers. Only people who are accepted for consecration have the right to expel demons in a healing service.[199]

Ramambason L.W. believes that the learning procedure was tougher in the early stages of the revival movement than now. He refers mainly to the Soatanana-branch and says that the course did not proceed unless what was taught had become part of the behaviour of the novices. According to Ramambason, the learning procedure has changed with time and especially in the Ankaramalaza-branch. He believes that the training there is more flexible with a more liberal discipline than before.[200] B.S. Lie is afraid that some places the instruction of the novices is far from thorough enough, especially where the novices are illiterate. The requirements may then be lowered and it is a temptation to consecrate people without sufficient qualifications.[201] Randrianarivelo J. complains that many shepherds do not have sufficient knowledge of the church constitution because they are mostly interested in spiritual and biblical matters. This may cause problems in the co-operation between shepherds and pastors.[202]

---

[198] According to my experience, it is normally the pastor who is in charge of the theoretical part of the instruction of novices in the local church.

[199] Tobilehibe 1997:33–34. This means that only novices in the closing stages of their instruction are allowed to cast out demons. This right does not include the prayer with the laying on of hands, which is exclusively reserved to the consecrated shepherds.

[200] Ramambason 1999:71–72.

[201] Lie 1981:6–7.

[202] Randrianarivelo 2000:44. The critical comments above may be legitimate. It refers to experiences of the practical carrying out of the instruction in local churches while my study is delimited to what the instruction is intended to be. Inadequate instruction may be some of the reason for the movements' effort to furnish more precise training programs and instruction manuals.

2.2.2.3 *Consecration*

The consecration of novices to become shepherds takes place in the church in a *toby* that has the right to consecrate.[203] It is done only once a year, on the annual commemoration day of the *toby*. Those who have finished the instruction may choose which *toby* they want to attend for consecration and the main centres (*tobilehibe*) are most popular if the novices can afford the cost of the journey.[204] The criteria for novices referred to above have to be fulfilled, but in addition to these, the eagerness during the instruction period and the seriousness of moral conduct has to be evaluated as satisfactory in order to be admitted to consecration.[205]

The novices wear their white dress on the day of consecration to have it consecrated together with themselves.[206] This dress is their personal property and they have the responsibility to have it sown and cover the expenses in this respect. The handbook gives detailed regulations about the style of dress in the Ankaramalaza-branch.[207] The dress should be loose, have open sleeves, be simple of solid fabric, well closed in the throat, have a wide collar and be long enough to cover all the other clothes. Men's dress is open in part of the front, with two white buttons, women's dress is open in part of the back, with three white buttons.[208] Old and experienced shepherds should sow the dress while they are praying for those who are going to wear it. The novices are not allowed to sow their own dresses, because the dress is God's clothing of them. The handbook instructs the dressmakers not to exploit the sowing to gain money but rather to take a reasonable coverage of expenses. A pamphlet with question and answers explicitly says that the dressmaker should claim no money to sow the shepherd dress, but this does not prevent gifts from the owner and the novices buy the textiles to be used for the dress.[209] The style of the dress is slightly different among the

---

[203] Not all the smaller *toby* have this right.
[204] Fifohazana miray ao amin'ny FFPM 2000:9–10, Randrianarivelo 2000:41.
[205] Tobilehibe 1997:37–38.
[206] Fifohazana FFPM 1980:no. 19.
[207] Tobilehibe 1997:60–62.
[208] The opening of the women's dress should not be in the front, in order to prevent the enemy from tearing apart the dress through the opening and thus dishonour her. Tobilehibe 1997:61. This caution seems to concern practical shepherd work with people showing severe manifestations during exorcism.
[209] Ankaramalaza 1997:39.

branches of the revival movement but all of them are white and reaching down to the feet.[210]

The consecration day is the year's climax in the *toby*. Since it takes place as part of the annual commemoration of the *toby*, a lot of people are gathered. The days leading up to consecration are filled with different services in the church, morning, afternoon and evening and the consecration day itself begins with prayer and exhortation.[211] In Ankaramalaza it is customary to start this day with a service of prayer, singing and preaching at 4 a.m., which lasts until 6.30 a.m. One person walks through the *toby* calling to prayer by shouting: "Now it is time to pray." As many as possible take part in this service and "God's word is falling like rain, so who is not going to feel well?"[212]

I attended the consecration service in the Ambohimahazo *toby* the 19th of June 1998.

> It started 8 a.m. and lasted until 2.30 p.m. My estimation is that 2–3000 people attended the meeting and only very few of them were able to find a seat in the church. The service started with about 250 novices and shepherds in line, all clothed in long, white robes, walking into the church to reserved seats. The service followed the liturgy of a Sunday morning service until after the sermon, announcements and collection. The President of the Avaratrimania church synod led the service and another pastor had a compelling sermon about the calling. The announcements mainly concerned the shepherds' work, how they should think about differences in the dress between the branches and their obligation to follow the customs of the *toby* where they were working. The collection lasted 2 hours. Then all the names of the people who were going to be consecrated were read.[213] The consecration liturgy consists of prayer, reading biblical passages[214] and singing before the novices kneeled at the altar rail, group by group. The Synod President and another pastor started from the middle of the altar rail and continued to the two sides, asking the questions according to the liturgy,[215] shaking hands as a sign of the "holy covenant", proclaiming that the novices are now workers in the church and

---

[210] See 4.4.4.

[211] Lie 1981:7.

[212] Fikambanana Toby Lehibe Ankaramalaza 1990:10.

[213] The number of novices who had been at Ambohimahazo for intensive training from the 2nd–19th June was about 100. 70–80 of these were consecrated on the 19th of June; the others had chosen to be consecrated elsewhere.

[214] Jer 1:4–10; Jn 21:15–19; Acts 20:28; 1 Pet 5:1–4; Mt 28:18–20.

[215] The liturgy for consecrating workers according to the liturgy book of the FLM is used, with some modifications (especially the great number of people praying for each novice and free prayer).

praying for God's strength to be with them.[216] Then 2 pastors and three shepherd leaders on each side successively prayed for the novices, all of them with the laying on of hands.[217] Apparently, it was a moving experience to be prayed for in this way. All the heartfelt prayers lasted for a long time and when all the novices were prayed for, one of the leaders in the movement had a speech of encouragement to the new shepherds.[218]

The consecration is interpreted within a biblical framework. It is considered a sign of God impressed on his worker and as such, it is necessary.[219] The authority given to the shepherds by God in consecration, places them in a special situation.[220] Consecration gives the strength needed to perform the shepherd work and gives God's gifts of grace. It is a shield against the enemy's power, it is an anointing of the Holy Spirit and it is an official installment to the service.[221] It is considered a covenant and holiness is one of its aspects. The handbook

---

[216] Pastor: "Will you do this holy service according to God's word?" Novice: "Yes." Pastor: "Do you promise to ask the Lord for strength and illumination from the Holy Spirit every day, in order to walk daily in the grace of our Lord Jesus Christ?" Novice: "Yes." Pastor: "Hear then the words of our Lord to his workers: 'He who hears you hears me, and he who rejects you rejects me.' (Lk 10:16). Thus says his word: 'Lo, I am with you always, to the close of the age.' (Mt 28:20). Let us shake hands as a mark of the holy covenant, which is done today. (And he continues) On behalf of the church I receive you as its worker in the name of God the Father, the Son and the Holy Spirit. May the Lord give you strength from above that you may fulfil your service, to bring grace to yourself, blessing to the church and honour to God, today and forever. Amen." Tobilehibe 1997:39 (my translation).

[217] The joint statutes say that there should be from 7 to 10 people praying for each novice. As far as I could observe, in Ambohimahazo only 6 people were praying for each of the persons to be consecrated.

[218] To the content of this speech, see 2.2.3.

[219] Tobilehibe 1997:35–37 has many biblical references. *Fanamarihan'Andriamanitra* (a sign of God) comes from the root *marika*, which is translated "marque, signe, modèle, plan". Abinal and Malzac 1930:434. Randrianarivelo J. mentions that *Mama* Nenilava was not consecrated like the other shepherds. According to the Ankaramalaza-branch, Jesus himself consecrated her and this was made official on the 2nd of August 1983, sometimes called the crowning of Nenilava. Limits of space does not allow me to comment on this here but see Randrianarivelo 2000:41, 32–36.

[220] The Malagasy word for "consecration" implies the idea of separation and the Handbook lists two basic meanings: separation from ordinary Christians and separation of the shepherd ministry from other services in the church. Tobilehibe 1997:36. Lie 1981:8 thinks that the aspect of delegation of power and authority is underlined too much both in the instruction of shepherds and in their actual practice, when compared to biblical teaching.

[221] Tobilehibe 1997:35–37.

uses the word "holy" in this connection but this does not seem to be applied directly to the shepherd's person.[222] In a report from a shepherd conference, however, it is said that "God's calling gives holiness (*hasina*)".[223]

After the consecration the shepherds receive an identity card with a photo and the pastor's signature. This card has to be stamped once a year by the district pastor.[224] It shows the shepherds as real workers in the church and they always bring their card when they practise exorcism outside their home church.[225]

Randrianarivelo J. sees the participation of shepherds in the consecration of new shepherds as a break with the rules of the Lutheran church which says that only ordained people, i.e. pastors, are allowed to consecrate all other church workers. He calls this practice a "new specific characteristic" of the revival movement and sees this lay involvement in consecration as an honouring and acknowledgement of the lay founders of the revival movement. He interprets this practice to be a tentative beginning of a break with the status of ordained pastors and wonders what the results would be if the church stuck to its regulations about consecration.[226]

Another problem raised with respect to consecration is that the Synod President has to be present at the consecration of shepherds, while this is not necessary at the consecration of other workers in the church. The Synod President's presence is elsewhere only prescribed at the ordination of pastors and people may think that the two are the same. Some even consider the consecration of shepherds as above the ordination of pastors, because more people take part in praying for the shepherds.[227] The Malagasy word to denote consecration is *fanokanana*,

---

[222] Covenant, Mal: *fanekena*. Tobilehibe 1997:39. The shepherds talk about God's holiness, the holiness of the shepherd ministry and perhaps the shepherds' holiness. Tobilehibe 1997:35–41 uses the word a holy service (*fanompoana masina*), a holy covenant (*fanekena masina*) and the holiness of the consecration service (*fahamasinan'ny fotoana*).

[223] Tobilehibe 1995:38.

[224] Mal: *mpitondra fileovana*.

[225] Lie 1981:7.

[226] Randrianarivelo 2000:99–101.

[227] IN 313 sees this as a problem. The participation of non-pastors and the Synod President's presence in the consecration of shepherds is a specific feature compared

stemming from *manokana*, which means to "isolate, put aside, separate, consecrate".[228] According to B.S. Lie, the word *fanokanana* is used about the ordination of pastors and consecration of shepherds alike,[229] but some of my written sources distinguish between these two acts by referring to the ordination of pastors with the word *ordinasiona*.[230] Randrianarivelo believes that this terminology aims at avoiding confusion between the two.[231]

Haus implies from her material that shepherds think that a lasting holiness is bestowed on them in consecration. She understands the holiness in relation to traditional culture, where holiness is a strong shield against evil. It can be a condition in consecrated people and these people preserve the holiness when they use it. She says that the holiness causes the shepherds to think that original sin diminishes or even disappears and sinlessness seems obtainable, at least while they are performing exorcism.[232] My research population of mostly leaders in the movement does not seem to support Haus' findings about holiness and sinlessness.

2.2.3 The shepherds' life and conduct

During the consecration of shepherds in Ambohimahazo on the 19th June 1998 one of the leaders in the movement held a speech of encouragement to the new shepherds. He started with a long prayer where the shepherds were referred to as God's servants, then he read Eph 4:1–6 and continued:

> To become a shepherd is God's calling; it is grace and does not stem from our own dignity (Eph 4:11). Do not forget "to lead a life worthy of the calling",

---

to the consecration of other church workers and may have an impact on ordinary people's understanding of the consecration of shepherds as something special.

[228] Abinal and Malzac 1930:712.
[229] Lie 1981:7.
[230] Ankaramalaza 1997:37, Fifohazana miray ao amin'ny FFPM 2000:10.
[231] Randrianarivelo 2000:100 says that the movement prefers to use consecration (*fanokanana*) for shepherds and not ordination (*ordinasiona*) or unction (*fanosorana*) (the Malagasy words in brackets are mine). Ramambason 1999:70 who writes in English, talks about shepherds who have been ordained, however. Lie 1981:7 says that what distinguishes pastors from shepherds in ordinary people's eyes is that only the pastor is given the authority to give communion.
[232] Haus 2000:148, 5, 93–94.

which should be characterised by godliness.[233] Remember that it is possible to be in service of the devil while we belong to God's kingdom. Jesus requests a worthy conduct full of lowliness. When you succeed in casting out demons this may cause pride and Jesus is set aside. Do not resist reproof. Do not make strife. We are called to carry the cross of Jesus in spite of the difficult living conditions. God does not bargain with the shepherds. If we are driven by love we are able to be patient with one another. The real shepherd is one with God and loves his neighbour. God's grace, revealed in our consecration, should lead us to repentance. Walk on the road of Christ![234]

Since the shepherds are given a special call to ministry they have to be admonished more strongly than ordinary Christians are.[235] Being a shepherd guides every aspect of life. The shepherds cannot live according to their own will but have an obligation to use every opportunity in the service of the Gospel.[236] Through consecration the shepherds receive a new obligation to live a godly life and renounce everything opposed to the Gospel.

A lot of pages in the handbook are dedicated to the shepherds' behaviour in all areas of life and with few exceptions several biblical references are given to each point.[237]

> The shepherd is to be a model in his everyday life and "what to do and not to do" covers one and a half pages. It continues with regulations concerning clothing and purity, because "you are Jesus seen by people". The exterior should mirror the interior and detailed regulations concerning fashion, colours, transparency of materials and different clothing for men and women are given. The purity concerns advise about fingernails, bad breath, worn-out clothes, a well-groomed body and the use of perfume. Then the shepherds' good conduct in relation to his/her family, to other members of the congregation, to society and to the co-workers are entered into in detail. It ends with one and a half pages of summary listing the shepherds' attitudes and behaviour and his/her everyday work and work as a shepherd.[238]

---

[233] Mal: *toe-panahy araka an'Atra*.

[234] O 343. This is a summary of his speech according to my observation report.

[235] IS 322.

[236] IS 201.

[237] As an introduction to the section about behaviour, it is emphasised that the shepherd's unity with Jesus is required in order to succeed in the work. Love for God's word, prayer, a continuing surrender to Jesus and reflection on the calling is underlined. Tobilehibe 1997:43–44.

[238] Tobilehibe 1997:44–56. It seems as the author notices the length and detail in his listing and on p.49 he says that it is advisable to ask for the Lord's mind and wisdom in all this. In the pamphlet with questions and answers from the

My informants exemplify the shepherds' behaviour primarily in three ways: opposition against the "turning of the corpse" ceremony, prohibition against cigarettes, alcohol and snuff and warnings against pride during exorcism. It seems that bad conduct has a special relation to their performance of exorcism.[239]

According to estimations 95 % of the population in the Antsirabe area take part in the "turning of the corpse" ceremony.[240] The revival movement opposes this custom and shepherds are not allowed to take part in it. One shepherd recounted that he heard rumours that one shepherd not only attended the ceremony but also invited others to follow him. "If this shepherd does not repent," he says, "I will ask the district committee to recall his/her certificate."[241] When one of my informants and his mother became shepherds, they withdrew from this custom because of the beliefs implicit in it. They met severe opposition from their family.[242] Shepherds oppose the "turning of the corpse" ceremony because they see the devil at work there.[243] Their opposition does not mean a total rejection of traditional cultural elements, however.

Ankaramalaza branch of the movement it is asked if the women shepherds should "work" during their menstruation period. It is strongly underlined that they should not do so, according to a saying of *Mama* Nenilava and several passages from the OT is given (the Levitical moral code). The pamphlet continues to say, on the basis of the OT, that a woman is unclean (*maloto*) during this period and whoever touches her will also be unclean. To lay hands on people during this period seems to be an absolute prohibition for women but in an emergency situation she may cast out demons. The author says that this practice does not concern salvation but it is a good custom in order to respect God's holiness. Ankaramalaza 1997:12–13.

[239] My material does not contain much on this theme because I have not specifically investigated it. The scattered references are mostly hints when discussing other themes but they may enlighten the shepherds' stress on good conduct.

[240] IG 331. Cf. 4.1.1.2 (Interaction between humans and ancestors, god, idols and charms/amulets, nature spirits, sacred power). The widespread practice may be one of the reasons why several of my informants take this as an example of traditional worship.

[241] IS 314.

[242] QS 57.

[243] IS 321. If it only had been a paying of reverence to the ancestors, in line with bringing flowers to the grave, without involving faith in other deities, my informant would not oppose it.

One informant underlines that there are many traits in the traditional Malagasy culture, which are consistent with Christian behaviour.[244]

Especially frequent in my material is the mentioning of cigarettes, alcohol and sometimes snuff as strictly forbidden for the shepherds. One shepherd says that this stems from the devil and if shepherds smoke cigarettes they have lost their way.[245] When another informant was about to become free from his demonic oppression he heard a voice inside telling him to stop smoking and drinking alcohol. He especially doubted that he could manage to stop smoking but the voice inside said: "... if the Son makes you free, you will be free indeed. You are not going to free yourself. I am going to set you free." My informant says that he after that had forgotten the smoking and drinking and when he once tasted it again, he did not like it.[246] The shepherds also rebuke others for using these things, especially pastors, which often causes problems between them. The leaders teach the shepherds to choose their words carefully when rebuking others and rather pray for them.[247]

Because of the visible results of their work shepherds may exalt themselves, but the pride has to be resisted in the shepherds' lives.[248] The devil sets in his attacks also against the shepherds and it is a temptation for them to think that they cast out demons by their own power.[249] The shepherds may say to a sick person: "We are able to heal you" but they have constantly to be reminded that it is God who heals.

Randrianarivelo J. sees several theological implications in the shepherds' preoccupation with behaviour: an attempt to seek sinlessness

---

[244] IS 201. A shepherd conference in 1995 stated that the revival movement is a native movement (not the whites' worship) by the work of the Holy Spirit. Tobilehibe 1995:9.

[245] IS 322. His wording is *mivily* (not to go straight) and he does not seem to think of perdition as a result of this. He refers to the statutes of the revival movement, which forbids cigarettes, alcohol and snuff. Fifohazana miray ao amin'ny FFPM 2000:20.

[246] CHIS 8. My informant characterised himself an alcoholic at this time and he had been smoking cigarettes regularly for many years.

[247] IS 322, IS 315. Shepherds also have problems with bad behaviour. IS 206 speaks about a shepherd who has a difficult mind and nobody wants to live together with her. Her ways of saying things causes trouble again and again because she is not able to judge the appropriate situations. Another tells about shepherds opposing pastors and the reason for this is not only the pastor's. IS 214.

[248] IS 322. IS 201 says that some shepherds have too strong faith and they are difficult to guide.

[249] IS 206, IS 323.

while still in this world, or a temptation to think that eternal life is granted because of the good conduct, or difficulties in believing that confessed sin is forgiven sin.[250] B.S. Lie is afraid that the shepherds' belief as a whole will be marked by formalistic and moralistic traits and that their casuistic regulations may lead the shepherds to condemn Christians who hold different views.[251]

2.2.4 Shepherds and pastors

In order to enlighten how shepherds define themselves in relation to pastors I will present my informants' observations of pastors' reserve to engage in exorcism, how the shepherds interpret this, what they consider to be the reasons for the pastors' reserve and how shepherds conceive of an ideal relationship.[252]

My informants suggest different ways to exemplify the distinction between pastors and shepherds. Pastors are occupied with word and sacraments while shepherds tend to underline exorcism.[253] Pastors emphasise theoretical aspects of the faith while shepherds focus upon interpersonal relationship in practical life.[254] The role of the pastor is to teach novices to become shepherds because of his theological education and the shepherds normally define themselves as being taught.[255] Pastors retire when they have reached a certain age, the shepherds' ministry continues until death.[256]

Many pastors do not engage in exorcism even though the General Synod of the Lutheran church has made clear that pastors may cast out

---

[250] Randrianarivelo 2000:81, 85.

[251] Lie 1981:18–19. The mentioned dangers connected with the shepherds' stress on conduct and behaviour should be taken seriously by the leaders in the movement. See 5.2.4.

[252] Many of my informants are either theological students or pastor-shepherds. I suppose that these informants possess a double identity of both being shepherds and (coming) pastors and this may influence their understanding. My choice of informants makes it relevant here to include a subchapter on the relation between shepherds and pastors.

[253] QS 69.

[254] IS 318. IS 312 comments that the well-educated (*manam-pahaizana*) are more reluctant regarding the shepherds' practice than others.

[255] QS 54. We have seen above that shepherd leaders and others also teach novices. See 2.2.2.2.

[256] QS 156.

demons by virtue of their ordination and this is confirmed in the statutes of the *Fifohazana*.[257] A story may illustrate many pastors' general reserve:

> We were evangelising and made visits to all the homes, where we prayed, sang hymns and shared the word of God. When we had done this in one of the homes, a woman there asked for "work and strengthening". All of us were waiting because there were four pastors in the team. Nobody opened their mouths. After a while one of us said to the woman: "There are no shepherds here, only four pastors" and we stood there looking at each other. Then we left the house.[258]

In many cases the pastors' reluctance is not due to opposition against the shepherds' work but they do not take part actively.[259] Pastors practising exorcism also see this as primarily the shepherds' task. One of my informants says that he occasionally joins the shepherds in expelling demons to guide them and help them in an exhausting work and he constantly prays for them. He underlines, however, that it is the shepherds' special call to engage in close fight with evil spirits.[260]

Some shepherds interpret the pastors' reluctance to cast out demons as lack of courage. Because of their anxiety they do not dare to engage in this fight.[261] This may lead the shepherds not to respect these pastors and even speak ill of them.[262] The pastors' reluctance to take part in exorcism can also be interpreted as unwillingness because they want to continue in their sins or that they do not feel any need for conversion and help to

---

[257] According to IS 212 there have been two decisions in the General Synod concerning this, the first around 1950. Fifohazana FFPM 1980:19.

[258] QS 69. My informant wonders what those in the family thought after the team had left. "When we were alone and the pastors were not together with us," he says, "we had a lively discussion about the pastors' and the shepherds' work. Are they different or are they the same?"

[259] IS 310, IS 322. QS 41 reports that he had never seen a pastor casting out demons prior to his internship during the study of theology.

[260] IS 214. The frequency of the pastors' practice of exorcism varies due to many factors. My point here is to underline that they tend to consider this as the shepherds' special ministry in the church.

[261] IS 213, QS 125. When describing the shepherds' interpretations of the pastors' reluctance to engage in exorcism, my informants tell me what they have heard and experienced through years and it does not necessarily express their own position.

[262] IS 320, IS 322.

resist the influence of Satan.[263] Some shepherds may see pastors' reluctance as the work of evil spirits and some shepherds call pastors not active in the shepherds' work "Satan who opposes us".[264] If they feel that pastors counteract their work, they will sometimes withdraw from co-operation.[265] Some shepherds classify pastors into two groups: "pastors being shepherds" (*pastora mpiandry*) and "only pastors" (*pastora tsotra*).[266] When pastors are not actively taking part in exorcism, this will cause some shepherds to think that they themselves are above pastors because they perform a work, which pastors do not dare to do.

My informants think that the reasons for pastors not engaging in exorcism can be classified into two groups: human and theological factors.[267] The human factors are that many pastors have little knowledge of the revival movement.[268] Some pastors are formalistic and want to control everything in the parish.[269] Shepherds give high priority to visiting people's homes and since pastors seldom have time to do so, people may think that pastors are lazy. It is normally easier for people to consult shepherds than pastors when they need spiritual guidance because they feel the shepherds are more on their own level. The average level of education for shepherds is low and theoretical argumentation is difficult. When pastors reprimand them because of this, problems may arise.[270] The shepherds are sometimes too eager in their work and they are straightforward when rebuking sin, which may sometimes cause the pastors' anger because of their different understanding.[271] Some of my

---

[263] IS 322, IS 212. QS 101 comments that there are some pastors who do not live according to the Gospel.

[264] IS 214, IS 213.

[265] QS 54, QS 84.

[266] QS 110. *Tsotra* can be translated plain and straight (Abinal and Malzac 1930:795) and it can have a pejorative meaning. Here it only seems to mean pastors who are also not consecrated as shepherds.

[267] The boundaries between these groups are fluid and several elements can fit in both groups.

[268] QS 84, IS 311. Some ask for more underlining of the practical elements in "work and strengthening" in the theological education. IS 320.

[269] When shepherds are asked to come to parishes where they do not live they must ask their own pastor for written permission. The shepherds sometimes feel these regulations too formalistic. IS 314.

[270] IS 210.

[271] IS 318, IS 315. The shepherds' severe regulations about alcohol and smoking of cigarettes often cause problems in relation to some pastors' more liberal views.

informants point out the root cause to be a competition of positions and honour.[272] In line with this is the pastors' anxiety of not being successful when engaging in exorcism and thus losing face in relation to the shepherds.[273]

Among the theological factors are diverging opinions about what should be cast out of people. Uneasiness with the shepherds' definition of who is in need of exorcism and the theological implications of demons being cast out of pastors and other Christians are connected with this.[274] Some pastors are also said not to accept that demons can enter people, but this is seldom stated publicly.[275] When shepherds speak about visions and auditions, which they understand as God's guidance, this causes problems for some pastors.[276] This is the case also when shepherds perform actions that seem to be against human logic because they believe it to be God's guidance.[277] More unspecified it is said that shepherds have little biblical knowledge and therefore they emphasise their speciality.[278]

The ideal relationship between shepherds and pastors is considered a fruitful co-operation. Verbs denoting mutuality abound when my informants describe this: help each other, give each other strength, teach each other, guide each other and especially frequent is complement each

---

[272] IS 213, IS 320.

[273] IS 217. A feeling of competition between pastors and lay people may lie behind.

[274] IS 311.

[275] IS 320. IS 321 underlines that this concerns younger pastors who do not know their Malagasy heritage. He says that they do not deny the existence of demons but their ability to possess people. Since only this informant mentions this trait, my material is too thin to make any further conclusions from this view. I have never encountered the view myself.

[276] IS 316 tells about an incident where he had visions/auditions telling him to break his evangelising program in another parish and return home. He reported this to the pastor but the pastor answered that he did not understand the shepherds' practices and refused him to go. Then the shepherd said that the pastor had to take the consequences for what happened if he stayed and only then he was granted permission to leave. Having returned home this shepherd became the instrument of one and a half years of continuing revival.

[277] IS 210 tells about shepherds bathing patients with pneumonia in cold water, an action which may lead to death. Pastors often react against such things, my informant says, because they are guided by their knowledge. The plain belief of the shepherds is that if they have faith, God can work in supernatural ways.

[278] QS 69. It is implied that their low biblical knowledge may lead to meanings and actions, which are not grounded in the biblical message.

other.[279] This is so since the two ministries share in the same goal: to take care of people's spiritual life, to preach the Gospel and to destroy the works of the devil.[280] They should be likened to "water and rice: in the fields they do not throw each other away, in the village they do not leave each other."[281] This mutuality can become a reality if the pastors are less focussed on problematic details than on the general blessing of the *Fifohazana*'s work, if they focus on the results of the shepherds' work and if they grant appropriate room to the shepherds' participation in church work.[282] When the relationship is relaxed the pastor can cooperate with the shepherds in many ways and even ask shepherds to come home to strengthen him and his family when problems arise.[283] It is admitted that there are problems but if both sides manage to show their best will the existence of both pastors and shepherds is a blessing to the congregation.

2.2.5 Elements in the shepherds' view of demons

This subchapter deals with some main lines in the shepherds' view of demons. Partly, it can be seen as an introduction, because several of the themes will be found in later chapters, seen from different angles. Partly, it can serve as a furnishing of some basic elements in the shepherds' understanding of demons.

When shepherds talk about demons, evil spirits, Satan, the devil etc. the point of departure seems to be their experiences with this reality and thus their main interest is these beings' relation to humans. The shepherds believe in something they have experienced, even if they are not fully able to explain it theoretically.[284] In the following I present the

---

[279] Mal: *Mifanampy, mifampahery, mifampianatra, mifanitsy, mifameno.* QS 79, QS 69, QS 3.

[280] QS 6, QS 105, QS 3.

[281] QS 103. Rice is cultivated in water, according to the traditional custom and if the water vanishes the rice will die. Unless cooked in water rice is unedible.

[282] IS 212, IS 310.

[283] IS 320. The underlying problem seems to be a thinking that the one who gives strength is greater than the one who is strengthened and thus a sense of competition may be present. Cf. 4.5.2.5 (A unique position of the shepherds?).

[284] IS 201 says that the Malagasy way of understanding is primarily practically oriented. He maintains that this understanding is in contrast with the Western, which he describes in this way: "If Westerners are not able to explain a phenomenon accurately, they renounce its existence."

shepherds' views on the demonic reality and demons' abilities, their dwelling places, their reported appearances and how the shepherds conceptualise the demonic fight with humans.

Demons are a spiritual reality and spirits are invisible. One informant talks of evil spirits not only surrounding us but rather filling the space around us like air.[285] To fight against demons is like fighting against air since spirits have no material body. It is made explicit that the shepherds see the spirits of the dead as devils or demons.[286] A sort of hierarchy seems to emerge in this spirit world, but it is not consistent.[287] What seems to be commonly agreed is that there is one leader in-chief, who gives his orders and assigns different tasks to his subjects. The different tasks of demons are deduced from their influence on humans.[288]

Demons are cunning beings with varied and widespread abilities and their goal is one: to prevent people from having a good life, by lying and making people faint-hearted.[289] Demons are able to communicate and when they are addressed in dialogue during expulsion of demons, the shepherds normally talk directly to the demons in the person.[290] The demons' answers may reflect the real state of being, but they can as well deceive the shepherds. This is so because demons want to frighten the shepherds to end their work of expelling them and therefore they may

---

[285] IS 323. Elsewhere he refers to *Mama* Nenilava's saying that evil spirits are in the air and this association with air (*rivotra*) may have led to his understanding of spirits filling the space around us. He uses the Malagasy words *manodidina* (to be around) and *manerana* (to be around/fill a space). In the context he refers to Eph 6:12.

[286] IS 210, IS 310.

[287] In IG 332 Satan is said to be the main chief, Be-el'zebul is the chief of the evil spirits, the devil is the tempter and all the demons have different tasks to undertake. Later in the same interview Be-el'zebul is the same as Satan.

[288] IS 212. Some evil spirits make their victim dumb, others make them insane, some show their capacity in avoiding outward manifestations, some love unclean places and some cannot stand the word of God. One informant notices that spirits stemming from the coastal areas seem to be more efficient as healers than those who were originally worshipped in the Inland area and this has caused many traditional healers to expound their array of spirits. IS 320. In some instances it is said that the demons show themselves with many appearances, which could mean that they are essentially the same and only appear to be different. IG 332.

[289] IS 321, IS 217. Mal: *manakivy*.

[290] IS 200. In spite of this general rule IS 315 reports of talking to the patient and not to the demons, if he wants to know anything about the demons in him/her.

refuse to leave or say that they are too many to be cast out.[291] An alternative demonic option is to make the patient leave the shepherds, either by causing him to run away or by making him unwilling to attend healing services.[292] It is believed that demons use a whole array of different means to enter into human beings and they change their tactics according to situation, place and person.[293] Especially in the changed conditions of life in the society nowadays the demonic has more means at their disposal and they enter into humans in indirect ways: by the use of drugs, by videos showing sex and violence and by the increase of immorality in society.[294] Nobody is safe from demonic attacks, not even Christians and only those who do not let him reign can resist the devil's tempting.[295]

In two consecutive articles in the magazine of the Lutheran church, *Ny Mpamangy*, we find a rather comprehensive teaching about the devil and his kingdom, presented as the biblical teaching.[296]

> The different names of the evil one are presented, together with explanations of what aspects of the demonic activity these names refer to. Satan's origin is drawn from Ezek 28:1–19 and Is 14:4–23 and according to Rev 12: 4, 7–9 the dragon and his angels were expelled from heaven to the earth.[297] Jesus' saying: "I saw Satan fall like lightning from heaven." (Lk 10:18) shows that subsequent to the resurrection of Jesus Satan is not allowed to present himself at God's throne in heaven anymore, like he did according to Job 1–2.[298] The kingdom of Satan is hierarchical: The rulers constitute the top layer: powers

---

[291] IS 217, IS 218.

[292] IS 206. It is reported that when the shepherds command the demons to leave, saying "Get out" (*mivoaha*), the person rises up and leaves the service. "The devil causes him/her to leave," my informant says.

[293] IS 210.

[294] IS 311 talks of "modern devils" (*devoly moderne*) and says: "The devil does not make himself known on the body but he gives his orders to the person." The context of this saying is that these people do not show manifestations.

[295] IS 210. Cf. 4.3.3.

[296] It is part of the teaching of novices preparing to be consecrated as shepherds, but presented as also useful for all Christians who read the magazine. Even if it represents the teaching of a pastor with the initials A.M.M.T. in France (*pastora A.M.M.T. Frantsa*)—he seems to be a shepherd himself, since he uses the inclusive 1st person plural "we shepherds" in the articles—what he writes is approved by the editorial office of the magazine since it is issued there and thus shows a general teaching of the demonic.

[297] A.M.M.T. 1999A:7.

[298] A.M.M.T. 1999S:7.

ESSENTIAL CHARACTERISTICS OF THE *FIFOHAZANA*

and principalities (Eph 1:21; 3:10), which are called the kingdom of nobles. Below the nobles are the authorities and on the bottom layer we find the demons (Mt 9:33–34).[299] Demons are divided into four classes: "religious" demons, demons working on the mind, demons working on the body and demons of bad conduct.[300]

Demons dwell in the air around us according to Eph 6:12,[301] and this means that they go wherever they want. They may even take trips to the church and hide among the believers and they are able to stay in people's houses.[302]

An interesting biblical interpretation on this theme is given in the church magazine.[303]

> According to the Bible there are three heavens/skies above us: the atmospheric sky, the planetary sky and God's throne. The devil's space is the atmospheric sky between the earth and the third heaven (Rev 12:9–12, Eph 2:2) and he has no more entry to God's throne, where Jesus is seated. Jesus is exalted far above Satan.[304]

---

[299] A.M.M.T. 1999A:6. The social distinction between nobles (*andriana*) and slaves (*andevo*) is still very much alive among the Imerina and the nobles clearly see themselves as above the slaves in the hierarchical structure. By using this label the author conveys a strong hierarchical understanding.

[300] A.M.M.T. 1999S:8. The "religious" demons (*demonia momba ny ara-pivavahana*) are said to show themselves in false doctrine and inside the Christian congregation in devils causing envy and devils causing strife. It should be noticed that demons and devils seem to be used interchangeably here! The demons of bad conduct (*demonia momba ny faharatsiam-pitondrantena*) seem to be equal to unclean spirits and when these demons are cast out they cry with a loud voice (Mk 1:26, Acts 8:7). The other Malagasy expressions are *demonia momba ny saina* and *demonia momba ny vatana*.

[301] IS 312.

[302] IS 200. IS 323 says that when a couple has moved into a new house and they constantly have bad dreams or feel that something is pressing them, this is a sign of evil spirits living there.

[303] A.M.M.T. 1999S:7.

[304] In French there is only one word (ciel) covering both "sky" and "heaven". This is also so in Malagasy (*lanitra*), but *habakabaka* can be used to denote the firmament. The author furnishes French equivalents to the Malagasy words: ciel athmosphérique (*habakabaka*), ciel planétaire (*planeta*), le trône de Dieu (*seza fiandrian'Andriamanitra*). He bases the idea of three heavens on 2 Cor 12:2 and Hebr 4:14 (when it is said about Jesus that he "passed through the heavens" the author adds "all three"). The Malagasy word *habakabaka* (firmament) is neither used in Rev 12:9–12 nor in Eph 2:2.

A notable feature of evil spirits is that they may enter into material objects or living bodies and thus these objects/bodies can speak with the spirit's voice. Their invisibility is a prerequisite for this capacity. The devil resides in the remedies of the traditional healer.[305] It is reported that during the burning of amulets,[306] these objects were screaming with a loud voice, saying: "We are going to die, we are going to die" and some of them even jumped out of the fire, but they were returned "in Jesus' name".[307] "If spirits were able to enter into pigs, according to the Gospels, how much more may they enter human beings," one informant says and uses this incident to urge the people in the church to pray during expulsion of demons. If not, the evil spirits, which are driven out of one person, may easily enter into another, who is not preparing himself in prayer to resist them.[308] One informant mentions two incidents of exorcism where there was a strange odour of sulphur in the room, but it was not from the breath of the patient. The informant smelled that odour when the young boy conversing with him cried: "now he is coming". He takes this as a sign of demonic presence.[309] An idea of the multitude of demons is given when the shepherd encounters a difficult case and asks the demons: "How many are you in there?" The sick may answer "Legion". Then the shepherd continues his "work" and when he asks again, the number is 500. Then it is reduced to 100, 50 and so on.[310]

In almost all instances the reported appearances of demons/Satan come from individuals in their state of illness. These reports, told by the patients after their recovery to a normal state of being, seem to be taken

---

[305] IS 210. In the traditional culture the spirits' ability to enter into objects or bodies is widespread. See especially 4.1.1.2 (Possession) but also 4.1.1.1 (Idols and charms/amulets).

[306] Mal: *ody*.

[307] IS 218.

[308] IS 212. He says that exactly this happened in Farihimena during the revival of *Dadatoa* Rakotozandry Daniel (1946–1947). Suddenly one person in the church turned insane while shepherds were expelling demons and this is taken as a sign of demons moving into him/her. "If an expelled demon find a wide-open door into another human, it may use this opportunity," he says.

[309] IS 318.

[310] IS 200. Another informant reports on the demons answering "there are 3 trucks full of us in here". He advises the shepherds to refrain from talking with the demons, because demons can easily lie and thus frighten the shepherds in order to be left where they are. IS 217.

over by the shepherds. Some informants recall their own experiences.[311] Only one shepherd tells about his own observations of materialisations of the devil without being ill himself. It happened while he was expelling demons and his story is quite in line with the others:

> He saw the front part of a snake creeping over the floor towards the door. It was so plain that he later searched in books to find out what sort of snake it could have been. It had big canine teeth.[312]
> Just before this he has reported what the woman herself told about her experiences under the exorcism session: A snake had coiled around her neck and would strangle her. Her face looked like she was about to be strangled, with the lips pointing outwards. When they had "worked" with her for some time, she said "It is over now" and the snake left her. This was the devil leaving her, my informant said.
> At another occasion this informant saw a creature, something resembling a cat and a dog, leaving a woman "assaulted by demons". The animal left by the door and headed for a tree in the courtyard. It collided with that tree and some days afterwards the tree withered.

Visions of the devil in the shape of different animals are common: a snake, a dog-like creature, the head of a lion, but also appearances of people occur, normally closely acquainted with the patient.[313] The human-like figures can be compared to phantoms,[314] but can also take the shape of a deceiving Christ.[315] Frightening voices or noise are also referred to, an owl's cry is reported,[316] and visions of tiny threads of plastic or small worms creeping into the ears or covering the mouth and the eyes. The function of the tiny threads/worms was to prevent the patient from hearing the word of God or to make him unable to talk or read. In addition the patient was so occupied with these animal-like

---

[311] CHIS 8, CHIS 12.

[312] QS 101. In the conversation with me he reflects on what he could have seen, because he has problems in believing what he saw. "Could it be that we were so tired of working with this women?" he wonders.

[313] CHIS 130 tells about two instances in the beginning of his sickness where known people appeared to him during the night. They were close relatives and one of them even encouraged him to pray. From the way they looked (a scary expression on their face), however, he was convinced that they were demons in humanlike form.

[314] IS 200.

[315] CHIS 130.

[316] CHISA 156.

disturbers that he was unable to concentrate on what was happening around him.[317]

Some of my informants have mentioned images in books, which have shaped their mental pictures and one book, which extends the biblical teaching, is mentioned specifically.[318] It is a translation to Malagasy of a pamphlet called "The human heart", originally published in France around the year 1750, according to the introduction. This pamphlet is printed in 7 editions from 1958 to 1972 and distributed in the church in a total of 140000 copies.[319]

> Through 9 pictures of the heart a human's life is depicted. The first picture of a "heart filled with deceit" depicts the devil in a humanlike shape: a strange face with big ears and horns, wings, a human body but cloven-footed and a big fork in his hand. Around him we find a turkey, a snake, a goat, a turtle, a leopard, a pig and a toad. Aspects of the demonic are in the text attributed to each of the animals.[320]

Attributions of colours to the demonic is not uncommon, especially black and red: a person wearing red clothes, an altogether black animal with red eyes, or a person in black, standing on the grave.[321] In the handbook the motive for not wearing clothes in dark black and red in healing services points to the traditional culture. These colours are used in idol-worship: red is connected with blood in the different sacrifices and black stands for the darkness connected with these practices.[322]

Several conceptual analogies are used when the shepherds describe the demonic fight with humans:[323]

---

[317] CHIS 8.

[318] QN 108, IS 217

[319] Unidentified 1972. This is an enormous number in the Malagasy setting. Normally books and pamphlets are printed in 1000 to 3000 copies.

[320] Unidentified 1972:5–18.

[321] One informant says that she knows the animal was a demon, since it was altogether black (CHIS 12) and another reports of his skin turning black and red as a result of fierce fights with the demonic during the night. CHIS 130.

[322] Tobilehibe 1997:48. The prohibitions concerning clothing are said to stem from instructions given by *Mama* Nenilava.

[323] According to Hiebert 1994:193–198 "conceptual analogies" denote the mental categories people use for thinking. Analogies are tools and they do not necessarily render the way people think reality is.

Every human being is viewed as being governed by a spirit, who gives orders to the mind. This can be the spirit of God or the spirit of the devil. Only on the basis of the person's actions is it possible to trace which spirit he/she is governed by. Adultery, lying and stealing points to an evil spirit of guidance, while a feeling of comfort and peace during listening to God's word and attending healing services points to the Holy Spirit. The spirit of God and the spirit of the devil seem to co-exist within the human and the person within whom they dwell gives them power. When the spirits engage in battle within the human, the person becomes tired and weak. The urge is to let God's Spirit reign and thus defeat the devil.[324]

Sometimes the human is viewed as having a fence around him/her. This fence can be strong or weak and it is not clearly stated what the fence consists of. The devil is always on watch, looking for weak points in the fence and exactly there he launches his attack.[325]

Demonic attacks can be compared to the eager activity of a mosquito trying to bite you. We use all possible means to get rid of the pushing mosquito: we beat it, we try chemical drugs and mosquito nets. Then it withdraws and it looks like it is beaten. But when the beating ends and the drugs and mosquito nets are not in use any more, the mosquito returns and tries to bite you again.[326]

---

[324] IS 311, IS 318.

[325] In connection with the image of a fence IG 332 refers to Satan's activities in Job 1–2 as eager looking for weak points in Job's life, to be able to accuse him before God.

[326] IS 213. The analogy is easily understandable and relevant in the Malagasy setting, where many people die every year from malaria stemming from mosquito bites. The context for my informant using this analogy was the demonic efforts to enter into humans and how important it is to defend oneself against these attacks. He also used Jesus' words about the spirit finding its earlier house empty, swept and put in order (Mt 12:43–45) to underline this point.

A more philosophical understanding of demon-possession is in terms of influence, which resembles the influence obtained by hypnosis. When hypnotised the person follows the will of the master and the master's power over the person continues until the hypnosis ends. The demons exercise this "hypnosis" over people and during the state of possession the demons control the person and can make him/her perform supernatural activities: glossolalia, levitation and hidden knowledge. When the demonic influence ends, the person has no such abilities. IS 217. My informant makes it clear that this is his own theory and that most shepherds consider the demonic dwelling in the person very concretely. He underlines that what matters is not the theoretical explanations but the real experiences of demons enslaving people.

2.2.6 Shepherds and traditional healers

Shepherds and traditional healers (*mpimasy*)[327] stand in sharp opposition to each other, but people also consult traditional healers with their problems, especially related to sickness. I asked the shepherds if there were people other than shepherds who expelled demons and the answers seem to reveal a lack of knowledge of what is going on in traditional healing.[328] About half of the informants had not seen any other treatment than the shepherds', or they had only heard some stories, or they just did not answer the question. Those who knew something about this seemed to have only rudimentary knowledge, with some exceptions. The rest of my informants, too, do not in general elaborate on this theme and when I have asked about it, the knowledge seems to be uneven.[329] However, in nearly 50% of my case histories it is said that the patients have consulted a traditional healer in order to obtain a cure.[330] My general impression

---

[327] The word *mpimasy* denoting a traditional healer is most frequent in my material and when I use it here it denotes all the religious traditional healers. The word base of *mpimasy* is *hasina*, which designates the mystical power innate in objects or people, that makes an object worthy of respect or fear. The meaning may be that the *mpimasy* is filled with this mystical power in a special way (cf. *ombiasy*, which may be translated "with plenty of *hasina*"), that he knows the mystical power in diverse objects and therefore is able to distribute remedies which may have a healing effect on a wide variety of diseases. *Mpanao fanafody* is another word which literally means "the one who makes medicine or remedies" (the word *fanafody* is used of both Western medicine and the different treatments prescribed by the traditional healer).

[328] See Appendix 1.

[329] e.g. only one informant mentions that royal spirits are considered different from evil spirits but he says that he has never observed how the traditional healer casts out evil spirits. IS 310. I have to take into consideration my way of asking, misunderstandings about what information I requested, influence from the biblical teaching or the informants' judgement of what was appropriate to tell me may count for some of their seemingly lack of knowledge. In spite of these possible sources of error the lack of precise knowledge may be a hint that my informants to some small extent are occupied with traditional healing.

[330] It may well be that an even higher number have done so without mentioning it explicitly, because it is so common in the Malagasy countryside to consult a traditional healer that it may not even be worth mentioning. Another reason not to mention it could be a feeling of unease towards the interviewer, especially since many of the people in the case histories were brought up in a Christian context (in about half of the cases this is said explicitly). Many of the interviewees were close family of the patients and they may have felt unease as Christians to openly admit to having consulted traditional healers.

through many daily conversations is that a majority of the patients asking the shepherds for exorcism have first been in contact with a traditional healer and I will call it a typical course of events. My point in the following is to describe briefly the shepherds' judgements about what is going on in the traditional healers' practice, if they are able to expel evil spirits, eventual similarities with the shepherds' practice and what Christians' contact with traditional healers may lead to.

According to the shepherds, healers are guided by spirits. They are able to command the spirits to obey them and when people consult the traditional healers, this opens a path for spirits to enter these people. On the one side the spirits operating in the practices of the *mpimasy* are really considered to be devils.[331] The *mpimasy* are, on the other side, blamed for trickery: they use the Christian Bible, some of them are skilful herbalists but tell people that spirits are the healing agents and they hide their needs of income by religious explanations. When people consulting them are given amulets and taboos, these people are closely knit to the traditional healers and become dependent on them.[332] This trickery is not considered neutral because it is obvious that God does not trick anybody and thus also the traditional healers' trickery has to stem from evil spirits.[333]

The shepherds' thinking of the traditional healers' ability to cast out evil spirits is not uniform. Some maintain that the *mpimasy* can perform miracles and many are healed by their practices.[334] The traditional healers may heal, says another, but the demons do not leave the person, or they may leave for a while and then they return.[335] In fact, this is nothing else

---

[331] IS 210, IS 311, IS 201. The Christian expressions are so common to my informants that one of them seems to lay the word "devil" in the traditional healer's mouth when the latter says to a patient that "there is a devil who wants to enter you and therefore the one who is already there has to be gently removed". QS 133. Only one informant in my material announces an uncertainty about what is cast out in the "expulsion of spirits of the dead" (*fandroahana lolo*): "I am not quite sure that it is demons," he says, "but I think so." QS 6.

[332] IS 210, IS 314.

[333] IS 318.

[334] IS 321, IS 318.

[335] QS 144. QS 114. When the demons return, the situation for the person will be even worse. QS 105. My informant indirectly refers to Mt 12:43–45. QS 54 believes that the traditional healers are only able to cast out spirits, which they have inserted themselves. If the devil has taken advantage of the illness, however, only the shepherds' treatment (sometimes together with the medical doctors') will heal the patient.

than putting the demons to rest, because the person is still bound inside.[336] One informant says that the traditional healers' treatment will lead to idol worship and the illness will sooner or later return.[337] The understanding of Mt 12 in connection with this seems to cause problems: how can Be-el'zebul fight with himself? Can his kingdom stand if he is divided against himself?[338] In some of the case histories there are detailed descriptions of the traditional healer's treatment and in two of the reported cases the illness was really cured by him. In most cases, however, it is underlined that the healer's treatment—sometimes for years—showed no positive results and it is sometimes said that the case grew even worse after the consultation. The main reason why some informants mention the traditional healer is to show the superiority of the shepherds' treatment.

The shepherds consider the similarity between traditional healers and shepherds to be the devil's imitation of the shepherds' practice but he can never create faith in Jesus. The decisive element in the shepherds' practice is that they do all their work "in Jesus' name".[339] In the capital there was a healer worshipping a spirit called Jesus. He performed healing and practised expulsion of demons with the laying on of hands but later on it became visible that he used "black magic".[340] The

---

[336] IS 332, QS 2. The many taboos that are to be observed show that the demons have not departed. QS 101.

[337] QS 41.

[338] IS 320 concludes that, according to his experience, the *mpimasy* casts out evil spirits. So his/her own spirits have to be stronger than those he/she casts out.

[339] IS 201, IS 210. Non-shepherds in my material also seem to agree with the shepherds' understanding that in spite of some similarities in practice between the shepherds and the traditional healers their sources of power are diametrically opposite. QN 7, QN 162. IN 313 lists some of the similarities: singing or music, prayer (the *mpimasy* invoke the spirits of the deceased), the patients show manifestations. He mentions differences, however: while the traditional healer sprinkles water on the sick, the shepherds pray for them with the laying on of hands.

[340] My informant had made some investigations in the capital so as to be able to decide by which power this healer worked. IS 210. IS 310 suggests that some shepherds also show magical thinking. They act in a way, which makes the exorcism-part of the healing service look like the traditional healer's practices. They take the place of other shepherds because they have experienced that patients often act erratically when they themselves "work". These shepherds do not bother with preaching but think that they are experts in casting out demons. My informant interprets this as due to these shepherds' magical thinking. He wonders, however, why the patients respond by acting erratically when these shepherds work and think it may be due to their especially strong voices but he admits that he does not know. My informant

shepherds' conviction is that traditional healers remove people's faith and the principal goal for evil spirits is to lead people away from faith in Jesus.[341]

2.2.7 The shepherds' terminology related to demons and exorcism

In this subchapter I present firstly, very briefly the shepherds' terminology of demons/devils and expulsion of demons. The second and main part of the following is the shepherds' varied and comprehensive terminology in describing a person in need of exorcism. Thirdly, I present a way of interpreting the terminological variety and refer to a few written sources on the issue of terminology.

The traditional Malagasy culture speaks of good and evil spirits. Shepherds may also say evil spirits (*fanahy ratsy*) to denote demons. The most common conception, however, is that all spirits except the Holy Spirit are called demons (*demonia*) and considered evil.[342] Most of my informants seem to equate demons and devils (*devoly*) and use the two interchangeably, while others try to define the expressions more clearly.[343] Both demon and devil are foreign words to the Malagasy language but they have become generally used in the church and by the shepherds. Since they are part of the Bible's language, I suppose that few reflect on them as being of foreign origin.

The shepherds' vocabulary when expelling demons is rather uniform. They mostly repeat the imperative *mivoaha*, which can be translated "get out", "leave", "go away" and the action of expelling demons is either referred to as *famoahana demonia/devoly* or as *fandroahana demoniadevoly* (expulsion of demons/devils).[344] The Malagasy expressions for "casting out" (*mamoaka, mandroaka*) do not

---

      does not suggest that these shepherds' attitude stems from the devil but he asks for a more profound instruction.

[341]   IS 314, IS 331.

[342]   See 4.6.1.

[343]   The equation of demons with devils corresponds with Haus' observations. Haus 2000:51. IS 323 says that the devil is the chief (*loha*). It was the devil who tempted Jesus, not the demons, but the evil spirits in people are demons and not the devil.

[344]   This variation of substantives seems to be due to individual word-preferences. IS 210. They stem from two different roots: *voaka* (*mamoaka*) and *roaka* (*mandroaka*), which have approximately the same meanings.

necessarily mean to cast out (spirits) from within (a person). They can also be used for chasing them away from a territory, to pursue them or even to reveal their presence.[345]

When the shepherds in my material describe the demonic influence on people, there is no uniform vocabulary, it seems to shift from one person to another and it contains a variety of meanings. The comprehensiveness causes difficulties in handling the material but in order to present the shepherds' understanding properly in the following chapters, it is of vital importance to somehow come to grips with this terminology. According to the frequency of use by the shepherds I present the material in 3 groups and then I give some of the shepherds' general comments on vocabulary.[346]

Firstly, the expressions composed of the Malagasy root *voa* (assaulted, hurt, wounded).[347] *Voan'ny demonia* is most frequent in this group and in my field material as a whole and it can be translated: "assaulted/hurt/wounded by demons".[348] The people described in this way are, by some, said to be unconscious (*tsy mahatsiaro tena*), or showing manifestations, especially swaying the upper part of the body (*mihetsika*) during exorcism. It is as if another force is guiding them.[349] Others describe the "assaulted by demons" as full of fear, constantly looking over their shoulders for someone chasing them and their faces

---

[345] Cf. the conceptual analogies above. *Mamoaka* contains many meanings: "faire sortir, sortir, accompagner en sortant, envoyer, expédier, chasser, livrer, montrer, manifester, découvrir, exhiber, dire, révéler, dénoncer, publier, prononcer, rendre compte." *Mandroaka* is rendered "pousser en avant, devant soi, chasser, expulser, exilier". Abinal and Malzac 1930:842, 539.

[346] I underline that the classification into 3 groups is mine. The overlap of meanings in these groups is apparent and it is not my intention to conceal this somewhat bewildering variety in the material. It should be noticed that substantives have neither gender nor number in Malagasy, so the choice of singular or plural in translation to English is a matter of estimation.

[347] Abinal and Malzac 1930:839: "atteint, touché, pris, attrapé, frappé, saisi, taché, blessé, sur quoi tombe, dans quoi entre."

[348] In general, my own usage during the fieldwork has been restricted to *voan'ny demonia*: in the written interview guides and at least as a starting point in the conversations/interviews. "Assaulted by demons" is also the most common rendering in this book.

[349] IS 218, IS 201. Some informants equal this state with the demoniacs (L 336), while others distinguish them from demoniacs. IS 210.

seem abnormal.[350] "When a person no longer fights against the temptations trying to cause him/her to fall away from fellowship with God, this person is "assaulted by demons" and no outward manifestations can be observed," another informant says.[351] There are several variations of expressions with *voa*: *voan'ny devoly* (assaulted by devils),[352] *voan'ny fanahy ratsy* (assaulted by evil spirits),[353] and *voan'ny fanahy mamitaka* (assaulted by deceiving spirits).[354] These are more rarely used in my material and their meanings seem to be in line with meanings covered by *voan'ny demonia*.

Secondly, the expressions composed of the Malagasy root *azo* (seized, taken, received, assaulted).[355] Both *azon'ny demonia* (seized by demons) and *azon'ny devoly* (seized by devils) are frequently used. It seems as mentally ill people (*very saina*) can be described as "seized by demons".[356] Such a person may think that he/she is a snake and behaves accordingly.[357] When people show manifestations, the shepherds may say that they are "seized by demons". One informant believes that exactly the visibility of their bad actions is a sign of being "seized by demons",[358] while another states that the actions of those "seized by demons" can be both visible and invisible.[359] Those who are tempted to sin and do not resist it can be called "seized by demons".[360] "Seized by devils" is by some used interchangeably with "seized by demons" and denotes the

---

[350] IS 206.
[351] IS 325.
[352] Devils are "knocking at the door" and want to enter the person. Anxiety and a feeling of being haunted are symptoms, which characterise this state. IS 206.
[353] IS 218. The context of this saying is the spirits at work at the traditional healer.
[354] IS 322. Pastors and shepherds fighting against each other are said to have been "assaulted by deceiving spirits". My informant laughed when using this expression, but he gave no hint of only joking.
[355] Abinal and Malzac 1930:69: "gagné, obtenu, reçu, pris, atteint, saisi, empêché, compris, pu."
[356] IS 205.
[357] IS 217.
[358] IS 210.
[359] IS 323. When the actions are visible this informant seems to equal the "seized by demons" with demoniacs.
[360] IS 218. When a person has fallen in sin and thus has followed the satanic will, this can also be called *azon'ny fanahy ratsy* (seized by evil spirits). IS 312. IS 218 says that both the non-Christians and Christians who are pretending are "seized by demons".

mentally ill or people who suddenly feel very frightened during the session of expulsion of demons because of demons moving into them.[361] One informant thinks of people having reoccurring frightening dreams or often feeling visited by spirits or constantly experiencing problems in their lives as "seized by devils".[362]

Thirdly, the expression *demoniaka* and equivalents. This seems to denote a severe state of being. The people are not mastering themselves (*tsy tompon'ny tenany*) and this is apparent to the surroundings. They are no longer acting according to their own will, but the demons cause them doing strange things. A demoniac is said to have devils (*misy devoly ilay olona*), which may indicate that the devils are believed to have entered into the person.[363] To be a demoniac seems to denote a rather permanent state and some informants see it as resulting from a lengthy influence of demonic forces but it can also show itself in fits.[364] The demoniacs are sometimes identified in relation to those characterised by other terminology.[365] The French word "possédé" seems to be avoided to a great degree by my informants.[366] The word implies ownership, dominion, rule. In the few cases where it occurs, it seems to be used as an equivalent to demoniac, denoting a severely ill person.[367]

---

[361] IS 210, IS 318.

[362] IS 321.

[363] IS 206 thinks that while devils usually are disturbing people (*kitikitihan'ny devoly*) with the goal of entering into them, the demoniac is a person within whom the devils dwell and the occurrence of this state of being seems to be rare. IS 210 talks about the devil entering into a person through the means of remedies from the traditional healer (*ilay devoly miditra ao aminy*).

[364] IS 205, IS 210. L 336 expects that a demoniac may have fits and IS 210 says that this state may last a long time (this does not necessarily mean that it is permanent). Maybe the expression *babon'ny fanahy ratsy* (taken prisoner by evil spirits) belong to this third category. It is used about Christians worshipping idols, which causes a great fight inside the person. If they are unable to resist the demonic forces they are said to be "taken prisoners by evil spirits". IS 202.

[365] Some informants use the expression *voan'ny demoniaka* (assaulted by a demoniac) and from this wording it seems that they consider *demoniaka* to be some sort of demon. IS 206, IS 322. It is also possible that it is just a way of expressing themselves, because it has the same meaning as *demoniaka*. IS 323 says that *voan'ny demoniaka* is a misunderstood expression and that the shepherds using this should be re-taught.

[366] Since Madagascar has been a French colony, French is the second language and many French words are used regularly in the daily conversations.

[367] IS 212 tells about a Christian communicant, who suddenly showed manifestations during exorcism. Outside the healing service he/she behaved like anyone else and

There are some expressions in my material, which are not, however, frequently used. A person is *ampiasain'ny devoly* (used by the devil) when his/her bad works are concealed.[368] When people are unwilling to go to church, the path is open for them to be "used by the devil" and some of the poor people living at the *toby* may be "used by the devil" to continue in their laziness.[369] The expression *iasan'ny devoly* (the devil is working through [him]) can be used for Peter's behaviour in Mt 16:21–23.[370] *Nidiran' ny devoly aho* (the devil entered into me) seems to be used as a confession of sin. It means that the person did not withstand in the situation of temptation, but yielded to sin.[371] One informant talks about a person who was "seized by demons" and when *idiran'ny fanahy ratsy* (evil sprits entering) he was given supernatural abilities.[372]

One shepherd comments on this variety of expressions and says that people have no clear picture of the different meanings.[373] Another maintains that there is no great difference between the expressions. The variety stems from the seemingly different ways of appearance of the phenomenon.[374] One informant says that all the expressions mean that the devil's spirit is dwelling inside them.[375] Most of my informants do not comment on the variety in terminology but underline that exorcism is appropriate for the people described in this way.[376]

---

when I asked if he/she was "possédé" my informant vehemently denied this, saying that the state of being he had described lies outside the scope of "possédé", which is a philosophical term denoting a person unable to master himself/herself since he/she is being governed by an evil spirit inside. Unfortunately, my informant did not use any fixed terminology to characterise the person. He only recounted the story.

[368] IS 210 says that when the bad works are visible, the shepherds say that the person is *azon'ny demonia* (seized by demons).

[369] IS 213.

[370] L 336 says that Peter accepted that the devil worked through him.

[371] IS 201 uses this expression as a synonym of *azon'ny devoly* (seized by the devil).

[372] IS 200. The expression seems to point to the fit or crises and implies that the supernatural abilities were not constant. The informant continues to say that the evil spirit was carrying him (*fanahy ratsy no nitondra azy*).

[373] IS 210.

[374] IS 310. He underlines as an important point that the treatment of all this is nearly the same.

[375] *Fanahin'ny devoly mipetraka ao anatiny.* IS 311.

[376] Some of my informants believe, however, that there are cases described by this terminology, which should not necessarily be treated with exorcism. IS 310, IS 321.

Non-shepherds in my material also use a varied terminology to describe demons influencing humans and it does not seem to be consistent. Pastors who think that

The shepherds' understanding may be enlightened by the linguistic theory of category—prototype.[377] I postulate that the name of the category in the shepherds' minds seems to be "assaulted by demons/devils" (*voan'ny demonia/devoly*), which is the mostly used expression. Within this category the prototype seems to be demoniac (*demoniaka*), which is rather clearly defined and fits best with the main idea in the category. Some of the shepherds use "seized by demons/devils" (*azon'ny demonia/devoly*) with about the same content as demoniac and therefore this possibly also refer to the prototype. The category of "assaulted by demons", however, contains many other conditions than demoniac. Observations, which only in some respect correspond to the prototype are also localised here and when people only say "assaulted by demons", it is only the context that can determine if they mean demoniac or other conditions. Within the concept of illness, where I think the shepherds have placed the category of "assaulted by demons",[378] also other problematic feelings, more severe temptations and some sinful actions seem to be localised. The boundaries to these surrounding categories are vague and consequently, what shepherds see

---

only their own proposals are worth anything and cause strife in the congregation are said to be "assaulted by demons". QN 119. "Assaulted by devils" does not manifest itself except that bad morals can be interpreted this way. IN 313. The demoniacs are severely suffering and seem to be equalled to the possessed (*possédé*). IN 313, IN 317. A person who swears, loves strife and is an adulterer is said to have many devils (*be devoly*). QN 133.

[377] In short this theory says that every concept is constituted by different categories, which are related to each other in a special way. Our observations are organised in categories and this helps us to create meaning in the world. It is important to be aware that different people have their own ways of categorisation and especially in a study across cultures this is essential. Our thinking is not bound to well-defined categories, according to linguists, but rather to prototypes with vaguely defined areas around them with no strict boundaries to other neighbouring regions. A prototype is then defined as the observation, which fits best with the main idea in a category, while other less distinct observations may be localised in the same category. The metaphor used by linguists illustrating this, is that our cognitive capacity is like a landscape with tops and marks, which are the prototypes, while the regions around these constitute categories with vague boundaries to other categories with their tops (prototypes). The idea of prototypes makes the category-theory less rigid and linguists claim that this is more in line with how we perceive of the world. Aase 1997:162–163.

[378] The shepherds normally label those "assaulted by demons" as ill. The Malagasy word "ill" (*marary*) is a general concept, it denotes a multitude of conditions and it is differently constituted than the corresponding word in English.

as demonic involvement in these other categories can also be labelled as "assaulted by demons".[379] The common denominator in all these conditions is some sort of demonic influence/control/oppression and all areas where the power of the devil is experienced or believed to cause a certain amount of trouble seem to be included in "assaulted by demons". Some of the conditions, however, may be so far from the prototype of demoniac that the expression "assaulted by demons" is felt unnatural to use and other expressions replace it.

In a regional church synod's statutes for the revival movement there is a sort of definition given to the expression "assaulted by demons" (*voan'ny demonia*). Two groups are distinguished: those who are tempted by the devil and those who are the devil's property and thus have no more will of their own. The second group is equalled to those "seized by evil spirits" (*azon'ny fanahy ratsy*). The statutes support the understanding that the people included in the expression "assaulted by demons" comprise more than those who are the devil's property.[380]

Haus takes her point of departure in the statute's definition and underlines that the Malagasy expression "assaulted by demons" (*voan'ny demonia*) only focuses on the demons' work on people and it does not say anything about the relationship between an individual and the demons' power. She concludes by saying that the demonic control over people can be characterised as "influence by the devil" (seen in

---

[379] Also, it is likely to think that some people with problems belonging to the neighbouring categories in the concept of illness, e.g. "cancer", "depression" come to the healing services. They do not think of themselves as demoniacs (may be they suppose some sort of demonic involvement) but because of their problems they seek a cure.

[380] Unidentified Undated:9–10. The biblical reference to those tempted by the devil is Mt 4:1 and these people are said to be in need of help to conquer the tempter. They should be treated with strengthening and the laying on of hands. Biblical references to those who are the devil's property are Mk 5:2 and Lk 8:27 and only this group should be treated with exorcism, according to the statutes. This view differs from most of the shepherds' understanding in my field material (see p. 91 above). Haus also comments that there seems to have been a shift of meaning from 1966 to the present. Haus 2000:66. The regional synod where these statutes originated is on the west coast (*Andrefana*). This is outside the area of my investigation but I have included it here since it gives interesting comments on terminology. The pamphlet is unidentified but it is possible to guess that Norwegian missionaries could have influenced its understanding of where exorcism is necessary and where there should only be prayer with the laying on of hands. By that time many missionaries were district pastors and it is not unlikely that some of them had positions in the *Fifohazana* committees.

temptation), "oppression by the devil" (seen in sin) and as "the devil's property" (as seen in possession). She believes that the different terminology does not state particularly the devil's amount of control over people, except for those who are the devil's property, where the devil rules over them and their own will is correspondingly reduced. She notices that the adequate treatment for all three conditions is exorcism, a point also underlined by most of my informants.[381]

2.3 Summary

The *Fifohazana* has been a movement of spiritual revival in the church in Madagascar from 1894 until the present time. All of the four great *Fifohazana* founders are now dead but the movement they initiated continues to grow, both as organised departments within the historical churches and as a renewal movement. When I refer to *Fifohazana*, I use the singular "movement", well aware that the revival in Madagascar consists of different movements (plural), also with differences in practice. Their starting point and further development are so similar, however, that it is relevant to refer to all of them as part of one movement. Three of the branches originated within the area of the Lutheran church. With respect to the subject of my study, it is worth noticing that the background of three of the four founders was traditional religion with its healing activity through charms and amulets.

The four branches of the movement have slightly different customs and practices but the shepherds acknowledge their unity in spite of this and they follow the practice in the *toby* where they are working. The differences may cause problems, however and the new practice of exorcism in the FJKM-church is an example of how difficult it is to live with this diversity.

The *Fifohazana* understands itself as God's work through the Holy Spirit. The word of God is the basis, the shepherds work within the churches, they see the *Fifohazana* as one and hold the *toby*-institution as essential. Preaching of the Gospel, exorcism and care for the sick characterise their work. A true calling by God is necessary to become a shepherd and several criteria have to be fulfilled in order to get

---

[381] Haus 2000:65–73. In spite of her awareness of the shepherds' wide understanding of the demons'/devils' work on people, Haus continues to mainly use the word "possessed" (Norwegian: besatt) to denote the people in need of exorcism. I do not find this relevant since it does not cover the variety of the shepherds' terminology.

admission to the two years theoretical and practical training program, usually taught by pastors and shepherd leaders. The novices are consecrated in their white, long dresses on the annual commemoration day of the *toby* and lay people also participate in the consecration. The relation between consecration of shepherds and ordination of pastors is a topic on which opinions differ. As for behaviour, the shepherds have detailed regulations concerning every aspect of life. In my material this is especially seen in opposition to the "turning of the corpse" ceremony, prohibition against cigarettes, alcohol and snuff and in counteracting pride because of visible results of their work. The tension between shepherds and pastors may be severe, often related to the issue of exorcism, but the possibility of good co-operation is at hand if both parties show their best will.

To the shepherds, the demonic form a rather elaborated hierarchy of spiritual and invisible beings. Evil spirits dwell in the air around people and can enter into any material object. Demons in the shape of different animals are most common and to conceptualise the demonic fight with humans, imagery of attack is often used. Shepherds talk about either being governed by God's spirit or by an evil spirit. They are absolutely opposed to traditional healers because even if the healers may be able to heal sicknesses, they ruin the faith of Christians by exposing them to demonic influence.

The use of vocabulary regarding demons and expulsion of demons is rather uniform while a varied and somewhat bewildering terminology is used to denote people in need of exorcism. I do not find the English word "possessed" to be suitable to render the shepherds' understanding. To them, demonic influence varies from a light degree to a state where the individual's personality is taken prisoner and therefore I use "assaulted by demons" to describe the people seeking the shepherds' cure. To some extent the shepherds use indigenous terms to denote people in need of exorcism and expulsion of demons but some of the main terminology in this area consists of foreign words, which are now well rooted in the church vocabulary. This observation points to the contexts of interpretation in this investigation—traditional Malagasy culture and biblical message—and suggests an overlap and a close relationship between the two.[382]

---

[382] See 1.3.3.2, 4.1 p. 145–146 and 4.6 p. 330–333.

From a broader perspective on the historical origin and the characteristic features of the revival movement in this chapter I will in the next chapter narrow the presentation to exorcism in its actual context. The task is to describe the elements in a healing service.

3 Elements in a healing service

The Monday morning healing service at the Ambohimahazo *toby* starts at 8 a.m., but few let the watch dictate their lives. Around 8 o'clock some shepherds may enter the church to arrange the room: A small table is placed just below the altar section, in front of the benches and a white cloth is placed on the table. A single chair is put on one side of the table, which is the place of the leader. The benches at the front of the church are placed in a semi-circle and it is an unwritten custom that the people who feel in special need for the shepherds' assistance will be seated there. Some straw mats are placed in a corner in the side aisle of the church.

People are coming little by little, entering the church by the side-door and walking quietly to find a place at the front of the church. They at first do not say a word to the one sitting next to them. Instead they close their eyes, fold their hands and pray. Afterwards they may shake hands with those sitting on both sides. Almost all attendants carry a Bible and a hymnbook and some of them also have oblong handbags made of cotton material. They are shepherds and they carry their white shepherd robes in the handbags.

Healing services are open to anyone and as many as possible in the parish are exhorted to attend the services. The audience on these Monday mornings counts 45 in average, men and women and less than half of these live permanently in the *toby*. They come from the town Antsirabe and from the countryside not far away. They know that healing services are held on a regular basis in the *toby* and when they have special needs, they attend the service if not prevented by other daily duties. The congregation is considered to assist the shepherds in their work by singing, preaching, testimonies and by praying, may be the most important of all according to the shepherds themselves. This participation from the congregation is one of the reasons why the shepherds arrange these services in churches and not in private. The healing services in the Ambohimahazo *toby* are held in the parish church on the campus of the *toby*.[383] The shepherds consider these services a normal part of the congregation's life in the parish.[384]

Healing services consist of prayer, singing, preaching, testimonies, reading from the Bible, casting out of evil spirits (*asa* = "work") and the laying on of hands (*fampaherezana* = "strengthening"). All these elements form an integral part of the service and may be understood as a fixed liturgy.[385] It is important for the shepherds to place exorcism in this genuine church setting and they consider all the elements as an integrated spiritual treatment.[386]

---

[383] The founders of the *toby* have often placed this institution near the parish church and so this church is the place of meeting for Sunday services, healing services and all other activity in the parish. This is not the case for all *toby*, but in Ambohimahazo the parish church is used by the *toby*.

[384] Sharp has also observed that the congregation's participation is necessary for several reasons. She mentions that prayer and hymns are imbued with the power of God's Word and that the singing of the congregation will help draw the spirits out of the patients. She also says that the parishioners become witnesses to God's work by attending the services. Sharp 1993:258. This partly corresponds with my own findings. See 3.1.2.

[385] In a meeting of the four main *toby* in 1995, where many different questions concerning the revival movement, church and state were discussed, a proposal for a joint liturgy for the exorcism part of the healing services was introduced. The very fact of the necessity of such a joint liturgy displays that the different branches of the revival movement have their own ways of practising this ritual and that some of them feel a need for more conformity. The liturgy presented in this meeting in 1995 is very close—if not identical—to the one practised in the Ankaramalaza-branch of the movement and up to now there is no common agreement in detail. This proposal is very close to the liturgy normally followed in the Lutheran church and therefore I will render it briefly here. It presupposes the first part of the service with prayer, singing and preaching—and it is explicitly said that the word of God is the basis for any healing—but the proposed liturgy itself is limited to the casting out of demons and the "strengthening"-part of the service: 1. The shepherds' preparing (beginning from the collection), 2. Hymn no.175 to let the congregation prepare itself for what is coming, 3. The shepherds line up in front of the congregation, 4. Prayer, 5. Readings from the Bible, which form the basis for the work (Jn 14:12–17; Mk 16:15–20; Mt 18:18–20; Jn 20:21–23), 6. Prayer, 7. Words of exhortation (*fitaomana*) (brief), 8. Work of expulsion of demons and repentance, 9. Laying on of hands with prayer, 10. A hymn and the Lord's prayer, 11. The blessing, 12. A closing hymn. Note: Individual spiritual guidance should be done after the service, if anyone asks for it. Tobilehibe 1995:59.

[386] It may happen during fits of illness in the patient's home or elsewhere that shepherds start their exorcism in the name of Jesus without making a long

In the handbook of the Ankaramalaza-movement it is affirmed that the basis of "work and strengthening" is God's word and that its purpose is salvation by faith in Jesus Christ. This affirmation is found before the more specific instructions concerning the different parts of the liturgy.[387] Therefore, there should be no "work and strengthening" if the word of God is not preached first. It is underlined, however, that God's voice is not only heard during the sermon, but also during expulsion of demons and the laying on of hands, which is a continuation of the sermon in terms of application for people's needs.[388] It is concluded that the "work and strengthening" is a sign of salvation, while God's word is the basis of salvation.[389]

Since this project is delimited mainly to exorcism in healing services in a *toby* and I have announced that exorcism will be described within the context where this practice belongs,[390] this chapter is dedicated to elements in a healing service, which can be observed, registered and described. The bottom line of the presentation is the liturgy of a healing service in the Ambohimahazo *toby*. The presentation is arranged thematically and all parts are given due weight, since the shepherds consider it impossible to isolate exorcism from the other elements in the service, but exorcism is the main focus of the following treatment. My fieldwork material is the guiding principle in the outline of the presentation and then corresponding themes in the written material are presented where it applies, whether they support or contradict my own findings.[391] I have 3 main subchapters: 1) Prayer, singing and preaching, 2) Expulsion of demons and 3) Prayer with the laying on of hands.

---

introduction, but this is only practised in an urgent situation. Even then they are advised to read at least one passage from the Bible constituting their work.

[387] Tobilehibe 1997:80.
[388] Tobilehibe 1997:82–83.
[389] Tobilehibe 1997:84. Mk 16:15–18 is given as a biblical reference.
[390] See 1.1.
[391] My participant observation of 27 healing services does not cover all elements with equal thoroughness and in these cases I lean more heavily on the available written material.

CH. 3: ELEMENTS IN A HEALING SERVICE

3.1 Prayer, singing and preaching

"Proclamation of the Word of God, repentance and prayer/exorcism are basic to every healing service".[392] The organisation of these elements differs to some extent from place to place but a liturgical pattern forms the bottom line.

3.1.1 Prayer

Prayer permeates the whole healing service and the abundance of prayer in the service indicates how important the shepherds deem this element. People pray when they enter the church, the first 15–20 minutes is free prayer, all the testimonies start with prayer, one of the shepherds prays when they are lined up before the congregation, there is a prayer following the four readings from Scripture, the shepherds pray quietly and the audience is encouraged to sit in prayer with closed eyes during "work and strengthening", almost all the audience are prayed for individually with the laying on of hands, a prayer by one of the shepherds ends the "work and strengthening" and the Lord's Prayer normally closes the service. Almost all prayer in these services is free prayer, the only exception being the Lord's Prayer. It seems like long prayers are preferred to short ones.

I will in the following comment on the different prayers according to the liturgy of the service. The exception is the prayer with the laying on of hands, which will be treated in a separate subchapter below.

When 5–10 people have come to the church, the prayer part starts without any signal from the leader. One verse from the hymnbook is sung by heart and the one who started singing, stands up and prays. When he/she is seated again, another starts singing and then stands up praying. This continues until the leader considers that it is time for testimonies and preaching. Some of these prayers are impossible to hear because of the low voice, but the content is often characterised by repentance, a feeling of unworthiness before God, or intercession: especially for the sick, that they may be set free from the devil's bondage.[393]

---

[392] Rasolondraibe 1989:349.
[393] This opening prayer part is often organised in other ways outside the Ambohimahazo *toby*, with prayer, singing and testimonies going hand in hand from the very beginning. In healing services with very many people present, this prayer

People are encouraged to testify to the work of God in their lives and primarily shepherds and novices do this. They start singing a verse of a hymn, while they proceed to the table where the leader sits. Facing the congregation they start their testimony with a prayer as soon as the verse is sung. Some of them also conclude their testimony with a prayer, before turning back to their seat. The most frequent content is a prayer of forgiveness, often in a crying voice and of assistance against assaults from the devil. Other themes are intercession for the sick and the shepherds, strength to bear the mockery from family and neighbours, that God will be present during the following "work and strengthening" and more generally that many people will come to the service or that a certain building project will come through.

When the shepherds are dressed in white robes, they line up in the front of the church facing the congregation. The shepherd at the utmost left seen from the congregation starts with prayer. This prayer stresses God's holiness and is a confession of sins. It is an urgent prayer, which centres on Jesus and the power from the Holy Spirit. The following exorcism is also prayed for as a holy work and a fight with Satan and the ultimate goal of coming to faith is underlined. Below is an extract of one of these prayers:

> ...In your presence of honour and holiness we are poor sinners, but you have still received us and let us hear your word. We are filled with thanks to you!
> Now, o Jesus, we pray eagerly: forgive our sins and have mercy with each one of us. There are still so much contrary to your will ... , which prevent us to see your glory.
> We cannot perform anything to remedy this situation, but ... we thank you for all your words, which has been given us freely in this service. We pray your Holy Spirit to open our hearts in order to be able to receive this word ...
> O Jesus, your sheep are gathered here and nothing is hidden for you about any of them. My wish is that you will bless them to be able to receive your word, so they can repent ...
> I pray eagerly to you, o Lord, that you will send your Holy Spirit to work in a special way, because when your Spirit works, whose hearts can be closed to you? ...
> O Lord, let your glory cover us so that we are not seen. Take away all boasting and daring of our own when we are doing your work and let us be led by your great power ... And let the words constituting your holy work, which we are

---

part may be omitted. Ambohimahazo *toby* 16 June 1998. The reason may be practical (people are unable to hear the prayer) but it may also reflect that this is no obligatory part of the liturgy.

going to hear, be living and powerful words, so they can open our hearts ..., because the evil one will always throw his arrows on us. ... Amen.[394]

According to the handbook, the prayer opening the exorcism session has two main functions. Firstly, to ask the Lord for mercy on behalf of the congregation so they can be saved. Salvation from sin, from the devil's traps and from God's wrath is explicitly mentioned. It should be an eager prayer that God will hear, provide the work and show his glory. Secondly, a prayer that invites people to the Lord, in order to repent, see his salvation and renew the will of serving him. It is underlined that this prayer is not on behalf of the shepherd's own sins or shortcomings, but carries out a mediator's role for the congregation. It is not allowed for the shepherd to display his/her own weaknesses and this is argued for by pointing to Jesus' example: he never rebuked his disciples in front of the crowd. This prayer should not use the pronouns "I" and "me", but "we" and "us".[395]

A new prayer follows the four readings from the Bible. According to my fieldwork notes the first part of this prayer is thanksgiving to the Lord for his word and the possibility to come together, the second part is a prayer of forgiveness for the shepherds and the congregation and the third part concerns the work, which is to start. It is a prayer that the Holy Spirit may be present and a petition of strength from Jesus, who will work together with the shepherds.

During the expulsion of demons it is not uncommon to see shepherds turning away from a severe case to pray quietly. Obviously enough, I have not heard the content of these prayers but the handbook advises the shepherds to pray during casting out of demons if they feel in need of strength. It should be a short prayer and the shepherd should move a little away from the rest of the shepherds/patients.[396] This prayer is not understood as a substitute for a praying attitude through the whole healing service, but underlines the centrality of prayer during expulsion of demons.[397]

When the prayer with the laying on of hands is finished, the shepherds line up again in front of the congregation and one of them

---

[394] Prayer before the Scripture reading in the Ambohimahazo *toby* 29 November 1993.

[395] Tobilehibe 1997:89–91. Note that in the displayed prayer above, the pronoun "I" is used and she also prayed for the shepherds and their work. Indirectly the weaknesses of the shepherds are displayed in this prayer.

[396] Tobilehibe 1997:107.

[397] The danger of disguise in front of the congregation lies very near.

prays. According to my notes, thanks and praise to God for what he has done is reflected in this prayer but it is also a prayer to prevent the evil forces from returning. Trust in Jesus, who will not leave his people, is also a theme. The handbook says that the aim of this prayer is to praise and thank the Lord for all his gifts and for having sent the Holy Spirit. It is also a prayer that God's word may grow to strengthen the faith. It should not be a repetition of confession, because God has already granted his forgiveness. Neither should it cause fear by having the devil as its theme. Instead the prayer should confirm the hope in Jesus.[398] The Lord's Prayer normally concludes the healing service, but it is preceeded often by a free prayer.[399]

3.1.2 Singing

There is an abundance of singing in a healing service. The singing during prayer and testimonies is initiated by individuals in the congregation and principally it is everyone's right to start singing if he/she feels compelled to do so. It is nevertheless advised that the leader guides the congregation in singing, to get an orderly service and so that the enemy will have no chance to insert inappropriate hymns.[400] Before every prayer at the beginning of the service, a verse from a hymn is sung and also before every testimony.

At the Ambohimahazo *toby* the congregation does not sing during the expulsion of demons. When the laying on of hands begins, however, the singing starts again and it is in this part of the service that most hymns are sung. One hymn follows immediately after another and it lasts until there are no more people who wish to be prayed for.

In the services, which follow the Ankaramalaza custom, it is only in the initial phase of the expulsion of demons that there should be no singing. The reason for this is that the beginning of the casting out of

---

[398] Tobilehibe 1997:119.

[399] Two times during my observations I had the feeling that the person who prayed was not sincere. A man about 50 years old had a long prayer, where he changed his voice all the time, sometimes very loud and afterwards so tender that it was almost impossible to hear. When he said that the devil moves around to catch whomever he may find, he was almost raging. The other time I heard a woman in her forties. She changed her voice, cried and seemed to appear theatrical. It did not seem genuine, but since I did not know the people, it is difficult to judge.

[400] Tobilehibe 1997:109.

CH. 3: ELEMENTS IN A HEALING SERVICE

demons-part is a time of repentance and the singing may disturb the congregation. When the casting out of demons has endured for some time, hymns which confirm the congregation's repentance and willingness to serve the Lord, should be sung.[401]

All hymns are taken from the hymnbook[402] and many in the audience know them by heart. I have made an analysis to find out which hymns are used in the healing services. I find a great range of hymns and many are used only once. I will in the following list the 10 most used hymns according to my material and comment briefly on their content.[403]

The first hymn to be sung when the testimonies and preaching are finished, is a prayer asking the Holy Spirit to descend among the congregation to guide the people. It also contains words of repentance and a prayer of cleansing. The Lord is asked to remind the congregation of these words and it ends with a prayer that the Lord will stay in the hearts of the singers.[404] The second most used hymn is another inviting the Holy Spirit to descend, "Come, o Holy Spirit".[405] Hymns with themes of confession of sins and repentance follow those of invocation of the Holy Spirit: "O, my father, who loves me. Your child, who has gone astray, come and repent before you...",[406] "O, sinner, do not say no when Jesus calls you, but repent...",[407] "My father, I left you long time ago, but now I will come home...".[408] The themes of God's love and compassion for sinners are always present in the most frequently used hymns: "God

---

[401] Tobilehibe 1997:110.

[402] *Fihirana FFPM*. This hymnbook is a joint project between the two largest protestant churches in Madagascar, the Reformed Church (FJKM) and the Lutheran Church (FLM)

[403] I use both the participant observation from healing services and questionnaires to shepherds. The questionnaires differ from the participant observation in their greater conformity in the hymns referred to. Many of them occur frequently, but even here a variety is present.

[404] *Fihirana* 175: *"Avia Fanahy ô! Fanahy Masina ô!"* ("Come, o Spirit, o Holy Spirit"). In some churches *Fihirana* 383: *O, ry mpanota, aza mandà, Jeso miantso, ka miovà* ("O, sinner, do not say no when Jesus calls you...") replaces the one mentioned, but I have never experienced that. The handbook says that this is a matter of organisation and the intention is the same, namely to make the people reflect on their own situation in order to repent. Tobilehibe 1997:110.

[405] *Fihirana* 176: *Avia, Fanahy Masina ô!*

[406] *Fihirana* 407: *O, ry Raiko, Izay malala, Tonga aho, zanakao, Izay nania, fa adala, Ka mifona aminao...*

[407] *Fihirana* 383: *O, ry mpanota, aza mandà, Jeso miantso, ka miovà...*

[408] *Fihirana* 417: *Nandao anao ela aho, Raiko ô, 'Zao dia te-hody aho...*

does not want anybody to be lost. He, your father, is full of love...",[409] "The poor people sought you, o redeemer, long time ago,... and everyone received your grace",[410] "Jesus, our friend, Jesus is ours, he will not go away, Jesus is ours...".[411] Confidence and surrender is another frequent theme: "O, father, who is full of compassion, here is your child... You feed me, you give me what my heart wants: great pleasure.".[412] The 10th hymn with an outstanding frequency, is a praise to the triune God, Spirit, Son and Father: "O Spirit, explainer, we wait for your coming...".[413]

Almost all the most frequently used hymns in my material correspond with the directions given in the handbook. But there are more general hymns proposed in the handbook, which do not occur more than once or twice according to my observations. This suggests that there is a set of almost obligatory hymns but outside of this set, the freedom of choice is great.[414] It should be noticed that the themes of the hymns primarily concern repentance and trust in God and the emphasis is not on a fight with evil powers or expulsion of demons.[415]

---

[409] *Fihirana* 28: *Zanahary tsy mba tia Ny fahaverezanao, Izy, Rainao be fitia,...*

[410] *Fihirana* 426: *Nanatona Anao, Mpanavotra ô! Ny olo-mahantra fahiny... Fa samy nandray ny indrafonao...*

[411] *Fihirana* 513: *Jeso Sakaizanay, Jeso anay; Sady tsy mahafoy, Jeso anay;...*

[412] *Fihirana* 444: *Ry, Raiko feno antra! Inty ny zanakao,... Hianao no mahavoky Hianao no manome Izay irin'ny foko, Dia hasambaram-be.*

[413] *Fihirana* 190: *Ry Fanahy Mpanazava! Miandrandra Anao izahay; Aza ela, fa tongava,...* This hymn is a very close translation of the Norwegian hymn: "Ånd fra himlen, kom med nåde" and the tune is the same. Sangboken. Syng for Herren 1983: no. 56.

According to Syvertsen, the hymns during the healing services are special revival hymns with a melodious time to the Malagasy mind. He has noticed that the time of the hymns are different from the ones used in the Sunday morning services. The voice is near to screaming and the intensity of the time grows stronger as the expulsion of demons continues. His assertion is that the time is near up to the time of the drums. Syvertsen 1983:176. What I have found, is that the hymns used in healing services are very common in all kinds of services, except *Fihirana* 175 and 176 and that many different hymns are used. I agree with Syvertsen, however, in respect of the intensity in the singing at healing services.

[414] The reasons for this similarity may be the rather fixed liturgy of the healing services and it may stem from the instruction given the novices before their consecration. Until mid-1990's, however, there was no fixed curriculum for the instruction and local pastors have been teaching according to what they found most important for the shepherds to know. See 1.3.2.

[415] This may be due to the range of hymns in the hymnbook, with few hymns in it concerning exorcism. Another possibility is that the choice of hymns in healing

The singing has different functions according to its place in the service. Invocation of the Holy Spirit and preparation of the congregation is the focus while the shepherds put on their robes to engage in exorcism. During the expulsion of demons and the laying on of hands, the intention of the singing is to turn the people's hearts to God and exhort them to repentance and surrender.[416] The handbook says that the singing of hymns give strength to the shepherds at work and facilitates the casting out of demons since the hymns are part of the sermon based on God's word and therefore mighty to defeat Satan.[417]

3.1.3 Preaching

After an initial clarification of what I mean by "preaching", I will describe the way of preaching, the preacher and the great range of passages read from the Bible. Then I concentrate on the most important in this subchapter: the content of the preaching, which I choose to arrange in 3 groups.

All parts of the healing service can be understood as preaching in a broad sense and the people may hear God's voice not only in the sermon, but also in the singing, the casting out of demons, the laying on of hands and in the other elements.[418] In my presentation of the material at hand, however, I delimit the meaning of "preaching" more narrowly to when a text from the Bible is read and commented on. This can be done in a short testimony or in a 20 minute sermon. I think this meaning of preaching is in line with the shepherds' general understanding.[419] I do not make any distinction between testimonies, sermons and a concluding exhortation, as long as, the above mentioned criteria are present.

---

services shows what the shepherds see as the most important point to stress in this situation.

[416] Tobilehibe 1997:85.
[417] Tobilehibe 1997:108.
[418] Tobilehibe 1997:82–83.
[419] According to this use of "preaching", the four readings from the Bible and the exhortation just before the expulsion of demons are not commented here, because the first is just a reading without any comments and the second is a general exhortation which is normally not based on specific verses in the Bible.

Preaching of God's word is obligatory in the healing service, but where and how it is done can differ from place to place.[420] At Ambohimahazo its place is normally between the prayer session and the exorcism and in addition the service often ends with a testimony. The preaching session normally consists of testimonies and a sermon.[421] Three to five people deliver their testimonies and the session ends with a sermon by the leader or by an elder at the *toby*. The form of presentation is stereotypical: the one who is going to deliver a testimony starts singing one verse from a hymn, while he/she moves in front of the congregation where the leader sits. He/she stands at one side of the table, prays and reads a passage from Scripture. He/she then comments on the text from the perspective of the time it was written and the testimonies show great knowledge about a range of biblical stories. The second step is normally an actualisation to the situation today. A short story may be told, or an exhortation to the congregation may end the preaching.[422] It is not customary to use a manuscript during the preaching. I can hardly recall having experienced that, even for sermons up to 20 minutes!

The preaching is enthusiastic with a strong appeal of repentance. It urges the listener to be actively involved and to choose whom to follow. It is not uncommon to see men and women weep before the congregation, either because of their feeling of unworthiness or because of all the people who do not believe in Jesus. The listeners easily understand the preachers' language and ways of expression.

The preachers are shepherds or novices, but in principle it is open to anyone to give a testimony. Sometimes the people are asked beforehand, but as a general rule the shepherds should be prepared to deliver a

---

[420] In an article where he describes the healing services in the Southeast coastal area, Syvertsen has observed that the sermon can be omitted and if it is held, it is normally short. Syvertsen 1983:176. My material contradicts this observation. The preaching of God's word is abundantly present, it is never omitted and the testimonies and preaching together may last for at least half an hour.

[421] At the Log 238, 67 Ha-*toby* in Antananarivo there are normally two sermons in each healing service, which was held daily at 8 a.m. and 2 p.m.

[422] In a hand-written manual used in the instruction of shepherds, Randriatsarafara 1998:15, Randriatsarafara J.G. gives concrete advise for the sermon: It should be based on verses from the Bible (Rom 10:17), which has to be read very carefully and the passage should be given a thematic heading and sub-headings. Another way of preaching is to comment each verse by itself. It is especially underlined that an actualisation to the congregation's situation is important. He distinguishes between sermon and testimony, in the way that a testimony has its starting point in the experiences of the preacher, while the sermon has its basis in a biblical passage.

testimony at any moment. The person who delivers the sermon is always appointed beforehand and it is usually the leader of the service. Sometimes it is said that those who are compelled by the Spirit should come forward and give their message. I can recall just one occasion when there was an awkward silence because nobody was prepared to give a testimony.

I have registered the gender of the people in the ordinary healing services delivering 74 sermons/testimonies. 39 of them were women and 35 men, a number, which displays the important role of women in these services. The Malagasy Lutheran Church does not allow women to become pastors, though they have several female theologians, but in the revival movement the women are in the majority.[423] The average age of the preachers according to my material is about 50 years old.[424]

I have recorded 87 passages from the Bible. Only 5 of these passages occur twice, so the span in choosing passages from the Bible is great. 27 of the passages read come from the Old Testament: Isaiah and Psalms are the most frequently used and 60 passages are taken from the New Testament: The synoptic Gospels have the overwhelming majority, but John, Acts of the Apostles and Romans are also used to some extent.[425]

---

[423] To make a comparison, I have also registered the gender of the preachers during the period of preparation to the consecration of shepherds at the Ambohimahazo *toby*. This period is special, with many people coming from the entire Avaratrimania church synod. The 3–4 days before consecration is like a festival, with different church meetings from morning to evening and among these are also healing services. Many people came to the healing services, from 140–500 and the preachers were to a greater extent asked beforehand. In these services 13 of 15 testimonies/sermons were held by men, which is rather astonishing compared with the pattern in the ordinary healing services.

[424] This is not based on information of exact age, but is due to my estimations of the age of the preacher. It is an average of 74 people. To judge the age of people is no easy task, but I have been living in Madagascar for almost 10 years, so my estimations of age should not be too far away. 50 years as an average is rather high and may correspond to the general thinking in the Malagasy culture that the elderly people are best suited to speak. It could also point to the fact that the shepherds in general are aged people with few young in their ranks. During my stay in Madagascar in 1998, however, I was told about revivals especially among young people in different places in the high plateaux and several of the shepherds who were consecrated in Ambohimahazo the 19th of June 1998 were in their twenties.

[425] The most used books of the Bible were the following and I am only mentioning books with more than 4 references: Ps: 6 passages, Is: 10; Mt: 12, Lk: 17, Jn: 8, Acts/Rom: 4 each.

In 56 cases I have recordings from the content in the preacher's testimony/sermon.[426] I have arranged the preaching in 3 categories according to content: Repentance to faith, the devil and Jesus, the Christian life, in addition to more general instructions.[427]

3.1.3.1 Repentance to faith

> 1 Jn 1:8–2:2: Very often people do not understand that they are sinners. They do not realise that they have done any wrong and they are not able to understand that misfortunes occur in their life or in their family. It was sin that in the beginning caused illness and suffering. When we confess our sins, Jesus will forgive our sins and cleanse us. Then we stand righteous before God and Jesus can also heal our illness...[428]

The most frequently recurring element in this group is daily repentance. Confession of sins is the way to repentance and belief in the salvation of Jesus, performed by his death is essential. The concluding words at the end of the service often confirm the obtained forgiveness and continue: "do not sin any more". It is explicitly said that belief in Jesus is more important than healing from sickness. A connection between sin and illness/suffering is apparent in the testimony above.

3.1.3.2 The devil and Jesus

> Rom 14:9: (after a lengthy theological explanation of Jesus, who is Lord of all men:) Jesus knows if you have a divided mind. When problems arise, you are a Christian, but when everything goes well, you forget Jesus. There was a man who used paraphernalia from the Malagasy traditional healer and became very rich. This man pretended both to serve God and the idols. Today he is severely ill, all his money is gone and his wife and oldest son are dead. The traditional healer is dead and now this man cries for help from the Christians.

---

[426] To group this content is no easy task. Every testimony/sermon contains more than one theme, so it is a matter of choice in which group to put it. In spite of the difficulties, not to group is not an option because that will prevent any overview of the material.

[427] I use broad groups and when different ways of grouping are possible, I choose what I find to be most important to the preacher.

[428] Testimony held in Ambohimahazo *toby* 23 August 1993. I have summarised the content of this and the 3 following testimonies, but have tried to preserve some of the urgent way of preaching.

> Lk 13:6–9: The accidents in the beginning of chapter 13 happened because of the sinful people. The non-Christians have celebrations with plenty of alcohol now and the traditional healer brings offerings to the dead. Why have you come here? Because of your illness, or the problems in your family. If no misfortune had happened, you would not have been here. God shows his love for you in this way. Do not think of the illness, but concentrate on Jesus. He needs your decision, because he has come to set you free.[429]

Recurring themes are the devil, temptations and illness but the preaching is always embedded in a firm faith that only Jesus can set people free. In this group it is also underlined that the expulsion of demons is dependent on the Holy Spirit and the congregation is encouraged to see God at work through the shepherds. Satan tested Job and he does so with people today, but Jesus is stronger. The devil is seen behind the mocking of the Christians in their daily lives, because the devil hates the Christians and demons may "assault" people through their worries, which are abundant in the severe conditions in daily life. The congregation is urged to have trust in Jesus, who has the power to heal.

3.1.3.3 The Christian life

> Ps 84:11: God is the sun, which means that life comes from him. It is our responsibility to tell others about God's blessings in our lives. God is our shield and his power is not ended. In a very difficult time in my life, he walked by my side and rescued me. He will never abandon you! Have trust in him![430]

Consolation in different severe living conditions is an important theme here. A reiterating sentence is that "God is not abandoning you, but follows you step by step". It is underlined that there is no happiness outside the life with Jesus, but rather spiritual death. The life should be transformed by following Jesus and this shows itself in Christian witness and in serving the sick and unable. "Are we willing to be servants for the "assaulted by demons"?" The life should be guided by fear of God and confession to Christ.

Many other themes were also present: God's word as nourishment of the souls, prayer and God's answering prayer, to keep firm to the

---

[429] Both testimonies were held in Ambohimahazo *toby* 25 June 1998, the day before Madagascar's national day.

[430] Ambohimahazo *toby* 24 May 1993.

Christian doctrine, God's calling of the shepherds to witnessing, Jesus' second coming, how it is possible to be hardened and instructions about the content of the laying on of hands.

The preaching is very closely knit to the Bible, with a great variety of texts. The special texts in the Gospels about casting out of demons are not present at all.[431] Jesus Christ as saviour is a recurring theme and the preachers talk about sin, repentance and grace. It looks like this part of the healing service is used as instruction in Christian belief and conduct. The motif of temptation and demonic involvement in human life is clearly present, but it does not seem to occupy a major place in the preaching. Most of the preaching displayed in all 3 groups could be heard anywhere in the Malagasy Lutheran Church.

Preaching is an essential part of a healing service as it is also to the shepherds' ministry in general. The shepherds are called "preacher—healers",[432] a name, which shows that the preaching is an important part of their work. This is also in line with the statutes of the revival movement, which says that preaching the Gospel and exorcism are the shepherds' main obligations.[433] When it is firmly underlined in the handbook that preaching is an integral and obligatory part of a healing service, this emphasising rests in the conviction that only God's word can create belief in Jesus, which is the main purpose of the service.[434]

3.2 Expulsion of demons

This subchapter will mainly be organised thematically and I group the content under 3 headings: Preparation, Scripture reading and Expelling demons. Themes to be treated in the following are: the arrangement of the patients, the organisation of the shepherds' work, the biblical passages constituting exorcism, the shepherds' movements and words during casting out of demons and the patients' reactions. The liturgy of

---

[431] Only two of the used texts from the Gospels refer to evil spirits: Lk 10:10–21 and Mk 16:14–20

[432] Rasolondraibe 1989:347.

[433] Fifohazana FFPM 1980:no 23.

[434] Tobilehibe 1997:82–84. Rajoelisoa A. too, underlines that God's word is abundant in the revival movement and there are no special passages which are preferred. They all centre around Christ, who is the pivot of the Bible, dead on the cross and risen from the dead. Rajoelisoa 1977–80:101–104.

112   CH. 3: ELEMENTS IN A HEALING SERVICE

the service is visible in the presentation, as is especially apparent in the structure of the 3 headings.

3.2.1 Preparation

3.2.1.1 *The congregation's preparation and organisation of people in need of exorcism*

When the congregation starts singing no. 175 in the hymnbook, an invocation of the Holy Spirit to descend, this is a signal to the congregation to prepare for what is coming. Some of the shepherds start arranging the straw mats stored in a corner of the church. They are now placed on the floor in front of the benches and replace the table and chair, where the leader has been seated. The expectation rises while the congregation watches the movements of the shepherds arranging the room. The congregation is expected to bow their heads, pray quietly and continue with the singing.

People with special needs often move to the first benches or sit down on the straw mats. It is not uncustomary that the leader of the *toby* or another elderly shepherd walk around and advise some people to move to the first benches or to the straw mats. I presume that the leader knows these people; many have stayed at the *toby* for some time.

The Ambohimahazo *toby* has a special practice when arranging the people in special need of exorcism. In healing services elsewhere only straw mats are used for these people, while in the Ambohimahazo *toby* the first benches, which form a semi-circle, have the same function. I have been told that this is just a matter of tradition, but I have noticed that sometimes people seated even on the first benches are advised to descend to the straw mats. To me it looks like the straw mats are reserved for the special difficult cases.[435] The majority of the people sitting on the first benches or the straw mats have no observable traces of sickness:

---

[435] People have a right to sit where they want and if a person takes a place on the straw mat, nobody will move him/her away, even if he/she looks as healthy as anyone. The leader's organisation of the sitting during the expulsion of demons should only be considered as advice, which most people follow.

I watch a young girl with nice clothes sitting on the first bench together with her mother, who is a shepherd. The young girl reads the Bible during the whole session of demon-expulsion.
A man in his thirties, dressed in white, moves to the first bench and during the session he keeps his Bible firm in his arms.
An elderly man who looks like an ordinary farmer from the countryside, has put on a rather nice jacket. He walks with a limp when he leaves his place to sit on the first bench.[436]

"I am attending the weekly Monday morning healing service at Ambohimahazo for strengthening ," a merchant selling at the market in Antsirabe told me one day as we were walking back to town together after the service. He sits on the first bench during expulsion of demons and is prayed for with the laying on of hands. He told me that he had been a Christian for a long time, but never wholeheartedly. When his child turned severely ill and his house burnt down, Jesus appeared to him and told him to become a shepherd. That is why he is a novice now and he attends the training program in his local church.[437]

When family members follow their relatives to the healing services, they normally sit close to them during the casting out of demons. This means that some of the people seated on the first benches/straw mats are relatives of the sick, who have not come to the *toby* for their own sake. Consequently, they should not be counted among the ill people, but in practice it is impossible to distinguish them from each other. All the people seated on the first benches/the straw mats are treated with expulsion of demons.

I counted the number of people sitting on the first benches or the straw mats in 12 ordinary healing services at Ambohimahazo. With an average of 45 people present at the service, 30 of them sat there. This means that 2/3 of the people present subjected themselves to the expulsion of demons. About 60 % of these people were women, a little above 30 % were men and a little less than 10 % were children.[438]

---

[436] These 3 examples are all taken from my participant observation of healing services in Ambohimahazo.

[437] O 340.

[438] I do not have detailed specifications of the children's' age, but I have sometimes made notes like: "baby at her mother's breast, below school-age, 3 years, 4 years, 10 years, 13 years". In healing services in the fortnight leading up to the consecration of shepherds, with many more people present, there were also more women than men, who sat at the front of the church, but the total number of people on the first benches/straw mats represented a lower percentage of the congregation than in ordinary services.

114   CH. 3: ELEMENTS IN A HEALING SERVICE

The handbook underlines the importance of the congregation's preparation. Citations from the Bible are used to confirm this[439] and its practical organisation is by singing appropriate hymns until the shepherds return from the sacristy.[440]

3.2.1.2   *The shepherds' preparation*[441]

As soon as no. 175 in the hymnbook sounds, the shepherds rise from their places and move into the sacristy. They first shake hands or kiss each other with a holy kiss.[442] Then they pray quietly while they put on their white robes. Afterwards the leader prays loudly, before they organise their "work": who is going to pray, to read the texts from the Bible and to give an exhortation—if this is included—before the expulsion of demons starts. The delegation of tasks can be done according to the shepherds' wishes, or the leader appoints people to the different tasks. Then one of the shepherds prays the Lord to give them strength to fulfil their work and all the shepherds walk into the church and line up facing the congregation.

The shepherds are expected to live in a continuing preparation because they are to engage in a fight and nobody can win a fight if he/she is not well prepared. This is underlined to the extent that the handbook says "the good result of the work depends on the preparation and willingness of the worker".[443] According to *Mama* Nenilava, Jesus gives the victory over the devil and the shepherds receive that victory in prayer

---

[439] Amos 4:13b: "... prepare to meet your God, O Israel." Mt 5:6: "Blessed are those who hunger and thirst for righteousness, for they shall be satisfied."

[440] Tobilehibe 1997:85. One of the leaders is advised to organise the time of preparation because the congregation should not be left on its own during this time.

[441] The shepherds' preparation is held in a separate room in Ambohimahazo and I have not taken part in this session. Since this element is an important part of the healing service, I describe it according to the handbook.

[442] In many churches, especially in the countryside, there is no separate room and then the shepherds put on their robes in front of the congregation. This is also the case in the Log 238, 67 Ha-*toby*, where I have conducted some of my fieldwork. In such cases this turns out to be a rather spectacular ceremony, which may disturb the congregation in their preparation. I also suppose that the shepherds themselves may be tempted to exaggerate their level of spirituality since they know that the congregation is watching them.

[443] Tobilehibe 1997:86.

before the healing service even starts.[444] It may be necessary that the shepherds ask each other for forgiveness in the sacristy. There may be unsettled matters between them and this should be wiped away before engaging in exorcism. In order not to delay the congregation's waiting, however, such a mutual forgiveness should be done in the special shepherd reunions apart from the healing service.[445]

3.2.2 Scripture reading

When the shepherds have lined up in front of the congregation, the singing ends, sometimes in the middle of a hymn. The shepherd at the utmost left, seen from the congregation, says "Let us pray" and starts praying.[446] After this prayer the shepherd standing no. 2 from the left says "In Jesus' name" and then starts reading the first of four texts from the Bible. Shepherd no. 3, 4 and 5 continues the reading, without repeating "in the name of Jesus" and the reading concludes with "Amen".

The shepherds must have their Bibles opened to confirm that the words really are God's word and in order to avoid boasting of their knowledge of knowing the text by heart.[447] The reading should be well articulated without mistakes to show respect to God.[448] The reading should be done in a prayerful attitude, so that the Spirit of God can work in the hearts of the listeners. The chapters and verses in the Bible where these texts are written are not referred to in this setting. Otherwise, citing the references is almost an obligatory custom.

The most important verses constituting exorcism are parts of Mk 16:17–18: "...in my name they will cast out demons;... they will lay their

---

[444] Tobilehibe 1997:86.

[445] Tobilehibe 1997:87.

[446] Cf. 3.1.1 to the content of this prayer and the prayer immediately after the four readings.

[447] Tobilehibe 1997:91. People who are unable to read the small letters in the Bible and do not have the possibility of buying glasses are allowed to copy the four texts from the Bible to a clean sheet of paper. They should use a special sheet of paper (*taratasy voatokana*) and handle it with care, in accordance with its holy use. It is emphasised that the sheet of paper does not replace the Bible and that the sheet should lie in the Bible when read. It is preferable to read directly from the Bible, however. Ankaramalaza 1997:8.

[448] I once heard a woman shepherd reading one of the passages with several minor mistakes. During the reading she was corrected by people in the congregation and they showed clearly that they disliked her reading.

hands on the sick, and they will recover".[449] The Malagasy wording for the role of the biblical texts in exorcism is that the Bible *mampiorina* this work, which stem from the root *orina*. The meaning of this root is the action of making something firm in the earth, to build, construct, especially with regard of foundations. The prefix *mamp-* is causative and strengthens the meaning that the word of God makes firm the foundations of the practice of exorcism.[450]

The four Scriptural passages are the following and they are read in this order.[451]

> Jn 14:12–17:
> "Truly, truly, I say to you, he who believes in me will also do the works that I do; and greater works than these will he do, because I go to the Father. Whatever you ask in my name, I will do it, that the Father may be glorified in the Son; if you ask anything in my name, I will do it."
> "If you love me, you will keep my commandments. And I will pray the Father, and he will give you another Counselor, to be with you for ever, even the Spirit of truth, whom the world cannot receive, because it neither sees him nor knows him; you know him, for he dwells with you, and will be in you."
>
> Mk 16:14–20:
> Afterward he appeared to the eleven themselves as they sat at table; and he upbraided them for their unbelief and hardness of heart, because they had not

---

[449] 1 Jn 3:8: "...The reason for the Son of God appeared was to destroy the works of the devil" and Jn 12:31: "... now shall the ruler of this world be cast out;" are also mentioned in the handbook as important verses constituting exorcism. Tobilehibe 1997:79.

[450] Tobilehibe 1997:79–80; 91, Abinal and Malzac 1930:470.

[451] The four fixed readings were agreed upon when the four branches of the revival movement were united into the Protestant revival movement (*Fifohazana FFPM*). Before that, each branch had its own readings, which caused a level of uncertainty about which to follow. IS 200. Rasolondraibe P. and L.A. Sharp mention only two texts that are read before exorcism: Mk 16:14–18 (Sharp: Mk 16:15–18) and Jn 20:21–23. Rasolondraibe 1989:349, Sharp 1993:259. In a thesis about *Mama Nenilava*, Pitaka D. says that she only read one or two passages from the Scripture before exorcism and not four passages as is the custom nowadays, which he cites as the following: Jn 14:12–17; Mk 16:15–20; Mt 18:18–20; Jn 20:21–23. Pitaka 1999:116. These observations point to a certain degree of caution as to fix the readings very firmly, but the main idea of biblical references as the foundation for exorcism is clear. In my material I have observed only once that only two passages were read. In all other instances, there were four readings, but usually the reading from Mark 16 started with verse 15. In the different sources there is a certain variety on Mark's reading, but the verses 15–18 are always present.

believed those who saw him after he had risen. And he said to them, "Go into all the world and preach the gospel to the whole creation. He who believes and is baptized will be saved; but he who does not believe will be condemned. And these signs will accompany those who believe: in my name they will cast out demons; they will speak in new tongues; they will pick up serpents, and if they drink any deadly thing, it will not hurt them; they will lay their hands on the sick, and they will recover."
So then the Lord Jesus, after he had spoken to them, was taken up into heaven, and sat down at the right hand of God. And they went forth and preached everywhere, while the Lord worked with them and confirmed the message by the signs that attended it. Amen.

Mt 18:18–20:
"Truly, I say to you, whatever you bind on earth shall be bound in heaven, and whatever you loose on earth shall be loosed in heaven. Again I say to you, if two of you agree on earth about anything they ask, it will be done for them by my Father in heaven. For where two or three are gathered in my name, there am I in the midst of them."

Jn 20:21–23:
Jesus said to them again, "Peace be with you. As the Father has sent me, even so I send you." And when he had said this, he breathed on them, and said to them, "Receive the Holy Spirit. If you forgive the sins of any, they are forgiven; if you retain the sins of any, they are retained."

After the reading there is no explanation of the text and when the 5th shepherd has prayed, the 6th shepherd from the left starts the casting out of demons by raising his right arm and commanding the evil spirits to get out in Jesus' name. This is the practice in the ordinary services in the Ambohimahazo *toby*.

In healing services where the local church follows the Ankaramalaza custom, the 6th shepherd from the left will give a short exhortation before the expulsion of demons starts. This in Malagasy is called *teny fampibebahana*, which means "words that cause repentance". The exhortation is a special mark of the Ankaramalaza-branch and is always practised in the *toby* and congregations, which depend on this branch of the revival movement.[452] The main content of the exhortation, according

---

[452] In Log 238, 67 Ha, which is one of the centres of the Ankaramalaza movement, there is always an exhortation before the casting out of demons. *Mama* Nenilava herself had no additional exhortation before the casting out of demons and the reason given for this is that the people had already repented during her preaching. She did not prevent her followers from having the exhortation, however, but she underlined that it must be very short. Pitaka 1999:115. The handbook underlines that the exhortation should never be omitted because the exhortation to repentance

to my material, is closely knitted to Jesus, the forgiveness of sins and Jesus' love to all humans. It is an urgent exhortation to kneel down before Jesus to receive his power.

3.2.3 Expelling demons

I have chosen to arrange the following presentation according to important themes in my field material, which I indicate by headings in the text and I refer to other written material under each heading. I start with some comments on the shepherds' dress and equipment while "working". Then I concentrate on the casting out of demons: the initial demon-expulsion, the concentration on the patients at the front of the church, the shepherds' movements, their words and possible dialogue with the evil spirits. I describe the general atmosphere during expulsion of demons and I present the patients' reactions to demon-expulsion. In the end of this subchapter I comment on the length and organisation of the session.

3.2.3.1 Dress and equipment during exorcism

The shepherds wear long white robes and in the left hand they carry their Bible and a handkerchief. The left arm is curved with the Bible pressed to their chest. In a few instances I have observed an old shepherd in Ambohimahazo casting out demons without having put on the white robe. He has then not been one of the team that lined up in front of the congregation, but has stepped in when he considered the situation

---

facilitate the casting out of demons. When a person returns to God, the evil spirits in him will dislike staying any longer and the exhortation strengthens the person's faith, which is the ultimate goal of the healing. The shepherd delivering the exhortation should not read a new text from the Bible, but he/she is advised to actualise what has already been preached during the service. The goal of the exhortation is to lead the congregation to self-reflection and to urge the listeners to make up their minds and to follow the Lord from now on. The words should be permeated by love; compulsion and fright have no place. The exhortation should never last more than two minutes. The handbook renders an example of how to attract the listeners' minds to repentance during an exhortation. Tobilehibe 1997:96–98.

demanded it, e.g. when a person close to him suddenly behaved in a strange way.[453]

The Bible is a sign of the invisible power of God and it is the shepherd's only weapon to conquer the power of the enemy. It is pressed to the chest in order to protect the shepherd but also to show people the holy book during the work. When the shepherd has to hold a person because he/she is acting erratically, another shepherd should take care of the Bible, or the shepherd should leave it in a safe place. The handkerchief has a practical function, to wipe away perspiration or spit, so that the patient will not suffer unnecessary and it is prohibited to use the handkerchief as a means to cast out evil spirits.[454]

3.2.3.2 *Initial casting out of demons*

The shepherd appointed to do so raises his/her right arm and says with a strong voice: "In the name of Jesus of Nazareth, the powerful, I command the work of the darkness and all the evil spirits: Get out in Jesus' name."[455] This is an obligatory opening sentence. All the shepherds standing in front of the congregation join in by saying the same words with loud voices. For some seconds the shepherds stay in their places, but then they begin moving around among the people sitting on the mats and the first benches. They shout in each other's mouths: "Get out in Jesus' name" and they move their right hand as if they are chasing somebody from the place. This command, together with the

---

[453] This is in line with *Mama* Nenilava's practice as well. She seldom wore the special white robe when she cast out demons, especially when she encountered people "assaulted by demons" during evangelism. The reasons for her practice are said to be twofold: She worked so hard and perspired so profusely that it was impossible to have enough clean white robes for her at hand and she would not confuse her practice with the practice of the traditional healers in the area, who also used holy vestments when they were in contact with spirits. *Mama* Nenilava underlined that although it is necessary to wear holy vestments, faith is most important for the work. Pitaka 1999:117.

[454] Cf. Acts 19:12, where it is said that "handkerchiefs or aprons were carried away from his body to the sick, and diseases left them and the evil spirits came out of them." The handbook explains that what happened to Paul is not meant as a general way of casting out spirits. The example of Jesus should be followed and he chased out the demons only by his words. Tobilehibe 1997:62–63.

[455] *Amin'ny anaran'i Jesosy manan-kery avy any Nazareta no andidiana ny asan'ny maizina sy ny fanahy ratsy rehetra: mivoaka izao, na koa, mivoaha hoy i Jesosy!* Tobilehibe 1997:101.

fixed opening sentence, is not addressed to any individual in the audience.[456]

During this part the shepherds sometimes walk down the gangway of the church addressing the evil spirits in a general way. In the Monday morning healing services at Ambohimahazo, however, the shepherds normally stay at front of the church during this opening part, but their initial commands are nevertheless addressed to the whole audience.[457] In the services prior to the consecration of shepherds, when many people were gathered at the healing services, the shepherds moved down the gangway shouting: "Get out, in the name of Jesus."

In the Ankaramalaza-branch of the movement, it is common that the shepherds spread themselves among the congregation casting out demons in this part and it is even advisable that the shepherds form a circle around the people when this initial casting out of spirits is finished. It is considered a visible action of cleansing the room from demons and guarding the congregation against new demonic attacks.[458]

In conversation with shepherds I have heard that leaders have advised the youths not to stand in the doorways or sit in the windows during the expulsion of demons. Instead of leaving the room, the evil spirits could assault those who sit there, they say.[459]

3.2.3.3 *The shepherds' concentration on the patients at the front of the church*

After the initial casting out of evil spirits the shepherds concentrate on the people who have shown that they are in special need of exorcism by seating themselves on the mats/first benches. Some of the shepherds look as if they have a definite aim and start casting out demons from individuals at once, while others walk among the patients as if they have

---

[456] Rasolondraibe P. calls this initial part of the exorcism session "the general challenge", because it is a general casting out of demons from the whole room. He says that shepherds think that the deceptive demons may hide among the Christians and therefore have to be challenged to come forth. Rasolondraibe 1989:349–350.

[457] Their practice may be explained by the low number of people, normally 10–20 people, who are not sitting on the first benches or on the straw mats. All attendants are seated in the front part of the church and so the whole audience is close to the shepherds.

[458] IS 323.

[459] IS 318.

not decided where to begin. The shepherds are rotating from one person to another, since the number of people who are seated at the front of the church is normally higher than the number of shepherds. I have not noticed any fixed pattern in how the shepherds organise their movements. They seem to address one person at a time, commanding the evil spirits to depart, but they are all operating on a limited space at the front of the church.[460]

The shepherds should face the patient when casting out demons and as long as a person acts erratically, the shepherd is not allowed to leave him/her. The shepherd is engaging in a battle and no soldier runs away from the battlefield.[461] *Mama* Nenilava looked directly in the patient's eyes when she cast out demons and she said that even the eyes of the shepherd looking at the patient could cast out demons.[462]

The handbook advises the shepherds to go together in pairs, so that the two can be close to each other if a severe case suddenly shows up. The reason for this is practical and it follows Jesus' example to send out his disciples two by two.[463]

3.2.3.4 *The shepherds' movements*

The most common movement when casting out demons from individuals is a gesticulating motion with the right arm in the air above the patients' head. The shepherds are using great force when they move their arms, normally starting from the right with the arm high in the air and moving

---

[460] According to J. Gonia's observations the shepherds concentrate on individuals when they discover signs of demonic assault on a person: closed eyes or a trance-like appearance, a rhythmic rocking of the body, or convulsions. Then they command the offending spirit to release the person and leave. Gonia 1993:26.

[461] Tobilehibe 1997:99.

[462] Pitaka 1999:119. Pitaka D. says about *Mama* Nenilava that the patients could not stand looking at her, because then they and the devil, saw Jesus' own glory.

[463] Tobilehibe 1997:88. The handbook says that there should be at least two shepherds to arrange a healing service. One shepherd alone cannot expel demons from a whole congregation and even Jesus himself was using co-workers. The metaphor of a fight is also used and one soldier is not waging war alone. Tobilehibe 1997:99–100. L.A. Sharp says that the shepherds prefer working in groups of three, reflecting the trinity, but that groups of other sizes are acceptable. Sharp 1993:257. I have never observed a fixed number of three and three shepherds working together and nobody has in conversation given me such information. When difficult cases are showing up, however, I have observed not only two shepherds but five or six working with the person at the same time.

it downwards to the left. It looks like they are chasing somebody away with great force, without touching their enemy.

At the Ambohimahazo *toby* there is a special practice during expulsion of demons, which I have not observed elsewhere: the shepherds lay their hand on the patients' head when casting out demons and all the shepherds are moving to each patient doing so. When they have been sweeping with their arms in the air for some time, they start casting out demons from the patients individually from two sides and they succeed each other until all the shepherds have laid their hands on and cast out demons from all the patients.[464]

I have observed that the shepherds not only lay their right hand on the head of the patients, but sometimes they bend the patient's head backwards to be able to look him/her directly in the eyes. If the patient is reluctant to do this, it looks like the shepherd forces the head to the desired position.[465] Many shepherds gesticulate vehemently and sometimes it looks as if the casting out of demons is to be done by the sole force of the shepherds' gesticulations. Some shepherds have their own special ways of placing the hand on the head of the patient. They hold their hand just above the head while they say, "in the name of Jesus" and then they place the hand on the head while they are commanding the demons. These variations are certainly on the account of individuality.

According to the handbook it is only allowed to touch the patients if they are in danger of hurting themselves. Then the shepherds should keep a firm hold of the patient and they must be cautious not to hurt the patient in any way. When the patient is acting erratically, it is advised that women shepherds work with women and men with men. In the

---

[464] IS 200 explained that this practice has become a tradition in Ambohimahazo and since this is a *toby* where patients stay for a period of time, the practice can continue, even if it is not in conformity with the main practice of the revival movement.

[465] Aa.J. Syvertsen has observed that if the patient is seriously ill and the shepherds have to work lengthily to set him/her free from the demons, they may shake the head of the patient very strongly, especially when it seems like nothing is happening by just commanding the demons with words. Syvertsen 1983:177. L.A. Sharp says that the exorcist may push or tug on the patient's body, or the exorcist may push the patient to the ground repeatedly and command him/ her to rise again. In a footnote she refers to Trexler, who reports of three instances of Lutheran shepherds' violence to the extent that the patients died. This happened in the early eighties. However, she has never herself seen an exorcist strike anybody. Sharp 1993:260; 309–310.

handbook there is quite a list of what the shepherds are not allowed to do and supposedly this points to a certain problem of behaviour with regard to touching the patient. The general rule is to act respectfully against any patient and the shepherd is not allowed to press the patient's body, to strike him with the Bible, or to force him to do any actions, which at that moment is impossible for him to perform. The main reason for not touching the patient during expulsion of demons is derived from Jesus' words in Mt 8:16b: "...and he cast out the spirits with a word...".[466] In accordance with the example of Jesus the expulsion of demons must be performed by words alone.[467] When *Mama* Nenilava cast out demons, her right arm was sweeping from the right to the left in a downward motion. This was done with great force.[468] The shepherds' motions should not be exaggerated, the handbook says, because this will only cause fatigue and will at the same time distract the people watching. But the motions are to reflect authority and thus underline the words of command to the demons.[469]

3.2.3.5 *The shepherds' words*

The gesticulating motions go along with the firm and loud commands directly to the demons to leave the patient. The opening sentence is obligatory[470] and all the shepherds follow, pronouncing the same words. Then the shepherds use their own words of casting out demons. Since the level of intensity in this part of the service is very high and the shepherds all shout their commands simultaneously, it is difficult to hear exactly what they say. Short commands are most common: "Leave in the name of Jesus" and "You are beaten by Jesus and have no more power; so leave in a hurry", but some of the shepherds use rather elaborate sayings,

---

[466] In the Malagasy translation of the Bible this sentence reads, "...by his word alone he cast out the evil spirits..." (*...ary ny teniny ihany no namoahany ny fanahy ratsy,...*), which put an even stronger stress on the word.

[467] Tobilehibe 1997:105–107.

[468] Pitaka 1999:117.

[469] Tobilehibe 1997:105. The question about the shepherds' movements while casting out demons is much debated in the church and I have often heard accusations of shepherds, who have acted unwisely in this respect. I have not observed any serious cases where this happened. Cf. 4.4.2.

[470] "In the name of Jesus of Nazareth, the powerful, I command the work of the darkness and all the evil spirits: Get out in Jesus' name."

which they repeat with minor variations as they rotate from one patient to another:

> In the name of Jesus Christ, son of the living God, who will tear down everything which is not coming from Jesus to have no part in this servant of God. Leave in a hurry! I command and cast out all powers and authorities in the name of Jesus.[471]

I have also heard words of comfort directed to the patients during expulsion of demons, such as "You belong to Jesus, who died at the cross".[472] Such sayings may be followed by a command directed to the evil spirits.[473]

Not only demons are chased off with the words of the shepherds. They also direct their commands against illness, suffering, fear, unbelief and worries. The casting out of illness is heard especially often. The shepherds underline in their commands that these things come from evil spirits and they cast out "deceiving spirits, spirits that cause doubt and unbelief, fear from the devil and all the evil spirits".

If the patient show any observable sign of being "assaulted by demons", usually a rhythmic rocking of the body,[474] the level of intensity in the shepherds' shouting will often rise and if this behaviour continues, more than one shepherd will concentrate on this person.[475] It is

---

[471] Ambohimahazo *toby* 29 November 1993.

[472] This may be due to a wish of strengthening the patient's faith but may also stem from some confusion about whom to address when casting out demons. One of the examples of sentences to be used, according to the handbook reads: "Go away, for he/she is Jesus' property. He/She is bought with Jesus' blood. Jesus died on the cross in his/her place. Hurry. Go away!" Tobilehibe 1997:101. If the shepherd confuses the personal pronoun in this sentence and says "you" instead of "he/she" (the Malagasy language does not differentiate gender in the personal pronoun), the patient will be addressed directly.

[473] Shepherds have told me with humour that when patients were attending expulsion of demons for the first time, some of them rose up and left the room when the shepherds said: "Leave, in the name of Jesus." They simply thought they were asked to leave the room and not that the command was directed to a supernatural force residing within them.

[474] Mal: *mihetsika*.

[475] The level of intensity in the shouting may rise because several shepherds are shouting at the same time, but I have also an impression of a more intense shouting from each shepherd in such cases. According to L.A. Sharp, both the shepherds' voice and the congregation's singing increase in volume. She believes that this happens when the spirit arrives. Sharp 1993:259.

EXPULSION OF DEMONS

understandable that the shepherds, who consider the casting out of demons as a fierce fight with the devil, will become more intensive in their work when they feel directly challenged by the enemy.[476] The voice to be used during casting out of demons should be the voice of a person chasing an enemy. Even Jesus used a loud voice when he addressed the epileptic boy, *Mama* Nenilava said.[477]

The handbook gives detailed instructions about which words the shepherds could use during expulsion of demons. It is underlined that the word is the sword of the Holy Spirit and since it is the Holy Spirit who is really at work during casting out of demons, the word is the basis of the work. The word in this setting is written with majuscule on the first letter,[478] which normally refers to God's word in the Bible and the biblical reference is 1 Pet 4:11. The saying in the handbook seems to have a twofold meaning, however, since there can be no doubt that the shepherds' own words are referred to here. Words of authority should be used, while reflecting love at the same time. It is not allowed to rebuke the devil using unclean words, because that is exactly what he likes. Concise and direct words are the best. Several examples are given of what words the shepherds could use when casting out demons:

> "Leave, you Satan, go away, get out. Jesus is commanding you. Go away. You are not allowed to cause pain to this person any more. You are not allowed to bind him any more. Get out, Jesus says."
> "You have no power over people. The power belongs to Jesus. You are a defeated enemy."
> "You are not allowed to whisper in his mind. You are not allowed to deceive his heart. Get out. Get out, Jesus says."
> "You are not allowed to cause him speak nonsense. Be quiet, Satan. Jesus is commanding you."
> "Go away, for he is Jesus' property. He is bought with Jesus' blood. Jesus died on the cross in his place. Hurry. Go away!"[479]

---

[476] I once overheard a conversation between shepherds about one of their co-shepherds, who had been trained in the Soatanana-branch of the movement. He used a careful voice when commanding the spirits to leave and he even addressed them politely by saying "please leave" (*miala tompoko—tompoko* means literally "my lord", but is used as a general addition to make an address polite). The shepherds who were discussing his words concluded by saying: "Will any evil spirit depart when commanded by such a careful voice?" O 342.

[477] Pitaka 1999:119–120. The rendering of "rebuke" in Mat 17:18 in the Malagasy Bible is *niteny mafy*, which may also mean: "to talk using a loud voice".

[478] Mal: *ny Teny*.

[479] Tobilehibe 1997:101.

It is also allowed to name the different types of spirits binding the person, such as deceiving spirits, spirits of answering in a rude way, spirits that make a person weak, etc., when casting them out. Likewise, the different ways of undesirable behaviour or attitudes, may be named and cast out: unbelief, simulation, self-justice, worries, faint-heartedness, the habit of accusing others and other bad habits.[480]

It may facilitate the expulsion of demons to encourage the patient to invoke Jesus' name. The shepherd says to the patient with a clear voice, "Let us pray and call on Jesus' name", or he/she should lead the patient to say, "Jesus, save me!" The shepherd must observe the patient and see that he/she is conscious before encouraging him/her in this way.[481]

3.2.3.6 *Dialogue with evil spirits*

During my observation in the high plateaux, I have not noticed shepherds in dialogue with spirits and when I have asked about this, I have been told that it has no positive effects. The shepherds' aim is to deliver the person "assaulted by demons", not to know whom the spirits are and where they come from.[482]

The handbook admits that some shepherds have the practice of engaging in a dialogue with the spirits, just like Jesus did according to the story in Mark 5:9. This should not be a common custom, but if it has to be done for some reason, it should be reserved to leaders and elder shepherds. In some cases it may facilitate the healing of the patient. It seems that through this dialogue the shepherd can get information of

---

[480] Tobilehibe 1997:100–102. The handbook often sees evil spirits behind bad habits. Both of them stem from the devil's work and should therefore be cast out. See 4.4.3.

[481] Tobilehibe 1997:107.

[482] I have seen shepherds in dialogue with spirits during my work in the Northeast coast of the island and in conversation with shepherds I have heard several stories of shepherds in dialogue with spirits. Sometimes I have had an impression of this practice as the shepherds' testing of the reliability of the demonic involvement in the person, or as an experiment of how far the shepherd could dare to go in investigating the spirit world. L.A. Sharp, who has done her research on the northwestern coast, has observed that the exorcist speaks directly to the spirit with the aim of engaging the spirit in dialogue. The exorcist asks who the spirit is, why it has possessed the person and what it wants. When the spirit answers, the exorcist is shouting back his commands to the spirit to depart from the person. Sharp 1993:260.

what harm the spirit has caused to its victim. The shepherd should observe closely if the patient has any taboos, or paraphernalia from the spirits, or if he/she has made a contract with the spirits. It is easier for the shepherd to lead the patient to repentance if he/she knows what has caused the patient's situation. It is strongly underlined, however, that it is no common procedure to talk with the spirits. If the shepherd really is in close contact with Jesus in doing the work, the Holy Spirit should be asked to reveal to the shepherd the causes of the patient's illness, without any conversation with the spirits themselves.[483]

3.2.3.7 The atmosphere

The atmosphere during expulsion of demons is very tense. All the shepherds walk around shouting to the evil spirits with a loud voice. They are gesticulating all the time, as though they are chasing an invisible enemy. The invisible powers in the room are the spirits of darkness and their leaders, which may cause fear since nobody knows where they will strike next. Sometimes the patients scream or shout loudly and some act erratically. They may stand up, but the shepherds hold them tight and make them sit down again. Sometimes this looks like a real fight and it is difficult for the congregation not to watch carefully.

The healing services in the Ambohimahazo *toby* are held in the church, which is rather big, but the services in Log 238, 67 Ha in Antananarivo are held in two small rooms, both of about 7 x 5 metres. With about 80 people sitting on the benches, chairs and mats and around 30 shepherds working, the atmosphere is almost indescribable.[484]

---

[483] Tobilehibe 1997:102–104. The handbook uses much space to show that the practice of Jesus according to Mark 5:9 is not meant as an example for his followers. By this Jesus showed the disciples who he really was (a Christological purpose) and it was not meant as a methodology in casting out demons. Only once in the Gospels we hear that Jesus asked a question directly to the spirit. Consequently, the shepherds should not think that they will be more successful in casting out demons if they engage in conversation with the spirits. On the contrary, a conversation with the spirits may have undesirable effects, since the spirits then may scare the shepherd or lie about the patient's situation and so the spirits will easily seduce the shepherd.

[484] I have written in an observation report from a service in Log 238, 67 Ha: "The heart is beating harder than normally and I am afraid that I will start showing the most common sign of being "assaulted by demons": moving the upper part of the body back and forth. It is an indescribable psychological happening." Antananarivo, Log 238, 67 Ha 01 July 1998.

It is worth noting that the congregation seem rather unaffected by the situation and the atmosphere. Even young children sit quietly in their mothers' arms and I have seldom heard any crying, which I would interpret as a sign of fear in these sessions. Other observers from outside have also been astonished by the congregation's calmness during expulsion of demons.[485]

3.2.3.8 Observable reactions

Let me start by presenting two case histories:

> He was about 55 years old. Before the healing service he went aimlessly around talking with different people. He addressed me in French, but I could not understand what he was trying to say. When the service was about to start, there were some noise outside and just afterwards the man came into the church with his hands tied up on his back. The reason for this was that he had struck a person with a spade the day before and they were afraid that he would hurt somebody again. His wife came together with him and he sat down on the first bench. One of the leaders showed him a place on the straw mat and he sat there for the whole service. During the testimonies and the singing, he was restless, turned around and looked at the congregation. At small intervals he shouted with a loud voice to a woman sitting next to him, saying "Go out, Satan". His way of saying this was a true copy of the shepherds' wording. During the expulsion of demons, however, he sat calmly.
> In the following healing service he was also restless during the first part of the service. Often he stood up, sat down again, stood up and shouted, "In Jesus' name, the devil has no authority". Then he turned around to the congregation, staring at the people. When the casting out of demons started, he first refused to sit on the mat, but after a while he sat down and stayed there during the rest of the service.
> During the expulsion of demons on the third day, he was surrounded by 5–6 shepherds, all men. They forced him to sit down on the mat and shouted loudly to the evil spirits to depart from him. In this service many people were present and many shepherds were working, so the leader gave instructions to the shepherds through a loudspeaker. When one of the shepherds started to pray in the loudspeaker, the shepherds working with the man ended the

---

[485] Stene Dehlin 1985:57–58. L.A. Sharp says that "Exorcism sessions are electrifying events that are exhausting for both exorcist and patient and they can be frightening for young children and for the uninitiated." Sharp 1993:258. In conversation with informants I have heard stories about shepherds scaring young children by their screaming and when the child has started to cry, the shepherd has interpreted this as a satanic reaction and a sign of being "assaulted by demons". So the shepherd has screamed even higher and the child has cried more, until the child's mother has been able to calm him/her down. I have never observed this myself, however.

casting out of demons. Then the man rose on his feet in the middle of the shepherds and shouted with a loud voice, saying "Get out, Satan". After a while one of the leaders of the *toby* reprimanded the shepherds saying that they had to watch out, so that the patients did not start to cast out demons from the shepherds.[486] The shepherds were working with this man even when the prayer with the laying on of hands started and they continued the casting out of demons for some time. But eventually one of the shepherds laid his hand on the head of the man and prayed for him.[487]

A young woman (20–25 years old) had been taken to the *toby* by her mother. The young woman walked out of the church and came in again many times during the service. Sometimes she nearly lay down on the bench, but a shepherd commanded her to rise up, in the name of Jesus.
A week later she was really upset during the whole service. While people shared their testimonies, she talked to herself with an audible voice and she repeated the preachers' referring to chapters and verses in the Bible. She was restless, moved from place to place and trampled on the floor. She also knocked the man sitting next to her and she spat on the floor in front of her.[488] The old leader of the *toby* moved from his place and sat down close to her, but she moved to another place on the bench and when he reprimanded her, she began to yell. When her mother tried to calm her, she answered by hissing at her mother. She started singing songs, but the tunes were wrong and she was not able to sing properly. She said repeatedly as if she was talking to herself: "Ghost" and "Mother's heart is sick; heal it/her".[489] While all this happened, the service went on as usual, but I observed that many of the people in church were occupied with watching this young woman.
She moved to a mat of her own, but when the casting out of demons started, she became quite fractious. She rose up, struck the people around her and tried to get free from the shepherds' hold. She shouted and screamed and pulled faces at the shepherds. She rolled around on the mat and after a while she started to cry sadly. The shepherds were standing around her and they tried to communicate directly with her, saying "Jesus loves you". They repeated this phrase, but she did not seem to listen to them. She just continued to cry sadly and she said loudly, "Aaaaaa".
After some time she started to cough, it looked as if she was going to vomit and she spat on the floor again. She opened her outer jacket and put her hand

---

[486] I spot a fine sense of humour in the leader's word, for even if expulsion of demons is a serious event, humour is never far away.

[487] The observation of this case was done in three days. Ambohimahazo *toby* 16–18 June 1998.

[488] It is very impolite to spit inside a house and this was even a church!

[489] A person sitting next to her informed me of the content of her saying afterwards. I could not hear it from where I sat. The English rendering is a translation of the Malagasy: *Angatra. Marary ny fon'i mama. Tsaboy izy*.

> on her chest as if she had problems with the respiration. Then the shepherds prayed for her.
> About one month later she was still there at the healing service. She still looked restless and during the casting out of demons she sat smiling and sometimes she repeated what the shepherds said. She was quiet, but my impression was that she disliked what was happening.[490]

In every healing service I have tried to observe the behaviour of the people on the first benches and the mats. I have noticed when there were reactions of some sort during the casting out of demons. The shepherds themselves normally use a standard expression about reactions during the expulsion of demons, namely *mihetsika*, which literally means to rock the upper part of the body back and forth, sometimes very gently and sometimes with great convulsions. In my observations I have tried to record any reactions during expulsion of demons: the gentle rocking back and forth of the body, the patient's talking to or answering the shepherds, the patient rising up and moving to another place and severe convulsions.[491]

I have included 27 healing services in my material and in nine of these I have observed no reactions during the casting out of demons. In three other services I have not recorded reactions explicitly and I suppose there were none. In eight of the services one person in each acted contrary to normal conduct, in four of the services two people showed such behaviour and in two services three people reacted in this way. All together, this counts 22 people, but some of these represent the same person in different healing services, so the exact number of people, who reacted in some way during the casting out of demons in my material is 16. When compared with the number of people sitting on the first benches or the mats signalling that they had special needs, this number is low. In the ordinary healing services at the Ambohimahazo *toby* 30 people on average sat on the first benches or on the mats and in other services the number was normally higher. From a total number of 700–800 people sitting at the front of the church, only 16 showed reactions to expulsion of demons as far as I could observe.[492]

---

[490] The observation of this case was done in healing services in Ambohimazo between the 29th of November 1993 and the 3rd of January 1994.

[491] As shown in the two case histories, there was unusual behaviour during the whole healing service. In the shepherds' view, these are reactions to the expulsion of demons, because the whole service is a challenging of the evil spirits.

[492] My general impression from healing services in the coastal areas is that a greater number of people sitting on the mats show observable reactions, which are contrary

Only 20 % of the people showing any observable reactions to the casting out of demons were men, the rest were women.[493] The number of people reacting during the expulsion of demons in my material is too low to make any generalisations but other researchers have also observed that there seems to be a predominance of women among the patients.[494] However, I have not seen any studies, where the people's reactions during the expulsion of demons are systematically recorded. It is interesting that the shepherds themselves, when they were asked to report case histories about severely ill people, reported a fairly even distribution of men and women among those "assaulted by demons".[495]

Three to five shepherds often work together when they encounter observable signs of reaction during the expulsion of demons. They shout loudly at the demons, command them to depart from their victim and strike the air around the patient. Sometimes these patients have severe convulsions, throwing their body up and down and they kick and strike everything around them. Then the shepherds have to hold them tight. I have observed these sessions to last up to half an hour.[496] It is very exhausting and I have observed shepherds dripping with perspiration. They replace each other succeedingly in the holding of the patient and the casting out of demons. If it looks like the patient will not calm down, the shepherds often bring him/her to a separate room, where they continue the casting out of demons.[497]

---

to normal conduct. In these cases, however, I have no accurate observation reports. Many of my informants have noticed that the number of people showing observable signs of being "assaulted by demons" seems lower in the high plateaux than in the coastal areas but I cannot verify this since my study is delimited to the high plateaux.

[493] 13 people were women and 3 were men.

[494] L.A. Sharp says: "The majority of patients are adolescent girls who are plagued by njarinintsy and other forms of possession sickness; older women (thirty or older) who wish to rid themselves of tromba spirits; and those whom kin label as mentally ill (*adala*)." Sharp 1993:257–258. Aa.J. Syvertsen says that most of the possession cases (Norwegian: "de besatte") concern women and he supposes that 80 % of the cases are women, but this is not due to any scientific recording. Other missionaries listening to the lecture challenged this conclusion of Syvertsen. Many of them had experienced that the majority of the "assaulted by demons" were men. Syvertsen 1983:178, 181.

[495] See 4.3.4.

[496] Aa.J. Syvertsen reports that they may last several hours. Syvertsen 1983:177.

[497] This is done not to keep the congregation waiting too long before the prayer with the laying on of hands can begin.

According to my observations, almost 98 % of the people sitting on the mats and the first benches sat quietly without any observable reactions during expulsion of demons.[498] They have come to the healing service and they have signalled that they are in special need of the shepherds' treatment by moving to the first benches or the mats. My informants have told me that the reasons for these people coming are diverse but they all have problems in their lives.[499] In general, the shepherds do not ask these people why they come.[500] They cast out demons and pray with the laying on of hands for all those who seek their service.

3.2.3.9 Shepherds and pastors on the first bench

In a few instances I have observed that shepherds have been seated on the first benches and thus subjected themselves to expulsion of demons. Twice the leader of the service has moved to the first bench when the exorcism session began.[501] She did not wear the white robe. I noticed that some of the shepherds skipped her as they moved from person to person casting out demons. It seemed to me that they used a lower voice when they came to her than with the other patients.

I once experienced that one of the shepherds at work also included the old pastor of the *toby* and an elderly shepherd while he was moving from person to person casting out evil spirits.[502] Only one of the shepherds did this but neither the pastor nor the old shepherd prevented

---

[498] When I asked the shepherds about the relatively low occurrence of reactions from the patients to the expulsion of demons, they often referred to the pre-history of the patients and their observable reactions in the opening phase of the treatment. I did not know all the patients' pre-history, so I cannot tell if some of them have had reactions to expulsion of demons prior to the services I attended.

[499] It may be marriage problems, a difficult situation for their children, some bodily sickness, poverty and distress because of the severe living conditions; they may have felt depressed for a long time, or they do not feel peaceful inside; they may feel that their faith in Jesus is fading, etc. See further 4.3.2.

[500] I have been told that some shepherds ask the patients why they have come and what their problems are but I cannot recall having observed this. The patients living in the *toby*, however, are well known to the shepherds.

[501] I was told afterward that she felt weak and sick and therefore she asked for her co-shepherds' treatment.

[502] They did not wear the white robe and sat at the end of the first bench because they were in charge of the service.

him from doing so. In another healing service a pastor from outside, together with his wife visited the *toby* and they were both seated on the first bench. When the expulsion of demons started, the shepherds cast out demons from them as they did with the other people sitting on the first benches and the mats.[503] I emphasise that these episodes are rare and some of them may have happened just accidentally, but they point to an interesting distinction between shepherds and ordinary people.[504]

3.2.3.10 Duration and organisation

According to my observations, the length of the expulsion of demons varies according to the visible reactions of the patients. In Ambohimahazo the loud shouting normally lasts for about 3 minutes and when the shepherds concentrate on the patients one by one, the level of intensity is lower. This normally lasts for 5–10 minutes. I have attended healing services, where the casting out of demons only lasted 2–3 minutes, but when severe cases show up, it may last half an hour.[505]

Since there is no singing during expulsion of demons in the Ambohimahazo *toby*, the whole congregation is expected to pray quietly but often both the patients and the congregation are distracted by what happens during the session, although most of the people present sit with their heads bowed. One of the elder shepherds had observed that the patients were distracted and he assumed that they were not praying, so he said that may be it would have been better that they were occupied with singing hymns.[506]

The handbook says that the length of this part is a frequent question asked by new shepherds, while it is implied that the experienced

---

[503] In this case I wondered if the shepherds did not know him or if he and his wife did not know the practice of casting out demons from all those on the first benches in the Ambohimahazo *toby*. In a conversation with this pastor afterwards he told me that he regularly subjected himself to the shepherds' exorcism.

[504] The handbook says that shepherds should not be prayed for together with ordinary people, but rather have their own reunions. Tobilehibe 1997:72–73. See 4.5.2.5 (A unique position of the shepherds?).

[505] Sometimes the patient then is taken into another room for a continued treatment or the patient is prayed for where he/she is. The shepherds continue the casting out of demons until the patient stops acting erratically. If the convulsions stop because the patient is exhausted or because the evil spirit is driven out of the person is not a matter of observation.

[506] IS 200. See 3.1.2.

shepherds know when the casting out of demons should end and the prayer should start. There are some guidelines, however and they are given according to the kind of service, the needs of the shepherds and the patients. A healing service should not last too long. Sometimes exorcism is part of a Sunday morning service and therefore limited. If the service lasts too long, this will be exhausting to the shepherds and the leader should keep this in mind. Sometimes it is wise to end the expulsion of demons when it has continued for a lengthy period and the patient still is not set free. The unsuccessful healing may be due to other factors, which have to be dealt with first: May be the patient still has paraphernalia from the traditional healer in his house. This must be delivered to the shepherds before healing can take place. May be he/she has offended other people, then mutual forgiveness is required before the patient can be set free. For severely ill people living in a *toby*, it is widely recognised that one single healing service not will set them free, so their treatment is expected to last for a period of time.[507]

When the casting out of demons comes to an end, the shepherds again line up in front of the congregation. It is time for the second part: "strengthening".

---

[507] Tobilehibe 1997:106–107.

In a handbook for the Reformed revival (*Sampana Fifohazana FJKM*) the liturgy, which now should be followed everywhere in this church is presented. When the shepherds have lined up in front of the congregation wearing their white dresses, one of them starts with a prayer prior to the four liturgical readings and after that another shepherd prays. Then it is casting out of demons: only one shepherd commands with a loud voice while he/she stands quietly in front of the congregation: "In the name of Jesus Christ from Nazareth.... In his name I command you and expel you, ô Satan. Leave to the burning pit ... You have to leave in the name of Jesus...". The other shepherds standing there are quiet (they do not say anything and they do not move). Then one shepherd prays and the people are summoned to come forward to be prayed for with the laying on of hands. They should kneel and the shepherd lays his/her hand on their heads and says: "In the name of Jesus I lay my hand on you. I do this work with the strength and authority of his name ...". When studying the handbook from the Reformed church we see that there seems to be an opening for individual casting out of demons but this is placed within the prayer with the laying on of hands: When needed, the casting out of demons should be done after the initial words of the prayer, says the handbook and then the shepherd continue the prayer with words of strength to the person. FJKM 1997:45–52.

3.3 Prayer with the laying on of hands/"strengthening"

The name of this part of exorcism in Malagasy is *fampaherezana*, which is a causative form from the root *hery*, meaning strength, energy, power and the noun can be translated as the action of "giving strength to" or "strengthening".[508]

I have never observed the expulsion of demons without a concluding "strengthening" and it should be noted how intertwined the shepherds view these two elements in a healing service.[509]

One of the shepherds prays and he/she may invite the congregation to start singing by referring to a number in the hymnbook. Sometimes the congregation just starts singing as soon as the prayer is done. Normally the shepherd will encourage those who are in need of intercession to show this by raising their hand. The shepherds then start praying for those who ask for it while the congregation sings hymns.[510]

The outline of the following presentation, firstly focuses on the people who are prayed for and secondly on the organisation of the "strengthening" and thirdly on its content. Then I mention specific traits, indicate the importance of the "strengthening" session to the shepherds and briefly describe how the shepherds bring the healing service to a close.

3.3.1 Who are prayed for?

When the prayer with the laying on of hands starts, the shepherds firstly concentrate on the people who are already seated at the front of the church.[511] They pray for all these people. Then people in the church raise

---

[508] In her dissertation L.A. Sharp translates *fampaherezana* with "empowerment", which is also possible lexically. Sharp 1993:257. In this section I refer to the prayer with the laying on of hands mostly by the English translation of the Malagasy rendering: "strengthening".

[509] The close connection between the casting out of demons and "strengthening" is strongly underlined in the statutes of the *Fifohazana*: "The casting out of demons and the laying on of hands are not separated and it is not allowed to separate them". Fifohazana FFPM 1980:no 25.

[510] In the churches and the *toby*, which follow the Ankaramalaza-branch, the "strengthening" follows immediately after the expulsion of demons and the singing continues without any break. As a consequence, the handbook advises not to have any prayer in public between the two elements. Tobilehibe 1997:118.

[511] Cf. 3.2.1.1.

their hands to show that they want to be prayed for. I once observed a 5 year old girl raising her hand as a sign to the shepherds and she knelt down and was prayed for. Often mothers with babies in their arms ask the shepherds to pray for them and their children.

In the ordinary healing services in Ambohimahazo almost all the people present are prayed for in this session, except the shepherds and the pastors.[512] The great number of people present who wish to be prayed for indicates that healing services are perceived almost exclusively as a service to the people in special need of the shepherds' treatment. In healing services with very many people present I have noticed that there are relatively more people who do not ask for intercession by the shepherds.[513]

In a few instances I have noticed that a patient has suddenly started acting erratically in the middle of the prayer session, when the shepherd laid his/her hand on the patient to pray. The expulsion of demons was finished and the prayer with the laying on of hands had begun but the shepherd immediately started casting out demons again. When the patient calmed down, the shepherd continued the praying.[514]

The statutes of the *Fifohazana* also specifies two groups of people to be prayed for: 1) the sick and 2) those of the congregation who ask for it separately.[515]

---

[512] To the question of shepherds being prayed for together with ordinary people, see 4.5.2.5 (A unique position of the shepherds?).

[513] Many devoted Christians are prayed for in the healing services and some of them have also been sitting on the first bench during the expulsion of demons. See 4.2.1.4.

[514] Pitaka D. says that there should be no laying on of hands if the person is still acting erratically or if the voice of the devil not yet has become quiet. He seems to take the person's confessing of Christ as a prerequisite for the "strengthening" and he says that the person should really repent before this prayer. On the other hand, however, he says that if the session lasts too long, the shepherds should pray for the people anyhow and they should also pray for the sick who are unconscious. Pitaka 1999:128–129. Pitaka seems to contradict himself on this point.

[515] Fifohazana FFPM 1980:no 24. Those who are labelled "sick" are the people who have been seated in the front of the church during the expulsion of demons, while it is open for anyone else attending to ask for the shepherds' prayers without any preceding individual casting out of demons.

3.3.2 How is the "strengthening" organised?

Some of the sick people on the first benches just sit on their places with bowed heads while the shepherds pray for them. Others kneel down before the shepherd on the floor[516] and when the prayer is finished, they move back to their places. The others may come to the front and kneel before the shepherd, or they may sit in their place and the shepherds move around to them and pray where they are seated. In healing services with many people and shepherds present, it is customary that some of the shepherds walk down the gangway from the very beginning of the "strengthening" session and start praying for the people who ask for their intercession. Kneeling or sitting during "strengthening" is optional at the Ambohimahazo *toby*. The handbook seems to favour kneeling and simply says that the person to be prayed for kneels before the shepherd.[517]

The shepherd places his/her right hand on the head of the person and often bows down a little, in order for the person to hear the words of the prayer. The shepherd prays quietly, but loud enough for the person to hear what he/she is saying. The people prayed for are expected to listen to the shepherds' prayer and not be distracted by praying themselves. Each of the persons asking for intercession is prayed for only once.[518]

The handbook says that the shepherds should lay their hand very softly on the head of the person and not bend it forcibly because the head is sensitive.[519] According to the statutes, casting out of demons and "strengthening" should not be done in a magical way.[520]

---

[516] One of my informants seemed to be embarrassed by the custom of kneeling down on the rude concrete floor of the church. In his opinion there should at least have been a straw mat to kneel on, or special chairs set up for those who asked for intercession. IS 205.

[517] Tobilehibe 1997:118.

[518] Cf. the expulsion of demons in Ambohimahazo, where all the shepherds cast out demons from each person seated on the mats or the first benches. See 3.2.3.4.

[519] Tobilehibe 1997:118. The Malagasy word, which I have translated "sensitive", is *saro-pady*. This is a compound word. *Fady* means taboo and *saro-pady* denotes that there are many prescriptions that should be observed concerning the designed object. L.A.Sharp comments on the submissive position of the patients and the shepherds' touching their head during casting out of demons and "strengthening". According to Malagasy thinking the head is sacred and should not be touched and she says that only elders and royalty may raise their heads above the others. Sharp 1994:540. The shepherds' understanding of "strengthening" will be dealt with in

3.3.3 The content of the "strengthening"

All the shepherds pray at the same time individually for different people and the congregation's singing is as loud as usual in the Malagasy church, so it is difficult to describe the exact content of the prayers by participant observation. Therefore I will in the following use the shepherds' answers in the questionnaires and other written material to supplement my own observations.

The initial words are to a great extent obligatory. When the shepherd has put his/her right hand on the head of the patient, he/she starts praying by saying: "In the name of Jesus of Nazareth, the mighty one, I lay my hand on your head and with the authority of Jesus I perform this holy work."[521] Then the shepherd goes on with the prayer, using different words according to the person to be prayed for.

One of my informants distinguishes between six categories of people to be prayed for and how to direct the prayer according to the person in question:[522]

> For adult Christians:
> I ask Jesus to receive the person and his wishes and I ask for Jesus' mercy. Then I turn to the person and says: "O brother in Christ. Jesus says to you: Do not be afraid, your sins are forgiven in the name of Jesus. Receive the Holy Spirit. Be strong and have faith in Jesus. May the things you are asking for be given to you! May the peace of God be with you. Amen."
>
> For non-Christian sick people and the mad (*adala*):
> "I heal you in the name of Jesus. In the name of Jesus you, Satan, will be cast out. Go away to the bottomless hole and to the burning hell. This person

---

4.5.2.5 but it is important for them to emphasise that they are laying their hands on the patients' heads because of the authority given them by God.

[520] Fifohazana FFPM 1980: no 24. Pitaka D. says that when *Mama* Nenilava observed hard-hearted people, she assigned several shepherds to assist her and place their hands on the person together with herself. She also did so when she observed that some people chose specific shepherds to pray for them, because she would teach the people to have confidence in any shepherd when they were prayed for. Pitaka 1999:130. Pitaka also underlines that the shepherds should not put their hand on other places on the body of the patients other than the head. It is explicitly stated not to place it on the shoulder or on the location of the illness. Pitaka 1999:129.

[521] Tobilehibe 1997:116, Rasolondraibe 1989:350.

[522] To a great extent I have preserved the words of my informant in the rendering, but I have not repeated the mentioned opening sentence, which is slightly altered according to the person in question. Only a summary is given and no prayer is rendered in full length.

belongs to Jesus and you have no authority over him. Go away in Jesus' name and bring with you all your belongings: sickness and all bad things..." There is no giving of the Holy Spirit if the person is not baptised or he/she is mad.

For children:
"In the name of Jesus, who loves the children, I lay my hands on you. For he said: Let the children come to me, for to such belongs the kingdom of God. God, bless the children so that they can grow up and learn to love you. In the name of Jesus, I give you the blessing, which he gave to the children who were carried to him. May he guard you from all evil that you always may stand in his grace. May you be given the things your parents wish for you. God's peace be with you." If the child is baptised, he should be given the Holy Spirit.

For young people:
This is very much like the above, but can be supplemented with: "Guard his youth and deliver him from all temptation..."

For church workers (pastors, shepherds, local church leaders):
"In the name of Jesus, receive the Holy Spirit, be strong and abound in the work of the Lord, who has chosen you. May you be filled with strength and be ready when our Lord comes back. May you be given what your heart desires! Peace be with you. Amen."

For widows and orphans:
"You are the protector of widows and the one who gives them their right and you are the father of the fatherless (Ps 68:5). Do not be afraid! I am with you always, to the close of the age (Mt 28:20). In the world you have tribulation; but be of good cheer, I have overcome the world (Jn 16:33)."[523]

What is especially striking above is the prayer for the non-Christian sick people and the mad. This prayer is held in a form of expelling the devil and most part of it is addressed directly to the devil and not to God! The extended use of quotations from or allusions to the Bible should be noticed. My informant has included prayer for church workers in her listing and she does not mention that prayer for them only happens in the special shepherd reunions.

The handbook mentions five different categories of people to be prayed for and there are many allusions to verses in the Bible.[524] The internal statutes of the revival movement maintain that the following words should be part of this prayer: "In the name of Jesus", "your sins

---

[523] QS 127.
[524] Tobilehibe 1997:115–116.

are forgiven", "receive the Holy Spirit", "peace be with you" and "amen".[525] The handbook gives advises as to the interpretation of these words and it is strongly underlined that the prayer should be oriented according to the person in question.[526]

3.3.4 Specific traits and importance of this session

According to my observations there is no preceding conversation between the shepherds and those who seek intercession. It has to be assumed, however, that the patients living in the *toby* are well known to the shepherds, but there are always people from outside the *toby* attending the services. I suppose that the shepherds cannot know these people's problems when they ask for prayer.

The atmosphere is very calm. The continual singing of hymns while the shepherds are moving quietly around and the congregation sitting with bowed heads or kneeling, gives an impression of peace and quietness. The contrast to the preceding expulsion of demons is striking. Experiencing the prayer is moving for people and it is not uncustomary to observe people crying while they are prayed for.

The "strengthening" part of the service may last for 10–40 minutes, depending on the number of shepherds and people present. As a general rule this part lasts longer than the casting out of demons and I have been told that many people come to the healing services primarily with the prayer session in mind.[527]

The laying on of hands with intercession is a special mark for the shepherds' ministry and it seems considered to be the heart of the shepherds' service. While novices in the last phase of preparation for consecration can take part in the casting out of demons together with experienced shepherds, they are not allowed to perform the "strengthening".[528]

---

[525] Fifohazana miray ao amin'ny FFPM 2000:9.

[526] Tobilehibe 1997:113–114. The ability of revealing God's will directly according to the people's need was a special mark for *Mama* Nenilava and therefore much of her time was spent on receiving people. She gave them advice and prayed for them and people believed that God was working through her in a special way.

[527] IS 321.

[528] Fifohazana miray ao amin'ny FFPM 2000:8. One non-shepherd says that it is the individual prayer with the laying on of hands, which in a special way distinguishes the shepherds' practices from those of the traditional Malagasy healers'. The traditional healer casts out evil spirits, he says, but there is no laying on of hands in

The handbook discusses the relation between the person's own wishes and God's will for him/her and the stress is on the shepherds' ability to become aware of God's will and pass this on to the person. It may be that the person's own wishes are contrary to God's will for him/her. While the shepherds are advised to pray for the Holy Spirit to reveal the person's situation, it also seems to be implied that the shepherds know the people they pray for. Conversation, advice and spiritual guidance are to be arranged outside the healing service.[529]

3.3.5   The closing of the healing service

As the shepherds have finished the praying with the laying on of hands, they line up again in front of the congregation and when all the shepherds have come to the line, one of them gives a prayer of thanks. Then the leader of the service suggests a hymn and sometimes one of the shepherds reads a short passage from the Bible and gives some practical advice to the people. This may be an encouragement to stay firm in faith, to read the Bible, or to continue praying when they are at home. The advice to attend healing services regularly, to bring remedies from the traditional healer to the shepherds and to take an initiative to mutual forgiveness in the family are often included. If anybody needs spiritual guidance or advice from the shepherds, they are encouraged to make contact about this after the service.[530] The Lord's prayer, said by the whole congregation, closes the healing service.

If there are specific announcements they are given at this time and sometimes a collection is made while the congregation sings another hymn. If not, the leader will just say that the service has come to an end and wishes God's continuing presence with the congregation.

The shepherds then go to the sacristy. One of them prays by thanking the Lord for the service and asks him to take care of the people when they leave. Then the shepherds remove their white robes and

---

his practices. IN 313. See 2.2.6. The laying on of hands while expelling demons in the Ambohimahazo *toby* is also allowed for the novices, when they work together with consecrated shepherds. Cf. 3.2.3.4.

[529] Tobilehibe 1997:114, 122. Aa.J. Syvertsen distinguishes between the sober-minded shepherds and those who are not. The sober-minded ask the people if there is anything special they want to lay before God in prayer, while others just pray without any preceding conversation. Syvertsen 1983:176–177.

[530] Tobilehibe 1997:121.

afterwards they may discuss shortly special observations during the service, how to follow up people by visiting them in their homes and may be some of the shepherds will wish to be prayed for by the others. More practical issues as fund raising may also be discussed. After a concluding free prayer, the shepherds leave for their homes.[531]

3.4 Summary

Since my project is delimited to exorcism in healing services in a *toby*, elements which can be observed, registered and described in this setting have been given weight in this chapter. The three main parts of a healing service have been dealt with: 1) Prayer, singing and preaching, 2) Expulsion of demons and 3) Prayer with the laying on of hands/ "strengthening".

There should be no exorcism if the word of God is not preached to the audience. My material reflects an abundance of prayer, a great range of hymns and Bible passages and it is striking that the theme of demonic involvement in human life does not occupy a major place in this first part. Rather Jesus as Saviour, sin, repentance and grace are emphasised and a belief in Jesus is said to be more important than healing from sicknesses.

Reading of fixed passages from Scripture constitutes exorcism and is obligatory. The sick sit on straw mats/the first benches, often together with some relatives. After an initial expulsion of demons not addressed to any individual, the shepherds cast out demons from all people having moved to the front of the church. The majority of them are women. The shepherds cast out demons by moving their right arm with great force in the air above the patients' heads and although they are not allowed to touch the patients, this prohibition is not always observed. They address the demons directly but may also command illness, different types of spirits, undesirable behaviour and bad attitudes to leave people. It is recommended not to enter into dialogue with evil spirits, even though Jesus did so, according to the Gospels. The shepherds use loud voices and the atmosphere during expulsion of demons is tense but the congregation seems calm. A very small number of the patients show observable reactions but all those who seek the shepherds' treatment are said to have come because they experience problems in their lives. As an

---

[531] Tobilehibe 1997:121–122.

exception, shepherds and pastors subject themselves to expulsion of demons in ordinary healing services, a practice prohibited in the handbook.

Prayer with the laying on of hands/"strengthening" always follows the casting out of demons. Almost all people present in ordinary healing services are prayed for, according to my material, possibly indicating that the audience consists of people with special needs. The shepherds place their right hand on the head of those who ask for it, in the name of Jesus and with Jesus' authority. The hand should not be placed anywhere else on the body. The prayer is altered according to the person in question and forgiveness of sins, the Holy Spirit and peace is given through the prayer. Normally, there is no preceding conversation between the shepherds and the people asking for "strengthening". The prayer with the laying on of hands is a special mark of the shepherds' ministry and is considered to be at the heart of their service.

We now turn to the shepherds' understanding of their practice of exorcism.

4 The shepherds' understanding of their practice

There is close correspondence between this chapter and the preceding one. In chapter 3 I described a healing service focusing on elements that could be observed and registered. Now I concentrate on central themes emerging from the preceding description, focussing on how the shepherds understand and argue their practice. Before doing so, however, I furnish some elements in what I consider to be the wider contexts for the shepherds' understanding of exorcism: traditional Malagasy culture and biblical message, as these contexts have been influencing them. The second subchapter (4.2) relates to prayer, singing and preaching (cf. 3.1). The third and fourth subchapters (4.3 and 4.4) mainly relate to expulsion of demons (cf. 3.2) and the fifth (4.5) to prayer with the laying on of hands/"strengthening" (cf. 3.3). At the end of this chapter (4.6) I give a few examples of how the wider contexts may be used as tools of interpretation to further enlighten the shepherds' understanding of their practice.

Chapter 4 is rather comprehensive and it is a conscious choice. I want to emphasise that the purpose of all the different subchapters is to highlight the shepherds' understanding.

4.1 The wider contexts of exorcism: traditional Malagasy culture and biblical message

My hermeneutic claim in this project is that the shepherds' understanding of exorcism cannot be fully grasped if this practice is isolated from the contexts in which it is functioning. The shepherds are Malagasy, brought up in the Malagasy culture with its assumptions about life and death, about the reality of seen and unseen powers, with affective reactions of the shepherds being Malagasy and evaluating themselves and their surroundings from their Malagasy point of view. At the same time the shepherds are Christians who belong to the church. Their practice of exorcism is seen as a function of them being Christians and it is performed as part of this church context.

The purpose of the following presentation is to draw some lines in the shepherds' horizons of understanding, i.e. traits in the traditional Malagasy culture and lines in the biblical message, which have relevance to exorcism. Traditional Malagasy culture and the biblical message are presented to shed light on my main theme by serving as horizons of understanding. By using the contexts as tools of interpretation I will be able to draw some conclusions as to how the shepherds seem to have utilised elements from the contexts in their practice and understanding of exorcism. My purpose with furnishing selected elements of the contexts is that in this way the shepherds' understanding of their practice of exorcism will be more clarified. When I describe the contexts, which presumably have influenced the shepherds, I am not asserting that the shepherds simply have taken over these lines of understanding. The shepherds' experiences, e.g. with exorcism may have altered some of their understanding on certain elements of the contexts. This possible expansion of understanding, however, is not a task for me fully to investigate[532] since my focus of interest is exorcism, as practised and understood by the shepherds.

By presenting the two contexts here before describing the shepherds' understanding of their practice, the reader is furnished with tools to make his/her own reflections. The contexts also emphasise the missiological perspective in this project, i.e. the shepherds' exorcism as an example of a Christian practice in the tension between traditional Malagasy culture and the biblical message. The two contexts are important as descriptions of the field, in which exorcism is practised and understood by the shepherds.[533]

---

[532] My fieldwork did not have this objective, so my data does not enable me to answer this question.

[533] See arguments for my choices in 1.3.3.2.

4.1.1 Traditional Malagasy culture

P.G. Hiebert's model of a Tribal View of Spiritual Encounters seems to be useful in order to present important traits in the traditional Malagasy culture.[534]

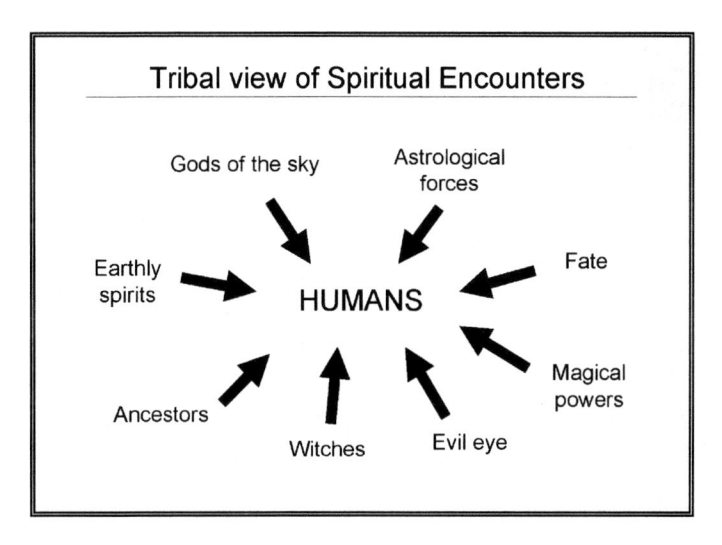

```
                Tribal view of Spiritual Encounters

                  Gods of the sky    Astrological
                                       forces
          Earthly                                    Fate
          spirits         →  HUMANS  ←
                                                    Magical
                                                    powers
              Ancestors
                           Witches    Evil eye
```

Figure 1: Hiebert's Tribal View of Spiritual Encounters
Model adapted from P.G. Hiebert and used by permission

The most prominent trait with a tribal worldview is that humans are in the middle of the battlefield between spirits, gods and forces, all of them unseen. Hiebert says: "For most tribal peoples ancestors, earthly spirits, witchcraft and magic are very real. The people see the earth and sky as full of beings ...."[535] All the spirits and forces relate to each other and they are involved in an ongoing battle for power. The forces are in essence amoral, but they relate to humans according to the way humans treat them. As a consequence, it is important for people to treat the unseen powers well and according to their wishes and requests.

My own experiences from Madagascar indicate that Hiebert's model covers important traits in the traditional Malagasy culture. It has to be

---

[534] Hiebert presents four sketches of worldviews: A Modern View of Spiritual Warfare, a Tribal View of Spiritual Encounters, The Myth of Cosmic Dualism, in addition to what he calls a Biblical View of Spiritual Warfare. Hiebert 2000:245–253.

[535] Hiebert 2000:247.

remembered, however, that this is a model and not photography of reality and as such it stresses some aspects while other aspects are more implicit. I will therefore make a few comments on the model to highlight my specific interest in this project.

The first impression of the model is that spirits and forces occupy a prominent place in this worldview. Most of the names in the model refer to spirit beings and forces. The Malagasy, too, seem to think that invisible spirits and forces are very real and they are part of everyday life and actions. A critique could be made that this model of worldview is polytheistic, with "gods" in plural and the question of polytheism and a high god is debated in the Malagasy setting.[536] The first subchapter will describe briefly important elements in the Malagasy universe of spirits and forces.

Secondly, the model shows the humans in the middle, surrounded by spirits and forces, a prominent trait in the Malagasy conception where human life is to a large degree determined by invisible forces. The forces may influence the humans, but the humans are also able to affect the forces. Thus the arrows in Hiebert's model should have gone both ways to render the Malagasy situation more accurately. The place of humans in the centre seems to indicate a basic anthropocentric orientation, where the human subject is pivotal. This seems to be true in the Malagasy setting, as well, but the model is not able to show that this should not be understood individualistically, but with weight on the human as part of a fellowship.[537] The relations between humans and the spirits/forces will be described under a second heading.

Thirdly, sickness and healing concerns to a certain degree the relations between humans and spirits/forces, as far as sickness is partly understood as caused by spirits and forces. In Hiebert's model this feature is present only implicitly, but it is important in my project. A third heading in the following description will deal with the traditional Malagasy conception of sickness and healing.

I am aware of the difficulties involved in structuring my presentation in this way, since the universe of spirits and forces, the relations between

---

[536] I cannot enter into the discussion here but see Ramamonjisoa 1997:80, Dahl 1999:33–34, Jaovelo-Dzao 1992:72–73. In the following presentation of traditional Malagasy culture I use "god" with minuscule, without taking side in the discussion.

[537] C. Nyamiti mentions four elements in an African worldview and one of these is "anthropocentrism": "Society and religion are centred on the human subject, whose welfare they are meant to procure. Humanity is the centre of the world. The world of nature and spirits is conceived anthropomorphically." Nyamiti 1995:41.

spirits/forces and humans and the traditional conception of sickness and healing are very much intermingled and depend on each other. Nevertheless, I will proceed as suggested above in order to make a brief overview of the field. The sources for the following description are researchers from the fields of science of religion, cultural anthropology and theology and the presentation is delimited to traits of relevance to exorcism.[538]

4.1.1.1 Traditional Malagasy universe of spirits and forces

Spirits and forces occupy an indisputable and prominent place in traditional Malagasy culture and nobody will question the existence of an invisible world parallel to the visible. These invisible waves of spirits and energies are able to influence the materiel world in different ways. The social order, the natural order and the cosmic order are closely linked and it is important that every action can be fitted into this order. The thinking is highly hierarchical and relational and it concerns everything that exists: spirits, forces and human beings.[539] The stability is delicate and can easily be turned to instability. The forces are battling one another and stronger spirits are able to conquer and take the place of lesser ones. Forces are constantly floating around like energies, circulating along invisible paths. Raison-Jourde calls the interaction of invisible spirits and forces in the world a "jeux des forces". There are negative and positive forces and they are seen as mediators between men, ancestors and god.[540]

Ancestors. The Malagasy have a comprehensive understanding of society: it consists of both the living and the dead. The dead members of the family are ancestors (*razana*). Raison-Jourde cites Feeley-Harnik, who compares the Merina thinking of the living as Westerners think of the top of an iceberg, with the ancestors as the hidden and most important part of society, since they are more powerful than the living.[541] The ancestors are thought to be the source of life.

The deceased become ancestors when they are buried in the family tomb according to the prevailing regulations. But those who are not

---

[538] See 1.3.3.2.
[539] Raison-Jourde 1991:78, 85.
[540] Raison-Jourde 1991:81–82.
[541] Raison-Jourde 1991:80–81.

considered as fully developed humans, such as babies, who do not yet have teeth and people who are ostracised, such as criminals and witches, will not be buried in the family tomb. This is a terrible fate and it is believed that the spirits of these people are drifting around disturbing the living.[542]

When the deceased become ancestors it is considered that the spirit of the dead has now become a mediator between god and the living, both as a spokesman and as a distributor of benefit and punishment. The ancestors are able to protect the living from invisible cosmic powers. They are considered as family and therefore it is felt that their interest is to protect. But, on the contrary, the ancestors may also be jealous of the living and cause illnesses.[543] They stand in an intermediate position. In fact, they cannot be bypassed if one wants to reach the invisible sphere. That makes them so important.[544] A famous Malagasy writer, Rahajarizafy, says that "The Malagasy's greatest fear was to incur guilt before the dead, and their greatest desire was to earn their favor".[545]

God. The Malagasy believe in a god who has many appearances and they have different words designating god, the most common are *zanahary* and *andriamanitra*.[546] The word *andriamanitra* e.g. can designate the high god and lesser gods but it may also be used about the ruler, charms and anything strange.[547] These entities can be called so because they take part in the same sacred power (*hasina*)[548] that is thought to dwell in *Andriamanitra*, according to Jaovelo-Dzao R.[549]

The most prominent feature of god's characteristics is that god is the creator but god does seldom intervene among humans. God is at the upper end of what is thought of as a hierarchical chain and as such, rather remote. When thinking of god, this causes fear much more than love and

---

[542] Dahl 1999:27.
[543] Skeie 1994:102.
[544] Raison-Jourde 1991:80.
[545] Cited in Olson 1970:20. See also Dahl 1999:26–27 for the centrality of ancestors in Malagasy thinking.
[546] There is an ongoing discussion of how to understand the etymology and the meaning of these two words. See Raison-Jourde 1991:77, Jaovelo-Dzao 1992:68.
[547] Cf Dahl 1999:33–34, who gives examples of the different uses of the word *andriamanitra*. *Andriamanitra* is the most common designation of the Christian God in the high plateaux.
[548] *Hasina* is a key concept in Malagasy religion. See below (Sacred power—*hasina*).
[549] Jaovelo-Dzao 1992:73.

the possibility of an intervention by god in person into the human scene causes a high sense of anxiety.[550] The Malagasy sayings confer many different characteristics upon god and some of them seem to contradict what has been said above, especially what concerns the remoteness.[551] The Malagasy thinking of god does not constitute a coherent picture, but presents a variety of meanings.

Idols[552] and charms/amulets. The Malagasy word *sampy* (idol) means a remedy wrapped in a cloth, with a long thread, which makes it possible to carry it.[553] An idol may be a piece of cloth or wood, sometimes decorated with silver or pearls. The so-called popular idols have integrated elements from nature spirits, ancestors, original inhabitants (*vazimba*) and nobles and are widespread.[554] The power from the "mother" idol is communicable to the "children", without emptying the "mother" for its power. The pieces taken from the "mother" idol are often called *ody* (charms/amulets) and they are owned and used by individuals. Some of these charms/amulets are swallowed in water or eaten with other food, others are carried around the neck, wrist or the ankle and some are stored in the house or put into the ground outside the house. Some of the charms/amulets used in consultations have curative effects because they are herbal medicines. J. Johnson asserts that people did not understand the way they worked and therefore attributed the same effects to all charms/amulets given by a specialist.[555] Rakotonaivo F. underlines that the pieces of cloth or wood are only the visible elements and not the real idol. It is god who dwells in these elements and god's power makes the idol holy and effective.[556]

---

[550] Raison-Jourde 1991:78–79.

[551] E.g. "god is everywhere and nobody can escape his sight". "God is not remote." Jaovelo-Dzao 1992:74–75.

[552] "Idol" is used here without any pejorative implications to designate "an image, representation, or symbol of a deity made or consecrated as an object of worship". Thatcher and McQueen 1980 Edition:420.

[553] From the Malagasy verb *misampina*, which means to carry over the shoulder as it is done with the special Malagasy cloth (*lamba*).

[554] Raison-Jourde 1991:90–91.

[555] Johnson 1914:50.

[556] Rakotonaivo 1997:21.

152   CH. 4: THE SHEPHERDS' UNDERSTANDING OF THEIR PRACTICE

Spirits of nature. The spirits of nature constitute the oldest layer in the Malagasy belief system, according to J.-M. Estrade.[557] These spirits and forces are everywhere in nature and this belief causes the Malagasy to be observant to places and territory.[558] The spirits are described in human analogies: they are unpredictable, their thinking is not easy to detect and they may revenge themselves.[559]

Sacred power—hasina. The word *hasina* covers a variety of meanings.[560] It stems from the root *masina*, which means holy, sacred, consecrated, sanctified. In Malagasy thinking everyone and everything is bestowed with a sacred power. This concerns particularly the original inhabitants, the soil, the mountain peaks, the sun, the moon, the ancestors, their places of burial, the sovereign and god himself. It is thought of as energies floating around in all possible relationships.[561] Kings and ancestors have much sacred power and consequently they are obliged to fulfil their obligations towards others by serving them in various ways.[562] In order not to cause misfortunes, the sacred power is surrounded by many taboos. If the taboos are broken, the sacred power can be dangerous and fatal.[563]

---

[557]   Estrade 1985:70. Rakotovao seems to classify these spirits as "spirits which origins cannot be traced". His two other classes are "spirits of the dead" and "idols". Rakotovao 1993:38–49.

[558]   Raison-Jourde 1991:83. Raison-Jourde mentions heights and lakes as special points of communication between world and heaven, because the first is close to the skies and the second reflects the skies.

[559]   Estrade 1985:70.

[560]   Vertu, force, puissance, la grâce, propriété naturelle ou surnaturelle, efficacité, santeté, sel, saveur, goût, vertu attachée à un objet, ce qui rend digne de réspect. Abinal and Malzac 1930:222.

[561]   Raison-Jourde 1991:84.

[562]   The kings had much sacred power in virtue of their position of power. The ritual of coronation in Merina displayed this: The one who was to become king was placed on a holy stone in the middle of the crowd. When he/she asked if he/she was holy—*masina* (i.e. if he/she had sacred power—*hasina*), the crowd answered holy (*masina*) and then the coronation was conducted. The place of this ceremony was called Mahamasina (= what makes holy/what gives sacred power). The sacred power of the ancestors was closely linked to the corpse and the grave. Birkeli 1944:7.

[563]   Raison-Jourde 1991:84.

4.1.1.2 *The relation between humans and spirits/forces*

Invisible spirits and forces are thought to be active in a variety of ways and they have a high position of respect in the traditional Malagasy society. Every really important action has a relation to the spirits/forces that are the true rulers of creation and humans must strive to be in harmony with this invisible universe.[564]

Interaction between humans and ancestors, god, idols and charms, amulets, nature spirits, sacred power. The deceased communicate with the living in dreams and when the ancestors complain that they are cold because their cloth is worn out, it is time to prepare the ritual of turning the corpse (*famadihana*). These rituals are characteristic elements in the Antsirabe district during the cold season.[565] The cult is the humans' part of fulfilling mutual obligations and in turn the ancestors will bless and protect the living.[566]

It is through the ancestors as mediators that people expect the gifts of god and according to J.-M. Estrade, the Malagasy do not make any offerings to god, make any temples to his honour or celebrate any cults in his name.[567] This is in line with F. Raison-Jourde, who maintains that the relationship with the divine is pragmatic, in order to obtain a favour and that the prayer is usually directed to what is thought to be the closest link on the hierarchical line between the ordinary man and god.[568]

People honour the idols, they ask for blessings and they make offerings. When people come to ask for blessings, the guardian distributes charms/amulets, which are taken from the idol and share the

---

[564] Estrade 1985:74.

[565] Up to 90 % of Lutheran Christians take part (the number does not refer to research, but is given in personal communication with church leaders in the district), even though it is said in the statutes of the Church that partaking will exclude them from communion. Fiangonana Loterana Malagasy 1984:53, §51,d. This exclusion is not carried out, however. In the latest edition of the statutes, reference to the ritual of turning of the corpse is almost completely removed. It is only said that Christians should be encouraged to have a single tomb "in order to avoid the turning of the corpse" (*mba tsy hahatonga ny famadihana*). Fiangonana Loterana Malagasy 2001:113.

[566] The ritual of turning the corpse cannot be elaborated on here, but the interested reader will find much literature on this subject. See Bloch 1971, Skeie 1994.

[567] Estrade 1985:75.

[568] Raison-Jourde 1991:79–80.

same power.[569] The distribution and use of charms/amulets is widespread and has a great impact on Malagasy everyday life. It is generally acknowledged that each charm/amulet has one or more taboos to be observed and if this is neglected, the power of the charm/amulet will diminish.[570] The consequences for the owner may be severe, since this is considered a break of contract. Sinning against a taboo also causes fear, which may have destructive consequences.[571]

Nature spirits complicate the existence of man, they are permanent objects of fear and they often serve as explanation of the mysteries of everyday life. Especially in connection with illness, which does not seem to have observable causes, spirits are supposed to be agents.

The sacred power (*hasina*) is communicable by touch, it can be weakened and rituals can reinforce it.[572] The sacred power is in itself a beneficial power, but depending on the way it is handled, the effects can be either positive or negative.[573] In the manipulative practices of sorcerers the sacred power can cause bad effects on agriculture, people and social relations. It is important to trace the possible relationship between the different forces circulating in the universe and this is foremost a task for specialists. In doing so, the hierarchical places given to everything in creation has to be observed. The striving for a proper equilibrium or harmony is vital. In Merina thinking the social order, the natural order and the cosmic order stand in direct correlation to each

---

[569] A charm/amulet (*ody*) is used as (1) a remedy to cure illness, as (2) a protection against illness, misfortune, evil spirits and ghosts, as (3) a remedy to harm others through witchcraft and as (4) a magical charm in love affairs. Rakotonaivo 1997:229–235.

[570] Johnson 1914:50–51.

[571] Rakotonaivo 1997:24–25. Rakotonaivo F. lists categories of taboos and what to do when a taboo is sinned against.

[572] The most famous of the rituals of reinforcement was the feast of the Royal Bath (*fandroana*), where the king's sacred power was augmented. Afterwards the water was sprinkled on the crowd and thus the king's sacred power benefited the people. Birkeli 1944:7. To the *Fandroana* ritual, see Larson 1997.

[573] Skeie 1994:93. K.H. Skeie argues against introducing a dualism in the concept of *hasina*, since that would conceal the fact that there is only one power in Merina ancestral worldview. Her point is to state the difference between the traditional Imerina and the Christian worldview, which she says is "strongly dualistic". E. Birkeli says that the evil force (*loza*) has nothing to do with sacred power, but it is considered its opposite and this seems to support Skeie's view of sacred power as a beneficial power. Birkeli 1944:8.

other and anything that affects one of them also affects the other.[574] Even if handling the sacred power requires special knowledge and wisdom, it is unavoidable for any individual not to be influenced by this power, since it is operating in all nature, in the agricultural activities, in the construction of a Merina house and in the making of a family.[575]

Possession. For the individual human being, to be possessed is accepting to be governed by forces stronger than the self. The person becomes a slave of these forces and this does not depend on personal choice. Either he/she is a victim of sorcery, as is the case in e.g. *ambalavelona*, or the spirits themselves chose whom to inhabit, as in the much more widespread *tromba*.[576] A general agreement is that *tromba* originated in Northern Sakalava, but has now spread throughout the whole island and despite minor varieties from one region to another, the homogeneity is great.[577]

Ramamonjisoa S. talks about positive and negative possession, good and bad *tromba*.[578] The positive possession is seen especially in the possession cults, while negative possession is understood as an assault from evil spirits and often use of sorcery and evil charms is connected with this suffering. The appropriate action in such cases is to expel the spirit in order to cure the victim. In her work on *tromba*, L.A. Sharp developed another classification. She talks about *tromba* possession, possession sickness and madness.[579]

---

[574] Raison-Jourde 1991:84–85.

[575] Skeie 1994:94.

[576] Ramamonjisoa 1997:71. Neither *ambalavelona* nor *tromba* is translatable into English. Ramamonjisoa S. calls spirit-possession a dominant theme in the Malagasy culture and it is so widespread that any Malagasy has an opinion on the subject. Ramamonjisoa 1997:68. Spirit-possession is also one of the most common themes in literature on Madagascar and especially *tromba*-possession is well documented. See literature on spirit-possession cited in Sharp 1993:19.

[577] Estrade 1985:105, Sharp 1993:116, Ramamonjisoa 1997:70.

[578] Ramamonjisoa 1997:69, 72. *Tromba tsara* (good *tromba*) and *tromba ratsy* (bad *tromba*).

[579] Sharp 1993:247. In the sakalava tribe possession and madness are distinct categories of experience, although they are somewhat overlapping. The experiences ranges from good and powerful in *tromba* possession, through possession sickness to madness, which is seen as a frightening illness.

156 CH. 4: THE SHEPHERDS' UNDERSTANDING OF THEIR PRACTICE

Possession cults[580] in the central high plateaux are performed at distinct locations. Different ceremonies are performed regularly, there are leaders in charge, clients attend, the possessing ancestors are identifiable and they impose taboos on the living.[581]

The essential element in the ceremonies is the sacrifice of an ox, but offerings of food, like bananas and honey always precede the prayers. These are considered as gifts to the ancestors. Ritual purification in water is obligatory. The clients' immediate concern is usually some form of illness, for which they seek a cure. They may ask for an individual ceremony and an important task is to detect the causes of the illness, for which the medium prescribes remedies revealed by the ancestors. Both when entering and leaving the possession state, the medium's body shakes. The possessing entities are most often ancestors of royal descent and this possession is considered positive,[582] but the possibility of other possessing entities, which are not easily recognised as ancestors or *vazimba*,[583] are also reckoned with. The mark of the relation between the ancestors and the living, outside the possession ceremonies, is the different taboos imposed by the spirits, usually food taboos. If a taboo is broken, the ancestor will react often by sending some illness or misfortune.[584] According to Ramamonjisoa S., possession in the high plateaux has been integrated into what claims to be Christian cultural and liturgical forms.[585] R. Cabanes notices that it does not seem incompatible

---

[580] *Tromba* possession can also be classified as a possession cult, but since *tromba* form a distinct group, I will describe it separately below. Here I concentrate on the original cults in the central high plateaux.

[581] The following is mainly taken from Cabanes 1972:38–63.

[582] This does not prevent the mediums from suffering and lots of precautions have to be followed by those who house a spirit. The community's general opinion about this possession, however, is positive, because of all the benefits obtained, especially healing.

[583] Spirits of original inhabitants. See more below.

[584] Possession cults in the central high plateaux are almost only confined to descendants of slaves and about a third of the Merina population belongs to this group. See Graeber 1997:374, Bloch 1994:134–137.

[585] Ramamonjisoa 1997:69. She refers to the story of a man she met, who started as a shepherd in *Fifohazana* in order to secure healing for a relative, but who experienced serious mental trouble himself afterwards. He felt invaded by something (French: entités), who imposed taboos on him and caused misfortune. Once he accepted the spirits to govern his life, he recovered from the illness. He was ordered to live as a poor man, to work against all evil around him and to serve Jesus Christ and his neighbours. Now he works as a healer, with laying on of hands,

for Christians to take part in the traditional cults[586] and in his article on the popular possession-cult of Ranoro in Antananarivo, M. Bloch says that most cultists are Roman Catholics.[587]

When a *tromba* spirit has chosen a host, it makes itself known through different means.[588] The most imperative and generally acknowledged is sickness. It is not until other means of healing have been tried that one suspects a *tromba* spirit to be the cause of sickness. Another way of making itself known to the elected host is dreams, e.g. where the spirit requests the buying of different items to be used in the ceremonies. A series of misfortunes, of which there is no explanation, may also be taken as a sign from the spirit world. If the person resists the spirit, this may cause her[589] great physical harm. Evil spirits preventing good *tromba* spirits to enter a person have to be expelled. The supernatural presence has to be authenticated by a *tromba* leader who performs different rituals to decide whether this is a *tromba* or not.[590] If the result of the tests reveal that a *tromba* is trying to make itself known, arrangements are made for the "clapping of hands" (*rombo*) ceremony. The aim is to permanently instate the spirit within her and in this way she will be healed from the

---

massage and medical plants. He wants his clients to repent and pray and he reports of many people who have been led to conversion through his work. His orientation is not the institutional churches, but the popular religiosity. He invokes the gods (*zanahary*) in the beginning of the ceremonies and he burns incense. His use of possession is twofold, both to instate the positive spirits (*tromba tsara*) and to exorcise the bad spirits (*tromba ratsy*). He has now a reputation as healer and exorcist (p. 71–72).

[586] Cabanes 1972:43.

[587] Bloch 1994:134. Bloch shows how this possession cult is being merged with Mary. In the middle of the shrine, there is a plaster statuette of the virgin.

The shepherds firmly oppose the development described by Ramamonjisoa, Cabanes and Bloch and disagree with their evaluation of the situation.

[588] The following description is based on Estrade 1985:105–132 and Sharp 1993:122–134.

[589] Sharp asserts that it is unusual that spirits possess men and 96 % of the *tromba* mediums she encountered in Ambanja were women. In line with this observation I use only the female form of the pronomen in the following.

[590] The *tromba* leader, also usually a woman, may use magical means, like a plate of water with silver coins in it, or—if the patient resists her methods—the patient may be bathed in cold water. If the patient shivers, cries, or moves the upper part of the body in rhytms, this is taken as a sure sign of *tromba*.

sickness and turn into a *tromba* medium. In traditional worship exorcism is no option in such a case.

Normally each *tromba* leader arranges two *rombo* ceremonies every month, following the moon's movements. Preparations are important and there is a need for different ritual objects: a plate with water, white kaolin, pieces of money, many sorts of charms, some modern objects the *tromba* likes (hats, keys, knifes, cards, mirrors, perfume) and an abundance of alcohol (rum is especially important). Musicians are hired to play a sort of zither (*valiha*), sometimes accordion and rhythm instruments. Music will entice the spirits to come.[591] In addition to the *tromba* leader's adherents, family and friends, several other mediums are also normally invited to these ceremonies.[592] The ceremony is expensive, because both the hired musicians and the other *tromba* mediums are paid to attend and in addition all the material objects needed have to be paid for. It is not uncommon that the ceremony is postponed several times due to lack of money.

The leader starts by invoking god the creator and different royal ancestors. The prayer is long, reciting personal names and Sakalava places. When the prayer ends, it is time to wait for the coming of the spirit. The atmosphere is full of rejoicing, because the spirits should be pleased. The musicians play. The air is filled with anticipation. It is not uncommon that neighbours and children crowd in the doorways at this time, watching the ceremony. All present are barefoot and have their heads uncovered. This is out of respect for the ancestors.[593]

The trance is normally preceded by trembling (slightly or more violently) and each possessed has her own style, according to the possessing spirit. The spirits have their own style of dress, behaviour and taboos to be respected. In this way it is possible for the audience to identify the possessing spirit, since the spirit's identity is constant over time. Most of the *tromba* mediums are women, as stated above and the spirits possessing them tend to be men. In trance, then, a female medium transforms into a male spirit, not just in dress, but also in voice and other behaviour. When the *tromba* spirit possesses the medium, her own spirit departs and remains absent until the trance state is ended. After the

---

[591] Sharp 1993:126.
[592] The reason for inviting other mediums is to ease the instating of the spirit in the new host. In the case reported by L.A. Sharp, one of these invited mediums officiated at the ceremony. Sharp 1993:127.
[593] Sharp 1993:128.

possession experience, the mediums do not remember what happened. It is believed that the *tromba* spirits live in royal tombs, but they leave this place temporarily to possess the mediums. Spirits of dead royalties come to life and interact with the living in these ceremonies. Some spirits are aggressive, others may be physically threatening, or playful and flirtatious. As more mediums go into trance, more alcohol is drunk, more clapping of hands and dancing is performed, the drama becomes even livelier.

The *tromba* mediums are both oracles and healers. When they are possessed, people consult them for different ailments and sicknesses and especially young children are often brought to the mediums. Even passers-by may drop in to ask for their services.[594] The speech of the medium is "*tromba* language" and rather incomprehensible and thus each medium has a translator, often the husband of the medium.[595] This translator passes on the spirit's advice and sometimes he may write the medical prescriptions on a piece of paper.

The climax of the ceremony is the arrival of the spirit in the patient. This may not happen until the last part of the ceremony. When it happens, the newly possessed, while still in trance, has several consultations with the *tromba* leader and her household and the discussion with the spirit does not end before it utters its name. It may happen that the spirit possessing a person is the same spirit who possesses one of the other mediums. This may cause difficulties instating the spirit, since a spirit only can possess one medium at a time and the spirit has to depart from one medium to possess another. Most *tromba* spirits are active in many mediums.[596]

It may happen that mediums leave the trance to eat during the night, but more often they stay possessed all the time. When the spirits leave, they do so in the reverse order and in a similar style to their arrival. The mediums are tired after the possession experience is over and they ask for a summary of what happened, but they do not seem to feel the effects of the alcohol they consumed during the ceremony.

Such large-scale ceremonies as briefly described previously happen when a new spirit is going to be instated in a person, when new family members are to be introduced to the spirit, or when the living have

---

[594] Sharp 1993:131.
[595] J.-M. Estrade mentions the phenomenon of xenoglossia in connection with *tromba* ceremonies, but he has never observed this himself. Estrade 1985:123.
[596] L.A. Sharp describes a *tromba* ceremony in detail. Sharp 1993:125–134.

160   CH. 4: THE SHEPHERDS' UNDERSTANDING OF THEIR PRACTICE

moved to a new house. Many mediums also hold small ceremonies in their homes with clients. The room has to be quiet and dark and only the client, the medium and the translator attend the ceremony. Sometimes a *tromba* spirit may arrive unannounced, outside ceremonies. This normally happens when the spirit is angered for some reason.

Once a spirit is properly instated in a person, it becomes part of the household and a permanent fixation of the medium's life until death. When asked, all mediums say that they suffer much. Nevertheless, according to L.A. Sharp's estimations, *tromba* spirits possessed 50 % of adult women living in Ambanja.[597] Estrade notices that many possessed hope to be delivered, especially because all the expenses at the nightly ceremonies are a heavy burden.[598]

Most *tromba* spirits claim that it is taboo for them to pray,[599] but influence from Christian practices can be seen in some ceremonies.[600]

All spirits are potentially dangerous, they can be angered and they may cause sickness and misfortunes. This is especially true with the evil spirits.[601]

Most theories about *vazimba* spirits maintain that they have a human origin. They were ancestors, whose bodies had been lost. The *vazimba*

---

[597] Sharp 1994:528. Sharp maintains that even though the mediums complained about their suffering, *tromba* possession has its advantages: a lucrative business of healing and a unique possibility of social acceptance for the non-Sakalava.

[598] Estrade 1985:258.

[599] Mal: *fady mivavaka*. It is the *tromba* spirit who has this taboo and it is also imposed on the host. "To pray" is the normal expression of going to church or to be a Christian. When Christians attend the *tromba* ceremonies, the spirit may try to calm them by assuring that they pray to the same god. Since praying is nevertheless forbidden, Estrade sees this only as apparently calming. The main reason for the *tromba* to resist Christianity seems to be the Christians' abandoning of certain customs important to the *tromba* and not the religion itself. Estrade 1985:124.

[600] The different *tromba* spirits have their own taste and Estrade mentions the song from the hymnbook: *Aza manadino ahy, ry mpihaino vavaka* ("Do not forget me, ô listener to prayer") as one of the songs used to make the spirits come. He also reports that in a ceremony the psalm "Te Deum" was sung and 1 Cor 13 read solemnly. Estrade 1985:117, 121.

[601] In some regions these are called "bad *tromba*"—*tromba ratsy* (Ramamonjisoa 1997:69), or "children of *tromba*"—*zanaky ny tromba* (Sharp 1994:529), or "*tromba* of no worth"—*tromba tsy manjary* (Nielssen 1995:50). H. Nielssen observes that in Betsimisaraka all spirits, irrespective of category, are called *tromba*. It is also only the *tromba* leaders who are able to heal illness caused by spirits.

were the ghosts of lost and dangerous spirits, angry because they had lost proper relations with their descendants. These spirits lack bodies and are mysterious.[602] *Vazimba* possession is connected with specific places, discovered as haunted by evil spirits because someone fell ill there. Exorcism is required. The curer burns things and the smoke and incense will cause the spirit to leave. Offerings may also be made e.g. honey, candies or bananas. The reason for this is to placate the spirit, so that it will remain in that place.[603]

Nature sprits present a bewildering variety and they are given different names according to the region. When the *jinn*, *lolo* or *biby* possess people in Betsimisaraka they cause illness and have to be exorcised.[604] The *tsiny* and *kalanoro* of Ambanja require mediums and although they are feared, they are respected as authority figures, specialists and healers.

The *kalanoro* spirits are found throughout Madagascar, sometimes under different names.[605] They are believed to have a humanlike figure, magical abilities and strange habits. The *kalanoro* mediums act as their guardians and they are said to keep these spirits. Clients are not allowed to view the *kalanoro* during the consultations but must sit behind a curtain. The spirits can be heard by a strange noise on the ceiling and walking on the walls when they are coming.[606]

Possession by evil spirits like *njarinintsy*, *masoantoko* and *shay-tuan* are classified by L.A. Sharp as possession sickness.[607] These spirits cause illness with strange symptoms and are visible in temporary fits of possession. The possession experience is characterised by a lack of recognition of known people and loss of memory of what happened. The spirits have to be expelled as soon as possible. If not, the illness will be aggravated and possibly turn into madness.

---

[602] Graeber 1997:383.

[603] A famous story in *Tantara ny andriana* tells about Ranoro, who periodically fell into trance, was possessed by a *vazimba* spirit and worked as a successful healer, performing remarkable miracles. Graeber 1997:384–387, 393.

[604] Nielssen 1995:52.

[605] One of the theories of *vazimba* origin suggests that the *vazimba* are the ghosts of *kalanoro*. Graeber 1997:383.

[606] Sharp 1993:138–139. Cf. the possession history by i.a. *kalanoro* spirits, told by a shepherd about his wife, in Austnaberg 1997.

[607] For a close analysis of *Njarinintsy*-possession, see Sharp 1990.

Sorcery/witchcraft, astrological forces and destiny. Malagasy in general think that hostile people are able to use some evil power to harm their fellows.[608] The belief in sorcery is pervasive and people believe that it is able to effect great damage and destruction.[609] Sorcery is hostile to the social order, because it is the negation of the *fihavanana*,[610] a core value in the traditional Malagasy society. One of the most common motives of sorcery is jealousy and revenge. The most generally known way of becoming a witch seems to be through the love poison (*ody fitia*). This is a charm used to attract a partner; sometimes one, who has had a proposal, but has refused and thus the motive is revenge. The offended party goes to a sorcerer who prepares a special charm. In some way or another the intended person is made to come into contact with this charm. The charm will drive the victim mad or it may even kill him/her.

It is widely recognised that sorcerers use poison to harm their victims and it may be given through food or drink, or by poisoning places the victim often will touch. Acute fear is another prominent factor. The witches active during the night frighten the household into shivering and the finger of a witch, pointed at a person while announcing that he/she will die on such and such a day, may be such an effective power that the victim will actually die.[611] Every sorcerer possesses and uses different charms and the possession of charms is essential to the practice of witchcraft/sorcery.[612] Their composition varies according to their aims and charms in the hands of a sorcerer can be used both to protect himself/herself during this activity and to harm other people. There are countless charms, according to the situations, people and aims, but their common feature is that they receive their power from another source.[613] No charm in Madagascar is used before it is consecrated to a spiritual being and if it for some reason, is supposed to have lost some of its power, it has to be consecrated again.

---

[608] To a brief discussion of theories on witchcraft see Hill 1996:326, 334.

[609] Rasolondraibe 1989:345.

[610] The meaning of *fihavanana* is comprehensive: kinship, friendship, solidarity, readiness to help, good relationship. As Ø. Dahl has pointed out, it is impossible to give this word a correct translation. Dahl 1999:85.

[611] Danielli 1947:266.

[612] Danielli 1947:267.

[613] Andrianjafy 1985:46–47.

The Malagasy believe that everything in this world functions according to *lahatra*[614], i.e. according to the orderly place that is given to everything and everyone. Both the individual and the elements of nature are intended to find their place in the world order. When confronted with joy and misfortune in life, most Malagasy see this as their *lahatra* and the appropriate reaction is to submit oneself to what happens.[615]

The universe is seen as alive and constantly striving for balance and harmony and as such, is a force to be reckoned with. This is to the extent that it is believed that there are cosmic forces, that by themselves restore the balance, which is especially clear in the concepts of *tody* and *tsiny*. *Tody* (retaliation) is understood as the working out of cosmic retributive justice, Rasolondraibe P. says, since every act, good or evil, is thought to bring out *tody*. Sooner or later the *tody* of your acts will return to you as an inevitable consequence of what you have done. The *tsiny* (blame) is another cosmic retributive force. It originates as blame by an offended party because of a mistake in word or deed and this turns into a negative cosmic force, which operates constantly until justice is completed, i.e. until the offended party has obtained his right.[616] In the concepts of *tsiny* and *tody* the forces relate to humans in an almost impersonal way, but the humans' actions themselves cause these forces to interrupt the humans.

The moon, the stars and the sun stand in relation to the humans and it is important to become aware of the individual *vintana* (destiny), because choices in life depend to a great degree on this knowledge. The different destinies are closely knit to the months of the year, pronounced with names coming from Arabic and interpreted by the *mpanandro*, who is a specialist in determining destinies. The Merina does nothing really important, if the destinies have not been thoroughly examined first and so this practice is an integrated part of everyday life. Andriamanjato R. sees this practice of divination (*fanandroana*) as an effort to confront or even change the destiny and by doing so a Malagasy tries to take responsibility for his own destiny. Andriamanjato tries to prove by this that the Malagasy are not fatalists, under control of unknown and blind

---

[614] *Lahatra* means order, organisation, arrangement. It also has the connotation of world order.

[615] Dahl 1999:71–72.

[616] Rasolondraibe 1989:345–346. The concepts of *tsiny* and *tody* are not identical. The *tsiny* can be eluded by avoiding it (*miala tsiny*) beforehand, while the *tody* inevitably will occur in due time. See further Dahl 1999:61–64.

164 CH. 4: THE SHEPHERDS' UNDERSTANDING OF THEIR PRACTICE

powers and Dahl, too, concludes that their tolerance is great, but they are not completely fatalists. He has found, however, that a common Malagasy tendency is to seek explanations for failure and success outside oneself.[617] An ambiguity between submission and control is seen in the humans' relations to the spirits/forces.

4.1.1.3 Traditional Malagasy conception of sickness and healing

The Malagasy words *marary* ("to be ill") and *aretina* ("sickness") cover a much wider range of meaning than the corresponding English words. They can be used to designate almost all sorts of undesirable conditions including depression, barrenness, feeling unwell and a bad mood. Sorrow and tears can be illness, or at least may lead to illness.[618] Rasolondraibe talks about a diminution of life force.[619]

The word *fahasalamana* may be translated health, peace, luck.[620] It is broadly defined and seen in relation to social and economic factors. To treat a person for something includes contributing to good health, to procure joy and strength in life and to give advice and remedies for ailments and sicknesses.[621] The word *fanafody* (medicine) can be used to refer to any substance that can bring about a change in an individual's state of health—be it beneficial or harmful. This can refer to pharmaceutical drugs, medicinal plants and different charms. The word is composed of *fanàfana* and *ody*, which literally means to remove the (effects of a) charm. According to L.A. Sharp, all medicine from the traditional healers includes substances with medicinal qualities and magical properties. Supernatural qualities are added to the medicine by the healer's sanctification, in actions made or words uttered.[622]

It is important to be aware of the different Malagasy connotations to the words when they are translated into English.

---

[617] Dahl 1999:69–71.
[618] Nielssen 1995:42.
[619] Rasolondraibe 1989:345.
[620] Santé, paix, bonheur. Abinal and Malzac 1930:565.
[621] Sharp 1993:208, Nielssen 1995:56.
[622] Sharp 1993:205–206. Sharp also notices that the term *fanafody* is used of different styles of healing, like Malagasy medicine (*fanafody gasy*) and European medicine (*fanafody vazaha*).

In general, the Malagasy go to a medical doctor/clinic when they get ill, if there is any within a relatively close range. They receive a prescription or vaccination and if they are able to find and buy the recommended drugs, they will do so. If the treatment is unsuccessful, however, they try other means. Then they often turn to traditional healers. The medical pluralism is a marked trait and alongside the pharmaceutical drugs also different sorts of traditional remedies will be used to secure a good result. Sometimes the medical doctor advises his patient to look up a traditional healer if he/she is unable to cure the illness.[623] Every crisis makes the Malagasy turn to the ancestral practices and the traditional thinking is still very much alive, but in different degrees from one person to another, Rajaonarison E. and Rakotomalala M.M. says.[624] When faced with a series of misfortunes or unexplainable happenings, people soon suspect some kind of sorcery and they normally consult some of the traditional healers,[625] mostly for divination of the causes and meanings of what has happened.[626]

Well aware that most Malagasy consult clinics when they get ill, I will in the following mainly concentrate on the cases where this "European medicine" fails, i.e. I will mainly deal with the "traditional" or "Malagasy medicine".

The causes of sickness. A common trait in the traditional conception is that sickness and misfortune stem from factors outside the individual and

---

[623] IN 324.

[624] Rajaonarison and Rakotomalala 1987:3. A non-shepherd in my material thinks that the spread of Christianity has changed people's attitude toward traditional medicine, but he admits that it depends on personal choice. He also maintains that those with a scientific way of thinking will refrain from attributing their sickness to supernatural causes. However, if the gravity of the sickness is great, he supposes that people will try all possible means. IN 324.

[625] Each Malagasy community possesses a whole array of traditional healers, each with their specialities: *mpimasy/ombiasy, mpisikidy, mpanandro,* different kinds of mediums, etc. They are all respected and people choose them according to their reputation.

[626] One of my informants gives an example of such unexplainable happenings: One day they found horse droppings in the food they had prepared and they did not have any idea where it came from. Another day they found the clothes of one of the children in the enclosure with the oxen (*valan'omby*) and shortly afterwards someone was throwing a stone at them while they were eating. The stone fell into one of the children's plate. These happenings caused great fear and the family was convinced that this did not happen by chance. IS 76.

are seen as an invasion of destructive forces. Etymologically, the Malagasy word *fahavoazana*, translated "misfortune" is even composed of the root *voa*, which means "being hit or hurt".[627] The Merina says that the sick *miafana* ("is purified") when he/she perspires profusely and shows symptoms of healing. Their unconscious understanding is that the sick person is polluted and healing is considered a purification. The perspiration is seen as an outward mark of the destructive forces.[628]

Illness and misfortune always have their causes, which is of great importance to discover. It is only in understanding the "why" that the appropriate cure can be given, even though the how may be quite obvious.[629] The "why" is a task for specialists and as a consequence the different practitioners are frequently visited. Especially when the causes are not directly observable or when several misfortunes strike in a short period of time, the causes have to be investigated more profoundly.

Spirits may be the agents. They are considered to be a living reality in people's everyday lives and are thought to be active in a variety of ways. Problems stemming from spirits can be physical, lack of fertility, conflicts in marriage, divorce, a problematic life situation or mental illness. All these problems are called illness (*aretina*).[630] The spirits of ancestors can send illnesses and misfortunes when angered.[631] Evil, malicious spirits may possess people temporarily and cause sickness and all sorts of problems. Evil spirits can be sent by *tromba* spirits to harm a potential host who is resisting possession. If such spirits inhabit a person, it is of utmost importance that appropriate action by the community is undertaken.[632]

---

[627] Rasolondraibe 1989:345.

[628] Rajaonarison and Rakotomalala 1987:3, 10. This emphasis on external forces is also noticed by other researchers. See Sharp 1994:529, 539, Skeie 1994:98. One of my informants understands the word "sick" (*marary*) as being hurt or hit by something, in the mind, the heart, or the body. This has consequences for the whole person. He/she becomes weak because he/she is being assaulted from outside. IS 320.

[629] Rasolondraibe 1989:344.

[630] Nielssen 1995:71–80. In H. Nielssen's study from a Betsimisaraka village all these problems are said to stem from *tromba* spirits. She explains this by saying that in her area all spirits are called *tromba* (p. 52), but this does not exclude that different categories of spirits are thought of.

[631] Sharp 1993:136.

[632] See the subchapter on possession above, where L.A. Sharp classifies sickness caused by these spirits as "possession sickness". Sharp 1993:141–142.

There is always a possibility that the causes of illness stem from taboos that are broken. Ruud ends his instructing study on taboo by saying that "every aspect of native life is influenced by taboos"[633] and the general impression from reading his study is that it is practically impossible for any human even to be aware of all the taboos that surround life. The mentioning of punishment belongs to the common taboo-formulation and Ruud's listing of the most common punishments includes many different illnesses, barrenness, banishment from home, suffering and death. He notices that all punishments are concerned with this life and the majority of them come from the powers behind the taboos. As the founding of the taboos referred to supernatural beings, the agents of punishment will be the same.[634]

Sorcery is another possible cause of illness. The background of sorcery is often problems and unsettled matters in the social relationships, which may lead to envy and a wish to harm the opponent. Illness and misfortunes may be the result.[635] According to Rasolondraibe P. and L.A. Sharp sorcery can also be effected through spirit-possession.[636]

Sickness may, by divination, be attributed to indirect unobservable causes, i.e. to *tsiny* and *tody*. These concepts also originate in social relations and the individual's own actions and show the importance of social behaviour/moral conduct in the Malagasy concept of sickness.[637]

When seeking the causes of sickness, an individual may come to the realisation of its positive purposes. This is especially visible in *tromba* possession. The intention of this sickness is to make the potential host willing to serve the community as a medium. In this light, the sickness

---

[633] Ruud 1970:301.
[634] Ruud 1970: 270–272.
[635] IN 324.
[636] Rasolondraibe 1989:345, Sharp 1993:141. M. Hardyman has studied *ambalavelona* sorcery and in her article she describes the symptoms of this illness. The main part of her article, however, indicates how the church ought to operate in this situation. Hardyman 1971.
[637] Rasolondraibe 1989:345–346. Rasolondraibe suggests three possible causes of sickness, which he calls: 1. direct observable causes (those established by ordinary observations), 2. direct "unobservable" causes (witchcraft and sorcery) and 3. indirect unobservable causes (*tsiny* and *tody*). He includes spirits as agents of sickness in the 2nd cause and talks about sorcery effected by spirit-possession. To the *tsiny* and *tody* concepts, see 4.1.1.2 (Sorcery/witchcraft, astrological forces and destiny).

serves as education.[638] When an individual falls ill, this can be interpreted as a message from the spiritual realm to the surrounding society. Divination may reveal the necessity of reconciliation and settling of problems in social relationships. It is also a possibility that sickness was sent in order to avoid a much more severe incident and this may turn out to be the cause of sickness.[639]

The healing process. The notion of healing as a long process is common in African thinking. K. Appiah-Kubi says that healing is "a process entailing a long, complicated interaction of other human beings, the community and above all the intervention of God".[640] Rajaonarison E. and Rakotomalala M.M. equate the healing process to "un itinéraire thérapeutique" and give by this the image of a journey, which may be more or less complex.[641] When H. Nielssen describes the *tromba* mediums' diagnosis of sickness, she gives the impression of a process: through the cult activity and the trance the medium forms the diagnosis little by little and by doing so she starts the healing process.[642] It is expected that healing takes time, that it involves many actors and that it cannot be studied without being aware of the relational aspects.

How is it possible to obtain therapeutic success? L.A. Sharp says: "… in this specific cultural context, ideas about therapeutic success are shaped by three points of view: the impressions and experiences of the patient, the patient's kin and the practitioner."[643] I will comment briefly these three points of view:

The patient is taken seriously. His/her experiences are real and they are the key to understanding the sickness and the correct diagnosis. When the patient reports an absence of troubling symptoms (be they restless sleep, depression, inability to articulate ideas clearly etc.) and

---

[638] Cf. above 4.1.1.2 (Possession).

[639] Rajaonarison and Rakotomalala 1987:5. Illness from an angry ancestor, mentioned above, can also be interpreted as a message with a positive intention, because it urges the living to take better care of the corpses and, by doing so, place themselves in a position to receive the blessings from the ancestors.

[640] Appiah-Kubi 1981:81, cited in Rasolondraibe 1989:346.

[641] Rajaonarison and Rakotomalala 1987:6.

[642] Nielssen 1995:82. This seems to impart nuances to my structuring of the presentation here: it is not a clearcut matter to separate the diagnosis from the healing process and my point is not to do that either. Rather I want to distinguish between them for the sake of clarity.

[643] Sharp 1994:526.

he/she is able to return to the former state of social involvement (behave according to the expectations of friends and neighbours), this is defined as therapeutic success.[644]

The individual is understood as part of a fellowship in the Malagasy setting and this makes the patient's kin important. Especially when the pressure of sickness is felt, the Malagasy shows his/her social character. The sick person does not want to be isolated from society, but rather he/she seeks a social confirmation of the sickness. In his/her orientation towards the social relationship the traditional healer is in danger of forgetting the individual and concentrating on the message conveyed by the sickness to restore the social order, Rajaonarison E. and Rakotomalala M.M. says.[645] According to Rasolondraibe P., the Malagasy is basically oriented towards the fellowship in times of illness.[646] In this way, the patient's kin is important in the healing process. Human presence brings power and activity from family and neighbourhood is valuable. L.A. Sharp has observed that especially in cases of spirit-possession it is important that kin and close friends care for, watch over and socialise with the sick. Their presence assures that the sick will be brought to a healer and that they watch the healing process and thus they are able to recount to the afflicted what happened.[647]

The practitioner's ability to empathise with and understand the patient is of utmost importance to therapeutic success. This concerns the worldview and conceptions of illness. If the epistemological realities of the practitioner differ largely from the patient's, this is a severe obstacle to success.[648] Rajaonarison E. and Rakotomalala M.M. describe the traditional healer, not only as a healer but also as an educator, who strives to be close to the patient and tries to redraw an image of the illness in understandable terms.[649]

---

[644] Sharp 1994:526.
[645] Rajaonarison and Rakotomalala 1987:5–6.
[646] Rasolondraibe is here citing Appiah-Kubi 1981:14 who says: . "The individual illness is derived from a sick or broken society. Society becomes the point of departure for individual diagnosis and the damage in the society must be repaired before the individual regains his health." Rasolondraibe 1989:346.
[647] Sharp 1993:143.
[648] Sharp 1994:526.
[649] Rajaonarison and Rakotomalala 1987:6–7.

With the understanding of healing as a process and the importance of the fellowship in mind, we now turn to the actual treatment. Since diagnosis is a task for specialists, the traditional healers also prescribe the treatment, according to the causes of the sickness.

If the cause of an individual's sickness is an angry ancestor, there are means to appease the spirit. This corresponds to the specific cause of the spirit's anger. If it is because the bodies of the dead are left outside the family tomb, the healer may instruct the living where to find the remains. If the reason is negligence of the tomb, the kin may be instructed to arrange a "turning of the corpse" ceremony (*famadihana*). The kin has to obey the spirit's messages, whatever they are, in order to start the process of healing.[650]

If the cause of sickness is a *tromba* spirit trying to make itself known to a potential host, this spirit has to be instated permanently through a ceremony. When the spirit is properly instated, the illness is healed and the person turns into a medium. Exorcising such a spirit is no option. It will only cause the sickness to be aggravated, since it is an attempt to counter the spirit's own will.[651]

If the cause of sickness is a break of taboo, different sacrifices are necessary to avoid punishment. The function of the sacrifice is to compensate for the life of the taboo-breaker and to restore what has been broken. The sacrifice reinstates the individual and the society into a dangerousless relationship with the powers. The taboo-breaker cannot bring the sacrifice himself/herself. It has to be performed according to a traditional ceremony (usually with praying, singing, sprinkling of blood and water) and it also includes the village, the ancestors and the gods.[652] Different sacrifices are also brought to the special water sources (*doany*), when people go there to ask for healing.[653]

For a *tsiny* patient, there is also a need of reconciliation with the offended party, in addition to a sacrifice. Forgiveness is contingent on the restoring of what is broken and this is a concern for the whole

---

[650] Sharp 1993:136.

[651] For more details, refer to the chapter on possession above.

[652] Ruud 1970:272–273.

[653] See Randriantsitohaina 1992. For a more detailed description of the sacrifice in Imerina, see Rakotovao 1993:33–88.

community. The offence must be addressed and removed in public in order to restore the harmony.[654]

If the cause of sickness is sorcery or witchcraft, powerful charms serve to protect and remove the evil. Sacrifices may also be required.[655]

When evil spirits possessing their victims cause sickness and misfortune, exorcism may be necessary. The first step in dealing with exorcism of evil spirits is to protect oneself, often by a strong charm. Only when absolutely necessary a special exorcism ceremony is organised, according to J.-M. Estrade. As long as possible, the healers try to caress the spirit, to make it content and to deceive it with sacrifices. If all this is in vain, the exorcism itself is very "polite": The spirit is awakened, honoured, appeased and made happy before it is asked to leave, often by offering it a new resort. The exorcism is so careful, because the healer fears the spirit's vengeance if it feels expulsed harshly or despised.[656] According to L.A. Sharp, an angry *tromba* spirit or a sorcerer may have sent the evil spirits and they cause temporary fits of possession. If the cause of the illness is diagnosed to stem from such spirits, the group of people around the sick provides a united front against the spirit and they try to give the victim strength to resist possession. They also arrange for exorcism as soon as possible. If these spirits are allowed to stay, they can cause madness and death.[657]

---

[654] Rasolondraibe 1989:347. Repentance and confession of sins are familiar concepts in connection with sacrifices. This is believed to ease complicated situations and "clear the heart", in order to let the force of the good flow freely. See also Ruud 1970:273.

[655] Rasolondraibe 1989:346–347.

[656] Estrade 1985:99–101. Estrade underlines that it is in line with Malagasy thinking to persuade, discuss and try to move the unwanted politely, instead of expelling and suppressing.

[657] Madness is according to Sharp's observations caused by external attacks from angry spirits. It is considered an extremely dangerous state of being. Sharp 1994:528. Sharp has observed that the healing process for people possessed by evil spirits called *Njarinintsy* is especially difficult. The spirits are uncooperative and the healer tries to strike a bargain with them. The healer presents gifts or leaves some goods in strategic places and by this he/she will make the spirit content so that it may leave the victim. Often several visits to different healers are necessary and when one spirit is driven out, there are often more left, since these spirits are said to work in groups of seven. Sharp 1993:141–142.

4.1.2 Biblical message

The purpose of the following presentation is to describe elements in the biblical message, which is part of the church into which the shepherds have been socialised and thus makes up the second part of the wider context influencing their understanding. I will do this through a close-to-the-text description of selected elements in the biblical material with relevance to exorcism.[658] It will be done in the tradition of biblical theology and mainly scholars in a conservative theological tradition, together with standard reference works, will be the sources for the presentation,[659] as argued for in the Introduction.[660]

In my close-to-the-text presentation I will be using P.G. Hiebert's model of a Biblical View of Spiritual Warfare as a theoretical point of departure. His model seems well suited to render a presentation of elements in the biblical message with relevance to exorcism.[661]

---

[658] Little weight will be put on the extra-biblical political, economical, social and religious contexts of the selected themes.

[659] The best way to delineate the biblical material might have been to study and present the kind of biblical message, which is prevailing in the Malagasy Lutheran Church today. Since this would be a new comprehensive project, however, I am not in a position to accomplish such a study.

[660] See 1.3.3.2. Some of the special Malagasy colouring of this message may become apparent when the "biblical message" is used as a tool of interpretation in a tentative analysis of selected elements in the shepherds' exorcism. Cf. 4.6.

[661] Hiebert's model with explanation and commentaries is found in Hiebert 2000:249–253.

Biblical View of Spiritual Warfare

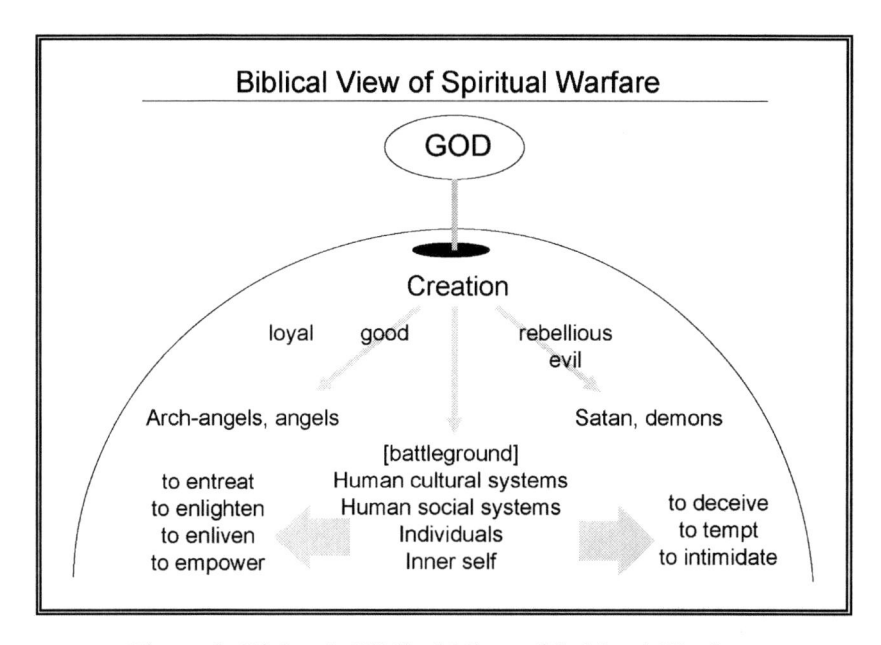

```
                    GOD
                     |
                 Creation
      loyal      good      rebellious
                            evil
 Arch-angels, angels        Satan, demons
                 [battleground]
  to entreat   Human cultural systems
  to enlighten Human social systems    to deceive
  to enliven   Individuals             to tempt
  to empower   Inner self              to intimidate
```

Figure 2: Hiebert's Biblical View of Spiritual Warfare
Model adapted from P.G. Hiebert and used by permission

Hiebert consciously delimits the presentation and is not attempting to include all elements in a biblical worldview.[662] Hiebert states the main points in the model as follows: God is eternal and good, creator and distinct from creation. On the level of creation, there has been a rebellion, which caused a break between good and evil. Satan, sin and sinners appear in creation. The biblical accounts of human rebellion and sin appear to a little extent in Hiebert's model. He only mentions Satan and demons in connection with "rebellious" and "evil" and may seem to leave out humans. This makes it somewhat obscure as to whether Hiebert's view of a "fall" only concerns cosmic history, or if the human rebellion against God is implied in his model. In his comments on the model, however, Hiebert talks about the humans as rebels, ever since the temptation of Adam and he states that the central story in the Bible is about God, humans and their acts, not about angels and demons.[663] Satan

---

[662] To what extent is it possible to talk about a biblical worldview? Is there only one worldview present in the biblical material or is it possible to trace different worldviews? And what is the relation between a biblical worldview/biblical worldviews and Christian worldviews? Limitation of space does not allow me to enter into this discussion but see Kraft 1996:67–68.

[663] Hiebert 1994:211, 208.

174   CH. 4: THE SHEPHERDS' UNDERSTANDING OF THEIR PRACTICE

and demons engage in a cosmic struggle with God and his angels. This battle is not about power, however, because God is sovereign. The battle is about establishing God's reign on earth. The weapons used and the goals of the two sides are contradictory. Satan deceives, tempts and intimidates people to prevent them from entering God's kingdom. God, on the other hand, uses the weapons of truth to enlighten and empower people, inviting them to the kingdom of God. The battleground is human cultural and social systems and human individuals. Humans are not passive victims but active and co-operative in the battle, permitting either God or the devil to have authority over their lives. It is not apparent in the model, but Hiebert argues strongly that according to the Bible the cross of Jesus is God's ultimate victory over the devil. It is a victory through weakness. On the cross Jesus carried the sins of the world and triumphed over all powers of evil. Hiebert says that if our understanding of "spiritual warfare" does not see the cross as the final triumph, it is wrong.[664]

The mentioned elements concerning the battle between good and evil seem to be relevant in the Malagasy Lutheran church, into which the shepherds have been socialised. I will briefly show some examples of this.[665]

The concept of God as creator is taken for granted by the shepherds.[666] On the level of creation, there has been a rebellion against the creator, which caused a break between good and evil. The humans' rebellion and fall are reiterating themes and dualistic vocabulary to

---

[664] As for presenting a biblical worldview, which takes the demonic dimension serious, Yung Hwa establishes 7 elements: 1. God is the creator of all things, visible and invisible. 2. Much of the created world has rebelled against God. 3. There is no metaphysical dualism. God is in power. 4. The universe is open and should not be divided into natural and supernatural phenomena. 5. Sin entered the world through the fall and sin is spiritual, psychological, social and ecological. 6. Jesus has conquered all powers on the cross. This is the root of Christian confidence when confronted with evil spirits. 7. Christian warfare depends on relationship to and belief in God, not human techniques. Hwa 2000:3–5. The resemblance between Hwa's 7 elements and Hiebert's model and explanations are striking.

[665] To support the relevance of the main themes from Hiebert's model as a theoretical point of departure, I refer briefly to my participant observation of testimonies/sermons in healing services. Cf. 3.1.3.

[666] God's essense and activities are not often referred to, but God and Jesus are talked of almost synonymously. God's continuing creation can be seen behind the words that "God gives us everything". Ambohimahazo *toby* 22 March 1993.

describe God and Satan, perfection and sin is used.[667] The shepherds presuppose an ongoing, cosmic battle between good and evil on an unseen level.[668] Humans are not considered defenceless in this battle. They can permit either God or Satan to rule in their lives and the shepherds are constantly urging people to let Jesus reign.[669] The battleground according to the model is human cultural and social systems, individuals and inner self. In the shepherds' perception, the main battleground between good and evil seems to be human individuals. Human cultural and social systems are to a great extent absent, while the battle within the inner self seems to be a matter of discussion.[670] Jesus' victory on the cross is a prominent theme in the shepherds' teaching and they have no doubt about who is the strongest one in the battle.[671]

4.1.2.1 *The concept of God*

J.J. Scullion asserts that "the one, exclusive, and only God is the centre of true Israelite religion".[672] He is no impersonal force, but has a personal name, by which he can be worshipped (Ex 3:15).[673] The God of Israel tolerates no other (Ex 20:3). The case is crystallised to such extent that Deutero-Isaia asserts there exist no other gods than Israel's God. The presumed gods are only ineffective works of human hands (Is 40:19–20).[674] The monotheism of the OT is everywhere assumed in the NT.[675]

---

[667] "God walks by our side, but the Devil will tempt us to fall." Ambohimahazo *toby* 10 May 1993.

[668] "Jesus is stronger than the Devil". Ambohimahazo *toby* 15 March 1993. Another preacher talks about "the power of darkness and Satan". Antananavio, Log 238, 67 Ha 07 April 1993.

[669] "The Devil will tempt us to fall." Ambohimahazo *toby* 10 May 1993. "Do not sin any more!". Ambohimahazo *toby* 13 September 1993.

[670] To the relation between bad habits and demonic involvement, see 4.4.3.3. A female shepherd talks about a boy "assaulted by demons" who was about to commit suicide, but she chased away the devil. The biblical passage she referred to was Is 59:1–2 about iniquities and sins, which make a separation between God and humans. Ambohimahazo *toby* 08 March 1993.

[671] "Jesus is stronger than the Devil." Ambohimahazo *toby* 15 March 1993. "Jesus has taken poverty, sickness and suffering with him on the cross." Ambohimahazo *toby* 25 June 1998.

[672] Scullion 1992:1042.

[673] Childs 1992:355.

[674] Scullion 1992:1042–1043.

"Creation marked the beginning of time, the start of an ongoing history, and the moment of origin before which there was no such reality apart from God".[676] Gen 1:1 draws a clear distinction between God and "not-God": "In the beginning God".[677] The world as a whole is God's and willed by him and he has arranged it as a good dwelling-place. The created world is the scene of God's activities and God as creator does not only refer to his work in the beginning. Creation is a fundamental aspect of all God's activities. God is caring for his world.[678] God is creator and sustainer (Ps 104). Because God is creator, he is Lord of the universe and history.[679] There is a close link between God as creator and redeemer. According to Deutero-Isaia, God redeems because he is the creator. In Is 45:14–25 the words "save", "rescue" and "Saviour" stand in close relation to God's creative activity and the Hebrew verb to create, בָּרָא, is used 17 times in Deutero-Isaia. As creator, God is the source of life and he is the life-giver (Rom 4:17).[680] The presence of God's life-restoring power is seen in the Gospels, in healings, exorcisms and resuscitations (Mk 5:1–20, especially v.15).[681]

God's uniqueness and creative activity show that there are no other powers at his side. Everything is subordinated to him. His concern for all creatures is rooted in creation and his purpose is to rescue.

4.1.2.2 Rebellion against God

Human sin is a reiterating theme in nearly every book of the OT, it is depicted as universal and as the fundamental human problem.[682] The basic characteristic of sin is found in Gen 3. It is the human aspiration to be like God, the self-centredness. The humans rebel in this way, turn their back on God and put the Ego on the throne. And the humans are

---

[675] Childs 1992:362.
[676] Childs 1992:385.
[677] Scullion 1992:1043.
[678] Hafner 1989:1385.
[679] Scullion 1992:1044–1045.
[680] Rom 4:17 is very close to the theme of *creatio ex nihilo*, a thought first found in 2 Macc 7:28. Childs 1992:391, Kratz and Spieckermann 1999.
[681] Bassler 1992:1051–1052.
[682] Cover 1992:33.

held responsible for what they have done.[683] The consequences of the human's disobedience were spiritual, psychological, social and ecological (Gen 3:7–19) and changed their lives fundamentally.[684] The story of Gen 3 plays a minor role in the rest of the OT,[685] but in Paul's view all men became sinners in Adam (Rom 5:12).[686] In the NT, the victory over sin through Jesus Christ is a main theme.

Gen 6:1–4 became a source of intense speculation in later centuries of Israel's history.[687] It is an obscure passage and some scholars see in this and a few other passages allusions to a "fall" of supernatural authorities.[688] B. Abijole maintains that the root cause of the disorderliness in the cosmos is the "fall" of man. The angels fell on the account of men and this was part of the cosmic "fall".[689] Y. Hwa presupposes that Satan and his minions have rebelled against God and he maintains that the humans' "fall" gave Satan authority over human lives and societies, but he admits that the Bible nowhere teaches this explicitly.[690] It has to be concluded that the relationship between the human's "fall" and a proposed cosmic "fall" is not clear from the biblical writings. Humans are in focus in the biblical accounts of rebellion and

---

[683] Unidentified 1989:1501. It was not until in later rabbinic sources that Satan was identified with the serpent in the garden of Eden. Hamilton 1992:988.

[684] Hwa 2000:4.

[685] Childs 1992:570. The problem of the origins of sin seemed to be of little relevance to the Israelite theologians before the Second Temple period. Human sinfulness was instead connected with its creatureliness. Cover 1992:33.

[686] Ladd 1975:568; 403–404.

[687] Allusions to this material in the NT are 1 Pet 3:19–20; 2 Pet 2:4. Bauckham 1983:50–51.

[688] O'Brian 1992:381 refers in addition to 2 Pet and Jude 6 also to Col 1:15–20, where a serious dislocation or break has to be implied and Col 2:15, which implies a rebellion against the creator before the disarming of the principalities and powers. P.T. O'Brian does not make clear if he sees this cosmic "fall" as prior or subsequent to the human "fall". I.H. Marshall says about Lk 10:18 that if it is understood as a vision, it may refer to an experience in Christ's pre-existent life. He also thinks that behind the battle in heaven, as told in Rev 12:7–10, 13, is the myth of the "fall" of Lucifer from heaven. There is a close relationship between Lk 10:18 and Jesus' exorcisms. Marshall 1986:428–429.

[689] Abijole 1988:123–124. His references to the angels' "fall" are Enoch and 2 Baruch and no biblical passage.

[690] Hwa 2000:4, 11. The same presupposition is found in G.E. Ladd, who says that the rebellious state of the world is not only due to the "fall" of man, but also to "the rebellious state of a portion of the angelic world". Ladd 1975:402.

178   CH. 4: THE SHEPHERDS' UNDERSTANDING OF THEIR PRACTICE

sin, while allusions to a cosmic "fall" are few and primarily relate to extra-biblical writings. The Bible provides no real answer to the origin of Satan and other demonic spirits.[691]

4.1.2.3   Cosmic battle

There are allusions in the OT to battles with the sea, chaos or other personalised demonic forces (Ps 89:10) and war imagery is found (Is 59:16–19).[692] In the Gospels a battle between God and Satan is seen especially in Jesus' exorcisms and Paul describes the Christian life as a battle "against the spiritual hosts of wickedness in the heavenly places." (Eph 6:11–12). Revelation gives visions of the spiritual powers at work behind the scenes of human history and the spiritual conflict is depicted as a conflict between Michael and the Dragon (Rev 12).[693] Thus, the existence of unseen, evil powers in opposition to the Lord and his followers is made clear in the Bible.

Satan and his kingdom. In the NT a "kingdom of Satan" with a uniform evil purpose to oppose God and his kingdom emerges.[694] The kingdom of Satan is organised on a cosmic scale,[695] and individual demons have no relative autonomy, but are subject to Satan.[696] The powers of evil in the NT are referred to with a remarkable variety of terminology.[697]

G. von Rad summarises the OT-teaching of Satan by saying "that in the true religious world of Israel the figure of the heavenly satan is not of central importance, and that there is thus no rigid consistency in the conception of this figure …". "It is striking how rarely the satan notion is

---

[691]   Hwa 2000:6–7.
[692]   Among God's attributes in the OT are warrior and king. Scullion 1992:1047. In later apocalyptic literature the imagery of conflict and battle is further elaborated as a cosmological struggle between God and Satan/Beliar with his fallen angels. Childs 1992:517.
[693]   Childs 1992:516–518, Ladd 1975:625.
[694]   Ladd 1975:50–51, Yates 1980:99.
[695]   Dunn and Twelftree 1980:222.
[696]   Foerster 1979a:18.
[697]   See Yates 1980:97 and Ladd 1975:401–402.

expressed in the OT."[698] In the few places he occurs, he is clearly connected with sin.[699]

Satan is mentioned 35 times by name in the NT, in addition to the use of ὁ διάβολος 32 times.[700] There are also a number of other titles attributed to him: "prince of this world" (Jn 12:31), "the prince of demons" (Mt 12:24), "the god of this world" (2 Cor 4:4),[701] and "the prince of the power of the air" (Eph 2:2). These titles seem to express that Satan has a hold on this world (this age), as is also expressed in Lk 4:5–6.[702] It also suggests a centralisation of all powers of evil under the leadership of one single will, as is seen in the attribution to Satan of a kingdom of evil (Mt 12:26). W. Foerster maintains that, "all the functions ascribed to Satan in Judaism are found again in the NT".[703] There is an absolute antithesis between God and Satan in the NT and the central purpose of Satan's activities is to hinder the Gospel and cause man's destruction and alienation from God.[704] It should be observed that Satan's reign is limited: he is judged (Jn 16:11), his power in humans' lives may be broken (Acts 26:18), he may be resisted (Eph 4:27), God may use Satan as his instrument (1 Tim 1:20) and his final defeat is in sight (Rev 20:9–10).

There are remarkably few references to demons in the OT and they appear only on the margins of the writings.[705] There is no connection in

---

[698] von Rad 1979:74.

[699] Hamilton 1992:986–987. The evolution of thought in the Apocrypha and Pseudepigrapha is interesting but restriction of space does not allow me to elaborate on this here. See Hamilton 1992:987–988, Foerster 1979b:75–78, Nel 1987:8–12.

[700] There seems to be no material distinction between the two. Foerster 1979b:79.

[701] The Greek word underlying the English translation "world" here is αἰών, which means this "age" and refers to the eschatological dualism underlying much of the NT thought. Ladd 1975:45–48.

[702] It is discussed as to whether this verse means that Satan has dominion over the world, or if he only lies. Y. Hwa suggests that he rules over a limited part of the world: "the 'world' of humankind in rebellion against God". He maintains that human sin gave Satan authority over human lives. Hwa 2000:10–11.

[703] Foerster 1979b:80.

[704] Foerster 1979b:79, Yates 1980:102.

[705] Foerster 1979a:10–11 sees a reason for this in the expulsion of witches in the days of Saul, as may be seen in 1 Sam 28:13.

the OT between demons and the figure of Satan.[706]

As a whole, the NT refers infrequently to demons, compared with much literature at that time, except in the possession narratives in the Synoptics.[707] A marked feature in the NT is that demons and evil spirits/evil angels are completely subject to Satan. They are not acting on their own, but form a unity under Satan and they are part of a kingdom of evil. Spirits of the dead and individual seducing spirits are not spoken of. Evil thoughts come from the human heart (Mt 15:19) and even though sin and flesh are considered as individual forces, they do not come from outside the human.[708] The subjection of demons under Satan is especially evident in the Be-el'zebul-controversy (Mt 12:24–29), where Jesus makes clear that two kingdoms stand in opposition to each other. Jesus regarded the casting out of demons from possessed people as a defeat of the kingdom of Satan. In spite of Jesus' victory over the demonic and the certainty of their final judgement (Mt 25:41), there is still a continuing battle going on (Mt 13:36–43). In the Gospels, demons are described as causing various physical afflictions (Mt 8:28). The NT gives no precise solution to the relation between sickness and demonisation, but it is clear that not all sickness stems from demons.[709] Certain individuals are said to "have" unclean spirits (Mk 1:23–26). The demons are spiritual beings and in several of the possession narratives they show knowledge, especially about who Jesus is, that is not common knowledge (Mk 1:24). Paul refers to demons in connection with idolatry and sees demons behind paganism (1 Cor 10:20–21). There seems to be an increase in demonic activity in the end time (1 Tim 4:1; Rev 16:13–14).[710] In the biblical writings there is no speculative interest in the powers of evil.

---

[706] Kuemmerlin-McLean 1992:140. To Pseudepigraphical Judaism, see Foerster 1979a:14–16, Dunn and Twelftree 1980:216, Ferguson 1984: 77–78, 94–95.

[707] Foerster 1979a:16, Reese 1992:140.

[708] Foerster 1979a:16, 18.

[709] Reese 1992:140–141, Foerster 1979a:18.

[710] Paul has summed up the powers of evil in his concept "principalities and powers" and suggests by this that they are united to a single will. Yates 1980:102–103. The content of this concept will be commented on below. Cf. 4.1.2.4 (Human cultural and social systems). It should be noticed, however, that Paul's many designations of supernatural beings do not suggest neither orders of angelic beings nor different kinds or ranks. Paul's main interest is to show Christ's victory over all evil. Ladd 1975:402.

Evil beings are recognised, but the interest is focused on their defeat in the person of Jesus Christ.[711]

God and his kingdom. The opening words of Jesus' public mission focused on the kingdom of God: "The time is fulfilled, and the kingdom of God is at hand; repent, and believe in the gospel" (Mk 1:15). By these words, Jesus established a connection to the concept of the two ages, found in Rabbinic literature and this constituted a framework of his ministry according to the Synoptic Gospels. The age to come and the kingdom of God sometimes seem to be interchangeable concepts and stand in opposition to the present evil age (Gal 1:4). The background in Hebrew-Jewish thought is that humankind in this age is dominated by sin, evil and death and is in need of rescue.[712] In the preceding paragraph I have shown that one of the characteristic features in the NT teaching of evil powers is that they form a kingdom under the rule of Satan. The main purpose of this evil kingdom is to destroy God's redemptive purpose with humankind and thus there is a cosmic battle going on between two opposing kingdoms. G.E. Ladd says that "the theology of the Kingdom of God is essentially one of conflict and conquest over the kingdom of Satan" and that this fundamental struggle is a vital part in Jesus' message of the coming of the Kingdom.[713] In Jewish pre-Christian views there is a strong expectation of an age, when Satan will be bound and his power broken.[714] Jesus declares in Mt 12:28–29, a passage containing the essential theology of the kingdom of God, that he has "bound the strong man" especially through his exorcisms. But "the whole mission of Jesus ... constituted an initial defeat of satanic power that makes the final outcome and triumph of God's kingdom certain".[715] Jesus' defeat of Satan is a victory in the spiritual world, but it is fought in history, because humankind is involved in the struggle. In his exorcisms Jesus confronted the kingdom of Satan directly. The exorcisms should not be seen as isolated incidents of Jesus' liberating power but as a demonstration of the presence and power of the kingdom of God.[716]

---

[711] Ladd 1975:51.
[712] Ladd 1975:46–48.
[713] Ladd 1975:51, 52.
[714] Ferguson 1984:95.
[715] Ladd 1975:66.
[716] Reese 1992:141. The above understanding of the kingdom of God prevents any reduction of the teaching of the kingdom to a general spiritual or moral category. It

A part of the angelic world has not rebelled against God and his purposes. These are the good angels.[717] In the NT there is a marked distinction between angels and demons and angels are generally seen as God's messengers.[718] They are incidental characters, mainly concentrated to the story of redemption and there is no systematic teaching on angels. Their main focus is salvation of humankind (Lk 15:10). Angels will have special functions in the end time and in the final judgement (Rev 10:1–7; Mt 13:41) and they are portrayed as warriors and with military imagery (Mt 26:53; Rev 19:14). In a final battle Michael and his angelic hosts will defeat the devil and his angels (Rev 12:7–9).[719]

Dualism. The strict monotheism of the OT does not leave any room for a metaphysical dualism. There is only one power, Yahweh, who created both darkness and light (Is 45:7).[720] The references to evil opposing forces in Is 27:1 seem to imply an ongoing cosmic battle, the result of which is certain: Yahweh is in power and one day this will be apparent to all.[721]

An eschatological dualism underlies redemptive history, as it is found in the NT: The contrast is between this (evil) age and the age to come, which Jesus has brought in a preliminary way by his coming to earth. No cosmological dualism is implied in this, because this world is not sinful in itself.[722] The world is God's creation and thus it is God's. But it has turned away from the creator and become a slave of evil powers. Ladd sums up the biblical dualism by saying that

> Neither in Judaism nor in the New Testament does this antithetical kingdom of evil opposing the Kingdom of God become an absolute dualism. The fallen

---

is in the centre of Jesus' message and is closely knit to his redemptive and liberating activity to save humankind. Dunn and Twelftree 1980:220.

[717] Ladd 1975:402.

[718] Foerster 1979a:16. Cf. Hiebert's model in 4.1.2.

[719] Newsom 1992:253–254.

[720] Dunn and Twelftree 1980:215. The major solution to the problem of evil was sought in the eschatological future, by believing in a God, whose ways and purposes transcended human understanding (Job 42:2–3). Watson 1992:678.

[721] Scullion 1992:1047. To the emergence of a dualistic theory of reality developed in the Apocrypha and Pseudepigrapha, see Nel 1987:9–12, Newsom 1992:251, 253.

[722] The Greek thought distinguished between the noumenal and the phenomenal world and the material world was a hindrance to the soul. This dualism was elaborated in Gnostic thought, where the material world in itself became evil. Ladd 1975:54.

angels are helpless before the power of God and his angels. In the New Testament, all such spiritual powers are creatures of God and therefore subject to his power. In the apocalyptic literature, they will meet their doom in the day of judgement.[723]

There is an ongoing cosmic battle between God and his angels and Satan and the demons. This battle is not about power because God is in absolute power, he has created all beings and the final judgement of evil forces is certain. The battle is about God's people, the human beings created by God.[724] The battleground is the world of humans.

4.1.2.4 Battleground

The biblical emphasis is primarily on humans as agents of evil powers and not on impersonal structures. Allusions to evil structures seem to be vague and not very frequent.[725]

Human cultural and social systems. Satan may work through the events of history. Jesus' ministry had relevance also to the political, economic and social structures. Both Jewish groups and the Roman government resisted him and the role of Satan is directly suggested in his entering into Judas (Lk 22:3). 1 Cor 2:8 seems to suggest a relationship between demonic powers and historical events. Even though the "rulers of this age" here may denote demonic powers, it is not unlikely that Jew and Roman authorities are also in sight as instruments bringing Jesus to the cross. According to Yates, Paul uses the words "principalities" and "powers" (Eph 6:12) "to lay special emphasis on the pressures which are brought to bear on the individual by the various social, religious and political collectives in which his life is involved; with particular emphasis on the political life of man".[726] Paul also seems to use the word

---

[723] Ladd 1975:50.
[724] See Ladd above. Hiebert 2000:250. This was also true in the community of Qumran, see Nel 1987:10.
[725] O'Brian 1992:384. According to Y. Hwa, an identification of evil with human structures may have erroneous consequences and restrict the activities of Satan. A demythologising of the texts only to structural evil does not render the biblical perspective of personal evil spiritual beings correctly, but it has still to be maintained that social structures and human institutions can be oppressive to human life. Hwa 2000:7.
[726] Yates 1980:103.

κόσμος as a wider concept, including the whole of human's earthly relationships, the world systems created by men (1 Cor 7:31). All worldly relations are transitory and should not be the centre of a human's deepest satisfaction. The true source of life must be sought on a higher level, because the world can stand between man and God (Phil 2:4–7).[727] The development from the state as the minister of God in Rom 13 to the state as an evil force in Rev 13 seems to suggest that earthly structures can become demonic.[728] Paul believes that all these powers, as created beings, are subject to Christ and he states firmly that they are unable to separate the believer from God's love in Jesus Christ (Rom 8:38–39).

Human individuals.[729] There is no teaching on the human as such in the NT. Humans are always seen in relation to God and as created by God evaluated highly.[730] A fundamental presupposition, however, is the fallen condition of man. The universal sinfulness of all humankind is spelled out in detail by Paul in Rom 1:18–3:20. This corresponds with the Synoptics' testimony (Mt 7:11) and John's talk about man living in darkness (Jn 3:19). Man is ruled by sin, in Paul considered as a personified power (Rom 7:15–20). The concept of sin places the human in the centre of the battle of allegiances.[731] It is on this basis that Jesus summons all men to repentance and belief in him. "Unless you repent you will all ... perish." (Lk 15:5). The whole of Jesus' coming and mission is thus seen in the perspective of salvation: "He has delivered us from the dominion of darkness and transferred us to the kingdom of his beloved Son," (Col 1:13). The battlefield is human individuals .

"In the Synoptics, the most characteristic evidence of the power of Satan is the ability of demons to take possession of the centre of men's personalities."[732] When a person is said to "have a demon" or is

---

[727] Ladd 1975:399–400.

[728] O'Brian 1992:384.

[729] The NT stands in the OT tradition, which considers man as a psychosomatic unity. When the NT uses different words to describe the human being, this is only "different ways to speak of the entire unified, integrated person". Taylor 1992:321. Because of this, I do not follow Hiebert's distinction in the model between "human individuals" and "inner self", but deals with the human under one heading.

[730] Taylor 1992:321.

[731] The exorcisms show to what extent "the realm of Satan and the demonic had gained a hold on the lives of men and women". Yates 1980:99. "We may think of this world as enemy-occupied territory." Ferguson 1984:22–23.

[732] Ladd 1975:51.

"demonised", it should not be associated with ownership, but rather with influence, control and domination over the person exercised by a demon.[733] This is not the place for a detailed analysis of the possession-exorcism accounts in the Gospels.[734] Suffice it here to comment briefly the much-debated relation between sickness and demon-possession because this is especially relevant in the shepherds' practice. In some cases sickness/infirmities seem to be a direct result of demon-possession: dumbness (Mt 9:32), dumbness and blindness (Mt 12:22) and epilepsy (Mt 17:15–18). Summary statements list demoniacs alongside other diseases and thus suggest that not all illness were attributed to evil spirits (Mt 4:24). The terminology used by the different writers is not consistent and O. Skarsaune suggests that if we take terminology as a point of departure, the border between sickness and possession seems to be blurred. When taking the phenomenon of demon-possession as a starting point, however, there seems to be two distinct categories of mighty acts: healings and exorcisms, each with their own structure.[735] The decisive point in the accounts of demon-possessed in the NT is to show Jesus' power over the demons, demonstrated in his exorcisms, which set individuals free and brought them back to normality. Jesus considered every exorcism as a defeat of Satan (Mt 12:22–29). According to J.D.G. Dunn and G.H. Twelftree the label "possession" should be reserved to those cases where an individual is totally dominated by an evil power.[736]

Possession is only one of Satan's strategies, however. The goal of Satan and his minions is to keep men away from the blessings of the kingdom of God and this will ultimately lead to destruction. All possible means are used to obtain this goal. The devil's temptation of Jesus, in order to lead him away from the divinely appointed mission, is the paradigm for the tempting of humans (Lk 4:1–12). Deceit, lies, accusations, disguise, disturbance of the reception of God's word, moral

---

[733] Reese 1992:140.

[734] See Twelftree 1993:53–129, where the NT data are dealt with.

[735] Skarsaune suggests that in the Synoptics the two concepts "possession" and "exorcism" should define and delimit each other mutually, in the sense of only talking of possession where exorcism is the adequate solution. Skarsaune 1997:165–166. To the question of possession and sickness, see Reese 1992:140–141, Thomas 2000:3–4, Ladd 1975:51–52.

[736] Dunn and Twelftree 1980:217. Dunn mentions the evil power using the individual's vocal chords, convulsing him/her and exercising superhuman strength as criteria.

disorder in the church, idolatry and magic are all demonic weapons.[737] The NT uses a varied vocabulary to describe demonic attacks on individuals,[738] the goal is always to get control over the person and man cannot free himself from the satanic yoke (Jn 8:34).[739] The death of Christ, however, defeated the evil powers and only belief in God's salvation can conquer them.

When baptised, believers enter a new sphere of life, where the evil powers do not rule. Thus baptism is an initial victory and Christians are summoned to live the baptismal life every day by renouncing sin (Rom 6:3–11).[740] Satan may thus be resisted, following the example of Jesus (Eph 4:27) and there are many warnings and exhortations in the Bible to oppose evil (Rom 16:19–20; 1 Pet 5:8–9). The most clear of these is perhaps Eph 6:11–13:

> Put on the whole armor of God, that you may be able to stand against the wiles of the devil. For we are not contending against flesh and blood, but against the principalities, against the powers, against the world rulers of this present darkness, against the spiritual hosts of wickedness in the heavenly places. Therefore take the whole armor of God ...

The evil forces are referred to here as a dreadful reality, but they constitute no threat to those who believe in the victorious Christ. Natural strength will not suffice to resist these forces, only divinely imparted strength, here concretised in a metaphorical use of armour. It is envisaged that as long as believers reside in this world, these "world rulers of the present darkness" will do their best to reclaim the people of Christ.[741] This tension between "now" and "not yet" is found in the Christian's relationship to the evil powers. The forces are subjugated to Christ and deprived of their power (Col 2:15). Yet the conflict continues and the final victory resides in the future (1 Cor 15:24). This same

---

[737] See above "Satan and his kingdom" for biblical references. In Acts 13:10 the sorcerer is called a "son of the devil". Foerster 1979b:80.

[738] S.A. Moreau gives an extensive list of Greek terms and he groups the attacks in four categories, according to activities: attacks on our holiness, on our functioning in ministry, on our person: gaining entry and on our person: enslaving. Moreau 1990:191–194, 85–90. It seems as Moreau primarily focuses on the believer in this grouping and humankind as such is to a certain degree absent. Cf. the listing of Satanic/demonic work in the world in Hwa 2000:7–8.

[739] Foerster 1979b:79.

[740] Abijole 1988:126.

[741] Bruce 1984:403–407.

conflict is found in each believer, since the flesh stays with him/her even after he/she has received the Holy Spirit (Gal 5:17).[742] Christians are called to live in this tension, in accordance with Christ's victory and in this way contribute to the final defeat of the powers.[743]

Mt 12:43–45 seems to underline that exorcism is not sufficient, seen in the wider framework of the NT. The positive force of the kingdom of God must replace the evil force of demons.[744] It is the Holy Spirit who banishes the powers of evil and gives the strength to live a new way of life (Rom 8; Gal 5).[745] Yates maintains that the majority of the references to evil powers in the NT concern this new way of life to be lived by Christians. In the young churches of Paul there was a constant threat to fall back to old fashioned ways of life and exhortations to let Christian virtues flourish are reiterated. Thus, a new way of life with good conduct is a major way of resisting Satan in the power of Christ (1 Jn 3:10).[746]

4.1.2.5 *The cross of Jesus*

God's ultimate goal with his kingdom is visible at the cross: the reconciliation of humankind, which constitutes the victory over the evil powers.[747] Jesus' prayer in Gethsemane shows his death to be God's plan (Mk 14:36) and Jesus knew that the death was the goal of his mission.[748] In light of the NT writings, atonement for sins (penal substitution) seems to be the basic model for understanding Jesus' death,[749] but another aspect is visible in some passages: his death is a defeat of evil powers:

---

[742] It should be noticed that this conflict is not between the flesh (σὰρξ) and the human spirit, but between the flesh and God's spirit. Thus this conflict only rages in the believers, who have received the Holy Spirit. Ladd 1975:469, 472. I suppose that it is this conflict within the human that Hiebert has called "inner self" in his model.

[743] Yates 1980:104.

[744] Yates 1980:106–107.

[745] Ferguson 1984:26–27.

[746] Yates 1980:110.

[747] Yates 1980:103, Hiebert 2000:252.

[748] Ladd 1975:249.

[749] In G.E. Ladd's NT theology, e.g,. he spends a quarter of a page to Jesus' death as a victory (in John) and one and a half page to the triumphant Christ (in the Pauline writings), while he reserves several chapters to other understandings of the cross. Ladd 1975:192, 434–436.

the Christus Victor model.[750] In short, this model takes its point of departure in the NT teaching of humanity under the power of Satan. Christ fought against and triumphed over the evil powers and in his death Jesus gave Satan a fatal blow. Christ's death is seen here primarily as the defeat of all hostile spiritual forces, which are thought to be the root cause of humans' problems. Those who believe in Christ share in his victory.[751] Fridrichsen argues that, from a historical perspective, it is probable that Jesus himself considered his death as the consummation of the fight with Satan.[752]

In Heb 2:14 the prince of death is identified with the devil whom Jesus destroyed through his death.[753] Col 2:15 makes it clear that Jesus triumphed over the cosmic powers on the cross: "He disarmed the principalities and powers and made a public example of them, triumphing over them in him."[754] The cross, as an instrument of disgrace and death where evil powers may seem to have conquered Jesus, was turned into an instrument which defeated the powers by him. In spite of the apparent weakness of the cross, Jesus triumphed and displayed to the universe the helplessness of all evil powers.[755]

How could the death of Jesus be conceived of as a victory over Satan? The defeat of the powers is in Col 2:14 clearly connected with cancelling the debt of human sin by Jesus' death.[756] When all the trespasses are forgiven (Col 2:13), there is no condemnation for sin and it seems as this forgiveness of sins has disarmed the principalities and powers (Col 2:15).[757] Expiation for the sins of the people is also the context of Heb 2:14 (v.17). The meaning seems to be that Jesus, through

---

[750] Referring to the famous book of Gustav Aulèn with that name. Hwa 2000:8. This is also called the classic model, because it is found to a great extent in the patristic period. For Irenaeus this was a key motif in his development of atonement and it seems like many early Christians thought that deliverance from demons was more important than deliverance from sins. Ferguson 1984:124, 127.

[751] Hwa 2000:8.

[752] Fridrichsen 1929:305–312.

[753] Bruce 1964:49–50.

[754] ἐν αὐτω can be read as either pointing to Christ ("in him") or to the cross ("in it"). Bruce 1984:108. Either way, the focus here is Jesus on the cross (v.14).

[755] Bruce 1984:110–111.

[756] Ferguson 1984:157.

[757] It will lead too far here to expose the theology of atonement. It should be enough to underline that forgiveness of sins is a major theme in many passages, which understands Jesus' death as a victory over the devil.

removing the humans' sin, destroyed the power of the devil. This constituted a victory over Satan, which was the purpose of Jesus' appearance.[758]

Col 1:20 seems to imply a cosmic reconciliation as the true goal of the shedding of Jesus' blood and not only the victory over all spiritual powers. If so, it underlines that God's ultimate purpose in the battle with evil is not victory but reconciliation.[759] The cross shows that in the battle between God and Satan, human sin is a central theme and that through forgiveness of sins Satan has lost his power over humans.[760]

Hamilton says that the death and resurrection of Jesus "constitute a victory over Satan in principle", but not until Jesus' Second Coming will all evil powers be destroyed.[761] Until then we may think of Satan as a wounded animal. He has received a mortal blow, but that makes him even more dangerous and increases his evil activity (Rev 13:3). Christians are to live in this tension between "victory in principle" by Jesus' death and the final defeat of Satan and his minions in Jesus' Second Coming.[762]

4.1.3 Summary

The unseen spirits and forces of the traditional Malagasy universe are integral parts of people's everyday life, as is seen in the widespread use of charms, the many taboos, possession cults and *tromba* possession and the need of divination in times of crisis and important moments. The spirits and forces are considered ambiguous and unpredictable and only the religious specialists are able to interpret the true meanings of what happens. In traditional culture possession by good spirits is considered positive and empowering but all spirits are potentially dangerous and it is important to get rid of evil spirits as soon as possible, sometimes by

---

[758] G.E. Ladd sees Is 53 as the background of Mk 10:45 and he maintains that the verse points to a substitutionary sacrifice for sin. He mentions, however, that the Greek fathers understood the ransom as a price paid to the devil, but he rejects this understanding on the basis of the wider NT teaching. Nowhere else is it found that Jesus' life was paid to the devil. Ladd 1975:187–188.

[759] Ferguson 1984:156–157. B. Abijole also includes Eph 3:10 as pointing to this cosmic reconciliation. Abijole 1988:125.

[760] Hiebert 2000:252.

[761] Hamilton 1992:988.

[762] Ferguson 1984:161, 163.

expulsion. The Malagasy conception of sickness is comprehensive, including a wide range of undesirable conditions and people seek, through the religious specialists, all possible means to regain health, to change destinies, to avoid the negative implications of their actions and to restore harmony. Healing is considered a prosess, where not only patient and healer are important but also the surrounding community and the spirit world.

Following Hiebert's "Biblical View of Spiritual Warfare" I have attempted a close-to-the-text presentation of the biblical message: God is unique as creator and redeemer of the universe. Humans rebelled against God and the consequences were severe. Evil beings exist but the Bible has no answer as to their origin, little demonology and relatively few references to Satan, except in the possession narratives. Evil powers constantly oppose the mission of Jesus and the NT focus is on their defeat in the person of Christ who brought the kingdom of God and bound Satan. The battle is fought in human cultural and social systems to a certain degree but the biblical emphasis is primarily on individuals as battleground. In their rebellion and sin humans are co-conspirators with evil powers and demon-possession is only one of Satan's weapons. He uses all means and every opportunity to destroy people. The cross is God's victory over evil. Through what appeared as weakness, Jesus triumphed and the paradox of the cross is the focal point in spiritual encounter. The final defeat of all evil powers awaits the consummation and until then Christians are urged to resist the devil by putting on the whole armour of God.

I have now given a brief presentation of selected elements in the two contexts, which I assert more or less influence the shepherds in their practice and understanding of exorcism: the traditional Malagasy culture and the biblical message alive in the church. I consider these elements as part of the shepherds' worldview assumptions, which to a certain degree may be unarticulated in their thinking. I have tried to make them explicit to furnish the reader with tools for deeper insight when reading the following presentation of the shepherds' understanding. They will also enable me, subsequently, to give some examples of a reasonable interpretation of the shepherds' practice and understanding in light of the two contexts.

We find elements in the preceding description of the contexts that seem to have been taken over and utilised by the shepherds in their practice and understanding of exorcism. Other elements may seem to constitute a break with traditional culture or biblical message, while some elements seem to have been joined, which will be apparent in the following presentation.

4.2 The closer context of exorcism: Christian teaching and God's word

The connection between exorcism and faith in Jesus, Christian teaching and God's word is so prominent in my material that I cannot leave it out when the purpose is to describe exorcism, as the shepherds perceive of it.[763] One of my informants says: "The devil is beaten when the Gospel is preached and people are converted. It is through conversion that the devils are driven out."[764]

The purpose of this subchapter is to describe how the shepherds explicitly connect exorcism with the Christian faith. It is divided into two headings, based on themes in the material. The first focuses on exorcism in the framework of Christian teaching and the second focuses on the actual use of the Bible in the shepherds' practice.

4.2.1 Exorcism in the framework of Christian teaching

In the following I present the role of the shepherds' teaching, both public teaching and consultations, some comments on the training of shepherds and a presentation of what shepherds understand as the most important aspects of exorcism.

4.2.1.1 *Public teaching*

The shepherds' public teaching is carried out mostly in the services at the *toby* or in the churches. "The shepherds' main task is to preach the Gospel. There will be no exorcism if the word of God is not preached

---

[763] This connection is also seen in an article on the teaching of novices, published in the church magazine, where the author lists the secrets of victory over the devil: unity with Jesus, the word of God, Jesus' name and the blood of Jesus. A.M.M.T. 1999S:9. The expression "God's word" (*ny tenin'Andriamanitra*) is much used by the shepherds to denote the words of the Bible.

[764] IS 202.

first."[765] "The basis of the revival movement is preaching of God's word and the *toby*-elders were primarily evangelists."[766] The shepherds' trust in the word of God and their underlining of this word ultimately stem from the example of Jesus who used words in both healing and exorcism.[767] "Exorcism rests on the biblical teaching and without God's word exorcism is futile (*foana*). When God's word is the basis, this word will lead to repentance and conversion."[768] In order to make the connection between Christian teaching and exorcism more visible, several churches have recently started to arrange "work and strengthening" within the liturgy of a Sunday morning service.[769]

> Preaching of the Gospel must always precede the accompanying signs according to Mk 16, exorcism can never be separated from God's word and it has to be performed in the framework of the church.[770] A continuing Christian teaching results in a grounded faith, which is necessary to prevent a person from returning to his/her former life. If the person does not continue the Christian training until his/her faith is firmly established, his/her situation will

---

[765] IS 322. Exorcism in urgent situations, often in the home of the patient, is normally only preceded by a short reading from Scriptures. IS 210 uses Acts 16:31 or Jn 20:21–23 in these cases.

[766] IS 310.

[767] IS 323.

[768] IS 311. Several non-shepherds in my material also emphasise prayer and preaching of God's word as necessary in the treatment. QN 62, QN 119. The Holy Spirit works by these means and the Holy Spirit is like a fire which devours the demons' power in a person. QN 78.

[769] Following the collection the shepherds put on their white dresses and carry out "work and strengthening". The pastor closes the service with a concluding blessing. IS 322 maintains that the philosophy behind this practice is both to show the connection between Christian teaching and exorcism and to underline that "work and strengthening" concerns the whole congregation. There is no "work and strengthening" when the service includes the Holy Communion, however. My informant has noticed that many people leave the church when the shepherds start "working". He interprets this partly as a lack of knowledge (they need more education) and partly as an indication that these people do not want to confess their sins and give their lives wholeheartedly to Jesus.

[770] *Mama* Nenilava made a close connection between the revival movement and the church and her example is to be followed. The church or the *toby* as the places of exorcism, appointed by God, is underlined in Ankaramalaza 1997:16, 40. If an urgent need arises, exorcism is allowed elsewhere but only occasionally. Treatment of sick people in the home of the shepherd needs special permission from church leaders/shepherd leaders and these sick people should be taken to healing services as often as possible.

be even worse than before.[771] God's word is like a developer, which causes the people to think through their lives. Both the law and the Gospel have to be preached and then the people are able to diagnose themselves. When this is done it is time for exorcism.[772]

It is believed that the preaching of God's word causes the evil spirits to reveal themselves.[773] One informant comments that this is the theology of the revival movement but he has observed that the demons more often manifest themselves during "work and strengthening".[774] Another tells about "work and strengthening" following a Sunday service. No observable manifestations were seen during the ordinary service but when the demons were challenged directly by the authoritative words in exorcism one person reacted with spasms (*nihetsika demonia*).[775]

4.2.1.2 *Consultations*

When patients come to the *toby* the shepherds usually have an initial consultation.[776]

> We pray and let the sick and his/her family briefly present themselves. Then the shepherds start the initial teaching and only when we have preached the Gospel, we cast out demons and pray with the laying on of hands.[777]

---

[771] The implied reference is Mt 12:43–45. The shepherds are aware of the danger of falling away from Christ and they mainly think this is due to a lack of Christian teaching to establish a firm faith. IS 312, IS 218.

[772] IS 323. This does not mean a lengthy period of Christian teaching without exorcism. Rather, the two follow each other as repeated elements in the spiritual treatment.

[773] IS 212. Several informants underline that the demons are challenged by the word of God.

[774] IS 318.

[775] IS 217. What causes evil spirits to reveal themselves seems to be a matter of controversy. Possibly, the shepherds do not only think of the sermon as God's word but also the shepherds' words in casting out demons, prayer and the singing through the whole service. Consequently, their theology of demonic manifestation through God's word seems valid to them. I will return to the question of diagnosis in 4.3.1.

[776] IS 206. The Malagasy rendering is *dinika*, "examination, consultation" (Abinal and Malzac 1930:106), which seems to include conversation about ordinary subjects but mainly spiritual guidance, concerning the Christian faith. Consultations are not delimited to the initial phase of the treatment but are seen as an integrated element all the way through the treatment. IS 323.

[777] IS 312.

Mama Nenilava's practice was to explain briefly the meaning of "work and strengthening" to the patient before engaging in exorcism and afterwards to have a lengthy consultation.[778] One informant seems to start with expulsion of demons and the laying on of hands and afterwards he continues with preaching and individual guidance.[779] Some shepherds say that when people consult them individually, they start with a profound consultation and afterwards they engage in exorcism.[780] When people come from the neighbouring districts to attend healing services in the church or at the *toby* there is normally no consultation preceeding the exorcism.[781] My informants seem to underline the importance of spiritual guidance in consultations but there seems to be controversy about whether a consultation should always precede exorcism. One shepherd explained that while conversation with the patients precedes exorcism in the Manolotrony-branch of the revival, this is not made a general rule in the Ankaramalaza-branch.[782] Sometimes the shepherds are able to discover the cause of the illness through an initial consultation.[783]

The content of the consultation may be to urge the family to mutually forgive each other if they have been in conflict, because this

---

[778] IS 323.

[779] IS 316. A brief conversation in the beginning does not need to be excluded in his practice.

[780] IS 314, IS 325.

[781] IS 314. The shepherds may know the patients living at the *toby* while people living outside the *toby* attend exorcism without any conversation with the shepherds. IN 317 maintains that the shepherds normally will know the patients' problems, either because the people themselves tell the shepherds while they still sit on the benches, or because people have had spiritual guidance with the pastor, who passes the information to the shepherds (nothing was said about confidentiality but I suppose that it was taken care of by the pastor). Lie 1981:14 maintains that the shepherds' practice of exorcism could be ameliorated if the patients always had a consultation, where the person had the possibility of confessing his/her sins, before exorcism.

[782] IS 323. The shepherd should know the sheep, the handbook says and sees the reason for this in Jesus' example. Jesus sought his sheep individually and he knew about them. It is easier for the shepherd to lead a person to conversion if the shepherd knows his/her problems. Tobilehibe 1997:100, 104. The importance of consultations in the shepherds' treatment is also underlined in Ankaramalaza 1997:15, 16 and Tobilehibe 1995:32. In Pitaka 1999:70–74 a lengthy description of *Mama* Nenilava's consultations is found and the author shows how important this aspect was in her ministry.

[783] IS 325.

may have caused the sickness.[784] Exhortations to pray, listen to God's word and to live a godly life are important elements.[785] The main objective is to urge the patients and their families to trust in the word of God by sharing this word with them and to lead them to wholeheartedly surrender to Jesus.[786] If a patient is unconscious, the shepherds will make arrangements with his/her family. These arrangements normally include advice about keeping the patient within the Christian church when he/she has recovered and if the family is non-Christian, to urge them to conversion.[787]

4.2.1.3 Training of shepherds

The quality of the Christian teaching of the patients and their families

---

[784] IS 312. "Come quickly to peace and forgive each other; then you will be healed, the word of God says." My informant does not give any reference for this verse but it is close to Jas 5:16.

[785] IS 323.

[786] IS 322. G. Haus maintains that the shepherds impose taboos on people through their teaching and when people break these taboos, they interpret this as a sin against the shepherds (and not against God). According to traditional community thinking such sins have to be confessed publicly, which means in a ritual context. Haus' point is that the shepherds make people dependent on exorcism through this teaching. Haus 2000:83. My informants have never talked of their teaching as imposing taboos on people but I have not investigated how ordinary people conceive of the shepherds' exorcism. If Haus is right, however, this may call for an even more profound biblical teaching.

[787] Cf. 4.5.2.4 (The role of the family). IG 331 tells about a family who earlier had brought their sick to a traditional healer. The deal, which the shepherds made with the family then consisted of whether the sick should continue as a Christian or return to traditional worship after recovery. If a recovered patient returns to a setting where the word of God is absent, the shepherds fear that his/her problems may return. Christian teaching in the home of the patient is important, this may augment his/her strength and the patient's own eager prayer to God seems to be able to prevent new fits. IS 206. CHIS 12 says that if she was unable to pray lengthily before going to bed she would have restless sleep. She seems to have interpreted her nightmares as stemming from demonic activity. See more of her story in 4.5.2.1 (Testimonies).

A question from a novice about the status of dreams in the Ankaramalaza-branch is answered in Ankaramalaza 1997:21–22 and it is stated clearly that the spiritual guidance should not be grounded in dreams but in God's revelation in his word. The possibility of dreams from God is not ruled out in special occasions, when God decides it necessary but it is subordinate to the word of God.

depends on the quality of the shepherd training. One informant has observed that some shepherds only use a few passages from the Bible and he infers from this that their knowledge of the Bible is too limited.[788] He sees a great danger for the movement in this and says that the task is to renew people's love for God's word. God's word has to be a guiding principle in the shepherds' lives and only theoretical knowledge will not suffice.[789] Several of my informants comment on the shepherd training.[790] During my conversation with one informant about what I had observed, he suddenly said: "If you deem the shepherds' actions to be contrary to the biblical teaching, just send them to me and I will gently instruct them."[791] This saying reveals willingness to a continuation of teaching. The continual teaching of shepherds does not seem to be given enough attention, however, both shepherds and non-shepherds underline this as a neglected area, which needs more attention in the future.[792]

4.2.1.4 The purpose of exorcism

My informants are careful in emphasising that exorcism has to be firmly grounded in the framework of Christian teaching and God's word. It is

---

[788] Cf. however, my observations of the preaching in healing services, where many different passages from the Bible are read and only a few of them occur twice. See 3.1.3.

[789] IS 210.

[790] IS 202 underlines the baptism when he teaches the novices because he sees this as the basis for the shepherds' ministry. IS 218 emphasises the fellowship in prayer, according to the model in Acts and Jesus as the pivot of the shepherds' lives and ministry. The occupation with the person of Jesus is a marked trait in the movement, especially underlined in the Ankaramalaza-branch. Several informants mention this. IS 201, IS 202.

[791] IS 200.

[792] IS 202, IS 210, QN 119. The standard two years curriculum for the shepherd training has a strong predominance of biblical teaching compared to the space granted to instructions concerning the practical performance of exorcism. Fifohazana miray ao amin'ny FFPM 2000:15–19. In this program "the shepherds' work (*asa*)", i.e. the practical part of their ministry, which in addition to exorcism also includes preaching, evangelising, visiting homes and prayer fellowship, only occupies one paragraph out of 5. The majority of Christian teaching and church history also marks Rasolondraibe 1994, while in Tobilehibe 1997 70 of 115 pages concerns Christian teaching. The rest is about exorcism. Due to space limitations I cannot elaborate on this theme. See 2.2.2.2.

CHRISTIAN TEACHING AND GOD'S WORD

against this background that they interpret the purpose of exorcism.[793]

> Exorcism assists people's faith, it shows them the truth about their lives and it underlines God's love for them. The message passed on by exorcism is that God wants people to wake up. The devil has no claim on them because they belong to Jesus.[794]
> Through exorcism the shepherds strengthen the people's minds[795] and afterwards people may be able to resist what causes trouble to them. The shepherds give strength and thus people understand that Jesus is able to help them.[796]
> The devil tries to make you think that you are lost but exorcism helps you to believe in Jesus, even if your problems are still there. Exorcism makes it plain that you have been deceived by the devil and therefore you have to be converted. When the shepherds walk around casting out demons I really remember to turn to Jesus.[797]

The above citations show that exorcism in the shepherds' understanding has many different effects, which cannot readily be observed in the expulsion of demons and the prayer with the laying on of hands. One of my informants talks about different pedagogical aspects of exorcism. "Firstly, it drives home that you are a sinner and that this sin has to be cast out.[798] Secondly, that you need to be converted every day and thirdly, it makes it clear for you that you have an enemy."[799] Conversion seems to be my informants' most reiterating theme when talking about exorcism and if exorcism does not lead people to conversion it is worth nothing.[800] This seems to be in accordance with the handbook, which

---

[793] Due to no uniform terminology in my material the following presentation may cause questions as to whether the shepherds talk about casting out of demons (the first part) or "strengthening" (the second part). As mentioned in 1.1 exorcism covers both.

[794] IS 201 says that exorcism passes on the positive elements and this is what the patients need. They already know too well the negative aspects of life.

[795] The Malagasy expression is *mampiakatra ny sainy*, which literally means "to raise the mind to a higher level". A lack of mental strength seems to be implied in the expression.

[796] IS 210.

[797] IS 202.

[798] Mal: *mila roahina io fahotana io*.

[799] IS 325 underlines that the pedagogical is only one of the aspects of exorcism. "Exorcism tells people that evil spirits are at work," IS 321 says.

[800] IS 312, IS 328. A real conversion shows in everyday life and it is not an exterior action, according to a shepherds' conference. Tobilehibe 1995:40.

198 CH. 4: THE SHEPHERDS' UNDERSTANDING OF THEIR PRACTICE

interprets "work" in a twofold way: causing people to convert (*fampibebahana*) and expelling demons. It says that what God really seeks is conversion. "Many shepherds are skilful in casting out the evil one," the handbook says, "but they do not know how to "insert" The Good One into people."[801]

> After the "work and strengthening" people have got strength to stay with Jesus, in spite of their problems and their trust in Jesus has grown stronger. Exorcism helps people lay their lives in the hands of the Lord.[802]

The purpose of the expulsion of demons in a healing service is to lead people to discover their weaknesses and be converted, to invite people to believe in Jesus and to make people firm in their faith.[803] The casting out of demons in this setting seems to be understood by some informants as a preparation to receive the second part of exorcism, i.e. the "strengthening" with the promise of the Holy Spirit and forgiveness of sins.[804] Casting out of demons aims at removing the power of the evil one to destroy the work of God. In this way the people may concentrate fully on God's gifts in God's word and the "strengthening".[805] Does the handbook focus more on the first part when it maintains that the expulsion of demons removes the obstacles for conversion?[806] One informant calls the casting out of demons a prophylactic treatment, in case spirits have had the opportunity to enter the person and this is always followed by the laying on of hands with prayer. He says that this is the way shepherds work and that this method has developed into an institution.[807] In the shepherds' practice casting out of demons and the laying on of hands should never be separated and this is based on both Mk 16:16–18 and the example of the founders.[808] Some of my informants realise that many of the people present mostly need strengthening of their

---

[801] Tobilehibe 1997:94–95. My informants' underlining of "work" as both causing people to convert and casting out demons seems to contradict Haus' observations. None of her informants distinguished between the two. Haus 2000:76.
[802] IS 311.
[803] IS 218.
[804] Ambohimahazo *toby* 08 March 1993.
[805] IS 321.
[806] Tobilehibe 1997:98.
[807] IS 214. The context of this saying is his understanding that everybody present at a healing service is treated with exorcism through an initial casting out of demons.
[808] IS 323. See 3.3.

faith.[809] Since "work and strengthening" has developed into a fixed liturgy, however, it is not possible for people to choose between the two parts. Everybody present receives both.[810]

4.2.2 The use of the Bible in the shepherds' practice

The present subchapter concentrates on my informants' actual use of the Bible when referring to exorcism.[811] The presentation here has to be distinguished from what I have previously presented as "biblical message", which furnishes a wider context of exorcism and is a tool of interpretation.[812] Most of the shepherds' explicit references to biblical passages will be found under the themes, to which they belong. I will in this subchapter point out the most frequent biblical passages used by shepherds in my material and try to show how the word of God constitutes a basic standard in their ministry. Then I give some examples of how shepherds have used biblical passages in their teaching.[813]

---

[809] IS 325.

[810] IS 321. Some of my informants point out occasions, where only "strengthening" is used, however. IS 201 says that shepherds may lay hands on a person without any preceding casting out of demons. His example is people in a healing service, who do not sit on the mats but in the second part they may ask for "strengthening". IS 312 says that if the shepherds are in a person's home they may pray for him/her without casting out demons first, if the person does not know the purpose of expelling demons.

[811] The Malagasy church is called "the church of the Bible" and the branches of the revival movement have always considered the Bible as an inspiration and a guide for their actions and as a reference for their ministry. Rajoelisoa A. especially underlines the indisputable position of the Bible in *Mama* Nenilava's ministry and he says that God's word is the backbone of every conversation with leaders in the Malagasy revival movement. He thinks that the success and permanence of the revival movement stem from the centrality of the Bible. The Norwegian missionary Dr. Borchgrevinck is cited, saying that the most remarkable thing about the revival movement is that it does not stem from the preaching of the Gospel but from the reading of the Bible. Rajoelisoa 1977–80:128–130.

[812] Cf. 4.1.2. Here (4.2.2) I present examples of the shepherds' actual use of the Bible in the context of their own experiences. I have no separate section in the book of the shepherds' references to traditional culture and the reason for this is found in the material itself. The shepherds do not seem to elaborate much on this theme, with the exception of traditional worship, which reoccurs in relation to several themes throughout my work. See however, 2.2.6.

[813] I do not include the shepherds' biblical references in sermons and testimonies in this presentation but the shepherds' preaching is considered a background. Many

4.2.2.1 Frequently used biblical passages

A general impression from my material is that the biblical universe (God's word, prayer, belief in Jesus, demons, the devil) is very much present and referred to by my informants, while direct biblical quotations are less frequent.[814] Some biblical passages/verses seem to be more used than others, however. The shepherds in my material most frequently refer to Mk 16:15–17.[815] The second most frequent is the Ger'asene demoniac in Mk 5, especially the part where the unclean spirits begged Jesus to send them into the pigs,[816] the boy with the dumb spirit in Mk 9, especially his convulsions and Jesus' words that "this kind cannot be driven out by anything but prayer",[817] the healing of Peter's mother-in-law in Mt 8[818] and the fight "against the spiritual hosts of wickedness in the heavenly places" in Eph 6:12.[819] The disciples' question why the man

---

biblical texts are referred to in the shepherds' preaching, but only a few of them concern exorcism directly. See 3.1.3. If this study had focussed on the shepherds' general use of biblical texts it would have been relevant to include texts used in sermons and testimonies here. Since my focus is on exorcism, however, I delimit the presentation in this way.

[814] In the handbook, on the other hand, biblical references to almost every theme abound and this may be taken as an indication of the importance of biblical support for the shepherds' practice and understanding of exorcism. I did not expect a lot of biblical references in mostly oral conversations and only occasionally I asked my informants how their understanding corresponded to the biblical material, according to their views. Two of my informants (IS 210, IS 323) make a lot of quotations from the Bible during the conversation, while the others only occasionally give biblical references. I understand the frequency in the two informants' usage as due to their individual way of expressing themselves and maybe to their wish of connecting the practice as closely as possible to the Bible. G. Haus' informants seldom refer to the Bible and she interprets this by saying that their biblical knowledge is low and that they orient their explanations primarily from the traditional religious context. Haus 2000:15.

[815] IS 310 do so in order to legitimate the primacy of God's word and IS 323, IS 200 refer to this passage to underline the connection between expulsion of demons and the laying on of hands. I will in the following footnotes give examples of how the mentioned biblical passage is used.

[816] This shows that spirits can enter into people and objects, according to IS 212.

[817] The reference is used to show the correspondence between the biblical story and what happens in Madagascar today (IS 310, IS 217) and the importance of prayer in exorcism. IS 210, IS 213.

[818] IS 217 says that the passage shows that Jesus cast out the sickness.

[819] This shows the existence of invisible forces, according to IS 312.

in Jn 9 was born blind and Jesus' answer,[820] Jesus' story about the spirit returning with 7 other spirits in Mt 12,[821] the Be-el'zebul-passage in Mt 12[822] and the tempting of Job are also mentioned more than once.[823]

4.2.2.2 *Biblical basis*

One shepherd says that the desired attitude in relation to God's word is found in Jas 1:22: "But be doers of the word, and not hearers only, deceiving yourselves."[824] The word of God is like a seed intended to fall on good soil, which is those who hear the word, understand it and live according to this word. There are lots of people who hear God's voice but they do not want to obey it.[825] The heavy emphasis on the Bible is inherited from the founders. *Mama* Nenilava, who herself had received several supernatural gifts and "her children" said that she had a direct contact with Jesus,[826] urged her followers always to be faithful to the word of the Bible. She even ordered them to correct her if she said anything contrary to the biblical teaching. "Do not follow Rainisoalambo or Nenilava," she said, "but obey the words of the Scriptures".[827]

Several informants point out similarities between the biblical world and what happens in Madagascar today, often by using general

---

[820] This is used to prove that what parents do has consequences for the children and in order to drive home the necessity of the parents' conversion to obtain a healing. IS 322.

[821] The future of those who are not firm in their faith will be even worse than the present sickness, according to IS 323.

[822] IS 320 uses this passage to show that traditional healers only remove evil spirits temporarily, because the devil cannot be divided against himself.

[823] Job's situation indicates that sickness may be a part of God's program for the person, according to IS 321 and IS 312 says that this passage shows that the devil is a tempter.

[824] IS 322. The rendering in the Malagasy Bible is *mpankato ny teny*. The verb *mankato* stems from the root *to* and has the meaning of "keep as true, accept" but also "be obedient to, execute". Abinal and Malzac 1930:704 has "accepter, tenir pour vrai, agréer, approuver, obéir à, accomplir".

[825] IS 322. Mt 13:23.

[826] "Her children" refers especially to Ankaramalaza revivalists. To her supernatural abilities, see Pitaka 1999.

[827] IS 323. To correct *Mama* Nenilava if she said anything contrary to the word of God would have been very difficult in the Malagasy context of respect for the elders but this saying may show how important she esteemed the word of the Bible.

statements like "the exorcism stories in the Gospels are quite similar to exorcism here in Madagascar".[828] In order to describe which symptoms the "assaulted by demons" have in the Malagasy setting, one informant pointed to the convulsions in the story about the boy with the dumb spirit (Mk 9:14–29) to find a relevant vocabulary.[829] Some of the informants notice differences, however, between Jesus' practice in the Gospels and the shepherds' practice. "Those who are really possessed need exorcism often, which is different from Jesus' practice. He cast out once and the person was free." My informant explains this by saying that "we are not Jesus".[830] My informants seem to have different opinions on similarities or differences between the Gospels and the shepherds' practice today.[831]

4.2.2.3 The shepherds' use of biblical passages

The shepherds' teaching is grounded in the word of God and the following example shows how a shepherd connects the biblical texts with the situation of the patient and his/her family.

> There are texts, which are frequently used ... We often teach the family of the sick because the patient is often mentally ill (*very saina*). It is about the family who brought their sick to Jesus. They removed the roof and let down the pallet. The sick no longer had any choice. He did not know what to do but he was saved by the faith of his family. We use this story to exhort the family to be eager in prayer, we tell them that their faith is precious and that they should do even more to progress in faith... The sick would not have come to Jesus at all without the faith of the family. We also use the passage when Paul was freed from prison and he called together the family of the jailer and urged them: "Believe in the Lord Jesus, and you will be saved, you and your household" (Acts 16:31)... It is important for us to teach the family of the

---

[828] IS 201.
[829] IS 322.
[830] IS 202.
[831] IS 315 seems to see a development in practice from Jesus' times to the present. He admits that Jesus only cast out demons from people coming to him, "like the sick and the deaf but now everybody has demons", he says, "and therefore we cast out demons of all people present. It is the demons which prevent people from having a good life." This informant is a Reformed pastor/shepherd and I cannot draw conclusions on his saying alone. A non-shepherd in my material (IN 313) has made the same observations as IS 315 and he also explains this as a development in practice. What is interesting here is that these informants observe a different practice from Jesus' but explain this by pointing to changed conditions in present times.

patients, because it often happens here in Madagascar that the sick and wounded are abandoned by their families. So we must give them special education and tell them that God sees your faith; he sees the whole family and in order to save this family member you must not deviate but make progress in your faith...

When the sick starts to recover we use other texts, e.g. about the person Jesus had healed and afterwards he said to him: "Take care that the sickness will not return to you." We tell the story about Jesus having cast out evil spirits from a person and then we say: "the evil spirit in you has now departed. If you are not eager and watchful, this spirit will return, bringing other spirits to help it. Then your sickness will become even worse than before"... We experience that these biblical passages have their impact and most of the former ill people keep to our advice.[832]

The shepherd connects the biblical world to the patients' situation and it is sometimes difficult to decide whether he talks about his own time or the biblical text. Another story from the same informant shows how biblical texts are used to interpret the sickness of the patients and give them strength to overcome.

There is a special group of people coming to the *toby*. Usually this concerns women and it often occurs about 3 months after they have given birth... They are sick because of lack of calcium. This state of health is exploited by the devil and they become unconscious. The women with lack of calcium are usually poor and they do not have enough to eat ... and we tell them the story of Daniel. All sorts of food were given to Daniel and his friends but they asked for vegetables and this simple food made them strong and healthy.[833]

We teach these women to do their best with the means at hand and use what God has given them. Our primary aim is to lead them to faith and a full trust (*hatoky tanteraka*) in God. When they trust in God, even the food they think is bad can be beneficial to them and thus their minds begin to become stronger... When the mind is strong this may cause changes in their bodily health. 99% of these patients recover after some time at the *toby*....[834]

Shepherds think the reason for the lack of calcium is found in Gen 3:17–18: " ... cursed is the ground because of you; ... thorns and thistles it shall bring forth to you; ..." Man is responsible for the curse of the ground and the destruction of the environment is increasingly felt nowadays. The earth does not bring peace but misery to the people. In the thinking of the shepherds the curse of the ground is still valid and this situation calls for a more profound

---

[832] IS 210. The biblical passages alluded to are Mk 2, Acts 16, Jn 5 and Mt 12.

[833] Dan 1:8–16. "At the end of ten days it was seen that they were better in appearance and fatter in flesh than all the youths who ate the king's rich food." (v. 15).

[834] My informant sees this high percentage of healing from this specific sickness as stemming from a special gift of grace, given by God to this *toby*.

faith and a more whole surrender to Jesus. Jesus is the only one who is able to remove the curse of the earth and he does that when a person becomes a Christian. Jesus has conquered the powers of nature as he showed in the story of the fig tree and in calming the storm and the people following him take part in his victory and experience his words: "Whatever you ask in my name, I will do it, ..." (Jn 14:13).[835]

Through this teaching, embedded in the words of the Bible, the shepherds give the patients a stronger faith, make them able to support their situation and they return home strengthened, in spite of their unchanged poverty.

4.2.3 Summary

The shepherds consider both public teaching and consultations important, their exorcism seems mainly to be understood as a revelation of God's love for sinners and it aims at leading people to conversion and trust in Jesus. The two parts of the exorcism liturgy, casting out of demons and prayer with the laying on of hands, are emphasised as inseparable. God's word is of primary importance to the shepherds. It is a guide for all teaching and practice and it should be obeyed. The word of the Bible plays a central role in the shepherds' actual teaching, where biblical texts are allowed to interpret the present situations.

There are several points of controversy among the shepherds: What causes evil spirits to reveal themselves? Should there always be a consultation before exorcism? To what extent is a continuing training of shepherds taken care of? Some informants recognise similarities and others see differences between Jesus' exorcisms and the shepherds' practice today. The shepherds' different opinions about the diverse purposes of exorcism seem somewhat obscure to me and this also seems to be differently understood by my informants.

---

[835] IS 210. My informant understands these people as "assaulted by demons" but he also explains the lack of calcium as the devil's indirect work on people through the created world. The amount of calcium in the cultivated products is so low that it does not suffice for the people living there, because of continued cultivation and no manure. The consequences are sickness. See 4.5.1.2 (The devil).

4.3 People in need of exorcism

Tokony havoaka demonia izy is a Malagasy expression and translates literally: "demons should be driven away from him." The verb *havoaka* is in the Passive tense and points to the agents of exorcism, i.e. the shepherds. A translation more in line with the meaning could go as follows: "this person is in need of exorcism." It is not uncommon to hear such sayings from shepherds in the Malagasy Lutheran Church.[836]

This subchapter aims at describing how the shepherds view the people who are treated with exorcism. Why do the shepherds deem this to be an appropriate treatment for these people? Since exorcism is the theme of my study, all people treated with exorcism by the shepherds are in focus here.[837] The first section focuses on identifying the "assaulted by demons". Reported signs and the shepherds' understanding of these constitute most of the space but other means of identification are presented. The second section raises the question of what causes a person to be in need of exorcism. The third section focuses on exorcism of Christians and a fourth section briefly comments on the shepherds' understanding of the distribution of gender related to exorcism.

4.3.1 Identifying the "assaulted by demons"

What conditions make exorcism necessary, according to the shepherds' estimation? Shepherds do not see diagnosis[838] as their highest priority but they report several ways of identifying demonic oppression in a person's life.

---

[836] IS 322.

[837] Cf. 3.2.1.1 and 3.2.3.8.

[838] IS 321 says that diagnosis stems from a scientific vocabulary while what is important to the shepherds is that God is able to heal whatever the sickness may be. The shepherds' orientation is towards healing of the person and they see no problem in sending the patient to a medical practitioner if they deem it necessary. IS 322 says: "To state a diagnosis is not the shepherds' task but rather to make firm the patient's faith in God's word." I use "diagnosis" here in a general, non-clinical sense, without any attempt to label people medically. It is used interchangeably with identification, as a general designation of the shepherds' attempts to identify a person's need of exorcism. The fact that neither the handbook nor Rasolondraibe P.'s instruction manual treat diagnosis separately may indicate that the shepherds do not use much effort in this respect. Tobilehibe 1997, Rasolondraibe 1994.

4.3.1.1 Reported signs[839] of demonic oppression: classification and numbers

My material contains a great number of signs and several possibilities of classification could be appropriate. The signs could e.g. be arranged according to their steadiness of appearance. Some are present constantly (e.g. madness), some occur as fits of illness (e.g. antisocial behaviour and bodily signs) and some are not apparent if not challenged in a special situation (e.g. resistance against the word of God, inability to pronounce Jesus' name).[840] Another possible classification is to group the signs in different categories. T. Engelsviken mentions 5 distinguishing signs of possession according to his field experience in Ethiopia: bodily, mental, supernatural, moral and religious signs.[841] My choice of presentation is close to Engelsviken's and focuses on the nature of the signs themselves. Since there is no consensus as to how to classify I have tried to keep as close as possible to my material and have arranged the signs in four broad categories, each with subcategories: signs which violate common conduct, bodily, supernatural and theological signs.[842]

---

[839] I mostly use the word "sign" in the following presentation but "manifestation" and "observable reaction" are used interchangeably with "sign", to denote visible aspects in a person' behaviour.

[840] The first and second of these classifications would be approximately the same as L.A. Sharp's distinctions in madness and possession sickness. Sharp 1994:528. The signs of the third category, however, are not mentioned in her work, probably because she has a different point of departure from my work. Sharp has chosen to differentiate between different categories of experience, but she has not attempted to give an overview of reported signs. Mentioned signs relating to possession sickness are: periodic bouts of bizarre, outrageous behaviour, sudden fits of possession, weeping uncontrollably, shout obscenities, attack people or wander aimlessly around, act as mad, try to beat people and shout or to cry suddenly. Sharp 1994:535. In her article on one category of spirit possession in South-Africa F.S. Edwards mentions several signs of physical illness and psychological disturbance: abdominal pain, unconsciousness, antisocial behaviour, confusion, depression, speaking in voices audible to anyone present. Edwards 1989.

[841] Engelsviken 1978:86–87.

[842] My categories differ from T. Engelsviken's because his point of departure is a classification on the basis of New Testament texts and exorcism practice during church history, while my point of departure is the variety of signs mentioned by the shepherds' themselves. Secondly, I see Engelsvikens' signs as selected examples, while I want go give a broader overview and this is why I also use subcategories. Thirdly, I find his category "religious signs" misleading to some extent in an African context where the whole life is seen from a religious viewpoint. I want to focus on the shepherds' specific Christian understanding of certain signs and I think

The space does not allow more than a listing of signs and I add few comments. I am not able to present the signs in the contexts to which they belong, i.e. the connection between the signs mentioned and the life-stories of the patients cannot be presented.[843] Any classification forces the material to some extent, but in order to get some sort of overview over complex material, I deem it necessary. While attempting a classification, however, it is impossible not to overlap to some extent and I am well aware of that. I present the signs in displays and indicate the number of occurrence in brackets. Occasionally I list the original Malagasy renderings.[844]

---

that the label "theological signs" covers that concern in a better way. Regarding the content, however, I find that all Engelsviken's categories are present in my classification, either in main categories or in subcategories.

[843] This would be a disadvantage if the study focused on an in depth understanding of spirit-possession. To my purpose, however, which is to exemplify how the shepherds identify the "assaulted by demons", my procedure may be satisfactory to give a brief overview of the material. Many questions cannot be addressed and argued for in this brief overview: The number of signs to be present before the shepherds label a person as "assaulted by demons", the necessity of different categories of signs to be present before a such labelling and how to count for individual differences of identification among the shepherds.

[844] Some informants mention that the family of the sick identify the illness to be caused by demons or labelling the patient as mad and some use special Malagasy categories of illness stemming from spirits: *ambalavelona, androbe*. According to a dictionary *ambalavelona* is a mental illness, which can cause madness, stemming from strong medicines by evil-doers (sorcery in connection with envy). *Ambalavelona* can cause illness in a greater population simultaneously and people say that it ends with death if not cured. Rajemisa-Raolison 1985:58. *Androbe* is the Malagasy Bible's translation of the Greek word σεληνιάζομαι in the New Testament (Mt 17:15) and the signs in Matthew, Mc 9:14–29 and Lk 9:37–43 are used by the shepherds to characterise this illness.

208 CH. 4: THE SHEPHERDS' UNDERSTANDING OF THEIR PRACTICE

Table 1: Signs violating common conduct[845]

Speech	Visible conduct	Moral	Other
Talk nonsense (*miteniteny foana*) (21) Swearing (*miteny ratsy*) (12) Shout all the time (*miantsoantso*) (5) Answer in a rude way (3) Use bad language about shepherds/Christians (3) Laugh strangely (3) Talk nonsense/answering during exorcism (2) Sing[846]	Run away (9) Scary conduct (*fihetsika mampitahotra*) (8) Remove clothes (6) Strange conduct (5) Jump around (5) Conduct violating common practice (4) No care about baby/family (3) Slander around Do not sleep indoors Let cattle into another person's fields	Beat other people (*mamono*) (19) Use violence (*mahery vaika*) (9) Eat unclean food (raw hen) (3) Love unclean places (graves) (3) Enter people's house without permission Drink alcohol	Stubborn (5) Fly into a rage (3) Accuse other people of being enemies Unable to participate in a conversation Stare into space Not conscious of what he did

---

[845] This category includes some signs, which as well could be classified elsewhere. While I nevertheless have kept this category, it is because of the occurrence in my material of conformity or discrepancy to common conduct as a weighty argument for identification.

[846] It is implied that it happened when singing was not an expected action.

Table 2: Bodily signs

Body in general	Eyes/face	Mouth/voice	Skin
Illness (16) Swaying the upper part of the body (*mihetsika*) (13) Swaying the upper part of the body during exorcism (10) Do not eat (8) Vomit (5) Spasms (3) Tremble (3) Walk aimlessly (2) Hurt oneself Spit Sleeplessness	Shifty-eyed (4) Red eyes (3) Strange glance (2) A scary face (2)	Dumb (17) Scream (*mikiakiaka*) (6) Foam at the mouth (5) The lips are moving, but no sound is heard (2)	Hands and feet seemed infected by leprosy, done by the devil (*nobokian'ny devoly*) Strong itching A darker skin[847]

Mental	Consciousness
Mentally ill (*very saina*)[848] (16) Anxious (10) Mad (*adala*) (8) Weak (8) Suffer (5) Cry often (*mitomanimany foana*) (4) Look troubled (3) Tired and disappointed Incomprehensible dreams Do not hear what the shepherds say during exorcism	Not mastering himself (*tsy tompon'ny tenany*) (21) Unconscious (*tsy mahatsiaro tena*) (16) Fall over (*torana*) (13) Fall over during exorcism (3) Do not remember what happened (2) Unconscious during exorcism (2) Faint

---

[847] The informant explained darker skin as a sign of demons.

[848] Some of the informants mention that the mental illness is not constant. Mal: *very saina nefa tsy maharitra, adaladala*.

210   CH. 4: THE SHEPHERDS' UNDERSTANDING OF THEIR PRACTICE

Table 3: Supernatural signs[849]

Visions	Bodily strength	Abnormal motions	Strange voice
Seeing strange things (animal trying to kill her; a lion's head; an open grave; an animal holding her tight; something black and big) (5) Visions in general (2) Dreams about death Talk with people he knew During exorcism he saw many animals and threads of plastic covered his eyes and mouth.	Amazing strength (14) Puzzled by their own strength (2) Untied her ropes They perform what is impossible for human beings	Jump from high altitudes without hurting themselves (a window four metres above the ground; a veranda on the 1st floor; ridge of a roof) (4) The feet above the ground when walking Climb the church bell Cling to the ceiling during exorcism	Voice of a dog/lion[850] (2) Another person's voice is heard through their mouth[851] (2)

---

[849] The signs listed under this heading refer to observations, which the informant is unable to explain and thus classifies to be outside what normally happens. It is open to discussion whether these signs would be classified as supernatural according to a Westerner.

[850] One informant says that the demons are using these strange voices to scare the shepherds.

[851] One informant refers to what was said: "there he has come to stay. He is on his way."

Hidden knowledge	Sense of a divided personality	Other
Mock people about things he should not know
Voices inside told him things they could not possibly know	It is as if another force is guiding him[852] (3)
Something is giving him orders[853]
She said she was a snake (and moved like a snake)
He felt that two spirits were fighting within him
He looks as if having seen a ghost	Voice which is scared (3)
Hear the owl's cry[854]
Sounds on the roof
The bed moved up and down
Suddenly a wind started blowing
Eat very much without staying in good health

Table 4: Theological signs[855]

Demons as agents[856]	Dislike of Christian message	No fruit in Christian life
The demons talk through the person[857] (8)
The demons refuse to leave the person
The demons may be raging with strong motions	Uncomfortable[858] during the sermon (9)
Do not dare (or: will not) pronounce Jesus' name (8)
Will not attend church meetings (5)	Cause strife in the church (2)
Their words/testimonies are contradicted by the deeds (2)
The prayer is no real prayer (2)

---

[852] Mal: *Toa misy hery hafa tao aminy*. One of the informants explicitly says he felt this during exorcism.

[853] Mal: *baikon-java-hafa*.

[854] The owl (*vorondolo*) is hunting during the night and is therefore believed to be the witches' bird. Hearing its cry is a bad omen.

[855] The theological signs refer to those, which the shepherds clearly relate to their Christian, theological universe.

[856] This subcategory is close to the subcategory "sense of a divided personality" above, but the signs referred to here are directly attributed to demons, while there is a sense of uncertainty of what is going on in the subcategory above. Ultimately the shepherds will attribute the signs in both subcategories to the demons' activity, but I have divided them according to nuances in the underlying material.

[857] They may reveal their number, or try to scare the shepherds by threatening them. Cf. the subcategory "strange voice".

[858] Words like tremble (*mangovitra*), be afraid of (*matahotra*) and not stand hearing (*tsy mahatanty mihaino*) are used here.

212 CH. 4: THE SHEPHERDS' UNDERSTANDING OF THEIR PRACTICE

	Will not be converted (4) Do not know Jesus as his saviour (2)	A spirit of heresy is guiding him (2) Abnormal singing of Christian songs

Self-justification	Reactions of the "assaulted by demons" during exorcism[859]
Self-boasting during exorcism (3) Pretend to be a better person[860] Justify himself	Accuse the shepherds (3) Do not understand what is going on Think of the shepherds as enemies Try to escape[861] Thrown to the ground by the devil Thoughts of being lost

The above signs of the "assaulted by demons" present a variety, it is not easy to spot the relatedness between them and the listing makes a somewhat confusing picture. This may be so because it does not seem a major task for the shepherds to identify signs. They often seem to take the situation for granted. They appear to have a clear opinion of who are the "assaulted by demons" and act accordingly. Some of my informants admit, however, that it is difficult to know exactly who are the "assaulted by demons" and that the signs they have mentioned have to be regarded as examples.

---

[859] This subcategory is difficult because many signs listed in other subcategories are said to be taking place during exorcism. I have chosen to keep this subcategory, however, as a supplement. All signs during exorcism could have been placed in one subcategory, but I have chosen to list them mainly according to the nature of the signs themselves and not according to where they occurred. In many cases it is not possible from the material to distinguish between the general signs of the patient and his/her signs during exorcism. The theme of the inquiry was well known to the informants and they may silently have implied where the signs occurred.

[860] Mal: *mihatsaravelatsihy*.

[861] The informant's understanding of his strong motions during expulsion of demons is that he was afraid of the shepherds and tried to run away. They in turn had to hold him tight so that he should not hurt himself.

4.3.1.2 *The shepherds' understanding of signs*

My conversation with shepherds about manifestations has been related mainly to signs during "work and strengthening" or crises when the sick stay at the *toby*.[862]

If a patient reacts severely to the shepherds' exorcism, they seem to suspect an active participation in traditional worship. Keeping and use of strong amulets and charms may cause manifestations[863] and some see a connection between the degree of manifestations and the category of spirits working in the patients. Several informants mention that *tromba* spirits cause severe reactions[864] and when the devil is cast out of people having the sickness called *kasoa*, he really shows observable reactions (*mihetsika*), another says.[865]

When spirits are confronted with the authoritative words of the shepherds for the first time the spirits are powerful (*mahery*) but it seems continued treatment with exorcism makes the spirits calmer (*malefaka*). So, signs normally show up in the initial phase of the treatment.[866] One

---

[862] Strange signs in ordinary social life are reckoned with but seldom commented lengthily. More often the shepherds speak about people who act quite normally in daily life but when taken to a healing service they may show observable reactions. IS 218, IS 311, IS 318. One informant (IS 328) e.g. speaks about the annual meeting in Ankaramalaza the 2nd of August 1991. *Mama* Nenilava sat behind a curtain but when she was to address the congregation the curtain was taken away. "Then all the demoniacs (*demoniaka*) showed observable reactions (*mihetsika*)," he said. Even one of the novices to be consecrated in that service had reactions. This person was taken to a separate room for casting out of demons and his consecration was postponed. To my question the informant wonders if it was *Mama* Nenilava's special holiness, which caused the demoniacs to react but he seems to reject this explanation and sees the reason in her continuous prayer life. Haus 2000:85 says that the devil causes manifestations when he sees the shepherds in their white robes but this understanding seems to stem from informants in the coastal areas.

The question of signs covers a vast field and I delimit the presentation here to make the point that different signs play an important role in the shepherds' identification of the "assaulted by demons".

[863] IS 311. "Playing with charms" (*milalao ody*) is seen by my informants as a marked trait especially among the coastal people and they seem to have experienced a more frequent existence of manifestations on the coast. IS 205. IS 321 says that the devil has other working methods in the coastal areas.

[864] IS 312, IS 321.

[865] IS 201. *Kasoa* is a sort of sickness with signs like madness. People think this sickness is connected with love affairs. Rajemisa-Raolison 1985:481.

[866] IS 318.

informant says that severe observable reactions are mostly seen at the annual meetings, where many shepherds are gathered. The families bring their sick members to these meetings and some of them may react very strongly to the shepherds' exorcism. My informant explains this with an example:

> It is like an animal living in an isolated place. It is calm there because nobody interrupts its actions. When suddenly somebody starts chasing the animal it rushes around. This is how the devil acts in a person. He has been calm in the home of the person because few or no shepherds have been "working" with him. When the patient is taken to a meeting where more than 10, may be 400 shepherds, are casting the devil out simultaneously with loud voices, he is stirred up (*taitra*) and shows severe observable reactions. The devil cannot stand the repeated "in the name of Jesus".[867]

Signs may be understood as the devil's attempt to prevent people from hearing God's word. A woman's talking during the service was seen as a demonic working method because then she could not listen to Jesus' voice.[868] A former patient spoke about a vision of snakes crawling on his body and this removed his attention from what the shepherds said, especially one snake, which curled on the patient's breast with its head close to his face, sneezing at him. This informant interprets his strong motions as a reaction against what he experienced in his visions, which made him afraid and he started screaming. Each time an animal bit him, he tried to escape and this caused severe manifestations.[869] When the devil is challenged through the shepherds' exorcism, this causes some people to react and this may be interpreted as the devil's uneasiness with the word of God.[870] In areas where the confrontation between idol worship and the preaching of the Gospel is especially apparent this may cause an inner conflict in the person because of the war between the good and the evil spirit. Manifestations may then be considered to point to the battle going on inside the human: the Holy Spirit is fighting

---

[867] IS 206. I did not understand IS 206 as thinking in psychological categories, e.g. that the loud voices caused the severe reactions. Rather he seemed to envisage that a great army of shepherds was able to frighten the enemy.

[868] IS 206.

[869] CHIS 8.

[870] IS 217. Pitaka 1999:118 reports that people's demons manifested themselves before "work and strengthening", while *Mama* Nenilava still had not finished her biblical teaching.

against the devil.[871] A former patient said: "Half of my head was filled with the devil, while the other half was filled with Jesus."[872] When a person is persuaded by the Holy Spirit and has decided to convert and follow Jesus, it is believed that the devil cannot stay any longer. His moving away may be seen in manifestations.[873]

Several of my informants say it is easy to identify the demoniacs.[874] This seems to be done on the basis of specific signs and a variety of signs are mentioned.[875] Others interpret the same signs differently and maintain that they may not point to demonic oppression. Thus signs alone are not considered sufficient to identify the "assaulted by demons".[876] When compared to the small percentage of people showing reactions in a healing service, observable signs are a mark of only a few of the people treated with exorcism by the shepherds.[877]

---

[871] IS 218. IN 313 once attended the baptism of an 18 year old girl. Her family were non-Christian but she had decided to be baptised. When the pastor was about to place his hand on her head, she opposed this, not intentionally but she did not master herself. Suddenly she turned mentally ill. The laying on of hands was omitted because she started with severe spasms and several people had to hold her tight. "This really had to be demons," he said, "because they [the demons] could not stand the coming of the Holy Spirit." The shepherds "worked" with her that day and the next morning before she regained her mind.

[872] CHQ 133. Some shepherds' understanding of this fight tend to postulate a clear-cut conflict between the kingdom of Satan and the kingdom of Jesus (IG 332), saying that everything that does not stem from the Holy Spirit has to stem from evil spirits. Ambohimahazo *toby* 16 June 1998.

[873] IS 218, IS 205. Pitaka 1999:118 talks of demons leaving people while they were screaming (*nikiakiaka*). It is not clear whether the people or the demons screamed.

[874] IS 322. "If a person shows strong reactions (*mihetsika mafy*) we know that he/she has devils". IS 312.

[875] IS 218, IS 311. Some of the non-shepherds in my material consider severe observable reactions during expulsion of demons as the most outstanding sign of demons (QN 108), at least that it is very difficult to identify a person as "assaulted by demons" if there are no manifestations. IN 317.

[876] IS 310, L 336. H.A. Virkler and M.B. Virkler give a condensed list of signs associated with contemporary Western demonisation, drawn from several authors of the subject. They conclude that a person who believes to be demonised, without being so could experience almost all the mentioned signs. An analysis of signs is therefore not sufficient, according to their view. Virkler and Virkler 1977.

[877] See 3.2.3.8. A near conclusion is that specific signs primarily are connected with the people labelled as demoniacs. None of my informants explicitly states this connection, however.

My informants emphasise especially some kind of reaction against Jesus' name as a valid sign of demonic oppression. Since it is taken for granted that the devil always is in opposition to the kingdom of God and hates Jesus, this sign seems to be expected in a multitude of different sickness conditions.[878] The identification is based on reactions when confronted with Christian preaching but unwillingness to go to church is interpreted in the same way.[879] It is counted as normal that a conflict arises when the Gospel confronts paganism,[880] but it is debated whether people "assaulted by demons" are able to pronounce Jesus' name. A sick girl, treated at a healing service, was exhorted to pray and when she mentioned Jesus' name, she fell to the ground.[881] "In the high plateaux people are accustomed to prayer and even the "assaulted by demons" may say the Lord's prayer without any manifestations," one informant said.[882] Another admits that some of the "assaulted by demons" may pronounce Jesus' name but afterwards they start swearing and this is understood as a reaction from the devil that cannot stand the name of Jesus.[883] The variety in understanding among my informants makes identification of the "assaulted by demons" along the lines above uncertain.

Lack of manifestations. From my observation of healing services I concluded that manifestations are rare[884] and the great number of questionnaire-informants who had not seen a person seriously "assaulted

---

[878] IS 201. L 336 maintains, however, that reaction to Christian preaching is only one of several criteria in an identification of demonic oppression.

[879] IS 201, CHIN 31.

[880] "When the light comes, the hidden demons have to show themselves." IS 212. When I asked IS 202 if demonic oppression was related to personality he denied this but answered that it was encountered most frequently in areas where Christianity and traditional practises stand in sharp opposition to each other.

[881] CHQ 161.

[882] IS 310.

[883] IS 201. When the devil does not manifest himself in the person he/she may be able to confess Jesus' name (1 Jn 4:3) but when the devil causes a crisis in the person, he/she is not able to do so. A.M.M.T. 1999S:10. This problem of identification also seems to be recognised by G. Haus, who says that the confessing may be an outward custom, while the heart is bound. Haus 2000:77.

[884] 16 people of about 700–800 showed any sort of observable reaction to exorcism. See 3.2.3.8.

by demons" points in the same direction.[885] Observable signs do not seem to be a necessary criterion of having demons. One informant says:

> Some people have demons but it is not visible on the exterior... Some show observable reactions with a crisis (*mihetsika ny crise*) when they are taken to a Christian service (*entina mivavaka*) and some have signs pointing to the existence of demons inside them ...[886]

Some of my informants think that the preaching of the Gospel for a considerable period of time in the high plateaux has caused a decrease in idol worship.[887] This seems to be interpreted as having reduced the number of people showing observable reactions to exorcism. The reason may also be that traditional practitioners seldom come to the healing services and consequently, the demons in them are not challenged by the shepherds' exorcism.[888] It may be that people are unwilling to let their demons leave and thus they show no manifestations,[889] or that signs were observable only in the initial phase of the treatment.[890] Several of my informants characterise the people in the high plateaux as not straightforward. They hide their actions and many embrace Christianity only as a custom. It seems to be implied that although these attitudes may stem from evil spirits, they do not manifest themselves in observable signs.[891] The attitudes of the people in the high plateaux have caused the devil to work differently, according to some of my

---

[885] 16 of 44 shepherds said that they had not seen such a person.

[886] L 336.

[887] At least the visible idol worship has diminished. The explanations of IS 200 and IS 312 seem to imply that demons have been expulsed from specific places due to the preaching of the Gospel. They mention water sources where demons resided earlier but which are now safe. My informants admit, however, that there is much hidden idol worship in the high plateaux.

[888] IS 310.

[889] IS 217 tells about four people who had been much involved in traditional practices. Three of them reacted to the expulsion of demons with observable reactions, while the fourth did not. The one who did not react was the leader. After one month of treatment with exorcism and preaching, one day the fourth person was persuaded and decided to convert. Then she suddenly showed observable reactions during expulsion of demons. Afterwards she said that during the whole month she had kept her demons because she was not ready to get rid of them. IG 332 refers to the magician's lack of manifestations in Acts 13:6–11.

[890] IS 318.

[891] IS 320.

informants. The devil may encourage people to be eager in church work but they never attend healing services and even dislike them. My informant says that if these people had been treated with exorcism, they may have reacted in some way.[892] The devil's working methods in the high plateaux are said to especially concentrate on people's attitudes and customs (*toetra amam-pomba*).[893] The devil pretends (*mihatsara-velatsihy*), he hides among the Christians and he encourages people in theft, unbelief etc. These things do not cause people to show manifestations.[894] Demons showing no observable reactions, however, are considered more difficult to cast out than those who can be traced on the exterior.[895]

Several sayings in my material imply that demons are at work in all people and if these sayings are taken literally, identification of demonic oppression seems superfluous. There are different opinions among the shepherds on this matter, however. Only a couple of my informants say directly that all those who do not believe in Jesus have demons. Their thinking seems to be that since the unbelievers are not on Jesus' side in the spiritual battle they have to be on the side of the enemy.[896] The demons in these people may show themselves through bad morals (adultery, theft, lying) and these actions cannot stem from God. Then they have to stem from the devil.[897] "Almost all people have demons, according to the teaching of *Dada* Rakotozandry," one informant says and he continues to define these demons as pretending, self-righteousness and unbelief.[898] According to another informant, pastors may have demons. He qualifies his saying by adding that "the work of

---

[892] IS 311. I have only a few examples in my material of people eager in church work who are suspected by the shepherds to be "assaulted by demons" and I asked this informant about the danger of labelling those who disliked the "work and strengthening" as having demons. He denied that conclusion and said that the demonic influence could be traced in their way of performing church work and in the results of their work. CHQ 6 also tells about a person eager in church work having demons.

[893] IS 320.

[894] IS 322.

[895] IS 320, IS 322, IS 323.

[896] IG 332.

[897] IS 318. IS 322 agrees in this logic.

[898] Mal: *Ny olona rehetra dia saiky manana demonia.* IS 205.

the devil also extends (*mihatra*) to pastors".[899] The demons seem to be at work in all people but to varying degrees:

> All people are used by the spirit(s) of the devil, but the demoniacs are used in a more serious way (*maningana*). The devil overshadows all people, devils are disturbing all people and it is important that there is a service in the church to help the people to fight against the devil.[900]

One informant says that all humans are sinners and therefore it is not problematic to cast out demons from anyone who wishes.[901] The sayings above show that shepherds in my material see it as a possibility that demons may work in all people, in some way or another.

Other shepherds in my material oppose the thinking that everybody has demons, however, but they realise that most shepherds, especially those in the countryside with little formal and biblical education, do not agree with them.[902] "It has to be admitted, however," one informant says,

---

[899] IS 213. His examples of such demonic work are envy, bad talk (*fitenenen-dratsy*), pride, boasting, hatred. This may be in line with the thinking of IS 320 when he says that shepherds do not think that demons may work in them. In the same interview IS 213 says that the shepherds should be careful not to cast out demons of people with fever. This saying implies that some shepherds may suspect demons where there are no demons at work.

[900] IS 311. This continuing presence of demons seems to be supported by Randrianarivelo 2000:92 when he says: "Malagasy Christians are aware that although there are no obvious manifestations of possession during worship, the demons are always working in each person's heart to tear away the believers from thrusting in God's words."

[901] IS 322. There is a saying in IG 332 that the devil enters people when they sin, but other informants in my material do not support this. Some of the non-shepherds in my material seem to be in line with the thinking that devils are working in all people. "All humans are sinners and therefore they all need exorcism," IN 313 says. "Those who are disobedient to God's will and trust other things are friends of the devil and I think they will be "assaulted by demons"," QN 38 says.

[902] IS 310. IS 321 says that many shepherds with little formal training are wrong (*diso ny fomba fiasany*). Shepherd leaders have to tell them not to suspect the devil behind everything. My informant especially calls for caution in relation to small children. The child may cry and try to escape during expulsion of demons and some shepherds think this stems from the devil working in the child and consequently, they become even more eager in their casting out of demons. The reason for the child's crying may be that the child is afraid, however and shepherds should be very careful with small children during expulsion of demons, according to my informant.

The shepherds' habit of suspecting demons behind any sickness and problem is also the most frequent mentioned accusation against the shepherds' practice by non-

220   CH. 4: THE SHEPHERDS' UNDERSTANDING OF THEIR PRACTICE

"that all evil stem from the devil," but this is quite different from maintaining that demons are at work in all people, according to his opinion.[903] Temptations stem from the devil but the tempted are not necessarily "assaulted by demons", another says.[904] As a consequence of this view, one informant maintains that only those who show observable reactions during expulsion of demons should be subjected to exorcism.[905] A couple of other informants also maintain that it is not right to cast out demons from all. Only those diagnosed to be "assaulted by demons" should be subjected to expulsion of demons, while the rest of the audience ought to sit in prayer for them.[906]

4.3.1.3   Other means of identification

A gift of discernment. Some shepherds are bestowed with a special gift from the Holy Spirit to discern the spirits working in a person and all shepherds are exhorted to have a praying attitude during exorcism in order to be open to the Holy Spirit's guidance.[907] Before the patients have said anything to the shepherds, the Holy Spirit may have made their problems known to the shepherds.[908] Sometimes the devils are invisible and hide and they may think that nobody is able to find them. Then it is

---

shepherds in my material. QN 27, QN 109. The consequence of this thinking is that all are treated with exorcism, which is opposed by many non-shepherds. QN 124, QN 78, QN 116.

[903]   IS 310.

[904]   IG 332.

[905]   IS 214. It is not clear whether he thinks of expulsion of demons as a means of identification here. Probably he has the initial casting out of demons in mind and he thinks that the shepherds should concentrate their subsequent expulsion of demons to people showing observable reactions.

[906]   IS 310. IS 321 says that he taught this to the shepherds in the beginning but now he is not stressing it any longer. The reason is that some shepherds then will say that he opposes their work. They say that it is impossible to know exactly who the "assaulted by demons" are and therefore it is best to cast out demons from them all. My informant has not changed his opinion in this matter but he does not seem to consider the shepherds' practice as totally wrong.

[907]   IS 323. The gift of discernment from the Holy Spirit is also mentioned by A.M.M.T. 1999S:9 and Haus 2000:45, 86, 101, 153.

[908]   IS 210, IS 322. IS 210 says that this is a characteristic of the revival (*mahafifohazana ny fifohazana*) and his saying seems to emphasise the shepherds' superiority, may be in relation to other healers. IS 210 sees the significance of a consultation with the patient/their family, however.

necessary to mention their names, revealed by the Holy Spirit. This is according to Eph 5:13: "but when anything is exposed by the light it becomes visible ..." and the devils then will be beaten.[909] Some of my informants have experienced this gift. A young married woman was in her second year of training to become a shepherd when she asked for a consultation with my informant and he received her in his home:

> She came because she had trouble in her marriage. Her husband accused her of an unwillingness to work and she admitted that something prevented her constantly. She worked for a week and then she was unable to work for two weeks. She identified the reason for this in something she was unable to conquer in her life. Earlier she had consulted her aunt who practised as a traditional healer (*mpitaiza*) but she had delivered all the items and they had been burnt at the *toby*. She said that she had forgotten one thing, however: some dust in a bottle and I saw that a battle started inside her when she said this. I prayed for her and after some time she told me that the content was dust from dead bodies. She asked for "strengthening" because "there is a strange spirit throwing shadows over my life," she said. She kneeled but before laying hands on her I wanted to pray and during this prayer I was convinced of expelling demons before the laying on of hands. I had arranged with some shepherds who sat in another room that they should come to my assistance if they heard any expulsion of demons. I started casting out demons in Jesus' name with an authoritative voice. Then the young woman answered me rudely: "O, you did not know the evil spirit there?" She was full of boasting. The woman did not master herself any longer and the spirit inside her talked. I did not doubt that it was the spirit of the devil. When the other shepherds came to my assistance the young woman suddenly jumped out on the floor and overturned the table ...[910]

This story shows both the ability of the shepherd to be sensitive to the Holy Spirit's guidance and the importance of getting to know the patient's life-story. The shepherd's arrangement with other shepherds and his knowledge of this kind of charm make it probable that his earlier experiences also were important factors in identifying the demonic oppression.[911]

The shepherd's discernment may be aided by the life-story of a patient and this may function as another indication of a possible demonic influence.

---

[909] IS 323.

[910] IS 323.

[911] IS 202 says that an identification needs experience.

Sometimes the shepherds seem to identify a spiritual problem in the person's life but in accordance with the practice in general medicine, the medical practitioner cannot tell a patient that he/she is gravely ill. The patients themselves have to tell their story: about scary dreams or the feeling of something pressing them. The patients' stories may assist in the shepherds' discerning but it is difficult for people to identify their own problems because of their weak faith.[912]

Since demonic involvement is considered a spiritual sickness, spiritual analyses are appropriate to identify the sickness and a person's involvement in spiritual matters is given close attention. The shepherds especially search for possible connections with traditional practices in the patients' past. This may concern the patient himself/herself or his/her family.[913] The start of the demonic influence may lie many years back and it is believed that a lengthy influence may aggravate the condition and cause bodily or mental sicknesses.[914]

A person's conduct may also assist in the shepherds' discernment of the "assaulted by demons". "Demons are involved in bad morals as prostitution and corruption," one informant says, "if the evil-doers refuse to be corrected and only follow their own minds."[915] "It is possible to discern if people are "assaulted by demons" from their attitudes (*ny toetry ny olona*)," another says and he mentions people who are quick-tempered and cause strife as examples of this.[916] Another informant talks of the "assaulted by demons" as having supernatural knowledge "but the things they do cannot stem from Jesus but rather come from Satan".[917]

---

[912] IS 323. What my informant means to say with "weak faith" is not clear but I suppose that he is thinking of the patient's inability to discover that his/her basic problem is spiritual.

[913] L 336: "Has the sick taken part in practices or worship related to demons? Has the close family taken part in demonic practices? Does the sick person live in a house where demons have been active?"

[914] IS 311. The influence may have started in connection with consultations with the traditional healer in connection with marriage or construction of a house but has been latent for many years. Suddenly it may show itself through a crisis in the person's life.

[915] IS 320

[916] IS 318.

[917] IS 218. He refers to Acts 16 and the slave girl who had a spirit of divination. He also mentions other signs to facilitate a diagnosis, like not taking care of the clothing, unnatural actions and a disturbed mind.

The logic seems to be that conduct contrary to the Bible cannot stem from God and thus it has to come from the devil.[918]

Expulsion of demons. The infrequency of the gift of discernment among the shepherds and their uncertainty about who are "assaulted by demons" may have caused them to use exorcism itself as a method of identification.[919] Some people may feel ashamed because they are "assaulted by demons" and they do not dare to show this by moving to the front of the room in the healing services. During the initial demon-expulsion the demons may reveal themselves in these people who can then be set free.[920] It seems as if the shepherds' ways of identifying these cases are observable reactions during expulsion of demons.[921] One informant says that casting out of demons from the whole audience aims at the self-diagnosis of the people. During the expulsion of demons people may examine themselves to see if they are "assaulted by demons" or not.[922] Another says that during casting out of demons it is God who distinguishes the "assaulted by demons" from those who are not.[923] Since the devil is a master of deception, expulsion of demons is a way to identify him.[924] The shepherds' expulsion of demons functions in practical life as a method of identification but the shepherds underline

---

[918] IS 322. My informant strongly underlines, however, that these people cannot be labelled demoniacs. Haus 2000:45 has observed that signs are interpreted in accordance with the patient's life and problems and that the same signs may be interpreted differently from person to person. She generalises by saying that shepherds understand all human conditions violating cultural or biblical norms as signs of possession (p.74).

[919] IS 200, IS 217.

[920] IS 217.

[921] IS 310, IS 217, IS 213.

[922] IS 318. See below (Self-diagnosis).

[923] IS 200. The way God does this is not clear but it seems as my informant thinks of people reacting to the expulsion of demons as appointed by God. The context of this saying is how to distinguish between the bodily sick and the "assaulted by demons". My informant seems to favour only the laying on of hands with prayer for the bodily sick but he does not seem to object an initial expulsion of demons for the whole audience.

[924] IS 321. IS 205 seems to relate pretending to the behaviour of people in the high plateaux: since most people pretend (*mihatsaravelatstihy*) it is not easy to know who are "assaulted by demons". "This makes casting out of demons necessary," he says. It seems probable that my informant sees demons behind the people's pretending.

that the purpose of exorcism is healing. If exorcism does not lead to the desired results, i.e. healing, the shepherds may try other means, e.g. drugs from a medical doctor.[925] Their basic faith is that nothing is impossible for God.[926] Since exorcism is conceived of as a way of showing God's love for the sinner, most shepherds assert that there seem to be no negative effects of subjecting people whom are not identified as "assaulted by demons" to expulsion of demons.[927]

Self-diagnosis. In many cases it is the family of the patient or the patient himself/herself who suspect the work of evil spirits and therefore they present themselves on the first bench/the straw mat during exorcism.[928] The family knows the patient's story and they are aware of what happened.[929] They suspect that the sickness is not natural. Healing services are open to anyone and the shepherds do not control the people moving to the front of the church when exorcism is about to begin. Thus it is the patients'/families' own judgement of their situation, which causes them to move forward. According to my informants the problems of these people are varied: problems in general,[930] the bodily sick, the

---

[925] IS 313.

[926] IS 321.

[927] IS 201. Cf. 4.2.1.4. Lie 1981:16–17 does not seem to agree with this logic and he accuses some shepherds of mistakes, especially when experienced shepherds continue to cast out demons although they know that the person is not "assaulted by demons". Lie has observed exorcism of mentally retarded and people with recognised sicknesses. He maintains that it is an easy solution for the shepherds to label any incomprehensible condition as stemming from demons.

[928] IS 321. This self-diagnosis is also mentioned by A.M.M.T. 1999S:9 and Lie 1981:16. In some cases the sick person come alone to the shepherds or to the *toby* and I asked IS 218 how it is possible for those "assaulted by demons" to seek the shepherds who are able to cast out the demons. Would it not be more natural that these people, if they are driven by the devil, avoid any contact with the shepherds? IS 218 explained this as a demonic attempt to disturb (*manakorontana*) the work at the *toby* but that, by the authority of Jesus, these people are healed. It seems to be implied in his explanation that Jesus played a trick on the devil and turned his bad purpose into something good. IS 210 explains this differently. He says that those who are "assaulted by *tromba*" themselves may come to the shepherds because there are periods when the spirits assaulting them have left and gone far away and then the people act normally (*misy fotoana toy ny hoe lasa lavitra niala tao ny fanahy dia mahatsiaro tena ilay olona…*).

[929] O 344, IS 315.

[930] IS 202: "When they have problems, they come to the shepherds."

wearied,[931] people pretending, self-righteous, those who are about to loose their faith,[932] people with pride, boasting, hatred,[933] those who need external help to fight against something and do not manage life alone,[934] people with evil dreams, people who have problems with family life or in work, poverty,[935] those who feel tempted,[936] lack of love, alcoholism, the desires of the flesh,[937] worries, kleptomania.[938] Many people mainly come because they feel in need of strength and they think that the shepherds' treatment gives strength in any kind of situation.[939]

It may happen that shepherds think that some of the people moving to the front of the church should not be treated with expulsion of demons. One informant realises the problem but sees it as impossible to tell one of the people sitting on the mat: "Leave that place because you are not "assaulted by demons"."[940] "When people come and say that they are "assaulted by demons", I investigate that thoroughly through an initial consultation," one informant says. Only if he is not able to trace the cause of the sickness to any "natural" condition he treats the case as having demonic origin and expels demons.[941] The preaching of God's word is said to aim at the patient's self-diagnosis. Then people see that they are sinners, in need of the salvation of Jesus.[942] They may "come to

---

[931] IS 200. It seems to be underlined that those who are tired (*reraka*) from a continuing fight between the spirits inside them (*adi-panahy*) need exorcism. IS 311, IS 312.

[932] IS 205.

[933] IS 213.

[934] IS 210.

[935] IS 311. This informant underlines that some people moving to the front of the church do not think of themselves as "assaulted by demons" but only that they feel troubled in life.

[936] IS 312. "Since we are tempted every day, we need exorcism," IS 312 says, "we are fighting against powers in the air."

[937] IS 322.

[938] IS 323.

[939] IS 210.

[940] IS 200. According to him this problem arises because the shepherds have not instructed the people properly.

[941] IS 325. With "natural conditions" he talks of psychological disturbances, problems in marriage/family, the patient's pre-history etc.

[942] IS 210.

themselves" and confess that they are deceived by their own heart or by evil spirits.[943]

To sum up, the shepherds use several methods in order to diagnose a person to be "assaulted by demons". The methods are not mutually exclusive but rather supplement each other. One of my informants tells how he identifies a person to be "assaulted by demons":

> A study of the person's life-story and prayer of the Holy Spirit's guidance to discern is important in the spiritual analysis. The study of the life story especially includes the person's relation to Christian faith, his/her contact with traditional religious practices and his/her moral conduct. A general analysis of symptoms, both bodily and mental, may assist the identification but some of the "assaulted by demons" show no manifestations. The identification may include a medical analysis in order to point out or exclude a bodily sickness. This medical analysis cannot diagnose a spiritual sickness [demonic causes], however.[944]

If the shepherds suspect any demonic oppression in a person's life, they think that he/she ought to be treated with exorcism.[945] "Exorcism is an appropriate treatment where spirits are at work."[946] It is worth noticing, however, that not all people treated with exorcism are labelled by the shepherds as "assaulted by demons" and especially not as demoniacs.[947] Thus the shepherds' exorcism covers a wider spectre of people than only those who are identified as "assaulted by demons".[948]

Several informants maintain that the shepherds do not know which people are "assaulted by demons" and which are not. In principle, there may as well be "assaulted by demons" among those who sit on the benches in a healing service as among those who sit on the first bench or on the straw mat.[949] "The shepherds are not prophets," one informant says, "and therefore everybody present at the service is treated with

---

[943] IS 323.
[944] L 336. This is an abstract of the informant's view on this matter.
[945] IS 213.
[946] IS 321.
[947] IS 323. Both IS 201 and IS 202 speak about sick family members who have been treated with exorcism and these people are not considered as demoniacs. Cf. 2.2.7.
[948] It also seems that any sickness could be treated with exorcism but I will return to the theme of sickness and exorcism in a separate subchapter so, I only mention it here. See 4.5.1.
[949] IS 323.

PEOPLE IN NEED OF EXORCISM 227

expulsion of demons, in case there are devils at work."[950] The shepherds are convinced that the devil is able to work in people in a variety of ways.[951] Thus the shepherds deem exorcism to be appropriate in many cases.[952]

This subchapter has focused on how the shepherds identify some people to be in need of exorcism. The following subchapter continues by asking why people are in need of the shepherds' exorcism.

4.3.2   What causes people to be in need of exorcism?

Is to be "assaulted by demons" a state, which hits arbitrarily or is it possible to trace specific causes?[953] Is there any relation between people's actions and demonic attacks? To outline the shepherds' understanding of these themes is the purpose of the following description.

In traditional Malagasy thinking it is necessary to understand the causes of sickness before an appropriate cure can be given.[954] To what extent are the shepherds occupied with causes and how do they evaluate the necessity of this knowledge in order to start the healing process?[955] My material shows that the shepherds are aware of several possible causes of demonic oppression, which seem to fall mainly into four wide groups, with some other causes only mentioned by a few informants. In addition, they talk about "God's program" in connection with the causes.[956] The grouping emerges from the material itself and I have tried to preserve some of the shepherds' own wording in labelling the groups: 1) idol worship, which is by far the largest, 2) lack of faith in Jesus, 3)

---

[950] IS 200.

[951] IS 321.

[952] G. Haus asserts on the basis of her empirical material that the shepherds are neither interested in, nor concerned with distinguishing between the tempted and those who are "the devil's property". They think all of them need exorcism. Haus 2000:78.

[953] Cf. 2.2.5 (Elements in the shepherds' view of demons).

[954] See 4.1.1.3 (The causes of sickness).

[955] Non-shepherds in my material criticise the shepherds because they emphasise causes too little. According to their opinion the shepherds ought to investigate the causes more thoroughly and have a close co-operation with medical practitioners. QN 62.

[956] In some of the material I ask specific questions on this theme but the shepherds' understanding of causes is also seen in their way of telling the stories of people being treated at the *toby*.

the devil's exploitation of problems, crises, sicknesses or an anxious personality and 4) temptations and sin.[957] There are nuances among the causes in each group, the borders between the groups are fluid and the grouping mainly serves to give an overview over the material. When creating such grouping, however, it is impossible not to overlap to some extent. Each informant normally mentions several possible causes and often it seems that a combination of more than one cause has led to the present situation. The story of one of my informants illustrates this well and causes belonging to each of the main groups are found in the following account:

> He was baptised as a little boy but could not remember if he had attended Sunday school. 11 years old he decided to leave the church because he did not understand what was going on there. Due to a lot of family problems his parents were divorced and this caused him to start with alcohol, which led to bad moral conduct. His mother brought him to a traditional healer to secure a good exam but he did not make good progress in school. He became more and more dependent on alcohol and cigarettes and one night a demonic attack made him unconscious and he became severely ill. The illness caused him to consult more traditional healers and he received lots of remedies. When a pastor from the congregation was sent for, he prayed for him and cast out demons. The pastor's understanding of his state was that "this is God's calling to you" ....[958]

In order to give an idea of the frequency of the different groups of causes in my material I present a table below, based on an attempt at counting causes in my material:[959]

---

[957] The more precise meaning of each of these headings will be elaborated on below.

[958] CHIS 8. I have only referred to a small part of his story in condensed form here.

[959] The table is not complete because my material is not produced to be analysed quantitatively. I have filled in the squares where the material enables me to do so. The table does not show how much each informant told about the mentioned cause, neither how important the informant considers the cause in relation to others. The grouping of causes is to some extent guided by my own judgements but the table reflects a clear tendency in my material. When e.g. I list 95 % "idol worship" in intervies with shepherds, this signifies that 24 of the 25 interviewees mention this cause. Each informant mentions more than one cause, which makes the total percentage more than 100 %.

Table 5: Causes for people to be in need of exorcism

Causes	Interviews with shepherds	Case histories			Question-naires shepherds
		Interviewed by me	Interviewed by field assistants	From the question-naires	
Idol worship	95 %	60 %	88 %	39 %	50 %
Lack of faith in Jesus	35 %				46 %
The devil's exploitation of problems, crises, sicknesses or an anxious personality	45 %	80 %	33 %		19 %
Temptations and sin[960]	40 %	40 %	22 %		11 %

In the following presentation of the material I offer a separate heading to idol worship because of its overwhelming frequency in my material. The other causes are described under a second heading, while a third subchapter deals briefly with the shepherds' understanding of sicknesses having positive purposes.

4.3.2.1 Idol worship

The shepherds normally use the expression "idol worship" (*fanompoan-tsampy*) as a general designation of everything related to traditional worship:[961] the traditional healers' work, everything connected with charms and taboos and sorcery/witchcraft.[962] Two of my informants estimate that 80 to 90 % of all demonic oppression stem from idol worship, which is not far away from the average counting of references in my material.[963] One informant defines the relations to idol worship as follows:

---

[960] In the questionnaires to non-shepherds 75 % mention "idol worship", 34 % "lack of faith in Jesus", 20 % "the devil's exploitation", and 22 % "temptations and sin".

[961] Cf. 4.1.1.1 (Idols and charms/amulets) and 4.1.1.2 (Interaction between humans and ancestors, god, idols and charms/amulets, nature spirits, sacred power).

[962] Practices like hypnosis, yoga, spiritism and sports from the East (Kung Fu, Karate) are also considered by some informants as idol worship and thus as a possible cause of demonic oppression. L 336, QS 166.

[963] IS 210 (80 %), IS 311 (90 %).

230   CH. 4: THE SHEPHERDS' UNDERSTANDING OF THEIR PRACTICE

> ... we call some people liberators (*mpanafaka*); they have made a pact with the devil, which enables them to cure people from sicknesses and it is with the devil's help they are able to do so. e.g. when a person has trodden on land, which is taboo and has been hurt by doing so, it is the liberator, which sets this person free from the devil's power over him/her.[964] They are called *ombiasy*, *mpimasy* ....
>
> The second group is people who seek the liberators' help and they receive things (*zavatra*) to place in their homes or on their body to protect them. ... When their worship of these things increases, i.e. there has to be taboos and when they worship the taboos, the devil and his kingdom grow within the people. These taboos give orders to the people and instruct them what to do and then they become really "assaulted" (*voa*) because the devil is ruling their lives (*ny tenany*). ... They think that these spirits bless them and only Christians are able to identify these spirits as devils. ... The people seek blessing and they do not pay attention to who the blessing entities are. ... The devils do not make themselves known immediately. As people worship them, they show their faces little by little. ...
>
> There are also devils, which may be said to be attached to the people, against the people's own will. A man may be in love with a girl but she does not want him. Then he consults the traditional healer (*mpimasy*) to obtain a love potion (*ody fitia*) ... and its power is mediated in a variety of ways, by perfume, by money etc. ... There has to be some sort of contact between the two persons. The love potion causes the girl to fall in love with the man and she seeks to come to him. ... Some of these girls resist this but they do not resist it fully and they turn mentally ill. We call this *kasoa* ...[965]

According to this citation there are three different relations to traditional worship. The first is voluntary where the liberator or traditional healer makes a pact with the devil, which involves demonic oppression regardless of his/her positive purposes. The second is based on a need on the part of the client. He/she asks for the traditional healers' services and little by little the nature of the demons becomes clear. The third may be classified as sorcery, where an innocent party is hurt by charms used by an adversary.[966]

---

[964] The shepherd uses a Christian vocabulary but his point seems to be that the traditional healer has means to relieve a person from his/her immediate suffering, which he sees as caused by the devil through a break of taboo. This does not mean that the person is freed from demonic influence, however, which becomes clear from the shepherd's continuation of the explanation.

[965] IS 201.

[966] Regarding sorcery, IS 201 maintains that some kind of agreement is implied in the shared items, e.g. the man asks for the girl's photo and she gives it to him, or he gives her perfume and she uses it. This may point to what my informant means by not resisting the attack fully (in the citation above). Syvertsen 1983:179 maintains

Pact, inheritance. There are few references to voluntary pacts with spirits in my material, presumably since these people seldom seek the shepherds' treatment.[967] In this connection it is mentioned as a possibility that the spirit of a traditional healer is inherited by one of the descendants.[968] According to one of my informants, the son of a great traditional healer turned insane in Farihimena. His father had decided that his spirit should move to the son who was obliged to receive it but did not want to. He had a feeling of two minds (*saina roa*) fighting inside him. Shepherds were contacted and after he had given away three baskets with charms and other remedies, he was healed.[969]

Remedies, taboos, conflict. The use of charms (*ody*) is widespread and this is my informants' most frequently mentioned cause of demonic oppression. One informant says that this custom is so common that family members have even secretly consulted traditional healers and given remedies to their sick at the *toby* during treatment there.[970] "Devils reside in the charms and if you do not have a power to resist their influence, the devils will ruin your life little by little."[971]

> The real traditional healer (*ombiasy*) is guided by a spirit, which directs him in the treatment of the patients. When the spirit directs the traditional healer in what to do, it inserts at the same time one of its spirit servants into the patient. This spirit resides in the patient. The patient does not know that the traditional healer also inserted a spirit when he handed over charms and gave instructions for different taboos to be observed. When the patient breaks a taboo he/she will turn ill and the spirit inside him will reveal itself. "There is a spirit inside you. You should not have broken this taboo but did and now we fight with each other."[972] Often the patient turns insane ... It is the great spirit of the

---

that what he calls "real spirit-possession" stems from pacts with spirits (e.g. *tromba*), use of remedies from traditional healers and sorcery.

[967] There are examples of traditional healers converting to Christianity, however. See Ankaramalaza undated:129–150. Voluntary spirit-possession is among the most common themes in literature on Madagascar, according to Sharp 1993:19.

[968] L 336, QS 3. IN 313 also mentions this possibility.

[969] IG 331. My informant took part in the exorcism. Charms are important in all the above mentioned relations to traditional worship.

[970] IS 206.

[971] CHIS 8. QS 181 even asserts that only to consult the traditional healers' rituals, without actively using charms, may cause demonic oppression.

[972] It is not clear if it is the traditional healer, which reveals the existence of a spirit inside the person or if the person himself/herself is made aware of this through the break of taboo.

traditional healer, which comes to the patient saying: "You have broken the taboo and have to be punished." There are people who are able to "take away [the penalty of] the taboo" (*manala fady*) by bringing sacrifices to the traditional healer or to specific places. Those who are not able to do so, however, will often turn insane because they are not obedient to the orders of the spirit ... The break of the contract has its consequences.[973]

According to the citation above the outbreak of the crisis took place when the patient broke a taboo and the thinking seems to be that the inserted spirit guards the taboos not to be violated.[974] Others connect the outbreak of a crisis specifically to a confrontation with the Christian message. The traditional healer inserts spirits through his healing practice but the person may act normally for years, until the spirit is challenged. A Malagasy studying abroad was taken to a traditional healer and given remedies of protection to bring with him, before he left home. Only years later, when this student started to worship in a congregation where expulsion of demons was practised, he suddenly started to act erratically.[975] In one of the case histories a person is called "a soldier of the idols" before his conversion to Christianity, because he frequently consulted traditional healers and seemed to practise as a medium himself. His sickness is interpreted as the devil's causing him to suffer because he withdrew from the devil's dominion.[976]

The shepherds do not rule out an element of conflict within the person when the Christian message confronts the traditional worship. This conflict is especially visible in Christians taking part in traditional worship.[977] "Most of the people coming to the *toby* in the high plateaux

---

[973] IS 210.

[974] The spirit residing in the patient seems to be considered as a representative of the great spirit in the traditional healer, or as a representative of the traditional healer himself. IN 324 also considers the break of a taboo as a cause of sickness and he calls it the "ancestors' punishment" (*kapoka avy amin'ny razana*).

[975] IS 311. "The devil caused him to suffer (*mampijaly ny nofony*) when he started to go to church and he was treated for one year before recovering." CHIS 12 interprets her demonic oppression as stemming from a consultation with the traditional healer many years earlier. He had then mixed some remedies with her blood. The crisis appeared when she became a committed Christian.

[976] CHISA 104. QN 147 reports of a person who had a really hard time when he withdrew from idol worship to become an eager Christian, because then the evil spirits let him suffer.

[977] IS 205, IS 218.

are Christians who are about to loose their faith."[978] The shepherds consider this double loyalty a dangerous situation.[979] In the high plateaux most people are supposed to know that charms and other remedies from the traditional healers oppose the Gospel. When they in spite of this knowledge continue their double practice, this causes a fight in their minds and they may be "assaulted". The explanation of evil spirits and the explanation of conflict within the person do not seem to exclude each other. "If we consider the human being in a holistic perspective," one informant says, "it seems as the psychological factors and evil spirits co-operate in causing the sickness."[980]

Sorcery. If some members of the family have brought remedies to the house, this may cause demonic oppression even to members living there who do not know about these charms,[981] but involuntary demonic oppression is especially connected to the practices of the sorcerer.[982] The use of a love potion is most frequently mentioned in my material.[983] Some of my informants talk about spirits moving by their own will or going where they are sent, or spirits forcing themselves to enter into

---

[978] Mal: *kristiana mangatsiatsiaka.* IS 312. Many of the case histories in my material show that the patients had some sort of Christian background, which is not surprising in the high plateaux where there is a large percentage of Christians. Shepherds maintain that hidden traditional worship is widespread in this area and this makes the theme of Christians worshipping idols a burning question.

[979] IS 312 speaks about the leader of a church committee who also consulted the traditional healer. He fell ill.

[980] IS 202. This informant also sees the handing over of remedies as solving the inner conflict and thus facilitating the healing. Human co-operation seems to be implied in several of the informants' understanding of causes but only a few (IS 202, L 336) uses a psychological vocabulary to denote this. Cf. 4.5.2.4 (The role of the patient). See also below, 4.3.2.2 (Lack of faith in Jesus; Temptations and sin).

[981] IS 323, IS 205.

[982] Hardyman 1971:215 says that people ascribe *ambalavelona* possession to sorcery and Rasolondraibe 1989:350 asserts that "demon-possessions are always attributed to sorcery". My material does not support Rasolondraibe P.'s assertion.

[983] IS 201, IS 206.

people.[984] I have a few examples where sorcery seems to furnish a possible explanation of an inexplicable sickness.[985]

4.3.2.2 Other causes

In some of my material some kind of circular argument emerges, e.g. lack of faith in Jesus may be considered by the shepherds as both a sign of demonic oppression and its cause. Similarly, a sinful life is believed both to stem from demonic influence and at the same time, to be a possible cause of demonic oppression. In the following I concentrate on these conditions considered as causes of demonic oppression.

Lack of faith in Jesus. Lack of faith in Jesus is the ground cause of demonic oppression.[986] "There may be many causes but they all stem from the fact that Jesus is not allowed to be Lord."[987] The inference from seeing lack of faith in Jesus as the ground cause of demonic oppression to think that non-Christians are "assaulted by demons" seems close. Some shepherds in my material seem to believe that non-Christians are necessarily "assaulted by demons" but the meaning may be that the non-Christians are more vulnerable for demonic oppression.[988]

Some of my informants maintain that some sort of power to resist demonic attempts to oppress people is needed and non-Christians may be considered as not having this power. This also seems to be the case for Christians with a fading faith. They do not have enough power to

---

[984] IS 322, IS 214. Sorcery is the explicit context of one of these sayings, while the context of the other concerns practising traditional religion and problems in the family.

[985] IG 331, IS 214. In both cases the shepherds furnish other probable explanations or have additional indications of sorcery. A non-shepherd maintains that the basis of sorcery is the people's own actions, mostly seen in faults committed against someone in the community. IN 324.

[986] IS 318.

[987] IS 201 sees this fact in connection with temptation to worship idols, i.e. traditional religion. L.A. Sharp summarises the causes shepherds state for an individual's sickness as lack of faith in Jesus. Sharp 1993:255.

[988] IS 213, IS 217. IS 318 and QS 69 seem to understand this theme in light of the absolute conflict between light and darkness. If the non-Christians do not have part in the light, they have to be on the side of darkness. "This does not mean that all non-Christians are demoniacs," QS 101 says.

conquer the evil enemy.[989] Going to church, listening to God's word and receiving Holy Communion give power and strengthen the shield against demonic attacks. To neglect these things makes the person vulnerable and opens the path for demons to assault him/her.[990] A woman at the end of her thirties was treated at the *toby*:

> She was mentally ill but when she recovered she decided to become a shepherd. At the time of her consecration she still had not recovered totally from her illness but *Mama* Nenilava said that she was to be consecrated in spite of this. After consecration she recovered quickly but within a month she fell ill again. She was treated at a *toby* and after 3 months she was able to work as a shepherd and she cared for ill people living in the *toby*. Four days before I met my informant she fell ill again. My informant interprets her illness as stemming from her not taking enough care. "If she is eager to pray she keeps in good health," he says, "but she works outside the *toby* and her work prevents her from attending all the services in the church." This is the reason for her relapses.[991]

The devil's exploitation. The devil seems able to exploit a variety of situations and human conditions in order to oppress a person. My informants especially mention sickness, difficult living conditions for the person or his/her family, problems connected to schoolwork (failing exams or studying too hard), an anxious or dependent personality and doubts or a weak faith.[992] Relatively new arrivals like drugs and video films may also lead to demonic oppression and the devil is able to take advantage of kinds of music to enter into people.[993] The devil's ability to exploit this seems to be common knowledge among the shepherds to the extent that some of my informants only mention the situation/condition itself, with no reference to the devil, as the cause of demonic oppression. One informant says:

---

[989] IS 206. The lack of power is also seen as a cause of demonic oppression by QS 121.

[990] IS 213, IS 218.

[991] IS 206.

[992] Sometimes the shepherds mention several difficult elements in a patient's story without stating explicitly that these may be the cause of the illness. One respondent's story includes a difficult situation at home, failure to pass an important exam, pressure from several people in her environment and she characterised herself as a dependent person. Her own understanding of the cause of her sickness, however, was a consultation with a traditional healer many years earlier. CHIS 12. Cf. 4.5.1.2.

[993] IS 210. Tobilehibe 1995:36.

We ask the family to forgive each other if there should be any unsettled matters among them. The patient may be sad because of incidents in the family and when the family members forgive each other mutually, he/she may be healed.[994]

Another informant tells a story to illustrate the connection between a difficult living situation and the devil's exploitation:

A man owns a cow but it dies or is stolen by someone. Then he thinks: "What will be my living now?" He does not know how to replace the cow and his mind is working hard (literally: "his mind leaves"—*lasa ny sainy*). His mind is not with him any more and he is not able to return it. This causes him to be "assaulted by the devil" and the demons enter him.[995]

Trouble-minded people seem to be targets for demons because they are already fighting, which means that their strength diminishes.

In addition the devil threatens them with discouraging words: "You will never accomplish this. It is right that you are poor and you will never manage through these problems etc." The people believe the voice of the devil and agree with him.[996]

It is believed that the devil uses the voice of people's conscience to discourage them because the work of the devil is to frighten people.[997]

Crises and problems may affect people's faith and people with weak Christian faith are considered to be targets of demonic oppression.[998] One informant talks about a person's inability to receive the Gospel, a state which evil spirits exploit.[999] Another talks about difficulties in believing the word of God and this seems to be considered a weakness, which may be exploited by the devil. When a person has doubts, evil spirits are able

---

[994] IS 312. My informant neither says that the devil has exploited this situation nor does he mention exorcism but both seem probable in light of the context of the saying.

[995] IS 206.

[996] IS 210. My informant refers to Adam and Eve in the Garden of Eden to support his saying. When they started to discuss God's words it was easy for the devil to seduce them.

[997] IS 210.

[998] Cf. above (Lack of faith in Jesus).

[999] IS 202.

to reinforce this state little by little and it may end with loss of faith. This is understood as the devil's exploitation of the condition.[1000]

One informant seems to think that the devil's exploitation consists in temptation to idol worship. He mentions difficulties like poverty and divorce, which make people seek some kind of support, they may especially call on spiritual assistance. Psychological dependent people always need something to rely on and if they do not depend on God they are open to any influence from the enemy.[1001]

Mental problems, crises in family or marriage and special elements in the patient's life-story are not necessarily exploited by the devil. Only if he is unable to identify any of these causes, which he calls "natural", one informant says that he treats the person's illness as stemming from demons.[1002] Another says that people may talk nonsense because their lives have become a mess and if these people are disturbed unnecessarily, their illness may even aggravate.[1003]

Temptations and sin. Every human being is tempted and temptations stem from the devil.[1004] The purpose of temptations is to cause a person to stumble and if the person is not on guard or if he/she does not have strength from the Holy Spirit within him/her, the person may give in and follow the temptation.[1005] "When a person stops fighting against temptations, he/she is "assaulted by demons", because then he/she is led away from God," one informant says.[1006] The relation between temptations and sin seems to be considered as consisting in some sort of co-operation between the devil and people, but is does not stand forth in an unambiguous way in my material.[1007]

[1000] IS 214.

[1001] IS 323.

[1002] IS 325. His information to this point is somewhat sketchy and I am not able to decide whether he thinks that the devil is able to exploit these situations or not.

[1003] IS 210. My informant seems to think of the tense atmosphere during expulsion of demons as a possible disturbance of these people.

[1004] IS 312, IS 318.

[1005] IS 218.

[1006] IS 325.

[1007] IS 202. My material does not furnish me with enough information to describe this relationship but I suppose that the shepherds' understanding is similar to what a non-shepherd in my material thinks about this theme. When IN 313 talks about the relationship between human responsibility and the devil's temptation he refers to Gen 3 and says that temptations will always exist, both from inside the human and

Temptations are not only related to moral conduct but some of my informants underline especially bad conduct as a cause of demonic oppression.[1008] Some shepherds think that a person's sin has caused demons to oppress him/her. Since he/she did not bother to follow God's will he/she now reaps the consequences of his/her own actions.[1009] One informant tries to define the difference between the fact that all people are sinners and sin as a cause of demonic oppression:

> ... when people sin they often come to themselves and repent. When they repent the devil looses his power over them. All human beings are sinners! When they remember to turn to Jesus, it is a pleasure (*mahafinaritra*).[1010]

It seems as if people who do not remember to ask Jesus for forgiveness of sins, or even want to continue in their sins, may be oppressed by demons.[1011]

Diverse causes. Some shepherds attribute the cause of demonic oppression to a sudden attack by the devil and this is especially common when committed Christians are hurt inexplicably. The shepherds say that the devil "wages war against" ... (*manafika*). It is said about an eager Christian, who was in the last months of her instruction to become a shepherd,[1012] about shepherds,[1013] or about a theological student who

---

from outside. The person is not obliged to stumble, however and the person is responsible for his/her actions if he/she accepts to follow the devil's voice. If the person stands firm in the faith, like Adam and Eve did before the "fall", he/she is not obliged to stumble. IN 313 uses two different expressions to denote the demonic influence and it seems as he will label a tempted person as "assaulted by devils" (*voan'ny devoly*) while he calls a person who has followed the temptation "conquered by the devil" (*resin'ny devoly*). There is no such consistency in terminology among the shepherds in my material but I cannot rule out that many of them would agree with this non-shepherd. See 2.2.7.

[1008] Sins related to sexuality and alcohol are especially mentioned (CHQ 6, CHQ 156) but IS 214 says that when pastors mock the shepherds they are visited by evil spirits. The story of CHIN 31 shows that when he was disobedient to his parents, joined the other youths and thus learned bad words, the devil "assaulted" him again.

[1009] IS 321. Tobilehibe 1997:104.

[1010] IS 218.

[1011] Cf. 4.3.1.3 (A gift of discernment), where bad moral conduct is a way of identifying a person as "assaulted by demons".

[1012] CHIS 12.

[1013] IS 206, IG 331.

suddenly fell ill.[1014] Sometimes, additional causes may be present[1015] and one informant says it happens because the people are not on the alert (*tsy miambina*).[1016]

Some of my informants assert that demons may move (*mifindra*) into people in the audience when they are cast out of the "assaulted by demons". One refers this to a saying from the great shepherd leader *Dada* Rakotozandry but others do not give any further explication.[1017]

Some informants say that they do not know the cause.[1018] This should not be taken as the meaning of not knowing what normally causes demonic oppression but rather that they do not have sufficient knowledge of a specific case and thus they cannot identify the causes.[1019]

4.3.2.3 "God's program"

During my conversations with shepherds about the causes of demonic oppression it has not been uncommon that they have understood a certain

---

[1014] IS 312.

[1015] Traditional remedies. CHIS 12. Sorcery. IG 331.

[1016] IS 312. He refers to the story in Mk 5 about demons entering into the pigs but also to a picture of "a heart not on alert" in a much spread pamphlet: Unidentified 1972:30. Cf. 2.2.5.

[1017] IS 318, IS 212, QS 142. IN 317 has experienced this during the great revival in Vatotsara. In her study from Southern Ghana B. Meyer talks of the practice of praying eagerly during exorcism in order to prevent spirits from invading the audience. Meyer 1992:119.

[1018] IS 206, IS 213, CHISA 81.

[1019] In her thesis G. Haus has a subchapter about causes of possession. Her material seems to be in accord with my findings concerning the important place of traditional religion in this respect. The shepherds think that everybody who uses the traditional healers' services will become "assaulted by demons" and the devil enters into remedies from traditional healers. Both active worship and storage of remedies may cause the spirit in the remedy to move over to the owner. Sin and the devil's exploitation of the human psychology as causing people to be "assaulted by demons" seem to be in agreement with my material. Haus does not mention lack of faith in Jesus as a cause of demonic oppression, however and the idea of God's program behind what happens does not seem to be prominent in her material (see the following subsection). Her supplement to my material seems to be that the devil is able to use riches and precious objects to possess people (e.g. through idol worship) and that spirits may possess people arbitrarily just because they like this person (the last cause seems to be attributed only to a few shepherds from the coastal area). Haus 2000:56–64, 71, 95.

case as "God's program" (*programan'Andriamanitra*).[1020] This emphasises that what happens is part of God's greater plan for the patient or/and his/her family and therefore God permits it to happen.[1021] It denotes that a sickness may have positive effects/results. An understanding of the case as "God's program" does not exclude other causes to be operative.[1022]

One informant talks about the difficult road God has led him on and he understands demonic oppression through years as God's testing of his faith. "Since all the tribulations did not kill me," he says, "I take this as a token that God will use me." When he looks back he realises that God has taught him a lesson not available to people who have not experienced this.[1023] Another admits that the sickness of his son has led him to experience a more committed Christian life.[1024] One informant talks about his sister who fell ill and when they brought her to *Dada* Rakotozandry, he said that this happened in order to call the whole family to be eager in faith and not divided.[1025] One respondent interprets her story as God's calling of the family. She and both her parents became shepherds as a result of the sickness.[1026]

One of my informants seems to interpret a case of demonic oppression as a test of the church workers. Are they willing to confront the devils or do they find excuses to evade the case?[1027]

In this subchapter I have presented the shepherds' views of the causes of demonic oppression, which I have shown also relates to Christians. In the

---

[1020] 25 % of the conversations during interviews on the theme of causes mention this.

[1021] IS 321. The biblical reference here is the story of Job and it is used to show that the devil has to ask permission from God before harming any human beings. God is not held responsible for what happens, however.

[1022] QS 104 mentions both idol worship and God's calling to faith as causes of the demonic oppression.

[1023] CHIS 130. A plain reading of the informant's story seems to attribute the causes of demonic oppression both to active use of traditional healers (*ody*) and to sorcery.

[1024] IS 214.

[1025] IS 205. *Dada* Rakotozandry even said that the sick person was the most pure of them all. My informant tells about remedies from the traditional healer, which were hidden in the house and he believes that his sister fell ill because of the work of these remedies.

[1026] CHISA 130. Consultations with the traditional healer are part of the story.

[1027] Only IS 214 mentions this and it is impossible to draw any conclusions from one saying alone.

following I focus more specifically on exorcism of Christians and this will inevitably overlap somewhat with what I have already presented, as will be seen below.[1028]

4.3.3 Exorcism of Christians

In my presentation so far, exorcism of Christians has occurred several times, in direct or indirect ways.[1029] Regarding this background it is relevant to ask how the shepherds understand expulsion of demons of Christians. Can Christians become "assaulted by demons" and how do the shepherds explain this?

When the shepherds comment on this issue they often define different ways of understanding the label "Christian". Further, they refer to their own experiences, which seem to have taught them that there is a possibility that committed Christians can become "assaulted by demons".

[1028] Part of the methodological approach in this project is to be attentive to what causes questions to my mind as an "outsider". See 1.3.3.2 and 4.6. Exorcism of Christians is somewhat obscure to me (and it is also a discussed issue in the Western debate on demon-possession), while my informants often mention Christians in connection with their practice of exorcism. Therefore I have chosen to comment this theme in a separate subchapter.

[1029] From my observations of "work and strengthening" I have noticed Christians sitting on the straw mats/the first benches. Cf. 3.3. Several of the "assaulted by demons" have some sort of Christian background. My material here is especially the case histories: Some have Christian parents, some are baptised, some have attended Sunday School but many of them have at the same time been in contact with traditional healers, which to the shepherds mean that they are not committed Christians. When "work and strengthening" becomes part of a Sunday morning service, most of the audience consists of Christians. Cf. 4.2.1.1. In the "strengthening"-prayer special words should be used when praying for "adult Christians" and for "church workers". Cf. 3.3.3. Earlier in chapter 4.3 I have mentioned the casting out of demons from a novice about to finish her instruction to become a shepherd (cf. 4.3.1.2, footnote 862) and the opinion of several shepherds that demons somehow are at work in all people. Cf. 4.3.1.2 (Lack of manifestations). I have also shown that some informants think that expulsion of demons includes everybody present in a healing service while others believe that not all treated with casting out of demons can be labelled as "assaulted by demons". Cf. 4.3.1.3 (Self-diagnosis). Concerning shepherds subjecting themselves to expulsion of demons, the fact that they were devoted Christians did not seem to cause any problems but rather that they did this together with the sick and especially if they had put on the white dresses. Cf. 4.5.2.5 (A unique position of the shepherds?).

At the same time they maintain that Jesus is able to protect his children from the devil. They try to explain this in different ways, which may indicate some sort of uneasiness with the occurrence and controversy in opinion. I will follow these lines of thought as an outline in the following.

4.3.3.1 Terminology

The shepherds see the label "Christian" as inaccurate and often when they are asked about cases where Christians have been "assaulted by demons", they define the word "Christian" more clearly.

The first group of answers characterises people who are not sincere in their faith: They are cold or immature Christians, whose faith is only a matter of theory and does not concern daily life.[1030] They are only Christians by name. They are baptised and attend Holy Communion but they do not know the Bible.[1031] They come to church only since it is a custom and they have not really made up their minds on whom to follow.[1032]

The second group of answers talks about Christians "with a divided mind" (*miroa saina*) who go to church but also have contact with traditional healers. These Christians have two lords and only one can have priority in their lives.[1033] According to the shepherds' understanding, these two groups of Christians are easy targets for evil spirits.

4.3.3.2 Committed Christians may become "assaulted by demons"

"When Christians are tempted, there is an evil spirit trying to enter the person and guide his/her actions. This causes a fight, which non-Christians do not know." The devil is always trying to seduce Christians

---

[1030] IS 312, QS 6.

[1031] IS 206.

[1032] IS 312. To receive Holy Communion is important to Christians in the high plateaux. The church is more crowded at communion-services (normally the 1st Sunday each month) than at ordinary services. This tendency of seeing baptism and Holy Communion as minimum demands to be called a Christian seems to be interpreted by shepherds as only having faith as a custom.

[1033] IS 217, IS 311. IS 315 says that they do not have their confidence in Jesus and their Christianity is seen as an outward matter.

to fall into temptation and according to my informant the word of Jesus has predicted this: The Christians are like sheep among wolves.[1034] Another believes that since the devil's work affects all people, the Christians are not excluded and the devil wages war especially against the Christians.[1035]

One informant tells about his old father who suddenly fell inexplicably ill, an event happening before my informant had become a shepherd. His father had worked as a local lay church leader (*katekista*), he had been a Christian through his whole life and he had brought up his family in the Christian faith.

> When he fell ill he did not speak [normally] but could hear what we said. He saw a flood of water, which made him cold and this vision lasted. Often he repeated: "Perhaps I will perish" (*angamba aho ho very*). We held a service there and afterwards I was convinced that my father needed "work and strengthening". The family was already gathered and we started the service. Then my father lay like he was dead, he did not say anything and could not move his hands and feet. Suddenly, he started to swear like he had never done during his lifetime since it was taboo to him. All of us prayed, asking for God's mercy and for forgiveness for our father and ourselves. So we started the casting out of demons and I continued for about 2 hours. There were no results. We begged God for salvation and help but my father mocked at us saying: "I will make you lose face" (*alaiko baraka*) and he uttered many bad words. We continued to cast out in the name of Jesus but after a while we decided to send for a shepherd. When hearing the word "shepherd" my father said: "Did you say shepherd?" (*mpiandry hoe*) and he continued: "I will not leave unless for a shepherd."
>
> They sent for a shepherd in the middle of night and he had to walk for one hour to come to the house. When the shepherd came he followed the liturgy of "work and strengthening" and when he had finished my father still did not talk. The shepherd said: "We have confidence that Jesus will work." So he left to go home. The next morning my father came to himself and wanted to eat. His mind returned and he told us in detail what had happened: what had hurt him and the visions he had seen. "This happened because of you children," he said.[1036]

Later on my informant reflected on this incident and he wondered what could happen to them when this had happened to his father who really had a living faith.

[1034] IS 311. This is a clear allusion to Mt 10:16.
[1035] IS 213.
[1036] CHQ 69.

4.3.3.3 *Jesus has power to protect his children*

At the same time my informants underline Jesus' power to protect his children. "If the Christians watch and pray, Jesus is not a passive Jesus."[1037] "Christ is powerful to protect his children," another says and he is convinced that Jesus does not let Christians who do not thrust in idols become "assaulted by demons".[1038] My informants emphasise that it is Christians taking their faith seriously whom are protected against demonic oppression. They use expressions like "really believe" (*tena mino*), "to really have part in Jesus" (*manana an' Jesosy tokoa*),[1039] "an eager Christian" (*kristiana mafana fo*),[1040] and a Christian who is "one with Jesus" (*miray amin'i Jesosy*).[1041] These Christians do not become "assaulted by demons" and they have no need of expulsion of demons, regardless of their own understanding of the situation.[1042] My informants see the protection closely knit to prayer to God for assistance and to the word of God.[1043] The demons have little possibility to work in Christians living by God's word because then they are filled with this word. When God's word is abundant, the person is always conquering.[1044]

[1037] IS 212.

[1038] IS 217.

[1039] IS 218.

[1040] IS 206.

[1041] IS 200, IS 202.

[1042] IS 200, IS 206. It is implied in this saying that such Christians may present themselves to the shepherds' exorcism but according to my informants they do not need this.

[1043] IS 213 also mentions the sacraments.

[1044] IS 321. The conceptual analogy seems to be a room, which can be full or empty: If there is no word of God, the room is empty and thus demons may stay there. In fact, there necessarily has to be new inhabitants. The existence of God's word and demons' work in a person seems to be inversely proportional: Much of God's word makes it difficult for demons to work while lack of the word of God opens the path for demonic activity. IS 206 tells about a patient who often left the *toby* because of economic difficulties (probably to ask for money from people he knew). As a result he was not attending all the services at the *toby*. My informant interprets this as follows: "Because of his lack of money his knowledge of God diminished and correspondingly the devil worked in him and made him run away from the *toby*...."

4.3.3.4 *How do shepherds explain exorcism of Christians?*

When Christians are "assaulted by demons" and there seems to be no obvious reason like traditional worship, my informants offer several possible explanations. It may happen in order to teach the family a lesson.[1045] The possibility of sorcery is a constant threat.[1046] Some say that such Christians did not watch (*tsy miambina*),[1047] another says that they did not defend themselves (*tsy miaro-tena*) with prayer to God[1048] and another that these Christians may not have repented (*mety tsy mibebaka*) or that the devil exploits some bodily weakness.[1049] Shepherds admit, however, that it is not always possible to trace the reason why Christians suddenly react with manifestations during casting out of demons and one informant emphasises that such reactions cannot be labelled as "possession".[1050]

In many cases Christians are treated with expulsion of demons but they show no observable reactions. "Christians do not attend 'work and strengthening' to have demons expelled," one informant says. "Exorcism to them means strengthening of their faith." He argues for this view by saying that Christians with a living faith are not freed from demons, i.e. during expulsion of demons, a saying I interpret to mean that these people normally do not show any observable reactions of demonic oppression during casting out of demons.[1051] Several of my informants

---

[1045] As in the story cited above (4.3.3.2).

[1046] QS 105. The son of one of my informants was a committed Christian but still he fell ill because of sorcery. He had been brought up in the Christian faith, had good moral conduct and attended church regularly. My informant saw his sickness as a result of him not being watchful. His son was too young to consider it a possibility to become targeted. IS 214.

[1047] IS 202. IS 312 bases his argument on Mat 26:41: "Watch and pray that you may not enter into temptation" and he says that Job's story shows the devil as a tempter.

[1048] IS 213 refers to Mt 12:43–45 and says that the devil really attacks those who have an empty and swept house, i.e. the Christians.

[1049] IS 202.

[1050] IS 212. According to his opinion, those who move to the straw mats in a healing service are not all "assaulted by demons". In this case my informant uses the French word "possédé".

[1051] IS 205. His saying is somewhat obscure and difficult to understand. In Malagasy it reads: *Raha ny tena finoana velona dia tsy afaka demonia ny kristiana*. It should be noticed that the shepherds' comments in this chapter both refer to Christians with observable reactions during casting out of demons and to Christians who present themselves to the shepherds' expulsion of demons (by moving to the straw mats or the first bench) without any manifestations.

have noticed that also committed Christians attend "work and strengthening" and it seems as they agree that many Christians come because they feel in need of strength. "They do not consider themselves as "assaulted by demons" but they believe that the shepherds' prayer gives them strength," one shepherd says and he adds that since "work and strengthening" is a fixed liturgy, everybody present receives both.[1052] "It is impossible to know why these Christians move to the straw mats," another says and he indicates by this that they also may come on behalf of their children, their wife/husband, or their family.[1053]

I have in this subchapter shown that the shepherds have different ways of explaining the exorcism of Christians, which I take to reveal controversy between their opinions on this theme. I will now briefly comment on the shepherds' understanding of the distribution of gender related to exorcism. This brings the presentation of the shepherds' view of people in need of exorcism to a close.

4.3.4 Distribution of gender related to exorcism

When I started to sum up and analyse my material, after having ended my fieldwork, I found two tendencies concerning gender in relation to exorcism. In some parts of the material there was an even distribution of men and women, or a slight majority of men, while in other parts there was a majority of women involved in exorcism.

[1052] IS 321. *Mama* Nenilava is said to have cast out devils from whoever repented during the preaching of God's word, without distinguishing between Christians and non-Christians. Pitaka 1999:121.

[1053] IS 212. Another shepherd says that although eager Christians are not "assaulted by demons", "they come and pray with us because they both want to receive strength and to share their strength with others." IS 218. The last saying seems to imply that Christians are expected to come to the healing services in order to assist the shepherds. Cf. 3 (Introduction). One non-shepherd in my material thinks that the casting out of demons and the "strengthening" are confused in predominantly Christian areas. His opinion is that Christians need much strength in their faith and they should strengthen each other (*fifampaherezana*), but he has doubts about the casting out of demons from Christians. He thinks that casting out of demons is appropriate when demons have entered the person and he/she has become a demoniac. QN 108.

The case histories show a slight majority of men among the "assaulted by demons",[1054] while people labelled as "assaulted by demons" living at the Ambohimahazo *toby* in September 1993 show an even distribution.[1055] In my observation material from healing services, however, there is a marked higher number of women than men and this concerns both the number of working shepherds and the people treated with exorcism in healing services.[1056] A browsing through the rest of my fieldwork material, searching for occasional examples of people considered as "assaulted by demons" in my informants' stories, shows a majority of women.[1057] I cannot attach any great importance to these numbers, however, since they are only mentioned as occasional examples.[1058]

The question of gender did not seem to be of special importance to my informants when I performed the interviews and I have only scattered references in my material.[1059] The handbook and Rasolondraibe P.'s instruction manual, too, do not elaborate on this theme.[1060] I present the available material to this theme in the following but the material is not

---

[1054] The 28 case histories, told by the shepherds, have 50 % of each gender. 4 of 9 case histories gathered by field assistants concern women and in my own in-depth interviews with people who formerly were "assaulted by demons" there is only one woman from a total of 5.

[1055] 4 men and 3 women.

[1056] 75 % of the working shepherds were women (of a total number of 189). Among those who were seated on the first benches/the straw mats about 60 % were women and a little more than 30 % were men (the rest were children). See 3.2.1.1. Among people showing observable reactions during expulsion of demons 80 % were women and 20 % were men (13 of a total number of 16 were women). See 3.2.3.8.

[1057] In the questionnaires given to shepherds two women are mentioned as occasional examples of people "assaulted by demons" and one man (the shepherds' stories of people formerly "assaulted by demons" are excluded from this number). In the interview material the number is 17 to 6.

[1058] The browsing of my material is done by computer and there may be errors, e.g. that some people occur more than once on the list. The numbers have to be considered as approximate.

[1059] In the perspective of my emic presentation, where the interview methods consisted of mostly open-ended questions, I have not pushed my informants to comment on the question of gender. The scantiness of references in my material to this theme seems to reflect my informants' interests.

[1060] The handbook advises that women shepherds are working with women and men with men, when the patient acts erratically. Cf. 3.2.3.4. This seems to be a practical measure to protect the shepherds against temptations.

sufficient to draw any conclusions on the shepherds' understanding of gender in relation to exorcism.

Only one of my informants comments on gender in relation to people "assaulted by demons" but he does not make any comparison between the number of women and men.[1061] He has observed, however, that during some periods mostly women come to the *toby* while in other periods there are mainly men. When I interviewed him in October 1993 he said that for about two years women had been in majority among those coming to the *toby*, but in the recent past more men were coming. I asked him what he considered to be the reason for this.

> What I have observed since I came here is that when the living conditions worsen, mostly women seem to be hurt,[1062] when life is difficult ..., especially the rise of prices for everyday commodities. In periods when food prices are cheaper, I have observed that men are hurt.
> *Question*: And what may be the reasons for this?
> Until now I have not solved this problem.
> *Question*: But this is what you have observed?
> This is my general impression. What caused me to study this is that the sick women coming here often talk about their lives, their difficult living conditions.
> *Question*: Do they tell their stories properly or are they unconscious of their talking?
> They are not mastering themselves at all. They just talk and talk and almost all they say concerns the difficult living conditions. This is the source of my assumption.
> *Question*: Do people consult traditional healers more often in difficult living conditions or is this theme without relation to what we are talking about?
> For most of these cases there may be a connection to traditional healers. Some people still believe that when they receive remedies (*ody*) from these people, they will earn money more easily. When young women experience difficult living conditions in their parents' home they may search for possibilities to escape. Then they look for young men who are willing to marry them and seek remedies from traditional healers to reach this goal. This is the love potion. After some time, however, this does not have the desired effect.[1063]

[1061] The only other mentioning of gender in my material is where IS 325 wonders why God has appointed so many prominent women to be leaders in the revival movement (with reference to a new outburst of the revival in Maropaika in the latter part of the 1990's led by *Mama* Christine). He does not propose any answers.

[1062] *voa* = *voan'ny demonia* i.e. "assaulted by demons".

[1063] IS 210.

The conclusion of my informant points to difficult living conditions but as he says, he is not able to explain the differences between women and men in relation to exorcism.[1064] My informant still maintained his explanation on the basis of living conditions when I interviewed him in June 1998. This time, however, he saw the difficulties in daily life as a reason why mostly young men (and not women) turned mentally ill and came to the *toby*. Their worries about how to manage through the difficult living conditions were too much for them to bear and this caused their sickness.[1065]

There seems to be a certain discrepancy on the theme of gender in relation to exorcism in my material compared to previous research on spirit-possession but the studies are not quite comparable.[1066] My material does not show any unambiguous tendency that women are in the majority among those "assaulted by demons".

[1064] In my fieldwork material which relates to other parts of Madagascar (and thus is not included in this project) I find two explanations as to why women seem to be more exposed to demonic assaults than men. The first sees the reason in women's many worries (*be ahiahy*), while the second is a referring to a non-Malagasy Catholic's opinion. This person did not believe that observable reactions during exorcism stemmed from Satan but from people's sentiments and since women more easily show sentiments, a larger number of them are diagnosed as "assaulted by demons". Aa.J. Syvertsen reports to have asked an evangelist why more women than men became oppressed by demons: "Women are much weaker than men," he said, "and they are unable to resist when the evil spirit or the traditional healer threaten them." Syvertsen 1983:178. B. Meyer has found that Ewe Christians in Southern Ghana think that women stand closer to *Abosam* (the devil) than men and the Fall is the biblical reference for this. Women's spirits are therefore more likely to be possessed by a witch's spirit. One of her informants also explained women's interest in prayer groups as a consequence of their closeness to the devil. There they would get a strength that men possessed naturally. Meyer 1992:117.

[1065] IS 210 mentions elsewhere that most young men come to the *toby* because of use of drugs, while women most frequently contract diseases because of lack of calcium. See 4.2.2.3.

[1066] L.A. Sharp found that 96 % of the *tromba* mediums in Ambanja were women. See 4.1.1.2 (Possession), footnote 589. Aa.J. Syvertsen supposes that 80 % of the "assaulted by demons" were women, according to his own observations, but other missionaries who maintained that the majority of the "assaulted by demons" were men challenged him. See 3.2.3.8, footnote 494. See J.-M. Estrade's explanations of why women are so prominent in connection with *tromba*. Estrade 1985:268–270.

4.3.5 Summary

Some of the "assaulted by demons" have manifestations and some have not. According to the shepherds, this depends on the category of spirits, the phase in the treatment and the devil's working methods. The shepherds do not underline the importance of diagnosis, but they use several methods in order to identify if a person is in need of exorcism: a variety of signs, the Holy Spirit's gift of discerning spirits, exorcism itself and the sick and their families' own estimation. Several of the methods are usually taken into account simultaneously.

Idol worship is by far the most frequent mentioned cause of demonic oppression in my material. This may happen through a voluntary pact with spirits, by actively seeking healing from traditional healers and involuntarily by effects of remedies in the person's home or by sorcery. The shepherds consider a person without faith in Jesus as an open target for the devil, problems, weaknesses, anxiety etc. may be exploited by the devil to oppress people, as is also the case with temptation to sin. The shepherds' understanding of demonic oppression as part of "God's program" for the patient or his/her family does not exclude other more direct causes.

Some Christians have faith only as a theory and they also consult traditional healers, which may cause them to be "assaulted by demons". Committed Christians may be affected by sorcery, lack of watchfulness, or because God wants their families to be saved but eager prayer and abundance of God's word make Jesus able to protect them from the evil one.

The question of gender is not much commented in my material but although it seems as though women are in majority among those who ask for exorcism by moving to the front of the church, I have also many references to men as "assaulted by demons".

There is controversy among my informants about their ability to identify and define the "assaulted by demons". Some seem to believe that demons are at work in all people, some that the devil is at work in non-Christians in general and others that exorcism is appropriate for people with a wide variety of conditions. Others oppose these views. When Christians are treated with exorcism, there are different opinions among shepherds as to why they need this.

The shepherds' evaluation of manifestations and lack of such and the ways some shepherds distinguish between natural problems/crises and the devil's exploitation of this seem obscure to me. This is also the case when shepherds deem exorcism to be appropriate for many different people, even for people who are not considered to be "assaulted by demons". It is difficult to grasp that the shepherds emphasise that Jesus has power to protect Christians against demonic attacks, while they at the same time admit that committed Christians may be "assaulted by demons".

4.4 Expelling demons and related issues

This chapter relates to the part of a healing service where demons are expelled. Only certain elements, which emerge from the material itself and are emphasised by the shepherds will be presented in the following. These elements are the relation between a general and an individual expulsion of demons, the shepherds' movements and the level of intensity in their shouting and the shepherds' expulsion of undesirable human conditions/attitudes and how they conceive of this. In addition to these elements I also present the shepherds' understanding of the dress and their use of water in connection with expulsion of demons, a custom, which seems to have been abolished by the movement in the middle of my fieldwork period.[1067]

4.4.1 Addressing the demons in general and casting out of individuals

During the hymn introducing the exorcism session, some of the audience move to straw mats or benches in the front of the room.[1068] According to some shepherds, the gathering of the people with special needs in front of the congregation is a matter of organisation. It is done to prevent the patients from hurting themselves, if they suddenly start acting erratically within the benches and to facilitate the shepherds' work.[1069] It may also signify other things. One informant believes that these people are aware

---

[1067] Other elements in the exorcism practice are treated elsewhere, according to what seems most natural e.g. people showing manifestations or lack of such during expulsion of demons (see 4.3.1.2) and shepherds treated with exorcism together with the sick. See 4.5.2.5 (A unique position of the shepherds?).

[1068] See 3.2.1.1.

[1069] IS 311, IS 312, Tobilehibe 1997:100.

of specific problems in their lives and do not want to justify themselves by pretending. By moving forward they ask for the shepherds' assistance.[1070] Another informant sees the moving forward as a sign of humility. He thinks that God may work faster when people make themselves humble and sit down on the mat.[1071]

The relation between the people on the straw mats and the rest of the audience during the expulsion of demons seems somewhat vague in my material. It is not always obvious which group the informants refer to and different aspects are underlined.[1072]

Demons are in the air around us.[1073] They may move everywhere, also to the church when God's people are gathering. They come in order to seduce people, to prevent them from listening to God's word and to frighten them.[1074] This belief makes it important to arrange an initial casting out of demons in the beginning of the exorcism session, with the primary aim of expelling the demons in the air among the congregation. The thinking seems to be that if the demons are left unchallenged they will not manifest themselves.[1075] During the initial casting out of demons the shepherds sometimes walk down the gangway among the audience.[1076] The understanding among my informants of the initial expulsion of demons varies. One says:

> It may be understood as a cleansing of the entire house where they are gathered. This strengthens the people because it implies that the devil has no

---

[1070] IS 323.

[1071] IS 328. A non-shepherd compares those who sit on the straw mat with Job who sat in the ashes, a strong sign of humility. IN 317.

[1072] Some of my informants seem to understand the casting out of demons in healing services as including all the people present (IS 311, IS 325), while others especially have those on the first benches/straw mats in mind. IS 310. A non-shepherd says: "When you attend a healing service, the shepherds cast out demons of everyone present" (*rehefa tratran'ny amoahana demonia ao, dia amoahany demonia*). IN 313.

[1073] IS 323 refers to Eph 6:12.

[1074] IS 200.

[1075] In an exorcism session immediately following the Sunday service one person showed manifestations. My informant says that during the preceding Sunday service the demons had not manifested themselves and he takes this as an indication that demons have to be challenged directly. IS 217.

[1076] A non-shepherd in my material is sceptical to this practice. "This is to no use," he says, "because the demons neither stick to people's bodies nor are all the people in a healing service demoniacs." QN 62.

room in the gathering but has to leave. Jesus is Lord of the place, only his work is to be done and this gives confidence to the people. This expulsion of demons has to be taken as a symbolic action: when the devil is expelled he is not given any room.[1077]

Another informant says that this initial casting out of demons aims more at the self-examination of the people gathered. It reminds them of the word of God in order to lead them to conversion and if they repent, the demons will leave them.[1078]

The shepherds continue by concentrating their efforts especially on those gathered on the straw mats/benches in the front of the room. The shepherds also seem to understand this differently and I mainly refer to two of my informants. The controversy is centred on an individual or a collective understanding. The following quotations refer mainly to the expulsion of demons from the people sitting on the mats but, from time to time, it seems as my informants have the whole casting out of demons-session in mind. The first informant explained:

> For me it is possible both to cast out demons from people individually and from many people together. The revival movement in Madagascar has chosen the second practice.[1079] In my earlier teaching of shepherds I told them that since not all people are demoniacs, they should not normally be subjected to expulsion of demons. I asserted that the demoniacs should be treated separately. My argument was Jesus' practice. He did not cast out demons in general but only from those who manifested themselves as demoniacs and came to him. And I told them that I am not willing to be labelled as a demoniac. ... In the Soatanana-branch of the revival those who manifest themselves with observable signs as demoniacs are "worked" with in a special room and the thinking in the Soatanana-branch is that people mostly need strengthening. In my opinion, the shepherds ought to know who are demoniacs and who are not before starting the expulsion of demons and thus they may expel demons from those in need of it.
> Even if this is still my view of how the practice should be, I do not emphasise it any more because I do not consider the shepherds' practice as wrong. And,

---

[1077] IS 217. My informant reflects on the possibility of some demons staying even after this initial expulsion but concludes that the action is a purposeful casting out and as such a renunciation of the devil.

[1078] IS 218.

[1079] His meaning seems to be that the way shepherds actually cast out demons has to be understood as an expulsion from several people at the same time.

in addition, if I underline my opinion too much, the shepherds will say that I am countering their work.[1080]

According to the informant above, he mainly understands the shepherds' actual practice as an expulsion of demons from many people simultaneously (collective) but another informant opposes his view. When the shepherds concentrate on those sitting on the straw mats, the second informant seems to understand this as an expulsion directed to each individual. He is afraid of the consequences of the new practice of exorcism in the Reformed Church (FJKM), where only one shepherd, standing in the front of the church far removed from the people, directs a general command to all demons to leave.[1081] "How is such a practice related to the Bible?" he asks.

> Jesus never cast out demons from a crowd, although he would have been able to do so because of his divine power. It is never recorded in the New Testament, however. The Lord seeks his sheep one by one (Lk 15). From a practical point of view it is not easy to imagine that a person sitting far back in the church can be freed from his demons if I stand far away casting them out. In fact, this is difficult to know but we assume that the devil is cunning and hides among people. If you, on the other side, stand face to face with a person, then God's power is present in a different way.[1082]

He refers to a testimony from a person formerly "assaulted by demons" to support his view of the necessity of being close to the patients when casting out demons. This person said that he barely saw the shepherds during expulsion of demons and he had problems with hearing what they said because something shut his ears to their words. My informant continues:

[1080] IS 321. My informant's way of referring to "the shepherds" does not mean that he himself is outside the revival movement. He is a pastor practising exorcism and his wording indicates controversy with some of his fellow-shepherds.

A non-shepherd also notices differences from NT times to the shepherds' practice: Then exorcism was only for those who came to Jesus, now it includes everybody present in the healing service. Jesus' exorcism was only for a few people, now it is for everybody, since we are all sinners. IN 313.

[1081] See 3.2.3.10, footnote 507. As far as I have observed, in the FJKM-setting nobody in the congregation moves to the front of the room until the prayer with the laying on of hands starts, after the general casting out of demons.

[1082] IS 323.

> The devil knows that if he is able to prevent people from listening to God's word he may conquer them. But if they hear this word they can use it to fight against the devil. When reflecting on this testimony it is worth asking if casting out of demons from far away really reaches the person. Does he/she hear what the shepherds say?
> Earlier, the casting out of demons in the 67 Ha church[1083] was only done from the front of the church. People far away did not hear and they only waited for the "strengthening". We decided to change the practice. Now the shepherds move around where people sit. This is according to Jesus' command: "As the Father has sent me, even so I send you." (Jn 20:21). He has sent us to save his sheep, i.e. to move where they are and not to be standing far away. ... Sometimes people want to move to the straw mats but they are prevented by the devil. They feel tied up to the chair. This makes it important for the shepherds to get close to the people. The theological basis for this is that no human seeks God because of their sins and the devil's hindrances but God is always seeking them. ... Every human is intended to have a close relationship to God and therefore the shepherds are taught to face each person individually. No demons will leave if the person does not understand that the expulsion of demons is done for him/her. There are no "church-demons" but only "individual peoples' demons" and the demons are different from person to person, as we also experience it in individual consultations.[1084]

This informant seems to admit, however, that the shepherds' actual expulsion of demons both includes an individual and a collective element. He says: "We have expulsion of demons both for all at once (*iray manontolo*) and for each person individually (*isam-batan'olona*)." None of them should be considered as impersonal and from a distance, however.[1085]

At least, the two cited informants accentuate differently what is going on in the shepherds' actual practice concerning the question of individual or collective casting out of demons.[1086] The most common

---

[1083] One of the Lutheran churches in Antananarivo, named after the district of the city where the church is located.

[1084] IS 323. The latter part of this citation seems to refer to the initial expulsion of demons, where the shepherds walk down the gangway among the congregation. It is unclear if my informant here also means to say that this happens during the whole casting out of demons-session. I have not observed that. The citation illustrates how difficult it is to distinguish between the initial casting out of demons and the concentration on those in special need of exorcism.

[1085] IS 323.

[1086] While the first informant's understanding seems to be based on observations of the practice itself (the shepherds' standing in front of many people casting out their demons), the second is firmly embedded in theological reflection, which has even caused changes in practice in the mentioned church. None of these informants

256 CH. 4: THE SHEPHERDS' UNDERSTANDING OF THEIR PRACTICE

opinion among shepherds seems to be that when demons are challenged by words of command during exorcism, they are normally cast out, wherever the people are seated.[1087]

4.4.2   The shepherds' movements and their loud voices

The shepherds are instructed never to touch the patients except when the patients are in danger of hurting themselves.[1088] Sometimes the sick may strike the shepherds but they should never strike back or use any force in their treatment.[1089] Sometimes, however, the shepherds exaggerate their movements, especially when they are stirred up by something, e.g. patients acting erratically. One informant tells about a group of German visitors coming to the *toby* Ankaramalaza videotaping the "work and strengthening". Then the shepherds' movements were similar to people pounding rice, which was not according to the teaching they had received.[1090]

There is no need for the shepherds to overstate their movements because demons are expelled by words alone. Strong movements rather tire the shepherds.[1091] It is wrong to cause pain to people, which may be the result if the shepherds touch the sick. *Mama* Nenilava was especially concerned with this and when she observed shepherds touching the patients unduly, she sometimes, after the service, showed these shepherds how it could hurt.[1092] Some of the sick are very tired and should not be disturbed either with exaggerated movements or with noise.[1093] The story in Mk 5 shows that the Ger'asene demoniac reacted

---

comment on the specific practice in the *toby* Ambohimahazo, where each shepherd moves around imposing their hands and casting out demons individually from each of the people sitting in the front of the church. This practice can only be understood as a casting out of demons from individuals.

[1087] IS 217, IS 311.
[1088] The traditional healers do not touch the patient during treatment, according to IN 313.
[1089] IS 210.
[1090] IS 323.
[1091] IS 323.
[1092] IS 323. *Mama* Nenilava never pushed or pulled the patient's body and she said that to do so is a result of the shepherd's insufficient strength. Pitaka 1999:120. A non-shepherd accuses the shepherds for touching the head of the patients so hard that it causes other sicknesses in addition to the demonic oppression. QN 136.
[1093] IS 210.

to Jesus only by seeing him. The demoniac knew the Spirit in the Lord and this proves that it is not the exaggerated movements that expel demons. Jesus was calm and determined when he commanded the spirits to leave.[1094]

How does the prohibition against touching the patients relate to the special way of casting out demons in the Ambohimahazo *toby*, where the shepherds lay their hands on each patient's head while casting out? One informant says that this laying on of hands is both to be understood as casting out of demons and healing of sickness, but he distinguishes this laying on of hands from the "strengthening". The laying of hands during the casting out of demons is no prayer—while the "strengthening" is— and all the shepherds lay hands on the sick successively in the casting out of demons session, while in the "strengthening" only one shepherd prays for each sick person. The practice of the laying on of hands is according to the word of Jesus: "they will lay their hands on the sick, and they will recover" (Mk 16:18). My informant admits that Jesus did not touch the demoniacs but he sometimes touched those who suffered from ordinary sicknesses when he healed them.[1095] Another informant also mentions that Jesus' touched some people when he healed them,[1096] and he says that the direct biblical background for the practice is Lk 11:20: "But if it is by the finger of God that I cast out demons, then the kingdom of God has come upon you." "The children of the revival think that the devil works in a variety of ways," he says, "consequently, it is necessary to touch (*fanendrena*) the sick."[1097] According to this informant's understanding all the *toby* have the practice of casting out demons with the laying on of hands. The practical arrangement of the liturgy, however, makes this more apparent in the Ambohimahazo- and Farihimena-*toby* because they have inserted a prayer between casting out of demons and "strengthening". In the Ankaramalaza- and Soatanana-*toby*, on the other side, there is no prayer separating the two parts and thus there is a soft transition from the casting out of demons to

---

[1094] IS 323. Since the spirits are invisible, it is in vain to chase them with exaggerated movements, according to QN 103.

[1095] IS 200.

[1096] He refers to Mt 8:3, Mk 7:33 and Lk 22:51.

[1097] IS 210. I have not been able to ask for further clarification of his sayings. It seems obscure to me why touching the patient is a necessary consequence of the devil's work in a variety of ways. The biblical reference of "the finger of God" seems to be used by my informant as stating the reason for touching the patient.

"strengthening".[1098] Another informant does not seem to agree with this argument because he asserts firmly that demons are cast out by words alone and he thinks that the Ambohimahazo-custom is an example of a practice that has been added to the founders' original practice.[1099]

When the shepherds emphasise that they cast out demons by words alone, this stems from Mt 8:16: "and he cast out the spirits with a word".[1100] They also see Jesus' practice in the NT as the background of their own practice in this respect: "And Jesus rebuked him, and the demon came out of him" in Mt 17:18 reads in the Malagasy Bible: "and Jesus talked loudly (*niteny mafy*) to him ...".[1101] What "talking loudly" means is in the handbook said to be "words of command full of authority". This is further explained by cautioning the shepherds not to exaggerate the level of their shouting, by prohibiting them to shout in people's ears and by advising the shepherds to be calmer when casting out demons from people with heart diseases.[1102] One informant calls for caution with respect to the level of intensity in the shepherds' shouting because there is normally children present in these services and loud voices may scare them.[1103] It is a constant temptation for the shepherds to think that they cast out demons by their own strength and they should be

---

[1098] IS 210. Thus, in the transition period some shepherds still cast out demons while others already have started the prayer with the laying on of hands. 67 Ha-church 10 April 1993.

[1099] IS 323. Even this informant recommends to cast out demons immediately if a person starts acting erratically in the middle of the prayer with the laying on of hands and afterwards to continue the prayer for the person. This probably points to a somewhat fluid border between the casting out of demons and the laying on of hands.

[1100] The emphasis on words alone stands in contrast to all the ritual symbols used in exorcism in AIC. In addition to purification in water, M.L. Daneel talks about a piece of red cloth to protect the patient, money signifying "divorce" between host and inhabiting spirit, blood from sacrifice on an unused plate, which are thrown away, to signify the separation from the spirit and burning of destructive medicines used in sorcery. Daneel 1990:233–235.

[1101] L 210. This is also the case in Mk 1:25, where the RSV has "rebuke" while the Malagasy Bible has *miteny mafy*.

[1102] Tobilehibe 1997:104–105.

[1103] IS 205.

EXPELLING DEMONS AND RELATED ISSUES 259

reminded of that demons do not depart because of the intensity of shouting, a point underlined by several shepherds.[1104]

4.4.3 What do the shepherds expel?

When the shepherds use the expression "casting out of demons", this normally signifies demons, devils, or the devil/Satan.[1105] Sometimes the shepherds are more specific in naming what they cast out, however and in the following subchapter I focus my presentation on this specificity.[1106]

4.4.3.1 *Naming human conditions/attitudes*

The shepherds mention a wide variety of human conditions/attitudes binding people. They do not attempt to give any exhaustive list and there seems to be no grouping of the conditions/attitudes.[1107] What should be cast out are exemplified as following: a depressed state of mind,[1108] unbelief,[1109] temptations,[1110] pretence, self-righteousness, hindrances to

---

[1104] IS 323, IS 325. "This is according to the Bible," IS 205 says but he does not refer to any specific passage. Several non-shepherds criticise the loud voices during expulsion of demons and one of them says that this will cause trouble to the sick, they may feel afraid and they will not be able to have a praying attitude. QN 103. One non-shepherd in my material emphasises, however, that commanding the demons with a loud voice is necessary in order to make them leave. QN 11.

[1105] The most common Malagasy expressions are casting out of demons (*famoahana demonia*) and casting out of the devil/devils (*fandroahana devoly*). IS 200, IS 206. See 2.2.7.

[1106] See 3.2.3.5. Casting out of sickness is perhaps most common but this is treated elsewhere and will not be dealt with here. See 4.5.1.3 (Expulsion of sickness).

[1107] The handbook talks of spiritual conditions/attitudes (*toe-panahy*) and conditions/attitudes in life (*toe-piaina*), which bind and scare people. These should be named and cast out. Tobilehibe 1997:101. In Malagasy only one word is used to denote all the referred conditions/attitudes: *toetra* and this word has no single English equivalent. In the following I use "condition/attitude" to convey the meaning of the Malagasy word but sometimes the English words do not seem to cover the meaning properly.

[1108] Mal: *fahakiviana*. IS 202, 217, 218.

[1109] Mal: *tsi-finoana*. IS 214, IS 217, IS 323.

[1110] Mal: *fakam-panahy*. IS 202, IS 315.

260 CH. 4: THE SHEPHERDS' UNDERSTANDING OF THEIR PRACTICE

pray/go to church,[1111] an unrepentant heart,[1112] weakness,[1113] adultery, pride,[1114] lack of love, envy, hatred, drinking of alcohol, lust of the flesh,[1115] worries, stealing.[1116]

Does my material indicate that the shepherds may be over-zealous when they expel all these different conditions/attitudes or do the shepherds state reasons for this practice? One informant admits that there are shepherds who "extend their abilities when working" because they are committed to their task but they are taught to primarily cast out demons.[1117] The shepherds are wrong if they e.g. gesticulate close to a person's head and command adultery to depart and the person is not committing adultery. Then he/she may be offended and even leave God, which is the opposite of the shepherds' purposes. The shepherds are advised to use less specific labels when they cast out.[1118] According to *Mama* Nenilava the command: "Leave in the name of Jesus," without any specific naming, expel every spirit, except the Spirit of God. My informant believes, however, that it may be helpful to name the spirits and his advice is to "cast out the devil and all his stuff".[1119]

Examples of admitted lack of wisdom among shepherds do not alter most of my informants' general opinion that undesirable human conditions/attitudes should be cast out. Some of them, however, emphasise that the shepherds should rather cast out the spirits behind these conditions/attitudes and not the conditions/attitudes themselves, because it is the evil spirits that exploit different human conditions/attitudes.[1120] They mention spirits of laziness, spirits leading

---

[1111] Mal: *fihatsarabelatsihy, fanamarinan-tena, ny tsy fahazoana ny mivavaka.* IS 205. According to my informant, *Dadatoa* Rakotozandry said that pretence and self-righteousness were demons ruling over people.

[1112] Mal: *fanamafisam-po.* IS 210.

[1113] Mal: *fahalemena.* IS 214.

[1114] Mal: *fijangajangana, fiavonavonana/fireharehan-dratsy.* IS 217.

[1115] Mal: *tsi-fitiavana, fialonana, fankahalana, fisotroan-toaka, filan'ny nofo.* IS 322.

[1116] Mal: *fiahiahiana, kleptomania.* IS 323. I have mostly arranged the listing according to examples given by each informant to enable the reader to get an impression of what is put together. Cf. similarities between this list and 4.3.1.3 (Self-diagnosis).

[1117] IS 217.

[1118] IS 322. My informant says that they e.g. may "cast out all sins and results of unbelief" (*ny ota rehetra sy ny vokatry ny tsi-finoana).*

[1119] Mal: *miala ny devoly sy ny forongony rehetra.* IS 323.

[1120] IS 214 says that since many shepherds do not reflect much on the words they use, they are not occupied with this distinction.

astray,[1121] deceiving spirits and all spirits not stemming from Jesus.[1122] The shepherds do not seem to consider the naming of human conditions/attitudes and different spirits to be mutually exclusive and some informants mention both, as does the handbook.[1123]

4.4.3.2 *The shepherds' reasons for expelling undesirable human conditions/attitudes*

All the conditions/attitudes mentioned above are considered as undesirable from the shepherds' Christian viewpoint. "They do not stem from a living faith in the heart," one informant says.[1124] Consequently, they have another source and have to be expelled. "They stem from the devil and not from God."[1125] The logic seems to follow a course of deduction:

> A quick-tempered person easily hurts other people and thus this condition/attitude cannot stem from God. Consequently, it has to come from the devil. ... This attribution of an undesired condition/attitude to have demonic origin does not mean, however, that the person showing this condition/attitude is without responsibility for this. Some people may accuse spirits in order to avoid punishment but a person who is willing to repent will not do so.[1126]

People living in these conditions/attitudes may know that these things stem from the devil and they have heard God's word about this but they are not willing to live according to God's word.[1127] Expulsion of these conditions/attitudes may be needed since these people have difficulties in believing God's word.[1128]

[1121] Mal: *fanahin'ny fahakamoana, fanahin'ny fampiviliana.* IS 213.
[1122] Mal: *fanahy mamitaka, fanahy rehetra tsy avy amin'i Jesosy.* IS 322. IS 315 talks of spirits causing a depressed mind (*fanahy mahakivy*).
[1123] The handbook advises the shepherds to name both types of spirits and human conditions/attitudes Tobilehibe 1997:101. Cf. below 4.4.3.3.
[1124] IS 205.
[1125] IS 322.
[1126] IS 318.
[1127] IS 322. My informant seems to hint to Jas 1:22.
[1128] IS 214. If undesirable conditions/attitudes are left unchallenged the result may be apostasy. IS 315. My informant especially underlines that temptations have to be cast out since their goal is to cause people to stumble and thus leave faith in Jesus. He characterises the undesirable conditions by saying that people do not get rid of

The shepherds' purpose when naming specific human conditions/attitudes is further that people examine themselves and this is considered a part of the shepherds' Christian teaching.[1129]

> When the shepherds cast out demons they mention several conditions/attitudes, which do not stem from God. They may for example command pretending to leave and when their words effect the listeners, this may hurt their hearts and they admit their own pretending."[1130]

The self-examination is expected to lead people to conversion and the shepherds' aim is to make people's faith in Jesus firm:

> When the shepherds command a depressed state of mind to leave, the message to the people is not that they are "assaulted by demons". It is more like the shepherds preach to people, commanding weakness and a depressed state of mind to come out. ... The depressed state of mind and all sorts of weaknesses can also be labelled as sin but the shepherds' commands make people think that Jesus is able to give strength, to take away their sorrows, to take away the depressed state of mind etc. The devil causes a depressed state of mind, the devil always frightens but Jesus gives us joy, peace, hope, love, humility, ...[1131]

The handbook says that some people only pretend to be Christians on the outside while their hearts are bound by conditions/attitudes like pretence, unbelief, a depressed state of mind, etc. The purpose of "work and strengthening" is to remove everything, which may prevent people from coming closer to God and receive his salvation.[1132]

---

    them. They come again and again (*miverina hatrany*). Cf. Lie 1981:15 who says that the Christians' habitual sins caused them to frequent the "work and strengthening".

[1129] IS 210, IS 312.

[1130] IS 318.

[1131] IS 218.

[1132] Tobilehibe 1997:95. "Work and strengthening" includes both naming different conditions/attitudes and casting them out, together with leading people to repentance through self-examination. Tobilehibe 1997:98.

4.4.3.3 *Relationship between human conditions/attitudes and evil spirits*

One of my informants tries to explain his understanding of this relation, admitting that it is a difficult question including both psychological and spiritual aspects.

> There is a power in every human being begetting all kinds of sin: hatred, adultery etc. The human weakness is like an open door for evil spirits. They exploit this condition/attitude. The person is unable to resist the temptation because of his/her weakness and yields to sin. Our weaknesses are unbelief. By saying this I think of people without the faith mentioned in Eph 6 [the faith is a shield to "quench all the flaming darts of the evil one"] and I am not thinking of the original human sinfulness and weakness. If faith is lacking the door is open to the tempter but humans have a choice. When the sin is conceived it comes forth, i.e. the person decides to follow the temptation and more than that, also to worship sin, which is a higher degree of approval.[1133] To give an example: If a person pretends[1134] because this brings the person benefits, it is not difficult to imagine that the spirit of pretence, which is a spirit stemming from the devil also comes.[1135] This spirit binds the person even more firmly to pretending. When this has happened, one may talk about the person as "assaulted by demons" because the evil spirits come from outside to the human. Then this person's pretence both stems from his/her natural condition/attitude as a sinner and from the spirit of pretence, i.e. from the devil who is a master of deception. When a shepherd is going to "work" with this person, Jesus will show the shepherd which spirit is operating there. Then the shepherd is able to name the spirit and he/she can say: "I command the spirit of pretence to leave", or "I command the pretence to leave". The shepherd's command includes both what stems from the person and what stems from evil spirits.[1136]

According to this citation pretence is a natural condition/attitude because of human sinfulness but evil spirits exploit it and there are evil spirits corresponding to the natural conditions/attitudes. Another informant takes doubt (*fisalasalana*) as an example and says that it is part of being human. This condition/attitude can also be exploited by the devil, which implies that another power enters the human. This informant believes that it is the devil coming from outside, which has to be cast out and not

---

[1133] Maybe this is an allusion to Jas 1:14–15.
[1134] Literally: if a person serves pretence as his/her lord (*tompoiny*).
[1135] G. Haus has noticed that shepherds describe external spirits with the same names as human conditions. Haus 2000:96.
[1136] IS 323.

the human condition/attitude.[1137] This opinion seems to contradict the citation above on the question of expelling only the evil spirit, or expelling both the spirit and the human condition/attitude.[1138] The handbook maintains that works of evil spirits and undesirable human conditions/attitudes often are dependent on each other and work together. Both are works of the darkness and need to be cast out. The shepherds should know the people they "work" with, however and should not let the naming of all kinds of different conditions/attitudes become a habit. Revelation from the Holy Spirit through prayer is especially mentioned as a means of identification here but also the shepherd's consultation with the person.[1139]

4.4.4 Understanding of the dress

The shepherds have to wear their white dress during "work and strengthening", as they did at their consecration[1140] and this vestment has a profound significance, as will be shown below. When my informants mention the dress, however, they seem most concerned with the visible appearance and the differences in headdresses between the branches are often mentioned as an example. In the Soatanana-branch men have headdresses, in the Ankaramalaza-branch women have them, while in the Farihimena-branch neither men nor women wear headdresses.[1141] The custom in the Soatanana-branch with men wearing headdresses causes a problem with regard to 1 Cor 11:7, which says that "a man ought not to cover his head, ...". One of my informants once asked *Mama* Nenilava how *Dada* Rainisoalambo could institute a practice contrary to a biblical

---

[1137] IS 214. The devil's ability to exploit human conditions and sicknesses is commented more lengthily in 4.3.2.2 (The devil's exploitation).

[1138] Two non-shepherds in my material see a danger in what they call expulsion of sins. QN 108, QN 139. QN 108 fears that the Christians coming to the healing services are unable to distinguish between sins and demons. They may think that the shepherds are able to cast out their sins, which may result in a belief in sinlessness after having attended "work and strengthening", or that demons inside them commit sin. Because of insufficient theological training of the shepherds, he is afraid that some shepherds, too, may think like this.

[1139] Tobilehibe 1997:102–103. To the work of the Holy Spirit in identifying the "assaulted by demons", see 4.3.1.3 (A gift of discernment).

[1140] Cf. 2.2.2.3.

[1141] IS 205, IS 212. IS 315 refers the use of headdresses to biblical regulations: "Women ought to veil their heads, according to the Bible" (1 Cor 11).

regulation. She answered that people later on had supplemented what the founders had taught and she emphasised that "the children of the revival" should always follow the Bible.[1142] Others ascribe the style of dress to the work of the Holy Spirit who gave directions to the founders about how the dress should look like. Consequently, it is difficult to investigate the differences and try to explain them, because the Spirit is free to act in his own way.[1143] Another informant sees a connection between the dress customs where the founders lived at that time and the style of the shepherds' dress. "Men wore headdresses in the Betsileo-tribe at the time of Rainisoalambo," he says, "and this is the reason why men in the Soatanana-branch have this custom."[1144] These differences ought not to create problems if the founders' different gifts of grace are respected as stemming from the Lord, according to another.[1145]

The handbook of the Ankaramalaza-branch of the movement gives detailed regulations about the style and significance of the dress. In the following I delimit myself to main points in the handbook's understanding of significance and I do not comment on style.[1146] The dress is called a "holy vestment" (*akanjo masina*) and it is underlined that Jesus has ordered the shepherds to wear it, through a vivid vision to *Mama* Nenilava. It is called a sign of holiness, consecrated by God and to God. The handbook furnishes a biblical background for the dress. It is a vestment of honour, given by God (2 Cor 5:3, Rev 3:18), it is the white dress of the righteousness from God (Zec 3:4, Lk 15:22), it is a sign of serving by working and fighting (Rev 7:15, 19:8) and it is a sign of the shepherd's covenant with God from his/her day of consecration (Is 41:9). The shepherds wear their white dress on the day of consecration, they should bring it whenever they depart for a journey (together with the Bible and the hymnbook) and they are supposed to wear it at their

---

[1142] IS 323.

[1143] IS 212, IS 322.

[1144] IS 210. According to this informant, men wear headdresses also in the Manolotrony-branch of the revival, due to this branch's origin in the Betsileo-tribe. See 2.1.1.

[1145] IS 322. IS 315, who is a Reformed pastor/shepherd, does not see the style of dress as decisive and when he is asked to visit sick people in private homes to cast out demons, he never brings his dress with him. By doing so he will emphasise that the holiness does not stem from the dress but from the person. A non-shepherd in my material, on the other hand, accuses some shepherds because they think it is impossible for them to cast out demons without wearing the white dress. QN 162.

[1146] For the style and regulations concerning the making of the dress, see 2.2.2.3.

funeral.[1147] The white dress and not ordinary clothing should always be used during exorcism but it should not be used when e.g. the shepherd functions as a local church leader (*katekista*) or deacon.[1148]

As a consequence of the profound significance of the dress, the shepherds have to store it and use it with care. Since it is holy it should always be kept clean. It has to be put in a holy bag (*kitapo masina*) and it should be washed regularly. Those who do not take care of this give the devil a possibility to ruin and dirty the dress.[1149] When not in use, it should be stored separately from other clothes in a high place, or on the top of other clothes, if the clothes are stored in one place. It is advisable to have two dresses. One is consecrated together with the shepherd and the new dress should be taken to the elder of the *toby* who prays for it, or consecrates it in a special liturgical service at the annual meeting of the *toby*. Every time the shepherds put on the dress, they should not forget to pray, to examine themselves and to remind themselves of the significance of the dress, in order to live according to what is mirrored by the dress. Shepherds who use the vestment as a nightdress are said to be on their way of apostasy and it should neither be used when the shepherds bath the sick in water.[1150] Those who reject use of the holy vestments do not understand that to wear it is a sign of respecting the shepherd's ministry. The shepherds' wearing of the white dresses mirrors the presence of Jesus (Ps 46:5, Ezek 37:28), it shows that Jesus leads the holy "work" and works together with the shepherds (Mk 16:20) and it protects the servants of God from all the enemy's work (Phil 3:2, 1 Pet 5:8). It is underlined that Jesus has not allowed the "children of Ankaramalaza" to use the white dress in everyday life. The holy vestment is dedicated for use only in gatherings for shepherds:

[1147] Their fellow shepherds put the holy vestment on the corpse and carry the coffin.

[1148] In urgent situations, where a sick person needs their service immediately, the shepherds are allowed to cast out demons without the dress but this is an exception to the general rule. Ankaramalaza 1997:7–8.

[1149] G. Haus cites a passage in the handbook and says that dirt and splits make it possible for the devil to enter into the dress and she connects this to the shepherds' belief that spirits love dirt and splits, in concrete and figurative meaning (e.g. smoke and alcohol are considered as dirty). She notices a tension between this and the shepherds' understanding of the dress as consecrated and holy. Haus 2000:59–60. The passage in the handbook equally well may be taken in a figurative meaning, however and thus it does not concern dirt and tears on the dress itself but rather points to the shepherds' handling of the dress in general.

[1150] Cf. 4.4.5 below.

consecration-services, "work and strengthening" and other special reunions where there is an agreement to use it.[1151]

4.4.5 Use of water while expelling demons: a controversial issue

The practice of bathing the sick in water during casting out of demons has been used by shepherds outside the healing service in the treatment of severely ill people.[1152] In the middle of my fieldwork in 1992–94 this custom seems to have been abolished. According to two of my informants this happened sometime before September 1993 but they do not agree on whether the prohibition is stated as a general rule (*fitsipika iombonana*) from the Protestant revival committee (*Fifohazana FFPM*) or as a request to end this practice.[1153]

A couple of informants mention that earlier there were shepherds with healing gifts who used to combine casting out of demons with bathing the sick in water. God let signs and wonders happen as a result of this and my informants wonder if these mighty acts in the past could point to the origin of the custom.[1154] This happened many years ago but my informants said that people's minds still stick to this way of healing: "They do not remember that this happened because people with gifts of

---

[1151] Tobilehibe 1997:56–60, 47. Many pages in the handbook (pp. 56–62) deal with the holy vestments and this indicates its importance to the shepherds. Randrianarivelo 2000:95–96 sees several dangers in such extended teaching on the dress: The shepherds may be tempted to consider the dress more important than the Lord and direct their faith towards a human product instead of turning to Jesus and his promise and he thinks that some shepherds may believe that the dress has a magic power because of all the interdictions surrounding it. He sees similarities between the shepherds' thinking of the dress and Zulu practices and refers to the Zulu prophet casting out demons by the veil of his robe. Sundkler 1961:230. According to my material, I question such a comparison with Zulu prophets, since the shepherds reject the use of any object while expelling demons. Cf. 4.4.2.

[1152] Another treatment briefly referred to in my material, which is not part of a healing service, is massage. IS 200, IS 210, IS 214. The handbook forbids the shepherds to use this practice in connection with exorcism. Tobilehibe 1997:83.

[1153] IS 200 said in September 1993 that the Protestant revival committee had made a general rule on this one month earlier, while IS 210 by that time said that the last meeting of the committee had requested that the shepherds should not bath the sick any more. I have not found any written minutes from this meeting and new decisions spread slowly, so it is likely that the practice continued for some time after August 1993.

[1154] IS 200, IS 210.

healing performed it. Some people think that expulsion of demons plus water is a liturgy of healing in the revival movement but it is not."[1155]

One informant explains how calm the "mad" (*adala*) became when cold water was poured over their body. In this way it was easier for the shepherds to deal with them. He thinks the calming effect has been the main reason for the use of water as a treatment but he agrees that it should not be used any more. It hurts the patient's body and it is better only to pray and wait for God's will with the person.[1156] In addition, he thinks that this custom changed people's focus from faith in Jesus to faith in the water and a visible action became the main interest. "People shall be healed only through faith in God's word," he says.[1157] Another informant gives another down to earth explanation to why the sick are bathed often: The sick often act erratically and may have severe spasms. This causes them to become exhausted and they perspire profusely, which causes a bad odour. Therefore, they have to be washed rather frequently. Since, according to my informant, many of them resist bathing because of their "madness" (*hadalana*), others have to pour water over their bodies and this way of bathing differs from how people normally wash themselves and may cause people to think that this water carries a special power. Shepherds take care of the sick and thus they also have to keep them clean and washed, which may have strengthened people's belief that this bathing has a special significance. The sick still have to be kept clean but non-shepherds should take care of this in order to avoid misunderstandings, according to the decision of the revival committee referred to.[1158]

Two of my informants report of treatment with water in connection with casting out of demons, prior to 1993. One of them experienced no

---

[1155] IS 210. One of the people treated at the toby who was still on his way to recovery when I met him, talked repeatedly about washing himself with soap and water in Jesus' name and if he did so, Jesus had told him that he would be healed. IN 207.

[1156] CHIS 8 also reports how the cold water made him suffer.

[1157] IS 200. A non-shepherd accuses some shepherds for thinking that the sick will not be free from the demons without use of water and he sees this as belief in a magical power of the water. "Such remedies were not used by the apostles but only the name of Jesus," he says. QN 60.

[1158] IS 210. There are people abandoned by their families and since shepherds take care of these people at the *toby*, it may be difficult to arrange the washing without the shepherds' taking part in it. Therefore, my informant says that shepherds may assist in the bathing of the patients but they should always do this together with non-shepherds.

lasting positive results from this. When the shepherds poured water over him, some of the animals crawling on his body left but they returned soon afterwards. He told the shepherds that they only tired themselves by bathing him. He saw that the animals still stayed in the basin, they looked like fishes and danced and they said to him: "We will not leave!"[1159] Another informant tells about a successful treatment of his son by the use of water together with expulsion of demons:

> At the *toby* they brought him to cold water two mornings and when the shepherds cast out demons, the sick said: "Do not expel us! Stop the casting out because we are disturbed by this." The second day the sick told that he felt that something powerful left him. To fight directly with the devil was hard work for the shepherds and in addition, they were standing in cold water whilst expelling demons.[1160]

At the Ambohimahazo *toby* there used to be a separate room where the shepherds poured water over the sick.[1161] Other *toby* used a river near by.[1162]

That some shepherds still make use of water in some way is seen in a pamphlet published in 1997 by the committee of the *toby* Ankaramalaza. One question concerns an observed incident of immersing a patient seven times into cold water. "Is this according to the Bible?" The pamphlet forbids the custom because it can be understood magically and the shepherds' working methods should differ visibly from the traditional healers' methods.[1163] The background of the practice

---

[1159] CHIS 8.

[1160] IS 214. One of my field-assistants also reports of positive results from bathing the patients in water together with expulsion of demons: When cold water was poured over a girl, she suddenly regained her conscience and noticed all the shepherds gathering there. CHINA 116.

[1161] Ambohimahazo *toby* 08 March 1993. Cf. the talk of a basin above.

[1162] IS 214. Use of water is important in exorcism practices in the AIC: It purifies, it expels evil and it can be used to take away evil through vomiting (often it is then mixed with salt, ashes etc.). Through baptism in water evil spirits are driven out. Water blessed by the leader is powerful and it may be sprinkled on people and houses to keep spirits out. Kitshoff 1997:6–7. Water is also the main ritual component in Bishop Nyasha's Pentecostal Church. Daneel 1990:232.

[1163] A non-shepherd in my material compares the traditional healers' and the shepherds' practices of exorcism and finds that there are several similar elements but addressed to different entities: singing (the traditional healers use music), prayer, a high level of intensity (in invocation of entities), followed by the patients' reactions with spasms. There is no prayer with the laying on of hands in the traditional healers'

270   CH. 4: THE SHEPHERDS' UNDERSTANDING OF THEIR PRACTICE

is said to be the treatment prescribed by the prophet Eli'sha to the Syrian Na'aman, found in 2 Kings 5 but this only happened once and thus it is not intended to be practised by the church in our times. "Jesus ordered baptism to be done in water according to Mt 28:18–20," the book says, "and this is the only relation to water in Christian practices."[1164]

4.4.6   Summary

An initital expulsion of demons is arranged in the beginning of the exorcism session and afterwards the shepherds concentrate on the people sitting on the first benches/mats. This casting out of demons includes both a collective and an individual element. The shepherds underline the example of Jesus in expelling demons. The shepherds are not allowed to touch the patients during expulsion of demons and they should be careful not to exaggerate their movements and the level of intensity in their shouting. In addition to casting out demons, shepherds also name a variety of undesirable human conditions/attitudes, or the evil spirits behind these, to be cast out. There are examples of shepherds being too zealous in their listing but my informants give several reasons for this practice. The relationship between human conditions/attitudes and evil spirits is considered a difficult question.

Shepherds always wear the white dress during expulsion of demons. Profound significance is attached to the dress and the biblical background of this "holy vestment" is underlined. Shepherds have used the practice of bathing the sick in cold water during casting out of demons in earlier times but because of a possible magical understanding, the custom is abolished.

There is controversy among the shepherds as to whether the casting out of demons in a healing service is to be understood as an expulsion of demons from many people at the same time or from individuals and whether the evil spirits leave because of the expulsion or because a person repents. They also have different opinions on whether it is the undesirable conditions/attitudes that are to be cast out or the spirits behind these, coming from outside and they differ in their understanding

---

ritual but instead he/she sprinkles water on the sick and their families. This water is mixed with charms (*ody*), which are taken from nature and is part of the remedies used to cast out evil spirits. IN 313.

[1164] Ankaramalaza 1997:11.

of the dress and how differences in dress emerged. Non-shepherds criticise shepherds because they exaggerate their movements and level of voice during casting out of demons, because they emphasise observable differences too much and because casting out of sins may have unintended consequences.

According to the shepherds, it seems as there are evil spirits corresponding to undesirable conditions/attitudes. I do not grasp, however, how the shepherds perceive of this. Why do they insist on casting out the undesirable conditions/attitudes? Why do they not address these conditions/attitudes with other means? It also seems obscure to me why the shepherds underline the importance of the dress so much.

4.5 Exorcism as healing

The purpose of this chapter is to enquire into the shepherds' emphasis on exorcism as healing, in a wide meaning of the term. Firstly, I describe the shepherds' understanding of sickness in relation to exorcism, nuances in the word "sickness", how they understand this theme, especially the relationship between sickness and the devil and the shepherds' views of different kinds of treatment. In this section I deal especially with sicknesses that can be observed in the body or the mind. Secondly, I focus on the healing process in the shepherds' overarching theological perspective: The shepherds' basic concern is faith in Jesus, they request a burning of all charms and they understand healing in a communal perspective. The shepherds consider the "strengthening" with prayer and the laying on of hands as the climax of their healing activity.

4.5.1 Sickness and exorcism

The shepherds firmly believe that God is able to heal any sickness, irrespective of its cause(s), if the sickness is brought to him.[1165] One informant cites Is 53:4: "Surely he has borne our griefs and carried our sorrows; ..." and adds that if we keep close to the text, it is written that the Lord heals any sickness.[1166]

[1165] IS 200, IS 321.

[1166] IS 323. A footnote in the RSV adds "or sicknesses" instead of "griefs" and the Malagasy Bible only has "our sicknesses" (*aretintsika*). IN 313 maintains that the

Sickness is an ambiguous word in the shepherds' usage and it has been used frequently in the preceding presentation. The main focus in this subchapter is the shepherds' view of sicknesses, which can be observed, in the body or the mind and the possible demonic involvement in sickness. Due to ambiguity in my material, I mostly use the word "sickness", without trying to define explicitly which kind of sickness the shepherds have in mind.

4.5.1.1 Bodily, mental and spiritual sickness: terminological considerations

The Malagasy words: *aretina*, *tsi-fahasalamana* (sickness), *marary* (sick) have much wider meanings than the corresponding English words and in accordance with my informants this wide meaning is reflected in my usage of the terms. *Tsi-fahasalamana* literally means "to be in a state of non-health", covering a wide range of different conditions. One of my informants explains "sick" by saying that some of the human strength, which usually is present, has gone.[1167] Sickness may sometimes be explained as stemming from an assault (*tafika*) from outside and if the person lacks the sufficient strength to resist this, he/she will turn ill: in the mind, in the heart, or in the body.[1168]

According to the handbook, a human consists of body (*vatana*), mind (*saina*) and spirit (*fanahy*)[1169] and sicknesses may refer to each of the parts. In my material, however, this distinction is not consistent and the demonic involvement is not necessarily delimited only to the spiritual. It is often difficult to decide which of these parts of the one human the shepherds have in mind when they simply say "sick" or "sickness".[1170]

---

      pivot of the shepherds' teaching on sickness is that Jesus is powerful to heal any sickness.

[1167] IS 210. When a person has a headache, some of his usual strength in the head is gone.

[1168] IS 210, IS 321. My informants do not make clear if "sickness on the heart" is the same as "spiritual sickness". "To cut one's finger is not considered an assault from outside," one informant says and the shepherds' underlying thinking seems to be that an assault is somehow considered to stem from the devil. IS 210. Cf. 4.1.1.3.

[1169] Tobilehibe 1997:125.

[1170] This ambiguity is reinforced by the fluid boundaries between body, mind and spirit and the view that sickness in one of the parts often effects the others. Haus 2000:18.

Examples of sicknesses referring to the body are headache, fever, cold[1171] and they are sometimes characterised in opposition to sicknesses stemming from sorcery, to demoniacs and to "uncommon sicknesses".[1172]

The Malagasy expression *very saina* literally means "lost mind" and the conceptualisation may be that the mind has left and it is impossible to trace it. When a mentally ill person recovers, however, this is expressed by saying that "his mind returns" (*miverina ny sainy*). One informant's explanation of the mad (*adala*) and the mentally sick (*marary saina/very saina*) is close to a personification of the mind. He says that "the mind leaves" and somehow the person is unable to return it, a condition causing sickness.[1173] Another informant characterises a mentally ill person by saying that only half of his mind is working or that his/her mind is sleeping.[1174]

Sicknesses connected to the spirit are by the shepherds called spiritual or demonic sicknesses. One informant says that the spiritually mad (*adala ara-panahy*) are "seized by demons" and some informants distinguish this group of sick at the *toby* from both the bodily and the mentally sick.[1175]

When my informants describe signs of the "assaulted by demons" in particular, i.e. the category of spiritual sickness above, they refer to the body in general, the mind and the consciousness. Illness itself often recurs among the signs.[1176] The listing of signs shows that there are various points of contact between demonic oppression and bodily or mental sicknesses and it is not ruled out that two of them or all three can be present simultaneously, another indication of the lack of a uniform terminology.[1177] Firstly, a demonic sickness may express itself through bodily sickness, like epilepsy, unconsciousness, blindness, dumbness, deafness, headache or different mental disturbances.[1178] Influence from

---

[1171] IS 76, IS 200. They are called sicknesses according to the flesh (*aretina ara-nofo*) and plain sicknesses (*aretina tsotra*).

[1172] IS 76, IS 201.

[1173] IS 206.

[1174] IS 210.

[1175] IS 200, IS 210.

[1176] IN 313 says that people in general consider bodily sickness a sign of evil spirits. See 4.3.1.1 (Bodily signs).

[1177] IS 217 distinguishes between psychosomatic and spiritual sickness.

[1178] L 336. IN 313 believes that some sicknesses are truly the fruit of evil spirits' work and it most often shows in mental illness.

the devil is said to effect the mind or the flesh.[1179] This means that an apparently plain bodily sickness, e.g. pain in a foot may turn out to be spiritual in origin.[1180] The devil is sometimes said to hide in the sickness.[1181] Secondly, bodily or mental sicknesses are believed to lead people into situations where demons are able to oppress them, e.g. if a person with fever is taken to a traditional healer and then evil spirits start to work in this person.[1182] One informant has observed that people using charms often contract asthma and cancer and he seems to have reached this conclusion because these sicknesses seldom are cured with Western medicine but rather through exorcism.[1183]

4.5.1.2 The understanding of sickness

"The Malagasy traditional belief that sickness has a cause is deeply rooted in the revival movement," one informant says.[1184] What he means to say with this is that the focus is on the causes and not on the sickness itself. This is supported by the ways shepherds understand sicknesses and the causes may be considered as natural, supernatural or both. In the middle of a severe bodily sickness one respondent was encouraged by the shepherds to ask God to reveal the reason for what had happened to her.[1185]

[1179] IS 311.

[1180] IS 218. In an incident with pain in the foot, the shepherds found that the demonic influence had come through the use of a special stick, connected with the blessing of the spirits.

[1181] QS 153.

[1182] L 336.

[1183] IS 323. His saying implies that people with these sicknesses often seek cure at traditional healers' practices, maybe because of the inefficiency of Western medicine. IG 332 says that the "assaulted by demons" are often sick or have a weak health because of all the taboos they are obliged to observe (many taboos concern food). This implies that these people have consulted traditional healers.

[1184] IS 210. He primarily points to spiritual causes of sickness, e.g. sorcery in exemplifying this. Rasolondraibe P. says that, according to the shepherds, "sickness always requires a deeper, mystical explanation" and that sickness either indicates a broken relationship with God, or an assault from the demonic on the faith of the patient. Rasolondraibe 1989:348.

[1185] QS 127. G. Haus maintains that in the shepherds' thinking every sickness has a spiritual cause. Haus 2000:101. Cf. 4.1.1.3 (The causes of sickness). A non-shepherd in my material asserts that those who believe in the Christian God and those who have a scientific way of thinking do not believe in underlying causes

When I in the following describe the shepherds' understanding of the devil's involvement in sickness, the possibility of natural causes without any connection to demons should be remembered.[1186] What I say below does not imply that the devil is the source of every sickness.

The devil. Many shepherds believe that all sicknesses in the beginning came from the devil and they support their view with the story in Gen 3.[1187] To further explain this view, one of my informants makes a distinction between the devil's direct and indirect work:

> Question: Do the uneducated shepherds (*mpiandry tsotra*) say: All sicknesses come from the devil?
> This is their general way of understanding but there are levels in the "... coming from the devil": In some cases the devil works directly and other times his work is indirect. This is the way we explain it now. The devil's direct work is seen plainly when people turn mad and we say that such people are "seized by the devil". There are also sick people like those who lack calcium and e.g. those with indigestion or headaches; it is the devil's work to cause sicknesses but these ailments are not the devil's direct and immediate work. These sicknesses happen because the devil works indirectly through the people's environment and this causes sickness.[1188]

The devil's direct influence in causing sickness is generally acknowledged as a possibility among the shepherds. The shepherds have no doubts that demonic oppression may show itself through bodily signs, either in different bodily sicknesses or in mental disturbances. Then the sickness seems to be considered a by-product of the demonic oppression. One informant exemplifies this with a person suffering from cancer:

---

behind sickness. Later on he seems to contradict himself by saying that the Christians believe that any sickness has a demonic origin. IN 324. Another non-shepherd thinks there are differences between city and countryside and he says that people in the countryside always think that sickness has a cause. IN 313.

[1186] I will only in passing comment on natural causes, however, but concentrate on the shepherds' understanding of supernatural causes of sickness.

[1187] IS 210. My informant says that if the human "fall" is accentuated in this story, sicknesses may be understood as originating from sin. If the serpent's temptation to sin is accentuated, the devil may be seen as the origin of sickness. He thinks that the second understanding rests on an insufficient biblical understanding. One of G. Haus' informants explains that sickness entered the world through the "fall" but since sicknesses are part of human life it is impossible to assert that the devil is the origin of every sickness. Haus 2000:104.

[1188] IS 210.

"When this person repented and returned to Jesus, he recovered completely and no traces of cancer were found in the medical tests," he said.[1189] He seems to consider the demonic oppression as the root cause of the cancer and when the devil's oppression was ended, the sickness vanished. Others report of an inability to speak, which ended when the person was set free from the demonic oppression.[1190]

The opinion that any sickness stems from the devil is debated. My informants gave examples of many sicknesses having natural causes, e.g. causes related to food, climate or too hard work, without any connection to spirits.[1191] At the same time, my informants seem to attribute the opinion to most shepherds that any sickness stems from demons.[1192] This opinion of a general demonic cause of sickness corresponds to little formal training and insufficient biblical education, according to some of my informants.[1193]

Mental illness especially seems to be attributed to demons,[1194] but one of my informants says that he is rather confused by this tendency among the shepherds in recent times. He admits that this sickness may

---

[1189] L 336. Even if my informant does not mention exorcism, the context of his saying implies this.

[1190] CHIN 31.

[1191] IS 214, IS 202, IS 321. Only one informant (the Reformed IS 315) says directly that "sickness comes from the devil" but he adds that it is, at the same time, God's testing. He may mean that sicknesses originally stem from the devil's temptation to sin but there is a possibility that he sees demons as causes of all sickness. His comments on this theme do not suffice to draw any sure conclusions.

[1192] IS 310, IS 210. That a majority of the shepherds attribute all sicknesses to demons seems to be supported by many non-shepherds in my material: "They [the shepherds] prophesise that sickness stems from demons". QN 27. "They are tempted to say that everything stems from demons although they know it is not." QN 109.

[1193] IS 321, IS 210. All shepherds in my material have a certain amount of formal training and in addition, their biblical education is profound, compared to the obligatory two years training program for shepherds. There are differences in opinion among them, however.

[1194] IS 318. IS 212 says that this is the theology of the revival movement and according to IS 200, the mad (*adala ara-panahy*) are "seized by demons". IS 210 says that according to traditional Malagasy thinking madness (*fahadalana*) is thought to stem from evil spirits' work, often through sorcery and that shepherds in general are much influenced by the traditional thinking and therefore many of them embrace the traditional explanations without further reflection.

stem from evil spirits but it may also have other causes.[1195] Another says that shepherds may suspect a sickness with natural causes if a mentally ill person has been treated with exorcism lengthily without recovering.[1196]

Some shepherds' understanding of epileptic symptoms is illuminating to the debate about whether there have been demonic causes or not. They maintain that this sickness is caused by the work of evil spirits, especially since it often has fits of illness.[1197] The shepherds call this sickness *androbe*, which is the Malagasy Bible's translation of "epileptic" in Mt 17:15.[1198] According to the biblical story Jesus "rebuked" the spirit and Mt 17:18 reads that "the demon came out of him and the boy was cured instantly". One informant says that many shepherds do not know that epilepsy has medical causes because they do not know the medical diagnosis. They treat these sicknesses at the *toby* and many people have been healed. The healed then speak about their experiences during the fits and how the devil worked with them and these stories strengthen the shepherds' belief in demonic causes.[1199]

[1195] IS 310. His saying seems to imply that the opinion of mental illness as caused by demons has grown stronger in recent times and my informant seems to feel uncomfortable with this development.

[1196] IS 321. The thinking may be that the spiritual sickness is healed by exorcism but there is still another illness, which needs medical treatment. Another possibility of interpretation is that a continued exorcism without results shows that the sickness stems from natural causes.

[1197] IS 321. IS 200 says that this sickness is connected to (literally: walks along with) evil spirits (*androbe miaraka amin'ny fanahy ratsy mihitsy*), which may suggest either that the sickness stems from the devil or that it is easy for the devil to exploit this sickness.

[1198] IS 200. The root of the Greek word σεληνιάζομαι is σελήνη, which means moon and the word is differently translated. The RSV has "epileptic", while King James Version has "lunatic", which is a more idiomatic translation of the Greek word (Bibelen, Det Norske Bibelselskap 1978 also has "månesjuk"). New International Version translates the Greek word with "have seisures".

Some shepherds tend to use biblical labels to characterise sicknesses. IS 218 diagnoses a person to have "a spirit of divination" (*fanahy mahavaly*), which is directly taken from Acts 16:16. Another shepherd tells about her sickness and says that a shepherd leader diagnosed it to be "paralysis" (*paralysisa*) because she felt so weak (Mt 9:2). O 341. The most common biblical label, however, is "epileptic" (*androbe*), where the symptoms in Mt 17 and parallels often are given as examples of the demonic oppression. CHISA 100, O 344.

[1199] IS 321. The patients' stories are considered as reality because they have experienced the condition. The tendency to build their conclusions on patients'

Shepherds familiar with a Western diagnosis, however, know that this sickness has natural causes and may advise treatment with Western medicine but they are far from denying God's ability to heal this sickness through the shepherds' treatment.[1200]

The devil's indirect causing of sickness is seen partly in his ability to work through people's environments and partly in the devil's ability to take advantage of sicknesses and through this oppress humans.[1201] Natural causes may be recognised as playing a vital role but, at the same time, the sicknesses may be attributed to the devil's indirect work. This is the case with the sickness due to the lack of calcium.[1202] One informant mentions people with cancer as examples and asserts that they are not demoniacs. He hints, though, that the devil's indirect work may have caused this sickness. He then thinks of smoking cigarettes or drinking alcohol, habits he attributes to the devil's work. He does not assert that this always is the case, however and says that the sick may neither have smoked nor drunk alcohol and still the sickness struck him/her. This saying seems to indicate that the shepherds do not always know the causes of sickness. "Anyhow," my informant says, "we ask Jesus to touch the source of illness and heal the person."[1203]

---

experiences is also found elsewhere in the shepherds' explanations. IS 323. Cf. 2.2.5.

[1200] IN 313 says that Malagasy in general consider epilepsy as stemming from demons (note the use of the Christian label: demon!), especially if the fits occur in a service or when the person listens to God's word. His own explanation is that this is a natural sickness, which may show itself with fits in noisy surroundings. He mentions pastors, which have had fits of epilepsy (*mifanintontsintona*) during the service and he thinks this may happen when the pastor is too tired. "He may have had this sickness since he was a boy and it is difficult to say that he is "assaulted by demons"," IN 313 says.

[1201] In my material, the devil's ability to exploit human sicknesses is most frequently mentioned. See 4.3.2.2 (The devil's exploitation).

[1202] IS 210. See 4.2.2.3. A non-shepherd in my material disagrees with the shepherds' understanding that sickness due to lack of calcium is connected with demonic oppression. He accuses the shepherds for believing that those with lack of calcium are demoniacs and thus spending much time with exorcism. The result, according to his view, is only that the sick grow weaker. The shepherds should have contacted a medical practitioner first, according to his view and afterwards they could have expelled demons, if they deemed it necessary. QN 136.

[1203] IS 322.

Bodily sickness often leads to a depressed state of mind and it makes the person weak, both bodily and mentally.[1204] The devil frightens the sick and one informant seems to understand the devil's exploitation of the sickness in terms of aggravating it.[1205] Another says that if a person has a chronic sickness (*aretina mitaiza*), especially a mental sickness, it is almost certain that the devil assaults him/her constantly to oppress him/her.[1206] My informants do not explain how the devil exploits human sickness. Sometimes the devil only seems to enter the human through sickness considered as weakness but there are hints about the devil's leading astray, which may point to contact with traditional healers.[1207] One informant's saying about the necessity of an urgent healing of the mentality (*eritreritra*) of the sick may also point in the direction of temptation to seek a cure wherever it may be found.[1208] It is implied in the shepherds' explanations on this theme that the devil's exploitation of sickness is a possibility and it does not always happen.

Positive purposes. The shepherds often understand sickness as having positive purposes.[1209] When I asked one informant if he considered all sicknesses to stem from the devil, he immediately denied this and said that sickness is God's working with a person. "If a Christian turns ill, I think that the bed is a High school, where God educates him/her," he says. He argues for his view of sickness as God's upbringing by saying that normally the person's time is spent on earning money. He/she has no thoughts of repentance and does not think much on God. When sickness

---

[1204] IS 202, IG 332.

[1205] QS 135.

[1206] QS 181.

[1207] IS 206.

[1208] IS 201. In 4.3.2.2 (The devil's exploitation) the devil's exploitation of human conditions is seen especially in frightening the trouble-minded, in a weak Christian faith, which may lead away from Christ and in temptation to idol worship. G. Haus' findings support the thinking that the devil is able to exploit sicknesses. She has found that the shepherds distinguish between human weaknesses and the devil's exploitation of these conditions, into which the devil has entered through spirit worship, sorcery, human sin, or temptations and that sicknesses exploited by the devil need exorcism. Haus 2000:86, 103, 104.

[1209] Cf. 4.3.2.3.

strikes, however, all this changes.[1210] Through sickness as upbringing God leads the person to repentance and if the sickness lingers, this may happen in order to keep the person dependent on Jesus' help.[1211] One respondent experienced God's calling to become a shepherd through her sickness and understands this as the positive purpose of what happened to her.[1212] Sickness may cause the family to seek help from Jesus. During the sermon at a healing service a shepherd called the family of the sick fortunate. If they all had been healthy, they would never have come to the service and they had not had the opportunity to repent and believe in Jesus. Sickness is thus seen as a calling of the family of the sick.[1213]

There is a short step from believing that sickness may have a positive purpose to maintaining that God has caused the sickness. Some of the shepherds' sayings may be taken in the latter meaning. One informant says that some shepherds think that the sickness is a "hit from God".[1214] Another tells about a pastor who opposed the revival movement but "God beat him by sending sickness to his son". Later on this pastor repented and was consecrated as a shepherd.[1215] One respondent says that "from then God started to strike my mind", in order to describe all the mental disturbances he experienced.[1216] One informant refers to Job's story but he asserts that even if God permits sickness to happen, God cannot be blamed as evil.[1217] He says that sickness may stem from human

---

[1210] IS 314. CHIS 130 also considers his suffering as an education to augment his talents. Lie 1981:9 says that it is often people's bodily sicknesses, which causes them to contact the shepherds and in this way they may be led to conversion.

[1211] IS 200. As a commentary to an interview with IS 316, IS 311 says that God may know that if the person had recovered, he may have left Jesus.

[1212] QS 127.

[1213] IS 322, IG 331.

[1214] IS 321.

[1215] IG 331. He was consecrated after his ordination because *Mama* Nenilava had ordered it. It is rather uncommon that ordained pastors later are consecrated as shepherds but occasionally it happens, usually because of an advice given by *Mama* Nenilava who has disclosed this as God's will.

[1216] CHIS 130.

[1217] IS 321. This informant includes the cause of sickness in the problem of evil but he does not attempt to solve the problem. IS 315 also refers to Job's story, saying that the devil cannot do any harm to humans before he has asked permission from God. He calls sickness both a test from God and a test from the devil at the same time. It is possible that some shepherds understand God's activity in relation to sickness in terms of his ability to make even evil to serve his positive purposes, but nobody refers to biblical passages as e.g. Rom 8:28.

sin in the meaning of Rom 6:23 as "wages of sin" and makes it clear that the people themselves are responsible for this, e.g. because of idol worship.[1218]

4.5.1.3 Treatment

The treatment of sickness characteristic of the revival movement is exorcism. They expel sicknesses in Jesus' name and they pray for the sick with the laying on of hands. As will be shown in the following, the shepherds understand these two parts of exorcism differently. In addition, shepherds may advise the sick to consult medical practitioners and to use Western medicine.[1219] This subchapter also includes how the shepherds distinguish between different kinds of sicknesses and give some comments on the training of shepherds in this respect.

Expulsion of sickness. Although shepherds are convinced that a certain sickness has natural causes they do not seem to oppose exorcism as an appropriate treatment. "The shepherds command sickness to leave, in the name of Jesus," one informant says. His own experiences seem to have persuaded him that the shepherds' practice of expelling sickness is effective: A sort of leprosy was cast out and afterwards the person recovered little by little.[1220] Another informant says that sickness has to be cast out since it stems from sin and thus it is opposite to God's will.[1221]

[1218] G. Haus has found that the shepherds consider sickness as God's punishment for human sin and God has a positive purpose for this. Haus 2000:84, 109.

[1219] In a pamphlet with questions and answers published by the Ankaramalaza-branch of the revival, one shepherd asks: "Are we going to "work" only with the people who we know are demoniacs? What about ordinary sicknesses (fever…)?" After having underlined the good co-operation between medical treatment and the shepherds' treatment the following answer is given: ""Work and strengthening" is the revival's way of treating all the sick, irrespective of their sickness" (*Amin'ny alalan'ny Asa sy Fampaherezana no fomba fanasitranan'ny fifohazana ny marary rehetra na inona na inona karazan'aretiny*). Ankaramalaza 1997:7.

[1220] IS 217. He realises that some shepherds may be over-zealous in naming the different conditions to be cast out but he believes that, as a main rule, demons and sicknesses should be expelled.

[1221] IS 322. In addition to stemming from sin this informant also talks of a possible demonic origin of the sickness, discerned by the shepherds. He exemplifies the shepherds' way of discerning this in recurring nightmares and that the devil will not let the sick fall asleep.

"The shepherds should cast out any sicknesses," another says, "because it is impossible to know which sicknesses the devil has exploited."[1222]

> If I am sick I may ask shepherds to come and "work". They expel the causes of the sickness, which may be evil spirits but may be other things and they expel the sickness itself. The meaning of exorcism then is that sickness should not rule over a servant of the Lord.[1223]

One informant emphasises that he sees no theological problems in expelling sickness. He bases this claim on reflections about the lack of knowledge about human beings. Even though Western science knows a lot about humans, there are still huge unexplored areas. He mentions the shepherds' healing activity as an example of one such area: "when non-health is commanded to leave, it leaves."[1224] Jesus' actions in the Gospels are referred to as extending human categories: "Not only did Jesus walk on the water himself but he invited Peter to do the same." My informant concludes by saying that nothing is impossible for God. The limitations rest with humans and our limited knowledge.[1225] Another informant admits that casting out of sickness it not rational but he supports the practice because he has seen many examples of healing through exorcism.[1226]

Some shepherds use the story where Jesus heals Peter's mother-in-law to support their practice. Some say that they follow the example of Jesus who expelled the fever, which seems to indicate a relation to demons,[1227] while others do not understand this story as an expulsion of demons but they still seem to support the shepherds' practice of expelling sickness.[1228]

[1222] IS 214. QS 127 tells about her own severe sickness and how she suffered. After having had surgery twice without any positive result, her husband called shepherds to "work" with her and cast out demons, maybe as a last option, since every other treatment had failed.

[1223] IS 321.

[1224] He has also experienced healing by telephone: A person from Dar-es-salaam contacted a person in Madagascar who prayed and cast out demons through the telephone. The person in question was healed. It is not explicitly said that the person who prayed was a shepherd but the context makes this very probable.

[1225] IS 217.

[1226] IS 202.

[1227] IS 217, IS 202.

[1228] IS 214. IS 323 refers to the Mt 8:14–15 version about Peter's mother-in-law. Only according to Lk 4:38–39 it is written that Jesus "rebuked the fever" and the

"Exorcism does not necessarily imply that a person is "assaulted by demons" but it implies that spirits somehow are at work there," one informant says.[1229] The biblical story about the woman who had had a spirit of infirmity for eighteen years (Lk 13:11–13) was the theme of discussion in a seminary session. Some of the shepherds maintained that this woman had been labelled as "assaulted by demons" by the teachers in their instruction to become shepherds and they all seemed to agree that her sickness stemmed from the devil. Most of the students would not call this woman "assaulted by demons", however.[1230]

One informant asserts that to treat a sick person with expulsion of demons does not mean that the sickness is thought to stem from the devil. It is rather that the sickness may cause depression and weakness and exorcism gives you strength to believe in Jesus, even though the sickness may still be there.[1231] His point seems to be that the shepherds' treatment with expulsion of demons does not necessarily imply a demonic cause of the sickness. One informant speaks about his own child to exemplify how he thinks about demonic oppression and sickness:

> Even the bodily sick, where there is no connection to spirits, may be healed through prayer: casting out of demons and the laying on of hands. These people need strengthening by the Gospel to regain their strength. Their mentality needs healing to prevent the devil from exploiting their faint-heartedness or their bodily sickness. This is what happened to my child who became sick and we cast out the devil and laid our hands on his head. This child suffers from asthma and he is not possessed (*possedé*) but his sickness caused many questions in our minds and so we "worked" with him and imposed our hands. And we preached the Gospel to him. The revival movement does not separate the two. We think that both the demoniacs and those who suffer from natural sicknesses (*marary tsotra*) may be healed through prayer.[1232]

---

informants referring to this story as an exorcism may rely on Luke's version. According to G. Haus' informants Peter's mother-in-law cannot be labelled as "possessed" but Jesus cast out demons from her. Haus 2000:101.

[1229] IS 321. "Since exorcism follows a strict liturgy everybody receives the same treatment," he says.

[1230] IG 332. This is a group interview with both shepherds and non-shepherds present.

[1231] IS 202.

[1232] IS 201. The shepherds' expression "healing through prayer" seems to be a paraphrasing of "exorcism", i.e. both expulsion of demons and the following prayer with the laying on of hands (see the beginning of the citation) but sometimes it only denotes the second part.

Prayer with the laying on of hands ("strengthening"). Some of my informants emphasise that the appropriate treatment of sicknesses is prayer with the laying on of hands ("strengthening"). When people come to the healing services, both those who suffer bodily and those who suffer from spiritual sicknesses move to the front of the church, as I have shown before. The shepherds treat all of them with exorcism. One informant thinks that this practice ought to be altered:

> The bodily sick should be separated from those who are "seized by demons" and unable to understand what is going on. The sick need laying on of hands but the "seized by the devil" are difficult to heal and should be subjected to exorcism repeatedly ... People with colds seldom come to be healed at the healing services but those suffering from pneumonia are frequent ...
> *Question*: Does this mean that especially severe sicknesses need to be cast out?
> Severe sicknesses do not really need to be cast out but need Jesus mediated through the laying on of hands. It is like the woman in the biblical story who said: "If I touch even his garments, I shall be made well" (Mk 5:28). People think that if they are able to touch the garments of these servants of the Lord, they will be healed, because the shepherds have a close relationship to Jesus and even bodily ailments may be healed through their work. The people hope that healing will be mediated from Jesus.[1233]

Since exorcism is a fixed liturgy with casting out of demons and the laying on of hands, it is not easy to split up, even though some shepherds seem to be convinced that people who are conscious and suffering from natural sicknesses only need prayer with the laying on of hands. Some informants see it possible to only pray for the sick, without any preceding casting out of demons, if this is what the person asks for but this may be an option in more private sessions, outside the ordinary healing services.[1234] One informant who supports exorcism of sicknesses because he thinks of it as a prophylactic method, in case the devil has exploited the sickness, attributes healing to God's answering of the shepherds' prayers and not to a casting out of the sickness. If I interpret this informant rightly, he thinks that casting out of demons has effect on the eventual demonic oppression of the person, while the prayer with the

---

[1233] IS 200. This informant makes it clear that it is the people coming to the shepherds who think like this. He calls it a magical view and gives examples of several of the revival movement's former practices, which are now abandoned because of such misunderstandings. See 4.4.5.

[1234] IS 201, IS 312.

laying on of hands may cause healing of natural sicknesses.[1235] "All the sick need prayer," one informant says, "but there are some sick who will be even more troubled in noisy situations."[1236] He certainly points to the casting out of demons with this saying about "noisy situations" and he exemplifies what he means by telling me about one person of his extended family who was about to turn mad because of drug use. They sent him to a *toby*, where he was treated with exorcism but his sickness was aggravated. My informant brought the sick person back to his house after 3 days and after a while he decided to take him to a psychiatrist in the capital. The day before I interviewed him, he had visited his sick relative and the doctor had told him that the boy was recovering. The psychiatrist instructed my informant to talk calmly to the sick boy, not to disturb him unnecessarily and not to be angry. Now my informant prays calmly together with the sick and he encourages his sick relative to pray. "I believe that shepherd elders in earlier times prayed calmly for the sick," he says as a concluding comment. If he is right, not all the sick were treated with casting out of demons, according to the shepherds' practice in the past but some were only prayed for.

Western medicine. A remarkably high number of my informants mention treatment with Western medicine as an option for the sick.[1237] "The

---

[1235] IS 214. He underlines, however, that nobody can request anything from God but that God is able to use the shepherds to mediate healing when he sees that the time is appropriate. Healing should always be considered as a gift from God in his mercy. Healing of ailments and sicknesses (*rofy sy aretina*) is also attributed to the prayer with the laying on of hands in Tobilehibe 1997:105 and Pitaka 1999:128.

[1236] IS 310.

[1237] Several reasons for this high number may be possible: Because of my informants' relative high level of education, they are familiar with Western medicine. In addition, they live in an area where there are pharmacies and at least some of them may have economic possibilities to buy and use this medicine. Since the interviewer is a Westerner, this may also have influenced my informants to relate the treatment to what they considered to be my frame of reference.

Two of the non-shepherds in my material reflect on people's ability to make use of Western medical treatment: Medical health care in the countryside is poor and people often live far away from the health centres. The medical personnel in charge are little trained and if they have knowledge to prescribe medicine, the pharmacies may be too far away to be an option to the people. Western medicine is expensive and one informant says that this is part of the reason why people consult traditional healers, where tariffs are lower (he does not mention the shepherds' treatment but their treatment is free of charge). Sometimes people do not have confidence in Western trained doctors because they consider them part of the official

revival movement does not see any problems with medical treatment," one informant says and refers to the internal statutes: "The revival movement is not allowed to prevent people from consulting medical doctors."[1238] The doctors are considered as having received a gift of grace, which enables them to treat natural sicknesses and Western medicine may be called a gift of grace.[1239] Doctors and medicines are tools in God's hands and the shepherds pray for the doctors' work. If a person is healed by the doctor's treatment, the shepherds consider this as stemming from God.[1240] It seems important to my informants to emphasise that the revival movement co-operates with Western medicine.[1241] One of my informants underlines strongly that the *toby* is no hospital and that it is necessary to have close contact with medical doctors.[1242] A few of the *toby* have dispensaries or hospitals, which are considered as complementing the shepherds' treatment in healing services but most *toby* have to rely on verbal agreement with doctors at public hospitals, if medical treatment exists not too far from the *toby*.[1243] "When people come with headache or when the shepherds suspect that the person's problem is purely medical, we advise them to consult a medical practitioner," one informant says.[1244] The people coming to the shepherds often suspect sorcery behind their sickness but the shepherds may propose that it may not be sorcery and therefore, they should seek medical treatment. Sometimes the shepherds may suspect demonic

---

establishment who are unable to improve the conditions of the poor. IN 313, IN 324.

[1238] IS 321. Fifohazana miray ao amin'ny FFPM 2000:12.

[1239] IS 310, IS 315.

[1240] IS 321. IG 332 says that even if the doctor is not a Christian, the shepherds should consider him/her a tool in the hands of God. Rasolondraibe 1989:348 maintains that the shepherds consider Western medicine as ineffective without the healing power of God.

[1241] IS 210, IS 202.

[1242] IS 325.

[1243] The need of a co-operation between the *toby* and Western medicine is also underlined by Tobilehibe 1997:125, saying that the medical treatment in the *toby* is the responsibility of the doctor, if there are any available at the *toby*. The reasons for starting a dispensary in the *toby* Ankaramalaza, according to Pitaka D. was firstly, the difficulties in bringing the sick to medical centres outside the *toby* and secondly, that more "children of the revival" became doctors and nurses. Pitaka 1999:154.

[1244] IS 210.

oppression but they cannot exclude that ordinary sicknesses also are present, which can be diagnosed by medical doctors.[1245] "The doctors know bodily sicknesses, while the shepherds know the spiritual."[1246] Some sicknesses ought to be cured by Western medicine but the shepherds are convinced that there are sicknesses, which cannot be cured by these means.[1247] The inability of Western medicine to cure spiritual sickness seems to be admitted also by some doctors trained in Western medicine. Several of my informants report of incidents when doctors have sent patients to traditional healers because they have been unable to give them a proper cure.[1248]

It is not clear whether the shepherds consider it important to treat the one before the other when a person suffers from both bodily and spiritual sickness at the same time. One shepherd says that the doctor may heal the bodily sickness but if this sickness is "brought by demons" (*entin'ny demonia*), the person will not be free from the demonic oppression.[1249] Another seems to mean that people with spiritual sicknesses should be treated with exorcism first and when the demons have left, treatment for natural sicknesses can start.[1250] The most common procedure seems to be that people coming to the *toby* are treated with exorcism and if they do not recover, the shepherds suspect other sicknesses and advise them to consult medical practitioners.[1251] The signs of bodily sickness may,

---

[1245] IS 321.
[1246] IS 213.
[1247] IG 332.
[1248] IS 311, CHISA 100. A Western trained doctor at one of the church's dispensaries also sent one of my respondents to the shepherds' treatment because he considered the sickness to be spiritual. CHIS 12.
[1249] IG 332.
[1250] QS 150. Haus 2000:100 asserts that, as in traditional healing practices, the shepherds have to deal with the magic-religious causes of the sickness before any medical treatment can be done.
[1251] IS 202, IS 321. IS 213 says that the shepherds should be careful in using exorcism with ordinary sicknesses like fever. When expelling demons they may experience that there are none and they conclude that the sickness does not stem from the devil but has natural causes. Lack of manifestations seems to be the way they discover that there are no demons to cast out of the person. Pitaka D. says that *Mama* Nenilava sometimes sent people directly to the doctor, however, after having had an initial consultation with them and this does not seem to include exorcism first. Pitaka 1999:155.

however, be treated with medicine alongside the treatment with exorcism.[1252]

I have a few hints in my material that some shepherds abstain from using Western medicine for themselves. "Some shepherds consult doctors rarely," one informant says, "because they trust in God and think that God has the power to heal them."[1253] He speaks about a "revival pastor" (*pastora fifohazana*) who suffered from epilepsy (*androbe*) and had taken appropriate medicines for a long time. He decided that he should stop taking the medicines because he thought that God would heal him, but his sickness returned. A colleague encouraged him to continue with the medication, "because this is the way God will help you," he said. The pastor did not listen to him. Then this colleague consulted *Mama* Nenilava and told her about his friend and she ordered this pastor to continue with the Western treatment: "This is God's tool to conquer your sickness," she said, "and the medicine is grace from Jesus." After having heard *Mama* Nenilava's advice the pastor continued with the medication.[1254]

[1252] L 336. QS 101 says that the "assaulted by demons" should be given adequate medicines in order to prevent them from becoming too weak and tired. L 336 calls "work and strengthening" for people having spiritual sicknesses a treatment directed to the main cause of the sickness ("traitement étiologique"), while he labels medical treatment for these people as directed towards the symptoms ("traitement symptomatique"). Pitaka 1999:156 calls "work and strengthening" a basic treatment (*fitsaboana fototra*) for the "assaulted by demons". A bodily treatment may go alongside this.

[1253] IS 321. IS 315 is the only informant in my material who never uses medicine. "Nobody is greater than God," he says, "and if God cannot remove the sickness, humans cannot." He says that he is often sick but he never uses medicine. When he falls ill, he just prays for God's deliverance and until this day he has recovered. He does not accuse those who use medicine, however and he tells them that they should not copy his practice if they are not convinced about it. He emphasises that medicine is God's gifts in his grace and he may advise people to consult a medical doctor.

[1254] IS 321. My informant does not explicitly say that this pastor is also a shepherd but from his attachment to the revival movement it is likely that he practises exorcism. Lie 1981:9 mentions that in the first decades of the Soatanana-revival there was a general understanding of all sicknesses as stemming from the devil, which in some periods was understood to mean that the shepherds could not use Western medicine. Lie believes that this thinking is abandoned today.

One shepherd in my material (IS 314) is a specialist in herbal medicines and when Christians consult him privately with a special sickness, he may treat them with this medicine. He will only do so if the patient asks for it. If the patient believes that

Distinguishing between different kinds of sicknesses. The shepherds' awareness of sicknesses relating to different parts of the human (body, mind and spirit) and their different ways of identifying people in need of exorcism show that many of them have their opinions about the problems of the people seeking their assistance.[1255] Most of my informants do not mention explicitly the necessity of distinguishing between the different kinds of sicknesses, however. Since they consider their own treatment as complementary with medical, my material does not postulate any problems with either of them.[1256]

A pragmatic attitude seems to characterise the shepherds. Since they firmly believe that God is able to heal any sickness, at least some of them seem to consider it unimportant what is tried first.[1257] The shepherds cannot know beforehand which means God will use to heal a certain sickness and therefore, they are willing to try all means at their disposal. One informants says:

> The way we distinguish the two [sicknesses cured by the doctors and demonic oppression] is that the shepherds "work" and cast out the demons; when they see that there are demons, they expel them. The person shows manifestations, the demons or the devil in the person make him swear or talk nonsense (*miteniteny foana*) ...

---

he/she will be healed by prayer with the laying on of hands, my informant considers it as sinful if he had treated such a person with herbal medicine. He underlines, however, that he cannot use herbal medicine in the treatment of non-Christians because they will think of him as a traditional healer. When this shepherd gives herbs to the sick he underlines that these are only tools in God's hands. He asks for God's blessing of the medicine and instructs the sick that they should not trust in the medicine but in God. This shepherd admits that his practice has not been without problems for some of his fellow-shepherds, since they think that this practice is connected with the traditional healer. When he discussed this problem with *Mama* Nenilava, she gave him her permission to continue the practice and said that open-minded people would not have problems with it. A non-shepherd also comments on the theme of herbal medicine and he seems to have no problem with Christians using this. The condition is that it is not connected with religious rituals. He says, however, that the weak in faith may have problems with it because they are not able to distinguish between biological-medical effect and the rituals normally undertaken by traditional healers in connection with this. IN 313.

[1255] Cf. 4.5.1.1 and 4.3.1.
[1256] Rasolondraibe 1989:348 also says that faith-healing and medical treatment are not mutually exclusive.
[1257] IS 321.

290   CH. 4: THE SHEPHERDS' UNDERSTANDING OF THEIR PRACTICE

> Let us say that a person has fever. The treatment for fever is Nivaquine or something similar but this medicine does not make the person recover. Then we see that it is the work of the devil, which has caused the person to fall ill ...[1258]

Some of my informants consider it important to identify and sort out people's problems prior to exorcism, however and not just treat anybody according to the liturgy.[1259] It can be fatal not to be able to diagnose common medical sicknesses. One of my informants has heard about people bringing their babies with critical high fever to the shepherds. "If the shepherds start with exorcism of these children and do not send them to medical treatment immediately, this may cause death," he says and he underlines the shepherds' responsibility in such cases.[1260]

Only one of my informants elaborates more lengthily on the theme of distinguishing natural sicknesses from demonic oppression. He says that doctors have the ability to diagnose medical sicknesses through different medical analyses while a study of the person's life-story may reveal possible demonic sicknesses, which will manifest themselves during exorcism. The sick will improve when treated with exorcism and when he/she repents. The most difficult, according to his view, is to distinguish demonic sicknesses from psychiatric sicknesses but he gives some guidelines to identify demonic oppression. 1) Life-story (contact with traditional healers), 2) lots of blasphemy and swearing, 3) symptoms not common in psychiatric suffering (head and feet turn backwards and after some time return to normal position; not eating for 40 days but still having normal strength), 4) medication, which normally improves the state of the patient has no effect and 5) absence of any manifest cause (like a strong blow to the head, loss of spouse or drug use).[1261]

Health education for shepherds. Shepherds need experience and training in Western medicine to be able to distinguish natural sicknesses from

---

[1258] IS 213.

[1259] IS 310, IS 325. Non-shepherds like QN 162 emphasises that the shepherds should investigate, through an initial consultation, the problems of the people coming and if they suffer from ordinary sicknesses they should pray for the sick and send them to a doctor.

[1260] IS 310.

[1261] L 336.

demonic oppression.[1262] A few of my informants emphasise this and they ask for a more thorough training of the uneducated shepherds in this respect.[1263] Efforts have been made in recent years to give shepherds in general some basic medical knowledge but this is reflected neither in the statutes nor in the handbook/Rasolondraibe P.'s instruction manual. It seems as this training especially is given to shepherds working in a *toby*.[1264] One of my informants complained of the difficulties in teaching shepherds to distinguish between natural sicknesses and demonic oppression and he sees the reason for this is their low level of general education. He believes that many of the shepherds are unable to understand this teaching and when they do not know how to distinguish the medical from the demonic in their own lives one cannot expect them to do so with their patients. Therefore, the leaders do not spend much time in teaching this.[1265]

4.5.2 The healing process in the shepherds' overarching theological perspective

According to the shepherds, healing is seen as a process and the purpose of this chapter is to present the shepherds' understanding of the healing process. Their understanding is guided by theological considerations, where "a healed relationship with Jesus Christ is of eternal worth and

---

[1262] IS 310.

[1263] IS 214.

[1264] IS 210, IN 313.

[1265] IS 210. The assistant director of the church's health department (SALFA) in 1998 was also the head of the *toby* Ankaramalaza and the general secretary of the Protestant revival movement, who was also the leader of the revival movement in the Lutheran church, was one of the leaders in this health department. One of the few psychiatric hospitals in Madagascar is situated in *Toby* Ambohibao (outside the capital) and the director for several years was a Western trained medical practitioner who is himself a shepherd. This situation, together with the establishment of dispensaries in some of the *toby*, may raise the shepherds' medical knowledge in the future.

G. Haus' informants also complain about the difficulties in training shepherds to discern between different illnesses. She has found that it is pastors who teach this subject (even where there are medical doctors available) and according to her informants shepherds do not need a lot of this teaching since God is powerful enough to heal any sickness. Haus 2000:111–112.

outweighs by far any temporal good".[1266] Within this orientation, any healing from bodily, mental, or spiritual sicknesses is seen as God's gift and longed for.

I start with referring to several testimonies and reports of healing from my field material and how the shepherds evaluate signs of healing. Then I move on to show how faith in Jesus is the shepherds' intended goal and how faith relates to healing. The healing process requires a renouncing of all powers opposed to Jesus, concretised in the burning of charms. I present the shepherds' communal understanding of healing: the family, the *toby* community and the patients themselves are all involved in the process but still there are some who are not healed. The climax of healing, according to the shepherds, is found in "strengthening", the second part of exorcism.[1267]

4.5.2.1 *Testimonies, reports and signs of healing*

The shepherds' success in healing has a wide reputation[1268] but my

---

[1266] Rasolondraibe 1989:348. Appiah-Kubi 1981:81 underlines healing as a process and Mugabe 1999:244–245 calls salvation a process in African thinking.

[1267] In literature on healing related to mainland Africa several of these themes occur, e.g. the importance of the community, search for spiritual causes, which emphasises a religious healing, a dual health system, etc. See Mugabe 1999, Saayman 1992, Igenoza 1999, Appiah-Kubi 1981.

[1268] In an article where she discusses the efficacy of the shepherds' treatment compared to treatment in psychiatric asylums, L.A. Sharp mentions that "many have become exorcists after they were or someone close to them was healed. Exorcists treat all forms of illness, including physical ailments such as lameness, blindness and headaches; troubled thoughts and restlessness; madness; and possession." Sharp 1994:531. She also describes the life stories of three people, who were treated by the protestant exorcists: Elisabeth was freed from her spirits, she converted to the protestant church and she is today a highly respected exorcist. After two weeks at the *toby* Vivienne felt stronger and three months later she returned to school. Elysé had lived at the *toby* for six months at the time of the interview and his father said that he was improving, but he still had crises. Sharp 1994:533–535. In her doctoral dissertation Sharp talks about the therapeutic efficacy of the Malagasy exorcists and in addition to the above-mentioned Elisabeth and Vivienne, she describes the life story of Zaloky, who had been a spirit medium. Ten years earlier the spirits were exorcised and she was at that time an elder in the church. Sharp also mentions an old man, who had a *tromba* spirit exorcised and later became a member in the church. Sharp 1993:266–268. Randriakoto A.W. says that "beaucoup de malades sont guéris par ces méthodes au toby Ambohimahazo", without naming any specific cases. He mentions that the first patient healed at the *toby* came from the *bara* tribe and he also refers to other insane people (*olon-dia*), who left the *toby* healed. He

informants emphasise that they refrain from creating publicity about this and from taking statistics of the success. There are shepherds in Antananarivo claiming that they may cure cancer and aids and invite people to come to them but one of my informants calls this a deviation from the real revival.[1269] If they take statistics from their success they could be tempted to boast of their results and take the honour themselves.[1270] Healing rests solely in God's hands, God decides and he will grant the healing in his appointed time.[1271]

Testimonies. Two of my in-depth interviewees are Honorine and Pascal:[1272]

> Honorine came into contact with the revival movement through a friend of hers, who was ill and had found no cure. Some of the friend's neighbours, who had themselves experienced that their son had been healed through the shepherds' treatment, advised her friend to go to the shepherds and Honorine followed her friend there. The preaching, singing and exorcism amazed her, because until then she had not been eager to go to church and she was deeply moved by the healing services. The pastor's and the shepherds' preaching impressed her and after some time, she decided to become a Christian.
> In the beginning she felt joy when reading the Bible, taking communion and going to church and her studies in school progressed well. She experienced a crisis, however, when she failed to pass an important exam. She became troubled and her problems led to her decision to begin preparing to become a shepherd. It was during the last phase of her preparation that she began to shake back and forth during casting out of demons.[1273] She attended daily healing services morning and afternoon and the symptoms lasted for four

---

sees the recruitment of sick people, who come to Ambohimahazo, as a result of the successful healing practices there and states that when people talk about the *toby*, they mention the miracles performed by the shepherds there. Randriakoto 1982:20–21, 23–24. These results are not documented scientifically by medical doctors or psychiatrists but, the great number of witnesses, who have experienced healing themselves or have seen that people in their close family have changed, testify to their trustworthiness. Even Sharp, who is critical to the shepherds' practice, admits that they are successful healers.

[1269] IS 323.
[1270] IS 322.
[1271] IS 322, IS 206.
[1272] I only present a summary of part of their stories here, mainly delimited to how they recounted their sickness and healing experiences.
[1273] When the shepherds observed her movements, they advised her to sit down on the mat. Cf. 3.2.1.1. Honorine told me how difficult it was for her to move to the mat during this period, since she was preparing to become a shepherd herself.

months. Then one day she vomited very strongly during the casting out of demons and afterwards she did not experience the shaking of the body anymore.[1274] She was consecrated as a shepherd and when I interviewed her, she had been a shepherd for six years.

She told me that when engaging in a harsh quarrel with her husband, she felt some of the symptoms coming back: her head was shaking, but never her whole body and she neither vomited nor foamed at the mouth. She now knows the symptoms well, so she is able to live a normal social life and she is a respected shepherd.[1275]

Pascal fell ill after he had failed to pass the baccalaureate exam. He began showing strange behaviour: destroyed a school notebook, ran away for several days, fainted and threatened his parents with a knife. In the beginning of the illness, he was testy and threatening, but later on he slept much and was not even able to go to the bathroom alone.

He was treated at two different *toby*, but his health did not improve. Therefore they made him take several medical exams in the capital, but even with the newest medical equipment, they could not trace any physical abnormalities. This made his family even more certain that this illness had supernatural causes.

In the first *toby* they treated Pascal with massage together with praying, preaching and exorcism. At another *toby* he was bathed in a cold river while the shepherds cast out demons. During this session Pascal repeatedly said: "We will not leave. Stop expelling demons because it makes us angry."[1276] After two days of treatment there he told the shepherds that he felt something strong leaving him, he recovered gradually and returned home. He had been ill for about five years by that time and when I conducted the interview he had just returned from this *toby*. Even if he showed signs of recovery, his family thought it necessary to let him go back to the *toby* and stay there for some time.

When I met the family again in 1998, I was told that Pascal had passed the entrance exam to a theological seminary and he was going to study to become a pastor.[1277]

Reports. In two other of my in-depth interviews both persons were healed by the shepherds' treatment. One of them was preparing to become a shepherd by the time of the interview, while the other had been

---

[1274] She thought that the vomiting was a sort of cleansing from impurity. Several years earlier Honorine's parents had brought her to a traditional healer: he scratched her forehead and some of the blood was mixed with charms to protect her.

[1275] CHIS 12.

[1276] Mal: *Aoka izahay tsy havoaka. Ajanony amin'izay ny famoahana devoly, fa mandrebireby anay izany.*

[1277] CHIN 171.

a shepherd for seven years by that time. The fifth person was still ill at the time of the interview.

In the case histories where my field assistants conducted the interviews, they reported the actual state of nine patients, treated by the shepherds. In many of them there are references to an improved state of health, although most of them are not completely healed. I refer to three of these reports concerning the results of the shepherds' treatment below:

> The fits of illness are more seldom than before and he feels relieved during the casting out of demons and the "strengthening". He is still ill, has hallucinations and does not sleep well. His speech is not normal, but he is not mentally ill.[1278]

> He is healed, but still it is difficult for him to take part in an ordinary conversation. After the exorcism he was free from the bonds and he experienced this as God's love towards him.[1279]

> She recovered gradually when her family decided to become Christians. But the illness returned after one year, two years and six years, the last time one year after her consecration as a shepherd. She was taken to a hospital and given sedatives for two weeks. Now she is filled with joy.[1280]

In the case histories told from memory by shepherds at a theological seminary, 18 out of 28 are reported to have been healed by the shepherds' treatment. Several of them showed antisocial or abnormal behaviour before and some have been cured from skin disease and an inability to talk. Eight of these people are themselves shepherds today.[1281]

[1278] CHISA 156. It is the patient himself, who gives the information to my field assistant.

[1279] CHISA 104.

[1280] CHISA 130. Another is reported to have recovered at the *toby*, but when she came home, she fell ill again. When she was baptised, however, she was healed. CHINA 116.

[1281] Cf. the displays of reported signs of the "assaulted by demons" in 4.3.1.1. The positive results are also reported by Rasolondraibe 1989:350 who mentions sicknesses attributed to sorcery, brain tumor, leukemia, stroke and advanced mental illness among those healed by the shepherds' treatment. In a book published on the 40th anniversary of the Farihimena revival movement, Ralisoa H. lists 12 people with names or other identifiable features, who are reported to having been healed during the ministry of the founder *Dada* Rakotozandry Daniel. Skin desease, blindness, mental illness, weakness and other undiagnosed severe illnesses are reported among the cures. Ralisoa 1991:18–20. In his Nenilava-biography, Tsivoery Z. says that people with different sicknesses (mentally ill, weak, *androbe*, trouble-

Some of my informants have experienced healing in their own lives,[1282] others have seen family members or other people they have treated themselves recover.[1283] In this way, my informants have been able to follow healing processes closely. My informants frequently mention a healing of one's spiritual life: "to become a Christian", "to have more confidence in Jesus",[1284] "eagerness in taking part in church life" and causing a spiritual awakening in individuals and the local church.[1285] Furthermore, they report of several family members who have become shepherds as a result of their experience[1286] and a feeling of relief after exorcism is mentioned in various ways. Some describe it as if a heavy burden has been taken away[1287] and another talks about a complete peace (*fiadanana feno*), which is different from the one obtained at the traditional healers' practices since it opens the mind.[1288] Exorcism is not considered an exemption from settling matters between fellow humans and mutual forgiveness is especially underlined.[1289]

Rakotomihantarizaka Organés who some time after the healing experience became a shepherd, tells the story of his wife, who was

---

minded because of severe life conditions) came to her and Jesus healed many of these people. He also describes two people "assaulted by demons", who were healed through *Mama* Nenilava's ministry and an 18 year old woman, who had been paralysed from birth. Tsivoery 1972/1991:24–25, 29, 35–36. In addition to healing stories mentioned by Tsivoery, Pitaka D. reports of healing from paralysis and witchcraft, which caused deafness. Pitaka 1999:104, 106.

[1282] IS 200, IS 206.

[1283] IS 214, IS 322. These stories were told spontaneously and they were not presented as a response to my investigation of the effectiveness of the shepherds' healing practice. In fact, the aim of my interviewing was not to obtain any comprehensive picture of the shepherds' effectiveness in healing. This could have been an interesting research task, which would have demanded a follow-up with a certain number of people "assaulted by demons" during a period of time. It would also have been necessary to co-operate with psychiatrists and medical doctors to document the patient's state of health before and after the shepherds' treatment. This is, however, not the purpose of this research project.

[1284] IS 218, IS 311.

[1285] IS 205, IS 316, IS 205.

[1286] IS 218, IS 320.

[1287] IS 311, IS 322.

[1288] IS 321.

[1289] IS 201. One shepherd refers to changes in appearance: While a person "assaulted by demons" was similar to a skeleton during her sickness, she regained her weight, became strong and had a nice face when she was healed. IS 218.

delivered by the shepherds' exorcism from being a medium having several spirits. He had himself experienced and taken part in the different phases of his wife's life story and when she was healed he especially emphasised the spiritual aspects:

> It started when Mama said to us Tuesday the 2nd of December 1980 that these devils would not return to my wife and up to this day there have been no traces of the spirits in my wife's life and she seeks Jesus sincerely. Nothing is more precious to her than the Bible...[1290]

[1290] Ankaramalaza undated:145, my translation. His wife's life story is presented in full length in p. 129–150 in the book. She was consecrated as a shepherd together with her husband.

Pitaka D. also tells about changes in the lives of people who have been in contact with *Mama* Nenilava: People using drugs, alcohol and cigarettes have ended these practices because they have understood that their bodies are temples of the Holy Spirit. Prostitutes and adulterers have left this lifestyle and people swearing and having a violent conduct have become calm and co-operative through their newness of life. A number of practitioners of traditional medicine and idolatry have left their practices and become Christians and they have surrendered all their amulets and medicines. People thinking that they were better than others have changed this attitude when they met God's word through *Mama* Nenilava and youths who feared school exams have been comforted by her. With the help of *Mama* Nenilava several of her "children" [refers to the adherents of the Ankaramalaza movement] have found work to secure their daily income and some of them have important occupations in the state administration. *Mama* Nenilava was not just caring about spiritual matters, but also the material parts of life. Pitaka 1999:106–110. T. Laugerud refers to a woman, who after contact with a traditional healer had been subdued to strong forces, but later on was delivered by a local evangelist (who supposedly was a shepherd). He knew this woman personally and noticed that after her healing, she was filled with joy. Laugerud 1993:70.

It is not possible, however, either from my fieldwork material or from the written sources, to estimate a percentage of success in relation to healing of people treated by the shepherds. The general impression is that healing occurs rather frequently, but it has to be remembered that stories of this kind also have functions of legitimisation and recruitment and it is natural that the stories are expanded as they spread. It is not easy to trace what really happened in the initial phase when a story has been told again and again over years. A rumour is not originated without any reason, however and the saying that "such diseases are healed through the revival movement" (*sitrana amin'ny fifohazana itony aretina itony*) are not just words alone. People having heard about or themselves having experienced healing spread such rumours. It has to be remembered that some of the written material from within the revival movement itself has the distinct aim of persuading people to believe in the mighty deeds performed by God through his servants. Such documents are by definition not very critical in incorporating stories, which from a scientific angle could be dubious. The Nenilava-biography by Tsivoery in particular

298   CH. 4: THE SHEPHERDS' UNDERSTANDING OF THEIR PRACTICE

Signs of healing. One of the questions in the questionnaire reads: "What are the signs by which you know that the demons have left?"[1291] I have made a display of the signs, which the shepherds consider to be crucial in the judgement of this. According to the groupings presented in the chapter concerning the signs of the "assaulted by demons", I list the signs in four columns: signs related to common conduct, bodily signs, supernatural signs and theological signs:[1292]

Table 6: Signs of healing

Signs related to common conduct	Bodily signs	Supernatural[1293] signs	Theological[1294] signs
A conduct contrary to his/her conduct when "assaulted by	Conscious[1296] (27) The illness is gone (9)	Do not remember what happened (2) A feeling of	Is able to/eager to pray[1298] (16) Invoke the name of Jesus[1299] (15)

---

resembles much on a writing of a biography of a saint. Nevertheless, much of the documentation rests on eyewitnesses and identifiable persons.

[1291] See Appendix 1.

[1292] See difficulties associated with classification in 4.3.1.1.

[1293] "Supernatural" refers to the shepherds' understanding of the sign as inexplicable in natural terms. This interpretation is done on the basis of the patients' own recounting of their experiences.

[1294] The signs presented in this grouping are closely knit to Christian religious practices.

[1295] If the person was violent, he/she is now calm; if he/she was unable to talk, he/she can now talk normally; if he/she could not see properly, he/she has now full vision.

[1296] "Conscious" is used as a translation of several Malagasy terms, e.g. *mahatsiaro saina, mahatsiaro tena, ary saina, tonga saina*. Most of the Malagasy renderings include *saina*, which means mind and generally these sayings could be translated according to their meaning as "not any longer have a disturbed mind".

[1297] The weariness and fainting refer to the moment when the patient regains consciousness and these are regarded by some as signs showing that the demon has departed.

[1298] The Malagasy word *mivavaka* can mean both to pray and to go to church and in this material both meanings are present. When these activities, which were not practised before, are felt as a joy for the patient, the shepherds understand this as showing that he/she is free from demonic bondage. One informant underlines that it is the prayer of forgiveness that is a sign of healing, not a prayer where the patient confesses that he/she is a sinner. QS 101.

[1299] This includes a confession of Jesus as Lord.

[1300] Intensifying expressions may be used here, like "he becomes a very eager Christian" (*mafana fo*); a surrender, which is complete/sincere.

demons"[1295] (17) Normal conduct (5) Calm (3) Understands a normal conversation (2)	Tired/weak (5) May faint (4)[1297]	power leaving the patient	Surrender the life to Jesus[1300] (10) The devil makes the patient shake violently (3) Filled with joy and peace in heart (3) The devil surrenders[1301] Handing over of amulets Accept the laying on of hands

It is not visible in the display but nearly ¾ of my informants include theological signs in their listing. This makes clear that, according to the shepherds' understanding, it is the person's relation to Jesus and Christian life, which is decisive in the judgement of healing.

Many informants see the signs of healing as closely knit to the person's conduct while "assaulted by demons" and the evaluation of healing has to be done by the shepherds who are "working" with the person in question. Signs are also judged in relation to what people normally do and when a person's conduct conforms to this norm, generally speaking, this is considered as a sign of health.

The display does not show how many different signs the shepherds mention together before they consider a person is healed, but my fieldwork material shows that they make their judgement on the basis of several signs. It seems like no sign by itself is conclusive but has to be judged with a view to the context and the person's situation.[1302]

As we have seen, the vast majority of people subject to exorcism show no observable sign of demonic oppression. Consequently, their signs of healing cannot be judged in relation to their former state, because it is impossible from outside to trace any sign. It is possible, however, to judge their surrender to Jesus and their Christian life. One informant mentions specifically these people's sincerity in conversion and eagerness to pray/attend church meetings as a sign of their freedom from demonic oppression.[1303]

[1301] The devil may say: "We are beaten and leave" (*resy izahay ka hiala*), "we leave" (*lasa izahay*). This points to the moment of liberation, according to the shepherds.

[1302] One informant reflects upon the demons' ability to deceive the shepherds and he says that one cannot be sure if some signs are really pointing to a healthy state or if they only reflect a deception from the demons in order to end the shepherds' treatment. QS 142.

[1303] QS 153.

4.5.2.2 The shepherds' basic concern is faith in Jesus

The shepherds' priority. By studying the stories shepherds tell when they explain their treatment to other people we may see some of their priorities. One of my informants told me about a visit to a sick man in his home:

> When we got there, we did not tell him that we had come to heal his illness but that we were shepherds and our task was to preach the Gospel. What is important is that you receive Jesus in your lives and when you have received Jesus, the rest depends on him, according to his word: "But seek first his kingdom and his righteousness and all these things shall be yours as well." Then the people in the house were led to conversion and it is astonishing but Jesus healed the man.[1304]

After having told a story of a man living at the *toby* who talks nonsense and tries to run away all the time, another informant asked me what to do with such a person and adds: "At the *toby* the treatment is prayer."[1305]

Sayings like the following are also found in my material:

> The goal for the shepherds' work is that both the patient and his/her family confess Jesus and this is far more important than recovery from sickness. If the patient dies, this may be Jesus' way of saving his/her life. Those who believe in Jesus have a living hope when they die and to the shepherds this is most important. Their task is to strengthen the patient and the family, regardless of healing or lack of healing.[1306]

Salvation through faith in Jesus is underlined in this citation and it is made very clear that confession of Jesus has a higher priority in the

---

[1304] IS 218. Later this man attended the healing services at the *toby* regularly and he witnessed how his healing had taken place. In this testimony, too, the shepherd's preaching is underlined. The visit certainly included exorcism, even if my informant did not mention it.

[1305] IS 206. My impression was that my informant primarily thought of exorcism as the *toby* treatment, although this does not exclude "going to church" as the most common translation of *mivavaka*.

[1306] IS 322. "The Lutheran revival movement follows the example of Jesus in Mk 2: forgiveness of sins precedes healing. Without the word of God faith cannot be firmly established and the goal of the Bible is not obtained only through healing." IS 323. G. Haus sees it as a problem that ordinary people mainly understand the revival movement in relation to sickness and healing, which is contrary to the shepherds' own underlining of God's salvation. Haus 2000:114. The shepherds themselves are aware of this danger and try to counteract it.

shepherds' thinking than healing from sickness.[1307] Preaching of the Gospel, conversion, a firm belief in Jesus and prayer seem to be the primary concerns of the shepherds.[1308] One of the shepherd's warnings against emphasising miraculous healing too strongly also suggests that this is not the focus of interest.[1309]

The relationship between faith in Jesus and healing. The main goal of the shepherds' treatment may be summarised as faith in Jesus. "The faith is a shield and without faith the path is paved for the evil one."[1310] Faith in Jesus is a goal in itself, the faith is seen as a starting point in the healing process[1311] and the shepherds aim at strengthening people's faith. The shepherds use "faith/believe" in a variety of ways: "to believe that…",[1312] "to receive the faith",[1313] "it gives faith",[1314] "little faith",[1315] "a shallow faith",[1316] "their faith is not enough",[1317] "if we really believe…",[1318] "request more faith",[1319] "need strength for his/her

---

[1307] A non-shepherd in my material says plainly that the shepherds do not fulfil their task if they only assist people in their daily problems. IN 324. They have to give spiritual education and underline this element even more than they actually do. He fears that some of the shepherds, who themselves have found relief from daily problems in the revival movement, are not aware of the real goal of their work. This calls for a profound training.

[1308] IS 314 says, as a summary of the significance of the revival movement, that God has used the revival movement to lead many people to conversion and that the main point for the shepherds is that people are converted to the living God.

[1309] IS 325. It should be remembered that it is a shepherd leader who says this and it may be implied that some (many?) shepherds in fact emphasise healing too strongly. Rajaonarison E. and Rakotomalala M.M. see the revival movement as the greatest enemy of traditional and neo-traditional medicine and accuse the shepherds for gathering curious people to the exorcism séances and exploiting this situation to lead them to conversion. Rajaonarison and Rakotomalala 1987:4.

[1310] IS 323. Eph 6:16 is the biblical reference.

[1311] Cf. 4.6.3.2.

[1312] Mal: *mino fa.* IS 200.

[1313] Mal: *mandray ny finoana.* IS 202

[1314] Mal: *manome finoana.* IS 202.

[1315] Mal: *finoana kely.* IS 202.

[1316] Mal: *finoana marivo.* IS 320.

[1317] Mal: *tsy ampy ny finoany.* IS 200.

[1318] Mal: *tena mino.* 67 Ha-church 10 April 1993.

[1319] Mal: *mitaky finoana bebe kokoa.* IS 210.

faith",[1320] "make the faith firm",[1321] "a living faith".[1322] To explain the exact content of these expressions in the shepherds' thinking is not my point here but rather to show that faith in Jesus is frequently referred to and in the shepherds' understanding there seems to be several degrees of faith.

There is a close relation between healing and faith in Jesus. One of the citations above indicates that when the family had been led to conversion, the patient was healed. Another informant suggests that Jesus will bring healing when the family has turned to him in faith and he gives the reason for this by saying that healing depends on Jesus and not on the shepherds' abilities.[1323] Several shepherds in my material report of experiences of healing in their own lives and some of them explicitly connect this with their decision to really take their faith seriously (*tena miroso*) and become a shepherd.[1324] One informant told me about a woman who had been ill for a long time when she came to the *toby*.[1325] It was difficult for her to believe that Jesus was able to save her. She thought she would recover through attending church services and giving collections to the church but "a healing can only come through when she believes that Jesus loves her and saves her," my informant says.[1326]

Healing in the shepherds' usage has a comprehensive meaning. In the conversation about the woman's healing just mentioned my informant quotes Jn 17:3 about eternal life, indicating that healing should

---

[1320] Mal: *fampaherezana ny finoany*. IS 321.
[1321] Mal: *miorina ny finoana*. IS 323.
[1322] Mal: *finoana velona*. IS 205.
[1323] IS 316. "The people's longing for healing is fulfilled when they come to Jesus," according to IS 323. In addition to a living faith, prayer to God is emphasised, as facilitating the healing. IS 206. When a severely ill person was treated at the *toby*, the shepherds living there asked several of their fellow shepherds in the surrounding area to come and assist them. They engaged in a continuing prayer for the person. IS 210.
[1324] QS 88, QS 100. To become a shepherd is often understood as a solid decision of following Christ whatever happens and to be dependent on faith in Jesus. It seems like some shepherds see this action of faith as the reason for their healing.
[1325] It is believed that when a person has been ill for a long time his/her condition has been aggravated and it is difficult to set such a person free.
[1326] IS 200. According to Appiah-Kubi 1981:104–105 the prophet-healer dr. Prah sees man's basic problem is the lack of a right relationship with his creator. For any healing process to be successful peace with God and a reception of his righteousness are needed.

be considered as far more than to recover from bodily or mental sickness.[1327] One informant complains because people come to the *toby* only to "seek the benefit of the flesh".[1328] His saying implies that healing from bodily or mental sicknesses is too narrow an understanding of what healing consists of.[1329]

When a person has reached the desired degree of faith he/she does not seem to need the shepherds' exorcism. People with a "living faith" have the necessary strength to "cast out demons from themselves" (*mamoaka demonia ny tenany*), as the shepherds put it[1330] and this state indicates that the people are healed (*sitrana*). "Even when Jesus did not say a word, the demons left, because they knew him and did not feel well in his company."[1331] This reflection is used to support the view that when Jesus lives in a person by faith, the demons flee away. "People cast out their own demons when they pray seriously (*tena mivavaka*)."[1332] "A thorough biblical teaching has caused demons to leave a person and set him/her free, even without exorcism."[1333] This "casting out of demons from oneself" is believed to happen quietly when people listen to the

---

[1327] IS 200. A non-shepherd says that to believe in Jesus and his work is genuine healing (*ny fanasitranana mahomby dia ny finoana Azy sy ny asany*). QN 143. G. Haus has also noticed that, according to the shepherds, health in its fulness means that the person has received God's salvation. Then the power of God's salvation will affect body, mind and spirit. Haus 2000:108.

[1328] IS 210. Cf. 4.5.2.4 (When the sickness lingers).

[1329] Dr. Prah's "divine healing and miracle ministry" in Ghana strongly emphasises that peace and righteousness are needed to secure a successful healing process. Man's basic problem, lack of a right relationship with God, has to be dealt with before any healing can take place. Appiah-Kubi 1981:104–105.

[1330] My material does not make clear if the "casting out demons from oneself" includes elements from the shepherds' liturgy of casting out demons. My general impression is that it does not include specific elements but the expression seems rather to be used to convey that some people manage their lives without any assistance from the shepherds' exorcism. When tempted by the devil their faith is strong enough to resist.

[1331] IS 214.

[1332] IS 318.

[1333] IS 325.

preaching and sing the hymns[1334] and it is presupposed that the patient then is conscious and able to receive the word of God in his heart.[1335]

> A Christian life in faith is a power, which conquers the devil, according to 1 Jn 5:4: "this is the victory that overcomes the world, our faith." The communicants have authority to resist the devil, since the Bible exhorts us in Eph 4:27: "give no opportunity to the devil."[1336]

The shepherds' use of "casting out of demons from oneself" seems to imply that exorcism is only for those who still need the shepherds' assistance in the healing process and some of my informants explicitly say that exorcism is not intended for all.[1337]

4.5.2.3 *Renouncing of all other powers—burning of charms*

When people consult the traditional healers, they always receive charms according to the problem in question and these charms are considered to carry power from the supernatural world. The shepherds and the

---

[1334] QS 68. My informant adds that this happens when the people are eager to do this, which seems to point to a certain involvement from the person. IS 212 says that it may not be known to the preacher that the demons have left.

[1335] IS 310.

[1336] IS 323. "The people who are not able to resist the power of the devil need the shepherds to convert them," QS 97 says after he has talked about how people who receive Jesus in their hearts may cast out demons from themselves. Only this informant uses the expression "need the shepherds to convert them", but conversion as a major aspect of exorcism may point to a thinking where the shepherds are seen as leading people to conversion.

[1337] IS 310, IS 318. I cannot infer that all my informants share this opinion. IS 320 says that pastors seldom subject themselves to exorcism because they think it is for people with a "shallow faith". IS 214 says that he does not encourage everybody to attend "work and strengthening". He fears that it then could evolve into a new sacrament. "Casting out of demons from oneself" and exorcism by shepherds do not seem to rule out each other. Both CHIS 8 and CHIS 130 tell about how they started to cast out demons from themselves after a period of treatment by the shepherds. One of G. Haus' main conclusions in her thesis is that "ordinary Christians" cannot be free from the devil's bondage without the help of the shepherds. Some shepherds in her material seem to think that prayer can remove minor temptations but the main impression is that the person's own prayer is not enough. Haus 2000:114, 78, 88. As far as I am able to judge, her main informants behind this opinion work in the coastal areas and there seems to be a discrepancy in opinion between them and my informants from the high plateaus.

traditional healers stand in sharp opposition to each other, because the shepherds define the sources of power, with which the traditional healers have contact, as demonic. Traditional healers are considered as opposing the true God, since they do not lead people to faith in Jesus, but show other ways of healing and comfort.[1338]

My case histories show that a majority of the people healed by the shepherds had first consulted a traditional healer and it is thus probable that they have brought charms to their homes. Several informants emphasise the handing over of charms obtained from traditional healers as a pre-requisite for lasting healing.[1339] Without cutting all the bonds to traditional religion, healing cannot be obtained.[1340] It is not uncommon that the family brings charms little by little, often when new fits of illness occur.[1341] When the charms are delivered, the person's feeling of conflict is solved and this makes him/her recover little by little, according to one informant. He implies that the person has been aware of the contradiction between his/her charms and the Christian faith but he/she has not before taken the consequence of this.[1342]

In the book edited to the 50th anniversary of the Ankaramalaza movement we find a shepherd's vivid testimony of how he and his wife were set free from bondage of the spirits. He describes in detail all the paraphernalia used in the cult of the spirits and how he had to deliver them all. When they met *Mama* Nenilava, his wife was struck with a sudden fit of demonic oppression. He tells how the shepherds started

---

[1338] See 2.2.6.

[1339] CHQ 12, CHQ 57. In one case we are told that a young boy did not improve because he lived with his family who stored remedies from traditional healers. When the pastor of the congregation moved this boy into his own house, he soon recovered. CHQ 41. The shepherd does not comment the social implications of the episode.

[1340] IS 205, IS 218.

[1341] Many of the remedies given by traditional healers are herbal medicine and some of these healers are experts in plant medicine. Normally the shepherds do not distinguish between this and the amulets and charms, which have the aim of protecting or harming people. Their argument for this is that all remedies given by traditional healers are put into the power context, in which they operate. Herbal medicines are also *voahasina* (made holy), i.e. made powerful in the sphere of mystical powers. Cf. 4.5.1.3 (Western medicine), footnote 1254.

[1342] IS 202. My informant seems to consider the inner conflict as an additional aspect connected with keeping and using charms, besides the shepherds' firm belief that charms have demonic origin. My informant does not seem to see any incompatibility between the two aspects, however.

with casting out of demons from his wife, but when she did not show any signs of recovery after a lengthy period, *Mama* Nenilava ordered him to rush to their house and bring all the paraphernalia from the spirit cult.[1343] He mentions all the items used in the cult and among them a large straw basket with medicines (*fanafody*), which he and his wife used in the curing activities of the patients consulting them. When he had torn down everything and carried it to *Mama* Nenilava's house, his wife was sitting there normal without any signs of being "assaulted by demons".[1344] All the paraphernalia from the spirit cult were placed at the foot of a huge tree at *Mama* Nenilava's house. Two days later, at an appointed time, shepherds and the family gathered there, dug a big hole in the ground, put all the charms into it and burnt it in Jesus' name.[1345]

The handbook underlines that the surrender of charms has to be done voluntarily by the patients and that this is a sign of their willingness to turn wholeheartedly to God.[1346] The "owner" of the charms himself/herself has to deliver them, by preference to an elder at the *toby*.[1347]

[1343] Rakotondrasoa R.N.M. describes the exorcism session in a healing service and he says that "if the case persists for more than two hours, this is a sign that the person is not yet really convinced and there is an *ody* (charm) in their house". He explains further that the shepherds will try to convince the family of the patient to deliver for burning "whatever *ody* they keep in their house if they want the relative to be free." Rakotondrasoa 1996:78.

[1344] The shepherds present at the exorcism told him later that his wife had behaved like a snake wriggling along on the floor while he was home, removing all the items they had used in the cult of the spirits.

[1345] Ankaramalaza undated:129–150, here especially referred to pages 140–145. See also Austnaberg 1997, where I have translated some of the testimony into Norwegian and commented the most important part of it.

[1346] Another pamphlet with questions and answers from the Ankaramalaza-branch emphasises this total rejection even more. Burning of charms (*fanafody*) is a mark of a person's renouncing and total resistance against everything connected to the former living and a confession of Jesus' total rejection of all sorts of idolatry. Ankaramalaza 1997:11.

[1347] In the story above about the handing over of charms it was the husband of the woman "assaulted by demons" who brought all the items used in the spirit cult. This does not contradict with the handbook's underlining of the willingness of the "owner" to deliver the charms. Tobilehibe 1997:123. In the mentioned case, both the wife and her husband had co-operated in the spirit cult. The wife was the medium, while her husband was the "interpreter" and thus they were both "owners" of the charms.

The ordinary procedure is that the charms are burnt, with the owner present. A big hole is dug outside the church or the *toby* and all the paraphernalia has to be thoroughly burnt in fire. One informant asserts that it is dangerous to burn charms without a proper teaching for the owner. He/she may then think that the devil is gone but it is wrong to consider the devil as destroyed together with these items. Such thinking can make people ill prepared to continue the fight with the devil and they may be hurt again.[1348] A short service is held and a liturgy for this is suggested in the handbook. It consists of prayers, hymns and Scripture readings. When the burning starts, the leader says: "In the name of Jesus from Nazareth, the powerful, we burn these idols (*sampy*), piece of wood (*tapa-kazo*) and charms (*ody*)." The singing should continue until all items are totally demolished by the fire.[1349]

The burning of charms from the traditional healer is an integrated part of the healing process but it is not performed in the setting of a healing service. The burning takes place at a time appointed by the shepherds and the owners of the remedies and only a few people are present at this moment.[1350]

4.5.2.4 *A communal understanding of healing*

In a Malagasy view of life every individual is viewed as part of a community, both dependent on the community and able to effect the community with its actions. The shepherds seem to share this communal thinking in their understanding of healing. In line with this way of understanding, I will in the following firstly present the role of the

---

If there are valuable objects of silver or gold among the objects, *Mama* Nenilava has advised the shepherds to let these items be subject to casting out of demons and prayer and then they should be handed back to the owner. If he/she refuses to take them back, they can be given as a gift to the church/*toby*.

[1348] IS 325.

[1349] Tobilehibe 1997:123–124.

The burning of charms as a part of the shepherds' treatment is well documented: Sharp 1993:260, Rasolondraibe 1994:42, Laugerud 1993:70.

[1350] There is no regularity in the burning of charms, because it depends on when people having remedies convert and decide to deliver them (L 210). I have not observed the burning situation myself, but I have seen charms delivered to the church and I have kept some charms delivered to the shepherds, which a pastor gave to me: a red cloth and a cup of clay with incense.

308   CH. 4: THE SHEPHERDS' UNDERSTANDING OF THEIR PRACTICE

family[1351] in the healing process, secondly, the importance of the larger *toby* community and thirdly, the patient's own role in the healing process. In a fourth sub-section I list how shepherds explain that some people are not healed. As will be seen, theological aspects prevail in the shepherds' understanding.[1352]

The role of the family. Severely ill people coming to the *toby* are sometimes unconscious or they are unable to hold a normal conversation. This is the most obvious reason why the family is important in the healing process but there are several more profound reasons.

> The 25th of April 1994 two *"pousse-pousse"*[1353] with three women came to the Ambohimahazo *toby*: a lady with her daughter and her niece. The niece was now in her thirties and lived in her aunt's house because she had lost her parents. She had showed symptoms of mental illness and strange behaviour since the age of 14 but they had never been able to really diagnose the illness. As a last solution the lady came to the shepherds and she wondered if she could leave her niece with the shepherds for treatment.
> At once a shepherd told the lady that the *toby* would let her niece live there, but he made the conditions clear. One person from the close family had to stay with her for at least the first two weeks to take care of her and the family had to cover all her expenses for the stay, such as food and clothing. ... The lady's problem was to find a person in the family who was able to stay at the *toby*. In response the shepherd underlined how important it was for the family to turn to God, if they wanted the niece to recover. They should also be taught the word of God.[1354]

The shepherds expect the family accompanying the patient to stay at the *toby* for some time, to provide for the expenses of the patient and to take part in daily services and Christian education.[1355] The shepherds offer

---

[1351] I use the word "family" here to denote the patient's primary network. This may be his/her parents, other family-members or those who bring him/her to the *toby*.

[1352] Saayman 1992:38–39 mentions four important signs in the understanding of sickness and health in African cultures: the community thinking, a religious (or spiritual) understanding of sickness, the communal healing centre and a dual health system. I find all these signs present in the shepherds' understanding of sickness and healing. See also Igenoza 1999:148, 150 who especially underlines the community thinking and belief in the spiritual causing of illness.

[1353] This is a Malagasy "taxi": a two-passenger carriage pulled by a man.

[1354] O 340.

[1355] It is not only in the *toby* that the family is expected to provide for the expenses of their ill members. This is also the case in hospitals. Family members stay with the patient, they cook for him/her or they bring food to the hospitals/*toby*. Sometimes, it

several examples of how important the family's contribution is in the healing process and they almost always underline the spiritual aspects.

> I remember a sick person who was sent to the *toby* Ankaramalaza. His parents brought him there and returned home. The boy did not recover and so I sent a message to the parents asking them to return. During a consultation I asked them about their spiritual life and said: "You should not think that it is enough to bring your child to the *toby*. God wants to use what is happening now to heal your whole family. What is the significance of Jesus in your life?" They answered and said: "One of our friends is a shepherd and when the child has a fit, we ask this shepherd to come and have an exorcism session."[1356] "So this is the way you follow Christ?" I said. When I investigated more thoroughly I found their marriage was in disorder and that their daily life was led according to this world's way of life and not a Christian living. And I exhorted them ...: "It is important that you confess Jesus, have a close relationship with him and abandon what opposes the Gospel. By doing so you may hope for a healing of your child. You do not even believe that Jesus will heal him... but just leave him here at the *toby* and wait for a miracle. God wants you to be converted. ... The crucial question is whether the family change their hearts, not the healing of this child ..."[1357]

The conversion of the family members, or at least their openness to Christ is considered important to a lasting healing. This close connection between the family's actions and the success or failure of the healing process is underlined by many informants. The shepherds say that if the family is unwilling to believe in Jesus, the healing of their sick is slow or does not take place. On the other hand, if the family is converted and believes in Jesus, the shepherds have often experienced that the sick are healed.[1358]

In line with this, shepherds often understand sicknesses as conveying a message to the family, especially when healing is delayed. Sometimes they say that "God requests...", e.g. their conversion or a

---

happens that families leave their ill members at the *toby* without taking care of them and then the shepherds have to take responsibility for both their material and spiritual needs (see below). In the following I mainly present the "spiritual aspects", in line with the shepherds' own emphasis.

[1356] My informant showed by his voice that the parents felt this question impolite and they answered him rudely.

[1357] IS 322.

[1358] IS 312, IS 322, IS 218. The same line of thought is found among non-shepherds in my material. QN 27. When one patient's parents decided to believe in God and handed over the charms, her fits became more seldom. When the parents were baptised, she recovered fully. CHINA 116.

strengthening of their faith/a wholehearted surrender, or that they become communicants.[1359] This reflects the shepherds' understanding of sicknesses having positive purposes.[1360]

Mutual forgiveness between family members is emphasised by the shepherds as facilitating the healing of the sick. There may be unsettled matters among them and one informant explains the need of settling the matters by saying that afterwards they have "a clean heart" (*madio fo*). He emphasises that the mutual forgiveness has to be done wholeheartedly.[1361]

> I will tell you about a sick person. His sickness resulted from his parents' divorce. He felt deeply disappointed and fell mentally ill (*very saina*). He was taken to a *toby* and treated there with "work and strengthening". The shepherds sent for his parents and talked with them (*dinidinika*). The shepherds preached the word of God to them and the parents and the family were told that "You have caused this sickness with your own actions and there is still an unclean spirit among you, which does not come from God." When the parents mutually asked for forgiveness, their son was healed and today he is a shepherd.[1362]

Shepherds sometimes refer to Jn 9:1–3 to support their understanding of the relationship between parents and children: "The activities of the family have consequences for their children," both positively and negatively.[1363] One informant says:

> Since the disciples ask Jesus this question in Jn 9:2 this shows us that the parents' actions may affect the children. And our experiences affirm this

---

[1359] QS 97, CHISA 130. The father of one of my informants who was not himself a shepherd also understood the severe sickness of his son as a message to the entire family: to become more eager in faith. CHIS 130.

[1360] IS 322 says that "it may be that God through the sickness saves his family" but he admits that it is difficult to have a decisive opinion about this (*mamantatra*). Cf. 4.5.1.2 (Positive purposes) and 4.3.2.3.

[1361] IS 312.

[1362] IS 322. When I asked my informant who should be labelled "assaulted by demons" in this case, he agreed that according to human logic it was the parents but he believed that the sins of the parents have consequences for their child. He said that God has his working methods, which sometimes are difficult for humans to understand.

[1363] IS 312.

because we often see that when the parents are converted the children are healed.[1364]

In one of the case histories the family's faith and prayers are said to carry the sick and the family does this on behalf of him.[1365] Other informants mention the difficulties of the sick when they are healed and return to their respective families, who do not have a prayer life. This may cause the sickness to return.[1366]

The shepherds' Christian witness and the education of the patient's family is one of the important tasks of the shepherds in the healing process and much of their time is spent on this.[1367] "They strive to lead the families of the sick to conversion ... to have confidence in God ... Then they [the family] can believe that "whatever you ask in my name, I will do it"."[1368]

The community life in a toby. The healing process at the *toby* may last for weeks, months or years.[1369] The shepherds are less preoccupied with the time of stay than with what the stay means to the sick.

The organised spiritual life in the *toby* Ambohimahazo consists of healing services Monday and Thursday from 8–10 a.m. and Tuesday and Friday from 2–3.30 p.m. The church at the *toby* is at the same time the parish church with services every Sunday at 9 a.m. Some Sundays "work and strengthening" is also included. Everybody living in the *toby* (shepherds, patients and their families) are expected to attend all these public services.[1370] The personal spiritual life consists of prayer morning and evening, reading of the Bible and an everyday life as a Christian.

[1364] IS 322. IS 210 refers to Jn 9 in cases where the sickness lingers because of unsettled matters among the family members. When these are settled the sick regains his/her health. IS 315 agrees that the healing of the children is dependent on the parents and he seems to consider the parents' belief as a prerequisite for healing but healing is not secured because of this. Healing depends on God alone!

[1365] CHIN 31.

[1366] CHIS 12, IS 322.

[1367] IG 331.

[1368] IS 200.

[1369] IS 210. Shepherds have several ways of explaining the absence of healing for some patients and I list these below (When the sickness lingers).

[1370] L 210. Wednesday mornings from 8–10 a.m. special gatherings are held for all those in charge at the *toby* and Saturdays from 8–10 a.m. there is education for shepherds and novices.

312   CH. 4: THE SHEPHERDS' UNDERSTANDING OF THEIR PRACTICE

This means that the patients listen to prayer, preaching and testimonies again and again and they are treated with casting out of demons and prayed for with the laying on of hands in every healing service.[1371] As they show signs of recovery, they are little by little taught by the shepherds to pray and read the Bible. This treatment is repeated until the patient is healed.

To give an impression of the length of the continuing treatment of these people, I will briefly list the patients labelled as "assaulted by demons", who lived at the *toby* Ambohimahazo in September 1993. My aim here is not to describe the symptoms of their illness, but to indicate that healing for the shepherds is considered a continuing process.

> A rather old man, who had stayed for a long time. A shepherd was taking care of him.[1372]
> A 43 year old man, who lived there with his mother. They had been living for some time at four different *toby*.[1373]
> A 22 year old man, who had stayed for one year and 10 months. His parents stayed at the *toby* together with him.
> A young woman living there with her mother, her child and her husband. They had been there for two months.
> An 18 year old woman who had come recently.[1374] She lived together with a couple who were both shepherds.
> A middle-aged man, who came the day before I visited them. His family was staying together with him.
> A young girl, who lived together with a blind woman and a very old, poor woman. I have no information about the length of her stay.[1375]

The indication of time is not exact, which may indicate that the shepherds are not preoccupied with the length of the stay.

Christian life and Christian faith permeate the *toby* and one of my informants characterised this as a place where people "are swimming in lots of God's word".[1376] This notion of Christian community is what

---

[1371] IS 202 talks about the continuing repetition (*iverimberenana*) of the treatment at the *toby*.

[1372] His parents had brought him to the *toby*, but they were both dead by then.

[1373] When I returned to continue my fieldwork almost 5 years later, this person was still living at the *toby*, but his mother was dead.

[1374] Mal: *vao haingana* (recently) can be a week or some months.

[1375] O 341.

[1376] *Milomano ao anatin'ny tenin'Atra maro ny ao amin'ny toby.* IS 311. During my fieldwork I experienced some of this feeling of "swimming" when going to healing

especially distinguishes the *toby* from everyday life in the village and such a life is, according to the shepherds, important in order to secure a lasting healing for severely ill people.[1377] The treatment takes place in a fellowship community, which comprises both the spiritual and the material aspects of life (body, mind and spirit) and the significance of this in the healing process is emphasised.[1378]

When it is a long time before the patients recover, some families forget their ill members and the shepherds at the *toby* have to take responsibility for the patients.[1379] One shepherd is appointed to take special care of each patient and sometimes a shepherd is responsible for more than one patient. It is not uncommon that this shepherd lives and sleeps in the same room as the patient and so the shepherd can be the patient's support in all sectors of life. The shepherds share what they have with the patients in their charge, both materially and spiritually: food, clothing and washing, if necessary and individual Christian education by reading from the Bible, praying and giving spiritual guidance.[1380] It should be remembered that some of the patients may be violent, act erratically and especially in the opening phase of the treatment the shepherds must be prepared to get up in the middle of the night if the patient has a sudden fit of illness. The shepherds use

---

services every day and listening to prayer, testimonies, Scripture reading, sermons and lots of hymns again and again.

[1377] IS 202 talks about the daily *toby* activities and says that "they are living in God's word".

[1378] Rakotondrasoa R.N.M. emphasises that the treatment in the *toby* is holistic when he says: "In the "Toby", ... the work of the "Fifohazana" concerns all aspects of human life in order to reintegrate people again in the socio-political life." (p. 117). Rakotondrasoa is citing the statutes of the Ankaramalaza *toby* to underline his statement, which says that the *toby* has concern for all aspects of human life since that is the meaning of the salvation God intends to give his people. Ankaramalaza undated:176–177. He rejects the view that the *toby* is a remote place to put away the sick and to fight with the evil spirits. Rather it should be understood as a place where God shows his mercy towards a hurt world. The *toby* is a place where people are united in community life and this integration into a fellowship is crucial in the Malagasy thinking. Rakotondrasoa 1996:116–118.

[1379] Cf. the family's obligation to cover the expenses. See above (The role of the family). The following information is based on observation and informal conversation during my stay in Madagascar.

[1380] Since the patients are not living in a separate place but together with the shepherds, the possibility of discipling the patients are good. The guidance in praying and God's word is the shepherds' special responsibility. L 210.

exorcism and prayer to assist the patient in fighting the evil spirits and they are encouraged to show love and compassion to any patient.[1381] The patients thus abandoned by their families are taken into the *toby* community and on a spiritual level, they are invited into the family of God.

The role of the patient. The shepherds assist the sick in order to raise their ability to conquer attacks from evil spirits: They strengthen them with words from the Bible through public teaching and special consultations and they cast out demons and pray for them.[1382] The patients themselves are not rendered passive in the healing process, however.

The patients' willingness to be healed is considered important. For the unconscious and patients unable to hold a normal conversation, this willingness is shown when the family brings their ill members to the shepherds.[1383] One informant talks about the person and the spirit oppressing her as co-operating in keeping this spirit and for a whole month there was no recovery. Through much preaching of God's word and Christian teaching, however, this lady one day discovered her true situation. Then she was able to renounce the spirit oppressing her. This was understood as a willingness to be set free and she soon recovered.[1384]

Even though the patient is willing to be set free, there is a complicated interaction between his/her own efforts and Jesus' work with this person. One informant says:

> We cannot be free [the temptations] if Jesus does not remove us from them, if the Holy Spirit does not clean us and enlighten us so that they may leave ... The Holy Spirit enlightens our lives and so we are able to conquer the temptations, we cast them out, we take them away ...[1385]

[1381] Fikambanana Toby Lehibe Ankaramalaza 1990:8.

[1382] IS 218, IS 210. Cf. 4.2.1.

[1383] "They [the patients] must have an eager wish to get rid of the evil one oppressing them," one non-shepherd in my material says. "The shepherds co-operate with the person in expelling the demons." QN 11.

[1384] IS 217. The AICs also emphasise the subjective co-operation of the patients in order to ensure a successful healing. This co-operation especially consists in the patients' confession of all their sins. The decision of the afflicted person to resist evil is requested by the healers; cf. the burning of charms in the shepherds' understanding. Kitshoff 1997:7, Daneel 1990:231.

[1385] IS 213. The inclusive 1st person plural "we" (*isika*) is used in the citation and I interpret this as the informant includes the interviewer in the sayings. There is a

This co-operation seems to be understood as a process where both the person's activity and Jesus' assistance are necessary to obtain the desired result.[1386] The inflicted person has to be willing and active in order to be healed but, at the same time, healing is fully dependent on Jesus' intervention.[1387] The goal of the healing process for the patients is that they have a living faith, which enables them to "cast out demons from themselves". Healing from observable bodily and mental sickness is seen as a possible result of this.[1388]

When the sickness lingers.[1389]

> Some of the people coming to the *toby* recover in one week, others have to stay for months or years and some have to wait their whole life. This situation makes many indifferent to the shepherds' treatment. People think that the shepherds' treatment resembles the treatment of medical doctors: When they come to a hospital, they receive medication and in 2 or 3 days they return healthy. People only seek the benefit of the flesh. When healing is delayed the patient or the family become disappointed and because of their many problems, they do not stay long enough. Sometimes they just leave their sick at the *toby*.[1390]

The shepherds' treatment aims at casting out devils and strengthening people's confidence in Jesus. This takes time, but "when severely ill people are taught continually over a period of time, in addition to "work

---

linguistic possibility that the Holy Spirit could be included in the "we" in the last sentence (i.e. the interviewee/the interviewer *and* the Holy Spirit ...) but I find this unlikely since the exclusive 1st person plural (*izahay*) is always used in communication with God.

[1386] In one of the case histories the patient's mother said: "Something is binding him and he is not standing up against it because he is not calling Jesus' name to help him. Jesus does not know how to save him ..." and the shepherd accompanying me interrupted and said: "Pray eagerly and conquer this devil so that Jesus can reign over him!" Both the patient and Jesus are considered to be active. CHIN 31.

[1387] The persons' activity is also important when demons attack. People defend themselves (*miaro-tena*) against demonic assaults, especially by prayer and God's word, which is understood as enlisting divine forces in the battle. It is the person's responsibility to "chase away the mosquito" by using God's weapons. If not, the devil will be able to work with these people, lead them away from Christ and make them vulnerable to all kinds of evil. IS 213. Cf. 2.2.5.

[1388] IS 205, IS 318. Cf. 4.5.2.2 (The shepherds' priority).

[1389] This refers to healing from observable sicknesses, bodily or mental.

[1390] IS 210.

316 CH. 4: THE SHEPHERDS' UNDERSTANDING OF THEIR PRACTICE

and strengthening", the work of the devil vanishes within them".[1391] One of the reasons why people are not healed is because they do not stay long enough at the *toby* to experience this. They do not wait for God's intervention.

Related to this is the case when the sick leave the *toby* in the middle of the healing process. Their state of health has improved but they have not yet reached a mature state of faith. Then shepherds believe that the sickness will become even worse.[1392]

Sometimes, this is connected with the situation in the patient's family and is believed to result from lack of prayer and spiritual life there.[1393] Other conditions in the family: unsettled matters, unbelief or the use and storage of charms may also hamper healing. To continue the healing process, these matters have to be settled.[1394]

As already mentioned, if the patients themselves do not come to a living faith in Jesus, healing is delayed or fails to come[1395] and the sickness may be considered as a means of upbringing for the sick, to keep him from leaving Jesus.[1396]

One shepherd admits that sometimes they do not know why a certain person is not healed. The patient's parents may be committed Christians but still there is no recovery. My informant says: "The human mind is unable to figure out the reason for this."[1397] When referring to Jn 1:12 one shepherd said in a testimony: "Jesus did not heal all the sick but he gave all those who believed in him power to become his children." This

---

[1391] IS 311. I have some testimonies from people who are healed saying that in specific situations their previous sickness threatens to return. CHIS 8 says that he still feels something pressing him at nights (the same symptoms occurred during his sickness) and he thinks that it is the devil, which he himself has cast out of other people "assaulted by demons" who disturbs him. CHIS 12 feels that some of the previous symptoms returns when she has engaged in a harsh quarrel with her husband and he is unforgiving. "He does not dare to do so any more," she says.

[1392] IS 323.

[1393] IS 322.

[1394] See above (The role of the family).

[1395] See 4.5.2.2 (The relationship between faith in Jesus and healing). A non-shepherd in my material accuses the shepherds of making the sick responsible for lack of healing. Shepherds say: "You do not believe, or you do not pray, or you do not endure." When the sick show no signs of recovery, the shepherds are less eager to "work" with them, according to my informant. QN 162.

[1396] IS 311 in a conversation with IS 316. See 4.5.1.2 (Positive purposes).

[1397] IS 322.

shepherd continues by saying that it is the reception of Jesus, which matters.[1398]

4.5.2.5 *The climax of healing*

According to the shepherds, what happens in the second part of the liturgy is the climax of healing.

> The "strengthening"[1399] ... makes firm and unites the purpose of the service and the "work", which is done, i.e. the encounter with God, the reconciliation with him and the renewal of the covenant with him, the reception of his words of promise and the firm staying within this [word].[1400]

The purpose of this second part of exorcism is to establish the kingdom of God.[1401] In spite of some differences in practice, imposition of hands is especially connected to the second part and it is the prayer with the laying on of hands, which distinguishes this prayer from all the other

---

[1398] Ambohimahazo *toby* 24 May 1993. Rasolondraibe P. says: "It is true that some patients are not cured (including some shepherds) and yet Malagasy Christians, especially the Lutherans, believe the Lord has visited his church with the power of his healing Spirit." Rasolondraibe 1989:350. In a joint meeting between several churches in Antananarivo, the discussion also concerned the revival movement and its healings. Pastor George answered on behalf of the shepherds: "... nous ne forçons pas la guérison. C'est une décision souveraine du Seigneur qui accorde ou non, une guérison. L'activité des mpiandry ne produit pas automatiquement la guérison. Et quand vous avez posé la question, en cas d'échec, que faites vous? Nous ne pensons pas qu'obligatoirement, on aura des succés ou la guérison. Nous faisons simplement la prédication de l'Evangile. Nous amenons les gens à se tourner vers Dieu, à reconnaître leurs péchés , et à accepter de s'engager dans la vie chrétienne. S'il est de la volonté du Seigneur de donner la guérison, c'est la libre volonté du Seigneur. ...". Ratongavao et.al. 1997:225.

[1399] Mal: *fampaherezana*. Cf. 3.3. In the present subchapter I normally use only "prayer" to denote the "strengthening" but it points to the prayer with the laying on of hands.

[1400] Tobilehibe 1997:111. QS 41 and QS 127 seem to use some of the same words as the handbook when they characterise the purpose of the "strengthening". QS 41 continues: "it causes the person to return to God and to receive Jesus."

[1401] Tobilehibe 1997:80. The first part (*asa*) is believed to tear down the kingdom of Satan. The necessity of both these parts, in this order, is drawn from Jer 1:10. Haus 2000:147 sees in this a parallel to the traditional belief, where they often (not always) cast out evil spirits before they can conduct negotiations with the good spirits. The goal is to establish a covenant between the spirit and the person.

318 CH. 4: THE SHEPHERDS' UNDERSTANDING OF THEIR PRACTICE

prayers in a healing service.[1402] This is so to the extent that shepherds often refer to this prayer only by saying "imposition of hands" (*fametrahan-tanana*).[1403] To deem from the ways shepherds refer to this part, they do not seem occupied mostly with the meaning of the laying on of hands, however, but rather with the content of the prayer.

One of the questions I asked the shepherds in the questionnaire was to describe the content of this prayer. The most reiterated answers were that "forgiveness of sins", "the Holy Spirit" and "strength" are given through this prayer. Others said that the shepherds bring the people to Jesus through this prayer and so the people are able to make a decision about following Jesus.[1404] The shepherds' answers referred to here furnish

---

[1402] The repetition of the prayer with the laying on of hands in every healing service is important to the shepherds. The practice in the *toby* Ambohimahazo, where shepherds repeatedly impose their hands on each patient during casting out of demons causes controversy among my informants. This imposition of hands is considered as an old custom in this *toby* and is clearly distinguished from the laying on of hands with prayer in the second part of exorcism. Cf. 3.2.3 (The shepherds' movments). The laying on of hands is often part of the healing activities in the AICs. Power is conveyed through this and evil spirits are driven away. Kitshoff 1997:9. The power-aspect resembles the shepherds' understanding of "strengthening" but in the Malagasy revival movement the overall practice is to cast out demons only with words, according to the example of Jesus.

[1403] Imposition of hands (*fametrahan-tanana*) and "strengthening" (*fampaherezana*) are used interchangeably by the shepherds. Ankaramalaza 1997:19–20. The main biblical reference for the practice of imposition of hands is said to be Mk 16:18.

[1404] The questions in the questionnaire were open-ended without any pre-set answers and most shepherds mentioned several things. From a total of 44 shepherds in this material, where not all of them answered this question, the numbers were as follows: forgiveness (26), Holy Spirit (23), strength (23), decision ... (10). Other content was that peace (9), blessing (6) and grace (5) is given through the prayer. In answering in this way my informants seem to follow the joint statutes of the revival movement, which says that "your sins are forgiven" and "receive the Holy Spirit" should always be part of this prayer.

I was surprised that only three people explicitly mentioned healing from disease. Healing from bodily sickness is often stressed in daily conversation as taking place in the "strengthening" and its base is the Scripture reading from Mk 16:18: "...they will lay their hands on the sick, and they will recover." Repeatedly I have been told that "work" is the casting out of the evil enemy, while "strengthening" is the place of healing from disease. Both Pitaka 1999:128 and Tobilehibe 1997:111 stress that healing is part of this prayer's results and they primarily connect this with Scripture passages pointing to the laying on of hands (Mt 8:3, 15, Mk 5:34, 6:5, Lk 4:40, Acts 28:8). It may be that the shepherds just implied the healing of desease without mentioning it explicitly, because it is so commonly thought of. Another possibility is that, since the shepherds do not distinguish sharply between bodily and spiritual

the background of the following outline. I describe the content of the prayer with the laying on of hands as forgiveness of sins, a giving of the Holy Spirit, strength through the prayer and finally, I comment on the shepherds' unique position.

"Your sins are forgiven." "When the devil is cast out, we turn to the person and say: "Your sins are forgiven"."[1405] Sometimes the shepherds' words in characterising this prayer can be misunderstood to mean that the shepherds forgive sins.[1406] Mostly, however, the shepherds only cite the mentioned phrase or they use the word "declare": "We declare (*fanambarana*) the forgiveness of sins from Jesus".[1407]

One informant connects the forgiveness of sins explicitly to baptism but he believes that often the shepherds are not aware of this link.[1408] In a pamphlet from the Ankaramalaza-branch the question is whether the shepherds should say "your sins are forgiven" to children during this prayer and this is affirmed by saying that forgiveness of sins is the basic meaning of baptism. Because of God's grace in baptism the child is transferred from the power of sin to the Holy Spirit's kingdom.[1409]

The shepherds' conviction is that only "people who are really converted should receive the "strengthening". Then they can be promised forgiveness of sins and peace."[1410] When it comes to practice however, everybody who asks for it receives "strengthening". The handbook says that people staying at the *toby* for a long time because of their continued treatment should also receive "strengthening", because this enables the Holy Spirit to work in them and may increase their faith.[1411] When I asked one of my informants how the shepherds could promise

---

    disease, they consider the spiritual part (receiving of forgiveness and the Holy Spirit) as the most important healing. Cf. 4.5.1.3 (Prayer with the laying on of hands).

[1405] IS 200.

[1406] "to forgive them their sins" (*famelana ny helony*). QS 54.

[1407] QS 57, IS 312. A non-shepherd in my material says that there is some discussion about the shepherds' forgiveness of sins in relation to absolution and he has noticed that people seldom consult pastors for confession with absolution because they believe to have received absolution from the shepherds. IN 313.

[1408] IS 202. In his instruction of novices/shepherds he always emphasises this connection, because as he says: "Baptism is the basis for all other things."

[1409] Ankaramalaza 1997:20.

[1410] IS 310, Tobilehibe 1997:96.

[1411] Tobilehibe 1997:107.

320   CH. 4: THE SHEPHERDS' UNDERSTANDING OF THEIR PRACTICE

forgiveness of sins to people who had not confessed their sins,[1412] he answered by saying that the shepherds note that the person shakes, which means that he/she is afraid. Then the shepherds ought to comfort the person by saying: "Have courage! Your sins are forgiven!" This shepherd takes the shaking as a sign of fear of death, which he, in light of my question, possibly understands as the person's conviction of sinfulness. On this basis, it is the privilege of the shepherds to declare God's forgiveness.[1413]

An implicit tension occurs since it depends on people's own choice to be prayed for, by raising their hand and my informants are aware that sometimes, people ask for "strengthening" because it has become a custom and they do not repent. The shepherds cannot refuse also praying for these people but their choice of words is important in such cases.[1414]

Forgiveness of sins is also intended to affect future life. "When the shepherds cite Jesus' words: "Your sins are forgiven", this summons the people to live in freedom and not return to the things binding them earlier," one shepherd says.[1415]

"Receive the Holy Spirit." The shepherds' references to the place of the Holy Spirit in "strengthening" seem to point in different directions. The sermon in a healing service used the following words: "We are going to receive "strengthening". What happens there? We receive the Holy Spirit. This is really what happens, according to the Bible."[1416] Another shepherd said that "if you have not yet received the Holy Spirit, you should approach the shepherds [i.e. an invitation to the coming

---

[1412] Implicit in my question is the confession of sins by using words, prior to the prayer session.

[1413] IS 200. The question of promising forgiveness without any preceding oral confession has been a matter of discussion for a long time in the church. One of the non-shepherds in my material recalls discussions in the seminary during his study. A foreign missionary did not accept the "strengthening" because, according to his opinion, only people who were led to a real conversion should be prayed for in this way. IN 317. Lie 1981:14–15 asks for spiritual guidance with confession of sins prior to the "strengthening" and maintains that a confession of sins before the prayer would have clarified the meaning of the Gospel.

[1414] IS 218. See below (Strength through the prayer). IS 310 says that some of the shepherds also think magically of this prayer and are not occupied with the word of God.

[1415] Ambohimahazo *toby* 17 June 1998.

[1416] Ambohimahazo *toby* 18 June 1998.

"strengthening"] and they will give it to you."[1417] Another said: "the people are given the Holy Spirit in the name of Jesus" in this prayer.[1418] Through this prayer the shepherds summon people to receive the Holy Spirit.[1419] These sayings seem to place the shepherds in a unique position.[1420]

Some of the shepherds' words concentrate more on content, however, i.e. what the Holy Spirit means to people. One of the shepherds cited above said in an interview that the phrase "receive the Holy Spirit" means that the Holy Spirit should lead the person, because only if the Holy Spirit leads people, they may get to know Jesus. "People are encouraged to come closer through this prayer," he said.[1421] Another says:

> When we say: "receive the Holy Spirit" this means that you should listen to what the Holy Spirit tells you. Obey the voice of the Spirit! There are many temptations but the Holy Spirit teaches us what to do.[1422]

Others again emphasise that through this prayer the Holy Spirit is asked to work with the person and to give him/her strength.[1423]

It is possible to understand the phrase "receive the Holy Spirit" in the meaning that the Spirit has not been dwelling in the person before. When one shepherd explains the prayer by saying that its result is that the Holy Spirit should be firmly placed (*hampitoerana*) within the person, this points to the Holy Spirit as already there, however.[1424] Other informants also make it clear that the Holy Spirit has stayed in the person since baptism.[1425]

[1417] Antananarivo, Log 238, 67 Ha 02 July 1998. G. Haus has observed that the shepherds' words emphasise that ordinary Christians have to receive the Holy Spirit through others. Haus 2000:148.

[1418] QS 97.

[1419] QS 54, QS 105.

[1420] See below (A unique position of the shepherds?).

[1421] IS 200. QS 181 understands the prayer as an opener of a person's life, in order that the Holy Spirit can renew his/her life again and again.

[1422] Ambohimahazo *toby* 17 June 1998.

[1423] QS 87, QS 76. The Holy Spirit plays an active role in healing and exorcism in the AICs and the main emphasis in the healing sessions is to be under total control of the Spirit. For a brief description of this theme in the AICs, see Kitshoff 1997:5–6.

[1424] QS 150.

[1425] IS 311 in Ambohimahazo *toby* 17 June 1998. The wording of IS 200 is that the person "has already received the Holy Spirit since he/she became a Christian". A non-shepherd's questioning of the words "receive the Holy Spirit" shows that this

The handbook briefly explains the meaning of "receive the Holy Spirit":

> The Holy Spirit is uncomfortable with sin, according to the words of *Mama* [Nenilava] and he easily withdraws from people when they sin (anger, non-belief, depression). Therefore, people need a continuing conversion in order to receive him again. The words "receive the Holy Spirit" is self-examination and watchfulness in relation to sin "which clings so closely" (Heb 12:1); it is a basic firmament and confidence in God.[1426]

A plain reading of this passage seems to suggest that the Holy Spirit withdraws when people sin and only by conversion he will return. Earlier in the handbook, however, it is emphasised that the shepherds' need of "strengthening" by no way means that the Spirit of God has withdrawn from them. The handbook says that the Spirit is given once but that his renewing work does not end until God's people have reached perfection.[1427]

Strength through the prayer. The joint statutes of the four branches of the revival movement (FFPM) regulate which words should always be part of the prayer with the laying on of hands but this does not mean that the

---

may cause misunderstandings. He says: "Have they received the Holy Spirit in baptism or do they receive him now?" IS 313.

[1426] The interpretation of these words is difficult. The Malagasy words are: *Araka ny tenin'i Mama, ny Fanahy Masina dia sarotiny ny amin'ny ota, ka mora mihataka amin'ny olona raha vao manota izy (fahatezerana, tsy finoana, fahakiviana,...), ary ilàn'ny olona fibebahana tsy tapaka, mba handraisany azy indray. Ny amin'ny hoe "raiso ny Fanahy Masina" dia fampahatsiarovan-tena sy fampitandremana ny amin'ny ota malaky mahazo (cf Heb. 12:1), ary fampiorenana sy fanomezan-toky ao amin'Andriamanitra.* Tobilehibe 1997:113–114.

[1427] Tobilehibe 1997:70. The handbook's choice of words here underlines that it is out of the question that the Spirit of God should withdraw: *tsy hoe sanatria nialan'ny Fanahin'Andriamanitra...* It may be argued that the handbook on p. 70 talks about "strengthening" of shepherds while in the citation above (p. 113–114) ordinary people are in mind and that these two groups possess the Holy Spirit differently. G. Haus seems to argue along this line. She takes the handbook in the plain meaning that the Holy Spirit vanishes when people sin and she infers that there is a possibility that the handbook thinks that the Holy Spirit will only return when the shepherds "put him back". Some of her informants seem to support this interpretation but as far as I can observe, these are ordinary shepherds from the coastal area. Haus 2000:93. I have no hints in my material that the Holy Spirit withdraws when people sin.

shepherds' own judgement is suspended.[1428] Their responsibility is to choose words under the guidance of the Holy Spirit according to the person to be prayed for. They also evaluate the person's recovery, consciousness, whether he/she is baptised, etc. in order to choose appropriate words.[1429] The shepherds supplement the obligatory words with their own when they pray, either because they deem it necessary or because the person asks for it.[1430]

The shepherds ask the Lord to give strength in the name of Jesus and they encourage the person to resist the devil and keep close to God.[1431] Through the prayer people are enabled to continue resisting what they feel difficult in their lives.[1432]

> Even though the devil is cast out the people are still weak. They think that they are severely hurt and that their sins are too numerous. Then we have to tell them that God Jesus forgives your sins when you confess them ... It is important to let them understand that the God they pray to is a loving God who is willing to forgive and receive all those who seek him.[1433]

The shepherds believe that the Holy Spirit guides them in their prayer.[1434] They may reveal secrets and say things by the Holy Spirit that they should not know but normally they are unaware of this themselves.[1435] The handbook advises that while the shepherds are praying they should simultaneously pray that the Holy Spirit reveals to them the desires and problems of the person.[1436]

When the people to be prayed for are unconscious, the shepherds do not use the obligatory words concerning forgiveness and the Holy Spirit[1437] and for the impenitent the shepherds may pray like this:

> Jesus, you know this person who has come here. We beg you to work with him/her with your Holy Spirit so that he/she may be really converted. You

---

[1428] Fifohazana miray ao amin'ny FFPM 2000:9. See 3.3.3.
[1429] IS 200, IS 218.
[1430] Tobilehibe 1997:114.
[1431] IS 200.
[1432] IS 210.
[1433] IS 200.
[1434] QS 69.
[1435] IS 210, CHIS 130.
[1436] Tobilehibe 1997:114.
[1437] IS 312, QS 3.

have brought him/her to this place and we have confidence that you will take care of this person and heal him/her. We give him/her over in your hands.[1438]

My informant thanks the Lord and says that when they often pray like this the Lord is working with his Holy Spirit and the person is led to conversion.

A unique position of the shepherds? The shepherds' roles as mediators between God and the people is seen in the "strengthening". They act on behalf of both God and people and these two functions operate side by side. The beginning of the prayer firmly states that it is God's authority that enables the shepherds to perform this service and it is their concern to give a message from God to the people. On the other hand, the shepherds assist the people when their burdens are too heavy and they bring the sick to Jesus. Through confession of sins and prayer of forgiveness the shepherds act on behalf of the people.[1439] They give strength and help those who are fighting and by this they prevent people from "loosing their mind".[1440] "When people are not able to shout: "Save me, Jesus!" they need help from the shepherds."[1441]

> When I feel weak, one informant says, I ask my wife [who is a shepherd] to "work". I am not possessed[1442] but the faint-heartedness itself stems from the devil and I am not able to resist it myself. She comforts me and give me faith—in face of my nearly giving in because of my problems.[1443]
> People have problems in their marriage. They may know that it stems from the devil, but the problems do not lose the grip on them. It is like he [the devil] has entered their marriage. Then they come [to the shepherds] because they are not able to resist the devil in it.[1444] The shepherds help them by casting out demons and with the words in prayer. The shepherds strengthen the people's mind so that they may be able to resist themselves.[1445]

[1438] IS 218.

[1439] IS 312.

[1440] IS 310. Mal: *fahaverezan-tsaina*.

[1441] IS 323.

[1442] My informant uses the French word "possédé".

[1443] IS 202.

[1444] Mal: *ny devoly ao anatiny*. This can point either to the marriage (the devil in it) or it can point to the people (the devil in them).

[1445] IS 210. This is not a word for word translation.

It seems as if people's ability to act for themselves may be weak or strong. When this ability has reached a certain low level, these people are in need of the shepherds' assistance. Then the shepherds resist the devil on behalf of the sick or give strength in order for the sick to be able to resist themselves.[1446]

The shepherds consider themselves to be God's deputies who bring the people to Jesus through prayer[1447] and they think that it is God who speaks through them. One shepherd says: "I believe that the words of the shepherds [in "strengthening"] are God's words." He also believes that people ask for this prayer because they want to hear what the Lord has to say to them.[1448] One of the shepherds told me about his experience of this prayer during his illness: "When the shepherd put the hand on my head, it did not feel like a human hand. I recovered through this because Jesus was at work through the shepherd."[1449]

The handbook says that this prayer shows the shepherds as priests and reconciliators, which emphasises the mediating role of the shepherds. The shepherds bring people to God and ask God to give them his grace, they declare God's forgiveness as a gift to the people, they distribute words of encouragement and they make firm the people's wishes to surrender themselves more wholly to God.[1450]

[1446] G. Haus maintains that the shepherds define themselves as high priests, who deputise for God and act on behalf of God. In this way the shepherds both assist God and the sick. Haus' conclusion from this is that "ordinary Christians" are made helpless in relation to evil and only the shepherds can break the devil's power through exorcism. People are made dependant on the shepherds' assistance. Haus 2000:135–136.

[1447] QS 21, QS 54, QS 69.

[1448] QS 142. B.S. Lie and G. Haus point to other reasons why people ask for "strengthening": Ordinary Christians perceive of the prayer as a communication of strength from the shepherds to the people, according to Lie 1981:15 and he fears that this prayer may be considered as a sacrament at the same level as Holy Communion. According to Haus 2000:127 several ordinary Christians believe that "strengthening" is similar to a strong charm, which protects them against their objects of fear.

[1449] CHIS 130. He refers to Is 53 saying that Jesus carried our sicknesses. Also the visiting shepherd had an experience of the presence of Jesus during the "strengthening".

[1450] Tobilehibe 1997:112.

This mediating role places a great responsibility on the shepherds. The condition for the Holy Spirit's work through them is their preparation in prayer and their absolute unity with the Lord.[1451]

On a few occasions I have observed shepherds asking for the laying on of hands together with the sick, always without wearing the white dress.[1452] It seems to be a matter of discussion whether the shepherds should receive "strengthening" publicly or not.[1453] One informant rejects this because of the social implications. People may think that the shepherd, too, is weak like them and needs exorcism. This may cause ordinary Christians to stumble. "Jesus never rebuked his disciples publicly but brought them to lonely places and he never let other people mock them," he says.[1454] Others do not agree in the practice that shepherds cannot ask for the laying on of hands publicly. They maintain that *Mama* Nenilava from the beginning practised both "strengthening" in private and publicly and that the common practice today may lead the shepherds to have a double set of morals, since it conceals that all humans are sinners.[1455] Another informant does not seem to make a big issue of this question and he seems to find a middle course. He maintains that shepherds already receive "strengthening", firstly, in special reunions only for shepherds, secondly, when they attend healing services without having a shepherd function and thus do not wear the white dress[1456] and thirdly, when they remove the dress in the sacristy after the "work and strengthening". Then they may lay hands on each other for

---

[1451] Mal: *mitokana mivavaka aloha*. IS 210. Mal: *firaisana tanteraka amin'ny Tompo*. QS 142.

[1452] See 3.2.3.9. "It is very seldom shepherds and pastors ask for "strengthening"," one of my informants says, "can it be that they do not think that demons can work in them (*tsy azon'ny demonia iasana*)?" IS 320.

[1453] My material is not clear as to this point, mainly because of the lack of uniformity in the shepherds' terminology on exorcism. This confusion will be seen in the following description. Generally, when shepherds attend healing services they are supposed to serve the others.

[1454] IS 323. This concerns both shepherds and pastors alike. IS 321 also agrees in this argumentation.

[1455] IS 201, IS 325.

[1456] According to IS 311 the shepherds cast out the demons from everybody present and not only from those who are seated on the straw mats or on the first benches. Consequently, shepherds just sitting in the benches during exorcism are subject to casting out of demons, too.

mutual "strengthening".[1457] Most of my informants seem to think only of the second part, "strengthening", while some may have the whole exorcism liturgy in mind when they discuss these matters. No shepherd in my material seems to object that when wearing their white dresses they should never ask for "strengthening" together with the sick.[1458]

The handbook refers to sayings of *Mama* Nenilava concerning shepherds asking for "strengthening". She instructed them to be strengthened in the special shepherd reunions. An absolute prohibition consists in that shepherds should never be strengthened while wearing the white dress.[1459]

[1457] IS 311. The casting out of demons is then believed to have been performed during the preceding "working", also including the shepherds who wore the white dresses, according to this informant.

[1458] IS 323. It is common to only have "strengthening" during the special reunions for shepherds but if some of the shepherds ask for "working" this is arranged. IS 321, IS 323. The practice of shepherds' "strengthening" each other is in change, because some shepherds seemed to obtain special places of honour. Now IS 323 proposes that the "strengthening" of co-shepherds should be a task of the elders, with reference to Jas 3:1. While still alive, *Mama* Nenilava was asked to appoint elders with the special task of "strengthening" shepherds but she was unwilling to do so, because she said: "When they are appointed you will not receive them." And she was right, according to my informant, because the appointed people were not the expected ones, they all came from one church and so the appointment was annulled again. IS 201.

[1459] Tobilehibe 1997:72–73. Jesus took his disciples aside when he strengthened and exhorted them in order not to cause the uneducated people (*ny olon-tsotra*) to stumble by seeing the weaknesses of the disciples. The absolute prohibition while wearing the white dress seems to stem from the shepherds' understanding of the dress. See 2.2.2.3 and 4.4.4. To do so would "make Jesus loose face" (*manala baraka an'i Jesosy*) and "remove the clothes in the devil's sight" (*miala tafy imason'ny devoly*). The handbook realises that the shepherds have weaknesses (*fahalemena*) and sins (*fahadisoana*) and therefore should repent. This has to be done in secret, however, before coming to the "work and strengthening" and not in sight of the people. The context of this saying is the shepherds' prayer in the beginning of the "work and strengthening" and Mt 6:6 is referred to. Tobilehibe 1997:90. G. Haus does not mention that the handbook's absolute prohibition for shepherds to ask for "strengthening" in a healing service concerns "strengthening" *while wearing the white dress* (italics mine) and in my opinion this causes her interpretation to be too categorical. Haus 2000:136.

4.5.3 Summary

The shepherds believe that God has power to heal any sickness. "Sickness" may refer to body, mind and spirit in the shepherds' usage and the terminology comprises wider meanings than the corresponding English word. The boundaries between the three parts of the human are vague and not consequent in my material and demonic sickness may express itself through bodily or mental sicknesses and on the other hand, natural sicknesses may lead people into situations where they become oppressed by demons.

Sicknesses may have natural causes but, according to the shepherds, sicknesses may also stem from the devil. In causing sicknesses the devil works both directly and indirectly. While a majority among ordinary shepherds tends to attribute all sicknesses to the devil, the shepherds in my research population do not hold this opinion. Some of them think that this view of sickness stems from insufficient formal education and biblical knowledge. Sicknesses can be understood as serving God's positive purposes, both for the patient and his/her family and some sayings in my material may be interpreted as attributing sicknesses to God's punishment, most probable as a result of human sin.

When the shepherds say that the treatment of sicknesses characteristic of the revival movement is exorcism, some of them seem to think primarily of expelling sickness while others mostly have the prayer part with the laying on of hands in mind. Treatment with Western medicine is recommended by my informants, they consider doctors as one of God's ways of healing and they underline the necessity of a close co-operation between shepherds and medical practitioners. Some shepherds have the ability to distinguish between natural sickness and demonic oppression but since any sickness may be treated with exorcism, it does not seem to be emphasised as decisive by most shepherds. The shepherds' general low level of formal education prevents them from benefiting from training in Western medicine. Some effort is made, however, in this respect, especially for shepherds working in a *toby*.

Healing depends on God alone and many people can testify to healing through the shepherds' treatment. My informants especially emphasise a living faith in Jesus, eagerness in church life, decision to become a shepherd, relief and peace as results of the healing process and these theological signs seem to be decisive in the shepherds' evaluation of healing, whatever the patient's problems may have been.

The shepherds' primary concern is to lead people to conversion and confession of Jesus, which is said to be more important than healing from sickness. Healing is by the shepherds connected with faith in Jesus. In the shepherds' understanding healing has a wide meaning and comprises bodily, mental and spiritual aspects, of which the spiritual seem to be emphasised as the most important. When people are able to "cast out demons from themselves" they do not seem to need the shepherds' exorcism but my informants disagree in whether exorcism is intended for all.

Traditional healers distribute lots of charms and according to the shepherds, these have to be handed over and burnt in order to obtain a lasting healing. When Christians keep charms this may cause an inner conflict but the existence of an inner conflict does not alter the shepherds' perception of the charms' demonic origin.

Healing is understood in a communal perspective. The patient's family are given important roles in the process because shepherds consider the family's willingness to believe in Jesus as facilitating and securing healing. The severely ill normally stay at a *toby* for an extended period and they are continually treated with prayer, preaching, testimonies, casting out of demons, "strengthening", Christian education and daily care. The inclusion of the patients into this Christian *toby* community is important. The patients are not rendered passive in the healing process, however and there is a close interaction between the patient's activity and Jesus as the healer. Sometimes, people do not experience healing of sicknesses and shepherds explain this with lack of endurance, hindrances from the family, or no faith in Jesus. They admit, however, that sometimes they do not understand why some are healed and others not but they constantly underline that it is the reception of Jesus that really matters.

The prayer with the laying on of hands is considered at the heart of the shepherds' service. In practice, everybody who asks for it is prayed for in this part, even the unconscious and impenitent but the shepherds should choose appropriate words according to the people. The shepherds declare forgiveness of sins and give the Holy Spirit, primarily understood as the Spirit's guidance and a willingness to listen to the Spirit's voice. The shepherds pray for strength in life and ability to resist the devil and they believe to be under the Holy Spirit's guidance in their prayer. It is the shepherds' task to bring people to Jesus through this prayer and this shows their roles as mediators between God and the people. To be God's deputies implies a responsibility for the shepherds to live a godly life.

The most important controversy in this chapter is probably the shepherds' understanding of sickness, especially its origin: Do all sicknesses stem from the devil and how are specific sicknesses to be understood? Other differences in understanding are seen in the relation between God and sickness: Does God permit or cause sickness, or even punish with sicknesses?[1460] Controversy is also seen when some shepherds think that sicknesses should be cast out while others maintain that God heals sickness through prayer,[1461] or when some shepherds see it as important to distinguish between natural sicknesses and demonic oppression while others seem to follow a more pragmatic attitude. The shepherds also seem to understand differently whether a living faith in Jesus excludes the need of exorcism[1462] and whether shepherds could submit themselves to "strengthening" publicly. The overall understanding of healing, however, seems to be shared to a great extent by my informants.

The shepherds' seemingly multiple meanings of healing, their understanding of sickness as an assault or lack of something and how they perceive of the casting out of sicknesses seem somewhat obscure to me. This is also the case with the relationship between faith in Jesus and healing from observable sicknesses, the shepherds' underlining that only the converted should receive "strengthening" in relation to the fact that all those who give a sign are prayed for with the laying on of hands. Their terminology of "casting out demons from themselves" is also obscure to me.

4.6 Crucial issues: An attempt at interpreting the understanding

The purpose of this project is to describe exorcism, as it is practised and understood by the shepherds. In order to reach this goal I have deliberately chosen a tool of interpretation: I assert that some sort of synthesis between biblical message and traditional Malagasy culture, as these two elements are handed over to the shepherds, has resulted in the shepherds' practice and understanding of exorcism. My goal is to describe what this synthesis looks like.

[1460] Cf. 4.3.2.3.
[1461] Cf. 4.4.3.
[1462] Cf. 4.3.3.

AN ATTEMPT AT INTERPRETING THE UNDERSTANDING 331

I do so, primarily by describing exorcism as practised and understood by the shepherds as correctly and comprehensively as possible on the basis of my fieldwork material. This is done in chapter 3 and so far in chapter 4. Basically my intention has been to give an emic presentation.

However, given the dual context and the synthesis mentioned a further focus on a few main themes may serve to elucidate the shepherds' understanding. The preceding presentation contains certain underlying assumptions, i.e. worldview elements. If these assumptions are made explicit, it is my assertion that I as a Western researcher may obtain a more valid picture of how the shepherds perceive of their exorcism. The purpose of the following then is to make explicit as far as possible some of these underlying assumptions and thus attempt to interpret the shepherds' understanding. This, too, is meant to serve an emic presentation. I will, however, inevitably move in the direction of an etic perspective in the interpretation since I use a theoretical framework, which is not used by the shepherds.[1463] This is based on my assertion that the biblical message and the traditional Malagasy culture furnish the wider contexts, within which the shepherds' exorcism has its proper place (*Sitz im Leben*). The contexts are both horizons of the shepherds' understanding and tools of my interpretation and the contexts may enlighten the shepherds' practice and understanding of exorcism to a Western audience.[1464] Since my main purpose is to give an emic presentation, I do not want to force the shepherds' own understanding in any direction. This calls for caution in the theoretical interpretation in the following.[1465]

In my search for underlying worldview assumptions of the shepherds' understanding I use three criteria for selection of themes: Firstly, there are controversial issues, which seem to be discussed, either among the

---

[1463] A clear-cut etic perspective would have been to analyse the shepherds' understanding from a totally different viewpoint (e.g. as a Westerner, from modernity) or to compare the Malagasy shepherds' understanding with other cultures' understanding of similar themes. None of these are my purpose and therefore my approach in the following interpretation can be called an intermediate position: more etic than emic but in the service of the emic perspective.

[1464] The presentation of the two contexts in 4.1 has been an attempt to define elements in two worldviews, which P.G. Hiebert calls assumptions on a deep level and these assumptions mould the shepherds' explicit understanding.

[1465] Cf. 1.3.3.2.

shepherds themselves or in the wider context of the FLM. This may indicate changes in worldview assumptions. Secondly, as an "outsider" several elements in the shepherds' understanding seem unclear to me, possibly because I am unfamiliar with the contexts. This is a drawback but in research it can be turned to an advantage: it forces me to investigate the issues more thoroughly and may enable me to discover elements in the shepherds' understanding, which seem to presume certain assumptions.[1466] Thirdly, themes and issues of special importance to the shepherds may not be discovered at first sight but, after having investigated a larger bulk of material, some main lines seem to emerge, which may contain worldview assumptions of considerable weight.

When I browse through my presentation of the shepherds' understanding using the above criteria there seems to be certain recurring themes in my material. I call them crucial issues. I suppose that controversy indicates some sort of crux. Other themes are crux to me, i.e. they seem somewhat obscure to me as an outsider and thirdly, according to my estimation, recurrance may indicate that themes and issues are crucial, i.e. of special importance to the shepherds. Further, I emphasise that only some of the themes emerging from this way of selection may point to the shepherds' underlying assumptions and I will only include a few main themes in my attempt of an interpretation due to limitations of space. The themes included should be considered as selected examples.

My interpretation is organised around themes and sub-themes. There is no pattern in the way I organise the crucial issues to the two wider contexts. Sometimes their relation to traditional Malagasy culture comes first, elsewhere the relation to biblical message, depending on what seems most natural. I refer to other researchers' works only when they contribute to the understanding of exorcism in relation to one of my chosen contexts, but, due to limitation of space discussion with other

---

[1466] I admit that this criterion rests on my subjective interpretation of meaning and depends on me as a researcher. Other researchers probably would have thought of other elements as "somewhat obscure" in the shepherds' understanding. My background, my presuppositions and my interaction with my informants guide me in using this criterion. Hummelvoll and Barbosa da Silva 1998:465. It is generally acknowledged in the hermeneutic approach that the foreknowledge of the researcher is a plus to research, when it is made explicit. Cf. 1.3.3.1 . The purpose of using my foreknowledge here is to select important themes for analysis, in order to serve the emic perspective and not to interpret the shepherds' understanding from my point of view.

researchers is reduced to a minimum. My attempts at interpretation should always be considered as tentative and I have obtained my goal with this part only if it enlightens the shepherds' own understanding.

In the following I attempt to give a theoretical interpretation of three main issues, which are found explicit or implicit in different parts of the presentation of the shepherds' exorcism: Firstly, the shepherds' identification of all spirits connected to traditional religion as demonic. Secondly, the shepherds' comprehensive use of exorcism and thirdly, the shepherds' conception of healing primarily as faith in Jesus.

4.6.1 All spirits in traditional worship are demonic

The shepherds regard all spirits connected to traditional practices as demonic. This feature underlies the shepherds' overall conception of spirits and is thus of special importance to them. At first sight, this seems to cause no controversy among the shepherds and they do not mention it frequently. Neither are the shepherds occupied with stating any reasons for this view, probably because they take it for granted. When investigated more thoroughly, however, what I call the shepherds' "either-or"-perspective is seen behind many of the shepherds' points of view, which also causes controversy among informants in my material. My assertion is that the "either-or"-perspective points to fundamental underlying assumptions for the shepherds.

The traditional Malagasy cultural understanding sees spirits as ambiguous depending on the humans' fulfilling of their obligations towards them. The spirits are neither entirely good nor only bad.[1467] This ambiguous role is also attributed to traditional healers. As mediators to the spirit world, they are seen as benefactors in the society because they protect and heal but they may also use charms in order to harm an enemy and as such function as sorcerers.

[1467] Ancestor spirits may distribute both benefit and punishment to the living. The gods/spirits that are dwelling in charms and amulets may heal and protect but when one of the taboos connected to a certain charm is broken, this may cause illness or misfortune. Nature spirits are believed to be able to heal but they are unpredictable and may revenge any offence. *Tromba* spirits are considered good but evil spirits may also possess humans against their own will, which is considered bad. See 4.1.1.1 (Ancestors. Idols and charms/amulets. Spirits of nature) and 4.1.1.2 (Possession).

Against this background it is surprising that the shepherds identify every spirit active in traditional worship as evil. Also the spirits of the dead, a decisive feature in the Malagasy spirit world, are redefined and incorporated into this hierarchy of the demonic, as are the traditional healers since they have a close contact with the invisible world. This is a consistent break with traditional understanding.[1468] G. Althabe also confirms this main point in the shepherds' understanding and says that the revival movement condemns violently most of the elements in the village-universe: the ancestors, the methods of divination, the ceremonies and the charms. He says that all these elements are placed confusingly in one single category and they are all seen as manifestations of the same demon.[1469]

The identification of all spirits connected to traditional religion as demonic may be explained on the basis of the influence from the missionary preaching, which labelled all traditional worship as Satanic and opposed to the true God. The missionaries' claims were possibly based on their understanding of the Bible and according to some critics, on their lack of understanding of traditional religion.[1470] Since the shepherds for more than 100 years have upheld this evaluation of spirits in traditional worship, however, there must be reasons for them to reject the traditional ambiguity.

G. Althabe, in his critique of the revival movement, furnishes another explanation of why the shepherds see all spirits in traditional worship as demonic. He postulates a double godhead in the shepherds'

[1468] All the informants in my material seem to share this basic evaluation but, as will be shown below, some of them nuance the "either-or"-perspective. Non-shepherds in my material also seem to confirm this picture. They believe that all spirits contacted by traditional healers are demons, but the non-Christians are not aware of this. IN 313, QN 108. In a handbook, published by the Reformed church and edited for the teaching of novices to become shepherds, the Malagasy names (in addition to names from the Bible) of the devils are listed as *tromba, bilo, ramanenjana, lolo, angatra, matoatoa, manankasina, manongay, vintana, fanahy, zavatra, ambalavelona, amalamaty, fanahin-drazana, fanahin-jazavavindrano, sy ny sisa*. It seems as if this list tries to be inclusive in saying that all the spirits in the traditional Malagasy worship are demonic. FJKM 1997:7. All Christians do not share this view, however and I have shown that especially Roman Catholics often take part in traditional cults. See 4.1.1.2 (Possession).

[1469] Althabe sees this condemnation as a continuation of the view already present in both Catholic and Protestant churches in Madagascar. Althabe 1984:203. L.A. Sharp also says that the shepherds re-label all spirits as demons. Sharp 1993:270.

[1470] Cf. e.g. Rakotomalala, Blanchy and Raison-Jourde 2001:410.

thinking and understands the positive part of God, closely connected to Europeans, to be characterised by white e.g. seen in the shepherds' white dresses. There is a tendency to see the negative part of the godhead, i.e. the demon as Malagasy, according to his opinion. It is characterised by dark skin and it seems to manifest itself in the ancestral practices.[1471] His postulated dualism in the divine (God and demon) is confirmed nowhere in my material. To the contrary, the shepherds never seem to understand God and demons to be part of the same divinity. Demons are created by God but have become his adversaries through their rebellion.

What elements in the biblical message, which have influenced the shepherds, may count for their strict condemnation of all spirits connected to traditional worship?

The point of departure in the biblical message is that God is unique as creator and every power is subordinate to him.[1472] A part of creation has rebelled against God, however and in the NT a kingdom of Satan emerges.[1473] Thus the invisible world consists of good and evil beings and there is no ambiguity: those stemming from God are good, while spirits and beings under the rule of Satan are evil. The purpose of Satan is to counteract the Gospel and cause human's destruction and alienation from God and in the NT there is an absolute antithesis between God and Satan, as rulers of two opposite kingdoms.[1474]

The biblical teaching of the uniqueness of God, the rebellion of part of the creation and the consequent division between good and evil beings according to their origin may be seen behind the shepherds' labelling of all spirits operating in traditional religion and in the practices of the traditional healers as demonic. By redefining as they do the shepherds have broken definitively with the ambiguity of spirits in traditional Malagasy culture.

One shepherd seems to be torn between two worldviews when he wonders how a traditional healer who is believed to be guided by evil spirits, can heal people, an act which has to be interpreted as good. In this shepherd's understanding of a biblical worldview the spirits operating in the traditional healers' practices have another source other than God and so these healers are evil. It cannot be denied, however, that the traditional healer makes an end to human suffering and consequently,

---

[1471] Althabe 1984:200.
[1472] See 4.1.2.1.
[1473] See 4.1.2.2 and 4.1.2.3 (Satan and his kingdom).
[1474] See 4.1.2.3 (God and his kingdom).

the spirits by which he operates are beneficial to humans. In the traditional Malagasy thinking such spirits would be considered as good since it produces positive consequences to humans.[1475]

The shepherds' evaluation of herbal medicine reveals controversy among them. As shown, one of my informants is an expert in herbal medicine and when people consult him, he sometimes uses this in his treatment. His evaluation of this medicine is positive because he sees its source as God's own creation and as such, good. Some of my informants agree with him in principle. This informant using herbal medicine has experienced how fellow-shepherds have tried to rescue him from this practice, however. These shepherds condemn all such medicine as evil and stemming from demons, whenever it is used.[1476]

4.6.1.1 The consistent "either-or"-principle

The shepherds who condemn herbal medicine altogether seem to pursue the "either-or"-principle consistently, without giving room for any nuances. The consistent "either-or"-principle surfaces rather frequently in the shepherds' understanding. In many cases the shepherds seem to infer directly that whatever does not stem from God has to stem from the devil. Bad and undesirable attitudes harm people, they do not stem from a living faith and so they are said to come from evil spirits. Many informants in my material believe that most shepherds think that all sicknesses stem from the devil. Sickness is considered evil and consequently, it cannot stem from God. Since there seems to be no third

---

[1475] When many Christians consult traditional healers in times of crises, they may use this line of argument: Since the traditional healer benefits them, good spirits have to dwell in him/her. This way of thinking is firmly opposed by the shepherds. K. Ferdinando sees the antropocentricity of traditional African religion as opposed to the theocentricity of the Bible. Ferdinando 1999: 382–383, 388. Traditional Malagasy thinking may also be characterised as anthropocentric in outlook: since God is relatively remote the spirits' moral character is determined in terms of their influence on humans, anthropocentric criteria are more important than determining the sources of power in distinguishing traditional healers from sorcerers and possessing spirits may be turned to the advantage of the possessed and the society and therefore possession can be actively pursued.

[1476] See 4.5.1.3 (Western medicine), footnote 1254. Some of the reason for this may be found in the close connection between this kind of medicine and traditional healers. When used by traditional healers the herbal medicine is consecrated and forms part of the spiritual realm, the healers seem to mix worship of spirits and herbal medicine and the patients are no longer able to separate one from the other.

possibility, it has to stem from the devil.[1477] Shepherds also tend to see spirits at work in a variety of situations, e.g. behind temptations, people's bad behaviour and many undesirable conditions/attitudes and they stand in absolute opposition to and condemn everything where they suspect evil spirits to be at work.[1478]

How is it possible to interpret the consistent use of the "either-or"-perspective in light of the two contexts?

One way of explaination is that the shepherds are mainly influenced by the biblical message but that some of them are forcing the message on this point. When they read biblical passages like Mt 10:30 ("He who is not with me is against me ...") and Jn 8:44 ("... the devil ... is a liar and the father of lies.") they seem to interpret them in terms of either God or devil. There seems to be little room for the human and they attribute sins like e.g. lying directly to the devil's work.[1479]

Another possible solution is to see the consistent "either-or"-perspective mainly as some sort of combination of a biblical and a traditional worldview. Powers and forces surround the humans and are seen as active in a variety of ways and humans are in the centre of the battlefield between forces and spirits. If this anthropocentric understanding of reality is combined with the biblical emphasis on the division in good and evil forces according to their origin, the shepherds may draw the conclusion that humans are controlled either by the one or the other.[1480]

The shepherds' inclination to see spirits behind undesirable conditions/attitudes, as well as a spiritual cause of sickness and misfortune is comprehensible in light of the traditional culture's preoccupation with spirits. When shepherds cast out both evil spirits and undesirable attitudes/sins, it follows that it is difficult to distinguish between sins and spirits. As a consequence of this thinking an externalisation of evil seems to take place, a common element in the

---

[1477] See 4.5.1.2 (The devil). In other parts of my fieldwork material alcohol, cigarettes and snuff are said to have so many negative aspects that they cannot possibly stem from God but have to come from the devil. The traditional healers' trickery in treating people is also said to stem from evil spirits since it does not come from God. See 2.2.3 and 2.2.6.

[1478] See 4.3.1.1, 4.3.1.2, 4.3.1.3 and 4.4.3. This spirit-perspective seems by some shepherds to be considered a major way of explaining evil but the spiritual activity does not seem to excuse from human responsibility when people yield to sin.

[1479] See 4.4.3.3.

[1480] See 4.1.1.

traditional understanding. In traditional Malagasy culture sin is considered in terms of its damaging consequences for humans and society and has to be removed to restore the harmony. If sin is understood in this way, the shepherds who are also influenced by a biblical worldview may infer that, as evil in terms of damaging consequences cannot stem from God, it has inevitably to stem from the devil.[1481]

The biblical influence may be seen in the division between good and evil according to their respective sources of power. It is possible, however, that the shepherds define the content of good and evil according to the traditional perspective of the ambiguity of spirits. This means that what is good and evil is judged by the consequences for human beings and not according to the sources of power. Then the focus of evil is everything that hurts humans and society, which may comprise a variety of conditions: sickness, misfortune, all sorts of problems, sin etc. It is then possible to conclude that all these things stem from the devil and occur as a result of demonic activity.

Not all my informants see the "either-or"-perspective as absolute, however. Those who do not, believe that sicknesses may also have natural causes without any connection to evil spirits and even if they admit that sin always is opposing God's will, they do not see any specific demons behind sin. Some of them see several of the undesired conditions and human problems (e.g. doubt) as part of being human in this world but they admit that there is always a possibility that the devil may exploit these human weaknesses in some way or another. A consequent "either-or"-perspective is by some of my informants, who themselves have to be considered as leaders in the movement, attributed to the insufficiency of formal and biblical education among many shepherds.[1482]

[1481] See 4.1.1.3 (The causes of sickness) and 4.4.3.

[1482] See 4.5.1.2 (The devil) and 4.4.3.3. The insufficient education is especially underlined in relation to most shepherds' opinion that any sickness stems from demons. Health education of shepherds is also difficult due to low formal education. It is especially non-shepherds that see dangers in some shepherds' equation of sin with demons because, when shepherds cast out sin, people may either think that they have no more sins or they may think that they are not responsible for this sin themselves.

4.6.2 The shepherds' comprehensive use of exorcism[1483]

The comprehensive use of exorcism is a salient feature in the shepherds' ministry. The shepherds consider exorcism appropriate for people with a wide variety of problems: for people showing manifestations during a healing service as well as for the great majority present without any manifestations. People with undesirable conditions/attitudes are treated with exorcism, people with bad conduct and people who have yielded to temptations. Exorcism is the shepherds' treatment of bodily, mental and spiritual sickness. Christians may be treated with exorcism, even pastors and shepherds. Exorcism may serve as a prophylactic treatment, in case evil spirits have entered the person and as such it functions as a means of diagnosis. Exorcism is even incorporated as part of the Sunday morning liturgy in some churches. This comprehensive use of exorcism, displayed in different parts of my description above, indicates its importance to the shepherds.

There is controversy among my informants, however, as to the limits of comprehensiveness: who are to be treated with exorcism and what is to be expelled? Some believe that only people diagnosed to be demoniacs through their reactions to Jesus' name are to be treated in this way and casting out of human conditions/attitudes, temptations and sins are opposed by some of my informants. They believe that it is only the demons coming from outside, exploiting human problems that are to be cast out. Some think that sicknesses are healed through prayer or the shepherds' special gift of grace and not through the shepherds' casting out of sicknesses. The purpose of exorcism of Christians is not to have demons expelled but to receive strength, according to some of my informants.[1484]

Several elements in the shepherds' comprehensive use of exorcism seem obscure to me as an outsider. What is it, e.g., that the shepherds consider necessary to expel? What about the different kinds of people,

---

[1483] It has to be remembered that the shepherds' exorcism consists in casting out of demons (*asa* = "work") and prayer with the laying on of hands (*fampaherezana* = "strengthening") and the word exorcism in my presentation is used with this meaning. Cf. 1.1.

[1484] There is another difference referred to in my material: Some shepherds mostly underline observable aspects of exorcism, an opinion primarily attributed to shepherds with low formal education, while others mostly emphasise conversion, faith and salvation. The second opinion prevails among my informants and they underline this aspect. Cf. the presentation in 4.6.3.

especially Christians, who are in need of exorcism, according to the shepherds?

In my attempt to interpret the shepherds' comprehensive use and understanding of exorcism, I will arrange different aspects of the theme under several subheadings. This is done to facilitate the reading but all the headings concern the introduced theme of comprehensiveness.[1485]

[1485] I do not exclude other perspectives than traditional Malagasy culture and biblical message to be important in interpreting the shepherds' comprehensive use of exorcism.

One such perspective may be the degree of general education. Augmented education brings much external influence, which may cause a feeling of inner conflict and may result in a changed worldview. A wider perspective is possible and an ability to see more nuances. Ideally, an increase in the level of education causes more reflection and a wider spectrum of meanings. I have not, however, investigated the degree of education systematically in my project and this is a conscious delimitation.

A pragmatic view is seen when some of my informants say that, since most shepherds do not have the gift of discerning spirits, they cast out demons from everyone present. IS 217, IS 321.

The shepherds seem to have different opinions as to the exact content of exorcism, especially the first part. At least, there are nuances in how shepherds emphasise the different aspects. It may mean casting out of demons, diagnosis, removal of hindrances for conversion, preparing of the strengthening, etc. If the shepherds understand what is going on in exorcism in different ways, it follows that they consider it appropriate in a variety of situations.

A more practical perspective is that the normal setting of exorcism is a healing service, open to anyone who wishes to be present. People's "self-diagnosis" is an important factor explaining why they come to a healing service, why they move to the mat/first benches during exorcism and why they ask for "strengthening". The shepherds allow them to come, they cast out demons and pray for all who feel in need of this. This means that the practical organisation of exorcism to a certain degree prevents the shepherds from controlling who should be treated with exorcism.

People's "self-diagnosis" highlights exorcism as seen from the patients' perspective. People may come to the shepherds' exorcism in order to have assurance of their salvation. Whatever problem may occur, they consult the shepherds who are able to purify them, expel all strange influence, reinstate them into a proper relationship to God and give assurance of their salvation. The widespread tendency in traditional Malagasy thinking to see a spiritual cause for all sorts of problems may contribute to such thinking. The main strategy in traditional practices when confronted with spirits is to be in harmony, to obey, to caress and to appease the spirits. It is possible that people come to the shepherds' exorcism with this in mind but with a "Christian" objective: to be in harmony with the Holy Spirit.

4.6.2.1 Frequency

Frequency is one aspect of the shepherds' comprehensive use of exorcism. How is it possible to enlighten this feature?

Casting out of evil, malicious spirits is practised in the traditional Malagasy religion. It seems, however, that expulsion of evil spirits is no salient feature in traditional Malagasy culture, especially in Imerina. This is contrary to G. Haus' assertion when she says that spirit-expulsion is as accepted and normal in the shepherds' practice as in the ancestor belief.[1486] The relation to spirits is rather characterised by a harmonious co-existence, where the spirits are honoured and made content with sacrifices. Casting out of spirits may be dangerous because of the spirits' power and the possibility of revenge is always threatening.[1487]

According to the presented biblical message the synoptic Gospels portray Jesus repeatedly as casting out demons and this element in Jesus' ministry belongs to the essential theology of the kingdom of God. This kind of mighty act is a decisive feature in the synoptic Gospels but sparingly found elsewhere in the NT.[1488]

Neither traditional Malagasy practices nor biblical message seem at first sight able to count for the frequency of exorcism in the shepherds'

They may understand exorcism as a means to obtain a proper relationship with God's Spirit since all other spirits are cast out and people are granted forgiveness and the Holy Spirit through the shepherds' liturgy. If the above understanding prevails among people seeking exorcism, then the shepherds are given an indispensable position in securing people's salvation. As people consulted traditional healers earlier they now come to the shepherds. G. Haus saw a tension between shepherds and ordinary Christians as one of the main themes in her thesis: Ordinary Christians are helpless with regard to the devil's power, they can never hope to be autonomous and will always need shepherds to cast out the evil and give them new strength. Haus 2000:153. People's understanding of exorcism is an important perspective but it is not systematically investigated in my project. My research population, mostly shepherd leaders, does not allow me to draw conclusions as to how the patients understand this practice.

[1486] Haus 2000:115. The relative infrequency of spirit-expulsion in traditional practices is indicated by the references to the index-words "exorcier, exorcisme" in Rakotomalala, Blanchy and Raison-Jourde 2001, which point to exorcism in Christian practices (*Fifohazana*/Pentecostal churches) in 6 of 11 cases. The infrequency of exorcism in traditional religion is supported by Estrade 1985:100 and Sharp 1993:243.

[1487] Cf. 4.1.1.3 (The healing process).

[1488] See 4.1.2.3 (Satan and his kingdom) and 4.1.2.3 (God and his kingdom).

ministry, even though Jesus' casting out of demons according to the synoptic Gospels certainly furnish an important background.

The traditional Malagasy inclination to consult religious experts in a wide variety of situations, however, should not be underestimated as a possible background. The traditional healers may handle all sorts of problems and they are both healers and consultants. If the shepherds understand themselves in correspondence with, but in sharp opposition to, traditional healers—and I suppose they do so to a certain extent[1489]—this element is a possible background of the frequency of exorcism in the shepherds' practice. In fact, people may intend to bring their problems to God but in accordance with traditional thinking, they have to do so through mediators, i.e. the shepherds.[1490]

The biblical teaching of God as creator may have been linked with the idea of the frequent consultation of religious experts in traditional culture. As shown, God's saving activity is included in the message of creation and Christians in the Bible are repeatedly exhorted to bring anything to God in prayer.[1491] This may, in practice, have contributed to the frequency of exorcism.

4.6.2.2 The structure of exorcism

The way exorcism is performed by the shepherds shows another aspect of its comprehensiveness. A decisive feature here is its division into two parts. While some of my informants see it as a possibility only to pray for people in some situations, without a preceding expulsion of demons, the common opinion is that each part of exorcism has a function in its own right and should never be separated.[1492] One informant refers to

---

[1489] Cf. the shepherds' roles as reconciliators, mediators, they assist people, etc. See 4.2.1.4 and 4.5.2.5 (A unique position of the shepherds?).

[1490] When people consult traditional healers they really seek assistance from invisible powers, with which the traditional healers have contact. This causes people to consult different healers to obtain their goals if they are not content with the contact with the invisible, obtained through the first healer. The focus of interest is not the healer but the spiritual reality behind. IN 324. See 4.1.1.3 (The causes of sickness). and 4.1.1.3 (The healing process).

[1491] Cf. 4.1.2.1.

[1492] When shepherds refer to the exorcism liturgy some call it casting out of demons (*famoahana demonia*) while others say "strengthening" (*fampaherezana*) to denote exorcism as a whole. This possibly indicates a somewhat different emphasis among them but it may also be understood merely as ways of expression.

exorcism with Martin Luther's famous distinction of law and Gospel: casting out of demons is law, while "strengthening" is Gospel. The two should not be separated and both are needed to lead people to conversion.[1493]

Sometimes my informants have hinted that, even if they consider that a particular person is primarily in need of "strengthening", exorcism is an institution and all the attendants take part in the whole liturgy, whatever their specific needs. This structure of exorcism as a fixed liturgy may contribute to its comprehensive use.[1494]

G. Haus asserts that, according to traditional thinking, rituals have to be performed accurately not to loose their power. She believes that this may be the reason why shepherds underline the necessity of both casting out of demons and "strengthening". If the liturgy is not performed in this way, it will not have the intended effect.[1495] This may be a possible background but it should be noticed that all the elements in the exorcism liturgy are found in the biblical message: casting out of demons, conversion, intercession, laying on of hands, forgiveness of sins and the Holy Spirit. The way these elements are combined into a liturgy, however, seems to be on the account of the shepherds.

The first part of exorcism seems to be modelled after Jesus' practice of casting out demons: Jesus commanded the spirits to leave only by using his authoritative word. This is seen as an ideal by the shepherds and although some of them may be too eager and sometimes touch the patients/overstate their movements, this is seen as aberrations.[1496] This first part is clearly different from spirit-expulsion in traditional practices, where a whole array of different items are used and where the casting out itself is as polite and insignificant as possible.[1497]

[1493] IS 322.

[1494] See 4.2.1.4. I have not encountered anybody in my material, shepherds or non-shepherds, who have denied that everybody needs to be prayed for (the second part). When J.-M. Estrade characterises exorcism by saying that mothers bring their babies to exorcism "pour les faire délivrer du démon", this does not seem to grasp the shepherds' full meaning with exorcism. Estrade 1985:322. It may be that the babies need to be strengthened, according to the shepherds, but because of exorcism as an institution, they take part in the whole liturgy.

[1495] Haus 2000:32, 76, 147.

[1496] See 4.4.2.

[1497] See 4.1.1.3 (The healing process). The shepherds themselves emphasise dissimilarity with traditional practices in performing exorcism, while they make efforts to show similarities with Jesus' practice.

The second part seems to go beyond the exorcism accounts in the synoptic Gospels. It may, however, be ascribed to the NT's view of exorcism in a wider framework.[1498] Mt 12:43–45 seems to underline that casting out of evil spirits is not enough; the "house" must be filled with the positive forces of the kingdom of God. Shepherds in my material underline that the casting out of demons is insufficient to obtain a lasting healing and they sometimes refer directly to Mt 12. Do the shepherds understand the second part of exorcism as "filling" the person with the positive forces of God, through the laying on of hands, prayer, forgiveness and Holy Spirit?[1499]

Another possibility for regarding the biblical message as background for the twofold structure of exorcism is the two kinds of mighty acts in the Gospels: exorcism and healing, combined in the shepherds' liturgy of exorcism.[1500] The shepherds use the same word to characterise both a person "assaulted by demons" and one suffering from some sort of observable sickness. They are both considered as "sick" (*marary*) and they are both treated with exorcism. Healing of observable sickness is further believed to happen through exorcism and one of the main biblical readings instituting exorcism is Mk 16:15–20, where both casting out of demons and prayer for the sick with the laying on of hands is spoken of.[1501]

[1498] See 4.1.2.4 (Human individuals).

[1499] When shepherds in my material emphasise that casting out of spirits is insufficient, they do not directly make this connection. Normally they talk about repeated exorcism, together with a profound Christian teaching, which leads the patient to a living faith in Jesus. Only when the person stays with Jesus, the shepherds consider the healing complete. See 4.2.1.4.

[1500] The distinction between the two kinds is not evident in the Gospels, especially if the point of departure is the terminology describing spirit-possession. If we take the phenomenon of exorcism as the point of departure, however and only talk of possession in cases where exorcism actually takes place, two rather distinct kinds of mighty acts appear. See 4.1.2.4 (Human individuals). In my conversation with shepherds I have sometimes challenged them on the distinction between exorcism and healing in the NT but usually they have not seemed to take my point. When I have said that Jesus never imposed his hands on the possessed but only expelled the demons with his authoritative word, shepherds have answered me that "exorcism is words" or "but Jesus imposed his hands on the sick". IS 323, IS 200.

[1501] It should be noticed, however, that the shepherds' exorcism comprises of even more than Jesus' exorcisms and healings, taken together. The prayer and the promise of forgiveness of sins and Holy Spirit cannot be explained in this way.

Still another way of explaining the background for the division of exorcism in two parts may be the structure of rituals in traditional religion. The ceremonies firstly, purify from guilt and punishment and secondly, restore what has been broken and reinstate the individual into a harmless relationship with the powers.[1502] In an analogy with rituals in traditional thinking, then, the first part of exorcism purifies from demons while the second part reinstates the person into a harmonious relationship with God.

The structure of exorcism with two inseparable parts results in the same treatment for both people primarily in need of the first part and people primarily in need of the second part. This may contribute to its comprehensive use.

4.6.2.3 *The wide range of people treated with exorcism*

The actual practice with an initial expulsion directed to all demons within hearing seems to imply that casting out of demons is directed to all the audience. Some of the shepherds in my material seem to oppose this. They maintain that casting out of demons should be performed only on those diagnosed as "assaulted by demons".[1503]

The biblical accounts show that when Jesus cast out demons, it was directed to the afflicted people only. There is no trace in the Gospels that Jesus cast out demons from people surrounding the afflicted and this difference between Jesus' and the shepherds' practice may be the reason for some of my informants' opinion.[1504]

Also when traditional healers expel evil spirits, this is only directed to the spirits causing problems and does not include those who bring the sick. The traditional healer may be aware of that some members of the family present have spirits dwelling in them but as these are considered good spirits, they are not to be cast out. There is another element in traditional thinking, which may have contributed to the shepherds' extended treatment, however, i.e. the community thinking. Sickness does not only concern an individual but the whole community and as the community may have contributed to the sickness, they also have

---

[1502] See 4.1.1.2 (Possession) and 4.1.1.3 (The healing process). G. Haus says that the main aspect of rituals is to purify from impurity and guilt and restore broken relations to God and the community. Haus 2000:29.

[1503] See 4.3.1.2 (Lack of manifestations) and 4.4.1.

[1504] Cf. 4.1.2.3 (Satan and his kingdom).

important roles in the healing process. The shepherds' treatment is exorcism and as they consider the family of the sick important in obtaining a lasting healing, they include the family in exorcism.[1505]

The shepherds' exorcism comprises of people with all kinds of problems ranging from temptations to severe convulsions. This seems to be in accordance with their terminology when describing people in need of exorcism, which is varied and seems to imply degrees of demonic affliction. Even people who are not labelled as "assaulted by demons", e.g. some who are bodily sick are treated with exorcism by the shepherds.[1506]

From the presentation of the biblical message it seems as Jesus' demon-expulsions were only performed on people who were seriously afflicted, possibly a similar group to those shepherds label as demoniacs. According to the biblical message, however, possession is only one of Satan's strategies. He uses a whole array of possible means, including temptation, deceit, lies, disguise, etc. to obtain his goal, which is to keep people away from the blessings of God. Have the shepherds included people with all these conditions in their treatment and whenever they suspect some sort of satanic activity they treat this with exorcism? By treating such a wide range of people with exorcism, they seem to have extended the biblical teaching on these matters. According to my preceding presentation, the biblical writers do not indicate that exorcism is an appropriate treatment to deal with all these satanic strategies. When attacked with Satan's widespread strategies, Christians are rather exhorted to oppose evil with the "whole armour of God", i.e. with divinely imparted strength.[1507] It is possible, however, that this is exactly what the shepherds intend to do, especially through the second part of exorcism: the "strengthening".

In the perspective of traditional thinking everything considered evil to the human should be addressed and removed. Some of the patients' problems may be seen as evil from a purely human viewpoint and thus should be removed. The shepherds' perspective, however, is rather what is considered evil in God's sight. If then people's temptations, sin, moral disorder, sicknesses etc. prevent people from having a living faith in God, these things are considered evil from God's viewpoint and consequently, they should be removed. If the shepherds follow this kind

---

[1505] See 4.1.1.3 (The healing process).
[1506] See 4.3.1.3 (Expulsion of demons) and 4.5.1.3 (Expulsion of sickness).
[1507] See 4.1.2.4 (Human individuals).

of logic, they may see exorcism as appropriate for people with a wide range of problems.

The extension of exorcism to include all people present at a healing service and the fact that the shepherds' exorcism comprises of a large group of people with diverse problems may be a consequence of the opinion that everybody has demons. My informants attribute this opinion to many ordinary, uneducated shepherds but usually my informants distinguish themselves from this thinking.[1508] My informants say rather that the devil/demons are able to influence all people in some way or another and that demonic activity effects everybody. According to traditional Malagasy culture the humans are surrounded by all kinds of forces, which relate to humans in a multitude of ways. This relationship is so complicated that people are not capable of knowing how and when spirits interact with them. Is it possible that the shepherds have extended this element in the traditional thinking, combined with the biblical teaching of the multitude of demonic strategies to lead people astray? These lines of thought may have resulted in their comprehensive practice of exorcism.[1509]

4.6.2.4 A variety of evils are expelled

There is controversy among my informants on what is to be expelled. Some maintain that it is only the evil spirits behind undesirable conditions or Satan exploiting human problems that should be cast out. Others extend the expulsion to human conditions and sicknesses, according to the way they understand Jesus' practice. The reluctance on the part of some of my informants may stem from the way they understand the discrepancy between what they find in the Bible and the

---

[1508] Shepherds from the coastal areas seem to think that a devil dwells in every human, a thinking G. Haus sees as stemming from *tromba* possession. In this cult it is said that "every human has a *tromba*", i.e. one or more good spirits dwell in all people. Haus 2000:81, 26.

[1509] One informant believes that all evil ultimately stems from the devil but he maintains that this is quite different from saying that demons are at work in everybody. Consequently, he does not consider exorcism to be appropriate for all. His reaction may be a consequence of his understanding of the biblical message, i.e. the Bible's silence about exorcism as a relevant treatment for people in such conditions. See 4.3.1.2 (Lack of manifestations).

shepherds' actual practice and they strive to preserve only what they consider to be supported in the biblical message.[1510]

I have shown that shepherds name and cast out all kinds of demons, sicknesses, undesirable conditions/attitudes, the spirits behind these conditions/attitudes, temptations, sins, etc. The comprehensiveness of this list seems to go beyond spirit-expulsion both in traditional practices and in the biblical message. As presented, in traditional religion mainly evil spirits are expelled, either because they cause suffering for the person or because they prevent good spirits to enter the person and in the biblical accounts only demons—and possibly sickness—is cast out.[1511]

The expulsion of evil spirits preventing good spirits to enter may have obtained a Christian interpretation in the shepherds' thinking: Evil spirits prevent the work of the Holy Spirit and this may be some of the background of the shepherds' eagerness in casting out demons.[1512] If this view is extended not only to concern spirits but also to everything the evil spirits can use/exploit, it is understandable that many things can be cast out. Then exorcism seems to be appropriate whenever the shepherds suspect some sort of demonic affliction, i.e. where demons are at work.[1513] Traditional thinking suspects a spiritual cause behind many kinds of sicknesses, misfortunes or problems in life and if this thinking is taken over by some of the shepherds, their understanding of exorcism has to be comprehensive to remedy this situation. One way my informants characterise a person who is no longer dependent on exorcism because he/she has a living faith, is that he/she is "able to cast out demons from himself/herself". This may only be an expression but it may also indicate the widespread understanding of spiritual causes in traditional thinking. If this is so, then problematic feelings, temptations, attraction to sin etc. may be interpreted as evil spirits trying to seduce the person and consequently, they should be cast out.[1514]

[1510] See 4.4.3.1 and 4.3.3.3.

[1511] See 4.4.3, 4.5.1.3 (Expulsion of sickness), 4.1.1.2 (Possession) and 4.1.2.4 (Human individuals). Expulsion of sickness depends on the way Jesus' healing of Peter's mother-in-law is interpreted but also on how to understand the connection between possession and sickness in Jesus' exorcisms.

[1512] This view is related to 4.6.1.

[1513] According to some shepherds' estimation exorcism may also be an appropriate treatment in cases where they do not consider spirits to be at work, e.g. in some sicknesses they think have natural causes.

[1514] See 4.5.2.2 (The relationship between faith in Jesus and healing). One of the main aspects G. Haus has found in her material is that the shepherds almost equal "devil"

4.6.2.5 *Exorcism understood as a fight between God and the devil*

When I have browsed my description of the shepherds' understanding, one line of special importance to the shepherds seems to emerge throughout the material: exorcism is seen as a fight between God and the devil. This constitutes a significant aspect in the shepherds' comprehensive use of exorcism. I assert that the shepherds understand their liturgy of exorcism as a counterpart to the fight between God and Satan on a cosmic level.[1515] This implies that the shepherds do not simply copy the way Jesus cast out demons according to the exorcism accounts in the synoptic Gospels. They rather seem to have modelled their comprehensive liturgy of exorcism according to the sustaining theology of Jesus' exorcisms. The theological framework of Jesus' exorcisms is an ongoing fight between the kingdom of God and the kingdom of Satan. The battle is not about power because God is in absolute power and through Jesus' death on the cross the final judgement of all evil forces is certain. The battle is about human allegiance. Created by God and as such good, the humans yielded to sin and in their rebellion became active co-conspirators with evil powers. The purpose of Jesus' mission was to summon all people to repentance and belief in him, while the main purpose of Satan's kingdom is to destroy this redemptive purpose of God. Within this framework, Jesus' exorcisms were no isolated incidents of liberation. Through these acts Jesus confronted the kingdom of Satan directly and the presence and power of God were demonstrated.[1516]

In the shepherds' thinking expulsion of demons is not enough. Exorcism is not only liberation from the power of Satan but it represents above all, connection to the kingdom of God. The shepherds interpret their work in accordance with the prophetic mission in Jer 1:10: "... to destroy and to overthrow, to build and to plant." The first part of exorcism (*asa*) tears down the kingdom of Satan, while the second part (*fampaherezana*) establishes the kingdom of God. The goal of exorcism is conversion, forgiveness of sins and reception/confirmation of the Holy Spirit, elements, which really connect people to the kingdom of God.[1517]

---

and "everything evil" and she believes that this opinion has caused an expulsion of everything evil, regardless of a traceable demonic presence or not. Haus 2000:136.

[1515] G. Haus also seems to see the centre of exorcism in the battle about human beings between God and the devil. Haus 2000:129, 153.

[1516] See 4.1.2.3–4.1.2.5.

[1517] See 4.5.2.5.

The shepherds understand themselves to be called by God, consecrated to this ministry and thus enabled by God for this fight. The shepherds are fighting on God's behalf, as his representatives and the fight that is going on in the shepherds' exorcism seems to be regarded as a battle between shepherds and demons, reflecting the battle between God and Satan on a cosmic level.[1518]

In other words, exorcism in the shepherds' basic understanding is not primarily considered a way of healing people from observable sicknesses. It concerns nothing less than salvation or condemnation. Mk 16:16 is one of the biblical readings constituting exorcism and it is read in the beginning of every session: "He who believes and is baptized will be saved; but he who does not believe will be condemned." Everything seems to be subordinate to this main perspective. People asking for exorcism only to obtain health have not grasped the real meaning of the liturgy, according to the shepherds and it is not most important that people are healed from their sicknesses. If the shepherds only assist people with their daily needs, they do not fulfil their calling.[1519]

The traditional cultural emphasis on a spiritual understanding of sickness and misfortune and consequently, a spiritual treatment to remedy the situation may be seen behind this thinking. The meaning of an incident does not lie in what can be observed but on a more profound, spiritual level. In the shepherds' thinking, this traditional feature seems to be understood in the framework of the biblical message handed over to them. The fundamental human problem is sin, which separates humankind from the living God. This "root cause" of all other problems must be addressed and when the fundamental relationship between God

---

[1518] If the shepherds understand their exorcism in an analogy with the cosmic fight between God and the devil, exorcism becomes important for people and the shepherds serving such a tradition become key people. Different questions as to the consequences of this arise: Should not everybody then be encouraged to come to exorcism or are the same results obtainable by Christian preaching and sincere prayer? Should exorcism be further incorporated into the liturgy of a Sunday morning service as it is already practised in some churches? What is the place of exorcism compared to the sacraments and absolution? What consequences will the above view of the shepherds' role in God's salvation purpose have for other church workers? These and related questions can only be mentioned within the frame of this project but they constitute important areas of further study for the church in Madagascar.

[1519] See 4.5.2.2 (The shepherds' priority).

and the person is harmonious/healed, then the symptoms of this broken relationship can be dealt with: sicknesses, problems, misfortunes etc. [1520]

If the shepherds' comprehensive use and understanding of exorcism mainly refers to the spiritual level, this may explain the opinion found among my informants that exorcism will not cause any damage to whatever person is treated in this way. Exorcism is considered as an assistance to oppressed people and people are assured that no demons are working in them, they are prayed for, receive forgiveness for their sins and assurance about strength and guidance of the Holy Spirit. God is demonstrated as victorious over Satan and the people are connected to the kingdom of God, which is the overall purpose of exorcism.[1521]

4.6.3 The shepherds' conception of healing as primarily faith in Jesus

Healing (*fanasitranana*) in the shepherds' understanding seems to cover a wide field of meanings and this corresponds with their perception of sickness (*aretina*), which comprises of a range of conditions. The spiritual dimensions of healing are especially emphasised in the fieldwork material and in the shepherds' frame of reference this is spelled out as a living faith in Jesus.[1522] Healing from observable

---

[1520] See 4.1.1.3 (The causes of sickness). and 4.1.2.2. More about this in 4.6.3.

[1521] See 4.2.1.4. The idea that exorcism easily hurts people is probably linked to Western thinking. Personally, I have felt uncomfortable when I have heard about people whom the shepherds consider as not "assaulted by demons" but still they are treated with exorcism. My informants do not seem to share this concern. The only direct reaction to mistreatment I can recall is when exorcism has excluded medical treatment, e.g. when babies with critical high fever are only treated with exorcism. The Malagasy shepherds' different cultural heritage and their overarching purpose with exorcism may explain the reason for their relaxed attitude. While in a Western cultural setting exorcism is associated with a witch-hunt and abuse of power, my informants seem to understand it as a remedy addressing the capricious invisible world surrounding them. And while a Westerner primarily sees exorcism as demon-expulsion, my informants consider it a means of mediating God's salvation to oppressed people. I have shown, however, that especially non-shepherds see theological problems in the shepherds' comprehensive use and understanding of exorcism.

[1522] The shepherds use "faith in Jesus" with many different nuances and it seems to cover different kinds or degrees of faith. See 4.5.2.2 (The relationship between faith in Jesus and healing). Faith as the goal of the shepherds' ministry comprises a

sicknesses, problems and misfortunes is still part of the area of meaning, however and a problematic life situation is normally the reason why people consult the shepherds.

The issue to be dealt with in the following is not the comprehensiveness of the shepherds' understanding of healing but their underlining of faith in Jesus as its main aspect.

I have chosen this theme, firstly because it is important to the shepherds. My informants constantly underline that a strong faith in Jesus is the purpose of their whole ministry, included the goal of exorcism. It is worth asking if my role as a missionary and seminary teacher has coloured this emphasis, because my informants may have given the information, which they supposed I would expect. This is not confirmed by other sources, however: The handbook, which is written to shepherds and novices, also emphasises faith in Jesus and L.A. Sharp has observed that conversion is the shepherds' ultimate goal. From participant observation of healing services, where the closer context of exorcism consists in Christian worship emphasising conversion, forgiveness of sins and belief in Jesus, it seems as the shepherds' strong weight on the spiritual dimension is more than an ideal.[1523]

Secondly, some controversy can be traced especially between my research population and other groups of shepherds. My informants seem to be rather unanimous in their emphasising of a living faith in Jesus as the most important healing but they seem to admit that some shepherds are more concerned with observable aspects.[1524] There are hints in my material that it is a temptation for shepherds to boast of their success in healing various kinds of sicknesses but my informants instruct their fellow-shepherds to concentrate on restoring the relation with God. My informants criticise other shepherd groups for creating publicity regarding their capacity of performing healing miracles.[1525]

---

conviction about Jesus as saviour who forgives sin and a trust in Jesus alone. When I talk about faith in this section, this kind of faith is in mind.

[1523] See 3.1.3, 4.5.2.2, Tobilehibe 1997:94, Sharp 1993:270.

[1524] Do the evil spirits depart because they are cast out or because people repent? Is the emphasis on God's word/conversion or on casting out of demons? Such questions, which may be raised on the basis of my fieldwork material, may point to different opinions among shepherds and indicate some shepherds' preoccupation with the visible aspects. Such questions may also reveal different emphases among the shepherds. Cf. 4.2.1.1, 4.4.1 and 4.4.2.

[1525] See 4.5.2.1. A.O. Igenoza sees in the African context a danger of "over-emphasising healing for its own sake rather than pointing the way to the Saviour"

Thirdly, the shepherds' understanding of the relation between healing as faith in Jesus and healing as a restoration of health seems somewhat obscure to me. The shepherds' understanding covers different aspects of healing at the same time and sometimes it is difficult to discern what they are actually talking about.

In the following I treat the issue of healing under two sub-headings, both are primarily focussing on healing as faith in Jesus. Why is a living faith in Jesus more important than recovery from sicknesses and is faith in Jesus necessary before healing of observable sicknesses can take place?

4.6.3.1 A living faith in Jesus is more important than healing from observable sicknesses

The people asking for the shepherds' assistance always have a feeling that there is something problematic in their lives. They come with their sicknesses, in a wide meaning of the term, bodily, mental, or spiritual sickness. When shepherds then talk about conversion and faith in Jesus, the background of the patients is their present problematic experience.

It is likely then that people coming to the shepherds primarily have their sicknesses in mind when they long for healing, while it seems as the shepherds' main orientation is to restore the relationship with the living God. An underlying issue may be the understanding of suffering. While for patients the concern is to get rid of a problematic situation, suffering seems to be understood in a biblical framework by the shepherds. The shepherds consider sickness and suffering evil but, as shown, the biblical message points to an even greater danger: eternal condemnation. Only those who believe in Jesus will be saved and consequently, this is an important issue. Healing of human suffering has consequences here and now while salvation has eternal consequences. The shepherds seem to have redefined suffering and in their understanding healing is primarily concerned with eternal salvation.[1526]

(Igenoza 1999:160) and A. Shorter asks several critical questions of exorcism in African churches, e.g. whether these practices lead people away from prayer and sacraments and whether they cause people to believe in Jesus. Shorter 1985:198–199.

[1526] See 4.1.2.4 (Human individuals). This is probably the background for the shepherds' understanding of sickness as having positive consequences or as "God's program". See 4.3.2.3.

The shepherds do not forget people's actual problems, however. Their practice may be said to follow Jesus' example in the Gospels. He proclaimed the kingdom of God as the focal point in his mission and summoned all people to repentance and belief in him but this did not prevent him from exercising his power to heal and exorcise, as part of his ministry.[1527] The shepherds' priorities may be said to reflect this. In an article Rasolondraibe P. calls the shepherds "preacher—healers" and he emphasises that being cured is in no way unimportant to the shepherds since a cure helps people to have a more firm hope in God's grace.[1528]

One feature in the shepherds' understanding of the demonic is that they tend to see demonic causes behind several human problems, or that demonic oppression may show itself in bodily or mental sicknesses. I have shown that this opinion may have been coloured by the traditional worldview, where spirits and powers constantly surround humans.[1529] According to the presented biblical message the cross of Jesus constitutes the victory over all evil powers and the "principalities and powers" are disarmed through forgiveness of sins.[1530] By preaching the Gospel of forgiveness of sins and faith in Jesus, the shepherds thus conquer the evil spirits. As a consequence, this victory may also address the concrete evil, experienced by the patients. In this perspective of forgiveness of sins with its consequences, it is understandable that to create a living faith in Jesus is important to the shepherds. By doing so, they both address the fundamental problem and its symptoms, i.e. they restore the relationship with God and thus enable a healing of the observable sickness/problem.

The spiritual explanations of sickness and misfortunes concern the "why" of sickness. The most important question in traditional culture when faced with sickness is to find the cause and evil spirits are suspected to be the agents of suffering in many cases.[1531] The sickness

---

[1527] See 4.1.2.3 (God and his kingdom).

[1528] Rasolondraibe 1989:347. Rasolondraibe distinguishes between healing as God's action and curing as a human ability. This is a specific use of the two English words and is done to render the African/Malagasy situation more accurately. Rasolondraibe depends on K. Appiah-Kubi in this distinction (p.348). Appiah-Kubi 1981:81.

[1529] See 4.1.1, 4.5.1.1 and 4.6.2.3.

[1530] See 4.1.2.5.

[1531] The shepherds are in accord with traditional thinking concerning the importance of this but they redefine the agent of affliction from ancestor spirits or gods to demons. Cf. 4.6.1. Rasolondraibe P. sees two possible agents of affliction in the shepherds'

itself, then, seems to be considered as a symptom of some underlying cause and the treatment should concentrate on the root cause to be really effective.[1532]

The shepherds' approach to sickness seems to be in line with this feature in the traditional understanding but their identification of people's fundamental problem seems to be defined according to the biblical message handed over to them: faith in Jesus addresses the ground cause of a person's problem.[1533] The relationship with Jesus determines people's eternal destiny and the shepherds make any effort to have this root relation healed.[1534]

Another feature in the shepherds' understanding, which may be supported by the biblical message, is that a living faith in Jesus provides a Christian with necessary strength to oppose the devil.[1535] As the shepherds may ascribe problems and misfortunes to demonic attacks, it is important to have enough strength to resist these attacks in order to stay healed in the future. The shepherds' treatment, which aims at creating a living faith, may then be considered as a prophylactic measure to avoid future harm from the evil one, which may be visible in different sicknesses and problems. Seen in this perspective, to create faith in Jesus is far more important than only treating the symptoms, i.e. sicknesses.[1536]

4.6.3.2 *Is faith in Jesus a prerequisite for healing of observable sicknesses?*

It is important to my group of informants to emphasise that shepherds are no miracle workers. They are "preacher—healers" with the distinct

---

understanding of underlying causes: either there is a rupture between the patient and/or his/her family and the source of life, or it stems from a demonic assault on the patient's faith. Rasolondraibe 1989:348. J.-M. Estrade talks about relieving the patients' bad conscience by means of ritual purifications. Estrade 1985:266.

[1532] See 4.1.1.3 (The causes of sickness).
[1533] The shepherds' opinion that separation from God is the ground cause of demonic oppression indicates this. See 4.3.2.2 (Lack of faith in Jesus).
[1534] Rasolondraibe P. affirms the centrality of faith in Jesus as the "root-relation" in the shepherds' understanding. Rasolondraibe 1989:348.
[1535] See 4.5.2.2 (The relationship between faith in Jesus and healing).
[1536] A living faith may also prevent Christians from consulting traditional healers, which are considered the main channels for demonic attacks, according to the shepherds. This is an indirect way of avoiding demonic attacks, by limiting the possibility of demons to influence people.

purpose of connecting people to the kingdom of God, by removing all possible hindrances for this to happen. They understand their ministry in line with the much-cited passage in Mk 16, where verses 15–16 talk about preaching the Gospel to faith and salvation, while verses 17–18 talk of the accompanying signs. In this orientation, faith in Jesus is the fundamental issue to be dealt with and healing from observable sicknesses is considered a sign, which the Lord let accompany their ministry. The shepherds often emphasise that a living faith in Jesus precedes a possible healing of observable sickness.

Does this emphasis in the shepherds' understanding make faith in Jesus a condition for the healing of observable problems to take place? L.A. Sharp maintains that the shepherds' "cure is conditional, based on conversion to a new faith" and G. Haus says that shepherds understand forgiveness as a condition for the healing of sickness on the basis of the account of the paralytic in Mt 9:1–8.[1537] Randrianarivelo J. criticises Sharp's assertion that the patients have to embrace the Protestant belief system to be fully healed. This is not the Ankaramalaza shepherds' teaching, according to his opinion. He says that the shepherds' aim is not to force the patient to embrace the belief system of any Christian church but to tell the healed person to believe in the Lord Jesus.[1538] The account in Mt 9 may well furnish some of the biblical background of the shepherds' understanding but do the shepherds here necessarily interpret forgiveness to be a condition for healing? My impression is that when the shepherds in my material emphasise faith in Jesus in connection with healing from observable sicknesses, their concern is not simply to say that healing will follow if a person has faith in Jesus.

More than thinking of faith in Jesus primarily in terms of condition for the healing of sickness, the shepherds, by their emphasis, seem to be preoccupied with fundamental causes. In the traditional worldview reconciliation and removal of sins by sacrifices are important. What is

---

[1537] Sharp 1993:274, Haus 2000:143. Haus asserts that uneducated shepherds see healing as a necessary consequence of forgiveness, while she has found that the theologians in her material distinguish between faith to salvation and faith to be healed (p.144–145).

[1538] Randrianarivelo 2000:90–91. Randrianarivelo's assertion seems to be an understatement. In my experience the shepherds strongly emphasise that to create a living faith in Jesus within the patients is the ultimate goal of their ministry.

broken has to be restored and since this concerns the community, it has to be done in public.[1539]

Elements in this traditional framework are found in the shepherds' understanding but the content seems to be moulded by the biblical message. The biblical message, which has influenced the shepherds, portrays sin as an offence mainly against God but also against other people.[1540] The shepherds are occupied with both the vertical and the horizontal: They see the relation to God as fundamental and what has caused this relation to be broken, must be restored. The shepherds preach the Christian Gospel about Jesus sacrificed for human sin, an act, which reconciled humans with God. But the shepherds also underline mutual forgiveness between the family and kin of the patient as necessary to enable the flow of healing to be effective. All this concerns underlying problems to be solved in order to enable healing from observable sicknesses. The observable sicknesses seem to be considered as symptoms of the fundamental issues.[1541] Without a restoration of the root relation a lasting healing of observable sicknesses is seriously hampered.[1542]

As argued for above, two kinds of miracles in the synoptic Gospels: exorcism and healing seem to be combined in the shepherds' exorcism.[1543] Several of the Gospel accounts of Jesus' healing miracles talk of faith, either the patient's or the family's faith. Whether this means faith in Jesus' ability to perform the healing or also includes faith in

---

[1539] According to J.-M. Estrade, the reconciliation has to be done both vertically and horizontally. Estrade 1985:266. Cf. 4.1.1.3 (The healing process).

[1540] See 4.1.2.2.

[1541] When I asked my informants to list signs of demonic oppression, they did not seem to have any uniform answers. A multitude of signs has been mentioned. May the reason for this be that the shepherds' focus is more on the underlying issues than on the signs? It may be that the shepherds mainly diagnose the demonic oppressed on the basis of what they consider to be fundamental problems and consequently, they only give examples of possible signs of these underlying causes.

[1542] I have some examples in my material telling about people who have obtained healing from observable sicknesses but who have not come to a living faith in Jesus. The shepherds seem to have experienced that these people will turn ill again sooner or later and some of them return to the *toby*. Cf. 4.5.2.4 (When the sickness lingers). These examples seem to indicate that faith in Jesus is not considered a condition for healing but rather expresses that an eschatological perspective moulds the shepherds' goal. See below.

[1543] See 4.6.2.2.

Jesus as God's representative is a matter of interpretation.[1544] Since shepherds know these biblical accounts of healing, it is natural that they underline faith as important in connection with healing from sicknesses. It seems, however, as these biblical texts are partly interpreted within the framework of the traditional worldview, which strongly emphasises fundamental issues. The faith, spoken of in the Gospel accounts does not, in the shepherds' understanding, primarily seem to mean confidence in Jesus' healing activity but most of all it seems to be understood as a living faith in Jesus' salvation. This understanding of faith may have further contributed to the shepherds' emphasis on the fundamental relation to be restored before a healing of the "symptoms" can take place.

G. Haus says that a condition to be healed from sickness, according to traditional thinking, is to admit the specific wrongdoing that caused the spirits to react. She thinks that the shepherds' understanding of people who are not healed partly corresponds with this traditional thinking. Haus does not clarify what this correspondence looks like but I understand her meaning to be that if the sickness lingers, the shepherds can always say that the person has not yet admitted the specific wrongdoing.[1545] My informants do not seem to be concerned with specific wrongdoings as explanations of a failure of healing. They rather emphasise the restoration of the fundamental relation with God as important in all cases.[1546]

My informants realise that some people do not obtain healing from observable sicknesses. As shown, they have several explanations that may count for this fact but sometimes they just have to admit that they do not know why.[1547] The admittance of this fact may impart a nuance to their emphasis on the underlying problem as crucial to healing. The tension between "already" and "not yet" in the biblical message handed

---

[1544] E.g. Jesus' words to the woman in Mk 5:24–34 that "your faith has made you well" (v.34) and Jesus seeing the faith of those carrying the paralytic in Mk 2:1–12. Since the shepherds do not distinguish between healing of observable sicknesses and healing of demonic oppression, the account in Mk 9:14–29 is also worth mentioning, where the father of the sick cried out and said: "I believe; help my unbelief" (v.24).

The suggested biblical background does not exclude that the shepherds may be influenced by the community thinking in the traditional culture, where family and kin have important roles in the healing process.

[1545] Haus 2000:110–111.
[1546] See 4.5.2.2 (The relationship between faith in Jesus and healing).
[1547] See 4.5.2.4 (When the sickness lingers).

over to them may have given them an interpretative framework to understand situations where people are not healed. Jesus has conquered all evil forces by his death on the cross but the final victory resides in the future. The tension between the old and the new stays as long as the Christian lives in this world.[1548] This perspective may furnish the background of both the shepherds' priority of a living faith over healing from observable sicknesses and their emphasis that only a restoration of the fundamental relation can enable a healing of sicknesses. When the shepherds focus on mending the relation with God they, at the same time, provide a full healing of all sicknesses and afflictions. In this world, this will only take place partially but the consummation will be characterised by a totally healed existence. This hope of an ultimate healing in eschatological terms makes it important for the shepherds to concentrate on creating a living faith in Jesus here and now. Only those who experience a healed relationship with God now can have a living hope of a healed existence in the consummation. This again confirms the results of the preceding section, asserting that exorcism in the shepherds' understanding has to be interpreted within the wider framework of salvation—condemnation.[1549]

4.6.4 Summary

I have chosen to focus on three areas in the shepherds' understanding of exorcism: their evaluation of spirits connected to traditional religion, one characteristic element in the exorcism practice itself and an important aspect in their understanding of healing. These are examples selected according to my criteria and I have shown how elements both from the traditional culture and from the biblical message handed over to the shepherds may enlighten the shepherds' understanding of the themes.

I have found that the shepherds' evaluation of all spirits in traditional worship as evil and demonic contrasts with the ambiguity of spirits in the traditional worldview and seems to stem from the biblical message. Some shepherds emphasise this point in the direction of a consistent "either-or"-principle, however, saying that whatever does not come from God has to come from the devil. This may be due to their understanding of certain biblical passages and to their belief in a widespread spiritual

---

[1548] See 4.1.2.4 (Human individuals) and 4.1.2.5.
[1549] See 4.6.2.5.

causing of human affliction, in line with traditional culture's preoccupation with spirits. It may also stem from their understanding of the biblical criterion for division of good and evil according to their sources of power, combined with the traditional understanding of the ambiguity of spirits as for the definition of the content of good and evil. Other shepherds seem to have combined elements from the two worldviews differently and react against the consistent "either-or"-principle. My informants seem to attribute the most consistent "either-or"-perspective to shepherds with little formal and theological training. It may probably be concluded that this group, at this point, is more influenced by the traditional culture than by the biblical message.

The comprehensiveness of exorcism is a salient feature in the shepherds understanding.
    Their exorcism seems more frequent than in both traditional thinking and biblical message. As traditional healers handle all kinds of problems, however, this may have contributed to the frequency of the shepherds' exorcism, together with the biblical exhortation to bring anything to God in prayer.
    The division of exorcism into two inseparable parts is significant and contributes to its comprehensive use. It may be ascribed to the New Testament's view of exorcism in a wider framework: the issue is not only to cast out demons but to fill the person with the positive forces of the kingdom of God. Perhaps we do see a combination of the New Testament's mighty acts of exorcism and healing into one in the shepherds' exorcism. However, the division into two parts may also be interpreted on the background of rituals in traditional Malagasy culture, which both purify the people and restore broken relations.
    The emphasis on life in community in traditional culture may furnish some of the background for the shepherds' extension of demon-expulsion to include a wide variety of people, while the variety of problems treated with exorcism may stem from the biblical teaching of Satan's diverse strategies to prevent people from entering the kingdom of God. The shepherds' conclusion that exorcism is appropriate for such a wide range of people does not seem to have any clear equivalent neither in the biblical message nor in traditional culture. Casting out of almost all kinds of evil may be the consequence if evil in the shepherds' thinking is understood as that which is evil to humans, as well as that which is evil before God. The traditional perception of demons constantly surrounding people and the biblical teaching of the devil's

ability to influence all people may have contributed to the comprehensiveness of exorcism. According to traditional thinking evil spirits preventing good spirits from entering a person are to be cast out. This may have resulted in the shepherds' expulsion of every spiritual influence, except for that of the Holy Spirit and also of everything which the evil spirits may exploit.

Basically, the shepherds' exorcism seems to reflect the underlying theology of Jesus' exorcisms as handed over to them. Exorcism is both liberation from the power of Satan and connection to the kingdom of God. Primarily therefore, the shepherds' exorcism concerns salvation or condemnation. This seems to reflect a basic spiritual understanding prominent in traditional thinking and this corresponds with the biblical emphasis on sin as the "root cause" of human problems.

The shepherds' understanding of faith in Jesus as more important than healing of sicknesses may depend on their understanding of suffering in a biblical perspective as primarily eternal condemnation. In line with Jesus' example they do not forget people's actual problems, however. The shepherds seem to understand sickness in traditional categories, by emphasising the ground cause but they define the fundamental problem of humans in biblical categories to be a broken relationship with God. They emphasise that faith in Jesus restores this relation and determines people's eternal destiny. Jesus' victory on the cross renders forgiveness, which addresses both the fundamental problem and the symptoms: Evil spirits are conquered when people's sin is forgiven and this enables a healing of observable "symptoms". A living faith in Jesus gives strength to oppose demonic attacks and therefore to create a living faith is more effective than treating symptoms.

The shepherds' emphasis on having a living faith in Jesus before any healing of sicknesses can take place may be drawn from the passage in Mk 16:15–18. Rather than thinking in terms of conditions for healing, the shepherds' preoccupation with faith in Jesus could be seen as an orientation towards fundamental causes, in line with the traditional worldview. Removal of sins through sacrifice and reconciliation is an important element in this worldview but its content in the shepherds' thinking seems to be moulded by the biblical message. My informants do not emphasise confession of specific wrongdoings in order to be healed. The prominent place of "faith" in the biblical accounts of healing may have contributed to the shepherds' emphasis but the core of the shepherds' understanding of faith is rather to restore a broken relationship with God than to have faith/confidence in healing of sicknesses. In the biblical perspective of "already—not yet" faith in Jesus, understood as salvation, guarantees a full healing of all afflictions in the future consummation.

As has been shown, there is no agreement among all the shepherds in my research population and there may be different reasons for the controversies. Some of my informants seem to react against what they see as going beyond their understanding of the biblical teaching. This, however, does not invalidate my suggestions as to how traditional Malagasy culture and biblical message—the dual contexts for the shepherds' ministry—together may serve to elucidate their understanding of exorcism.

5 Concluding summary and emerging questions

5.1 Concluding summary

I have focussed on one aspect in one sector of the revival movement in Madagascar, i.e. exorcism as it is practised and understood by shepherds in the Malagasy Lutheran Church. The word exorcism in the study is used with a special content denoting the shepherds' practice with expulsion of demons and prayer with the laying on of hands. My basic assumption has been that exorcism constitutes some sort of synthesis between traditional Malagasy culture and biblical message, as these two contexts have been decisive forces influencing the shepherds. The study design has been explorative and descriptive in order to grasp how the shepherds themselves understand this interesting but until now scholarly unexplored field. My findings cannot be summarised in a sentence or two but I will try to recapitulate some of the main traits and tendencies. The outline of the summary relates to my research questions, i.e. to explore and describe a) basic characteristics of exorcism as practised by the shepherds and b) the shepherds' understanding of people in need of exorcism, the expulsion of demons and the healing process.

A) I have investigated exorcism as it takes place in healing services in *toby* centres. The practice follows a rather strict liturgy. The services consist of an abundance of prayer, lots of hymns and a continued preaching of God's word. The emphasis in this first part of the service is not on demonic involvement in human lives but rather focuses on Jesus as Saviour, sin, repentance and grace. This reveals the main purpose of exorcism according to the shepherds' understanding, which is to lead people to conversion and trust in Jesus.

Exorcism consists of two inseparable parts and the shepherds believe that both the expulsion of demons and the prayer with the laying on of hands are needed to fulfil the purpose of exorcism. Although a person may be seen by some shepherds to be primarily in need of the second part, all attendants take part in the whole liturgy, since exorcism has developed into an institution. Elements in the biblical message may have contributed to the one liturgy with two parts: Jesus' exorcisms and healing miracles seem to have been combined into one and the expelling of Satan and the filling of a person with the positive forces of God may also have caused the twofold liturgy. Rituals performed accurately in order not to loose their power and the two parts of rituals in traditional practices, where ceremonies firstly purify and then restore what has been broken, may also be seen behind the two inseparable parts of exorcism.

Before the expulsion of demons starts people with special needs move to the first benches or straw mats. The shepherds put on their long, white robes and fixed passages from the Scripture are read, the most important seems to be Mk 16:15–20. The shepherds start moving their right arms in the air above the patients' heads, commanding all the work of darkness to depart. They are not allowed to touch the patients but this sometimes happens. The shepherds firmly command Satan and evil spirits to leave people, but also sicknesses, undesirable behaviour and attitudes, which are considered evil are commanded to leave and the shepherds all shout simultaneously with loud voices. The shepherds' words are direct and full of authority and they may encourage the patients to invoke Jesus' name. Only a few of the people sitting on the first benches/mats may show observable reactions to the expulsion of demons. According to my observations 98 % of the people sitting in the front of the church may sit quietly and do not show any traces of sickness but they all subject themselves to casting out of demons.

After the expulsion of demons the shepherds place their right hand on the head of the people on the first benches/mats and other attendants asking for "strengthening" and pray quietly. Almost all people present at ordinary healing services are prayed for and the shepherds do so in the name of Jesus and on his behalf. They choose words according to the people in question and declare forgiveness of sins and give the Holy Spirit and peace. The shepherds know some of the people but persons living outside the *toby* attending healing services usually do not have any preceding conversation with the shepherds. The prayer with the laying on of hands is the climax of the service and only consecrated shepherds can perform this.

B) The shepherds' terminology describing demonic influence on people is varied, with "assaulted by demons" as the most common. The usage is not consistent and it has been imperative to explore what terminology the shepherds' actually use and the connotations in order to grasp the nuances in their conception. The English word "possessed" is in most cases unsuitable to render the shepherds' understanding.

Many people with a wide spectrum of different problems, often without any observable signs, are treated with exorcism. Even people who are not labelled "assaulted by demons" may be treated in this way, since exorcism itself may function as a way of identifying demonic influence on people. There is controversy among my informants on these matters, however. Traditional Malagasy culture sees the human surrounded by spirits and forces and the shepherds seem to have combined this trait with the biblical view of all the different satanic working methods. This may have led to the shepherds' understanding that the devil is at work in all people but to varying degrees. Shepherds identify people's need of exorcism on the background of a multitude of different signs, by the spiritual gift of discerning spirits, or the sick and their families decide their own needs and consult the healing services. Observable signs seem to be considered as manifestations of underlying problems, in line with traditional thinking and therefore signs as such are not considered important compared to the underlying issues.

With regard to the shepherds' conception of Satan, demons and evil my investigation shows that the shepherds are interested mainly in these beings' relation to humans. They see an absolute antithesis between God and Satan and consider idol worship to be the most frequent cause of demonic oppression, either by a voluntary pact with spirits or by actively seeking healing from traditional healers, or involuntarily by sorcery. There is often an outbreak of a crisis when these people are confronted with the Christian message. Lack of faith in Jesus is considered to be the root cause opening the path for demonic influence and the devil is able to exploit a variety of situations and human conditions in order to oppress a person. The shepherds may also interpret demonic oppression as part of God's program for the person or his/her family.

There is controversy among my informants as to why Christians need exorcism. The shepherds explain this need differently with regard to Christians not taking the faith seriously and committed Christians. There seems to be a tension between God's ability to protect his children and the devil's ability to affect even Christians with his diverse strategies. The premises for my project have caused the question of gender and exorcism not to be a major subject. My material does not show any clear tendency, however, that women are in majority among the "assaulted by demons".

There are nuances in the shepherds' understanding of the exact purpose of the first part of exorcism. It may mean casting out of demons, a way of identifying demonic oppression, removal of hindrances for conversion and preparation for "strengthening". The initial expulsion aims at expelling demons in the air around the congregation. Evil spirits have to be challenged to manifest themselves. The shepherds include a multitude of conditions/attitudes to be expelled, all of them considered undesirable from their Christian viewpoint. Some shepherds rather expel the evil spirits behind the undesirable conditions/attitudes. Since the shepherds do not distinguish consequently between degrees of demonic assaults, exorcism seems to be considered appropriate for all conditions where the power of the devil is believed to cause a certain amount of trouble for people, may it be through influence, oppression or control. All the satanic strategies to assault people according to the New Testament may have contributed to the shepherds' inclusion of people with a wide range of problems in their exorcism. In traditional thinking everything considered evil to the human should be addressed and removed. The shepherds may have extended this trait to include also what is considered evil from God's point of view and then a variety of things should be expelled. According to traditional thinking evil spirits may prevent good spirits from entering a person. The shepherds may understand this to mean that not only evil spirits, but also everything that such spirits may exploit, prevent the work of the Holy Spirit and consequently should be cast out.

Shepherds firmly believe that God has power to heal and healing in the shepherds' understanding is considered a process, where an extended and repeated preaching, expulsion of demons, prayer with the laying on of hands and a loving fellowship in a *toby* all contribute. Healing has a wide meaning and comprises of bodily, mental and spiritual aspects, of which the shepherds constantly emphasise the spiritual as the most important, summarised in a living faith in Jesus. Conversion and confession of Jesus are the shepherds' primary concerns and this is considered more important than healing from sicknesses, which sometimes does not happen. The shepherds seem to have combined the traditional search for fundamental causes with a biblical understanding of suffering. They define the main problem of humans to be a broken relationship with God, which ultimately will lead to condemnation. Healing is understood as liberation from the power of Satan and connection to the kingdom of God and thus the battle between shepherds and demons taking place in exorcism concerns nothing less than salvation or condemnation. This seems to be considered as an earthly counterpart to the cosmic battle about humans between God and Satan. In this perspective, human suffering and sickness have consequences here and now while faith in Jesus has eternal consequences. Healing of bodily and mental sickness is important for the shepherds, however and they expel sicknesses and pray for the sick, but my informants' understanding of a possible demonic origin of sicknesses differ. A lasting healing requires that the person terminates all contact with traditional healers and the conversion of family members is considered important. Sickness is often understood as conveying a message to the family of the sick. Through the prayer with the laying on of hands the shepherds declare forgiveness of sins and give the Holy Spirit and peace, which again points to the climax of healing in the shepherds' understanding. The shepherds act as mediators between God and the people through the "strengthening", they declare God's gifts and assist people with heavy burdens.

My research has shed light on the shepherds' practice and understanding of exorcism, viewed—as has been shown—in the context of traditional Malagasy culture and biblical message. My basic assumption of exorcism as a synthesis of these two contexts seems to have been verified as a fruitful approach. I have been able to give a comprehensive presentation of the shepherds' practice and understanding of exorcism with the two contexts as horizons of understanding and to interpret some main themes in the shepherds' understanding in light of the contexts. The general picture emerging from the study seems to be that while some aspects of exorcism primarily have their background in traditional culture and others in biblical message, in most cases both contexts appear in some kind of synthesis.

5.2 Emerging questions

Since exorcism in the revival movement in Madagascar until now has been insufficiently covered by scholarly research, I consider my contribution to be a comprehensive but basic description. Many aspects of the Lutheran shepherds' exorcism need a more thorough analysis than can be given in one study alone. I will therefore briefly highlight some theological questions, which seem to emerge from the preceding presentation.[1550] I delimit myself to questions most directly connected to exorcism and I only mention some of the most important ones according to my own estimation.[1551]

5.2.1 Demonology and demonic involvement in human life

The shepherds have no normative, written, systematic demonology but they seem to have a rather fixed view of the demonic reality, to a large extent reinforced by their own experiences. This concerns demons' abilities, some sort of hierarchy, classes of demons, communicative skills, a set of different tactics, ability to enter into material objects or living bodies, materialisations and conceptual analogies. This view of

---

[1550] These are meant as areas for further research and as challenges to the revival movement and will mainly be related here to the biblical message presented in 4.1.2. The consequences will have bearing on biblical, systematic theological and practical theological issues.

[1551] Premises in the instruction program for shepherds, the theology of consecration, the shepherds' dress, the preoccupation with life and conduct, the relation between men and women and the connection between conversion and healing, are some of the questions I have to leave without comment.

It is tempting in closing to refer to the opinions of researchers of the AICs on exorcism and reflect on what I have found among the Malagasy shepherds. Cf. 1.2. Is exorcism a threat to the progress of the African? Does the practice encourage dualistic attitudes, cause fear of demons and make people demonise their experience of suffering? Are people diverted from prayer and sacraments? Does exorcism degenerate into a power-phenomenon and not a prayer-phenomenon? What about failures in healing, disorderliness and the unscientific aspects? Is there a danger of magical interpretation and a stigmatisation and enslavement of the victims? On the other hand: What if exorcism attacks the roots of witchcraft and causes freedom from fear? Does it counter the danger of superficial Christianity? Does it allow the possibility to construct a Christian worldview to meet the religious aspirations of African Christians? What about the real and lasting healing? The aim of my study, however and the limits of space do not allow me to enter into the above questions in this work.

demons, probably unconsciously taken for granted, forms the basis for the shepherds' practice and understanding of exorcism. Does the shepherds' view of demons take sufficiently into account the biblical monotheism, God's uniqueness and the subordination of every power to God? What about influence from elements in traditional culture and other written or oral sources, which may not be conform to the biblical message?

The variety in terminology denoting the demons' influence on people is a challenge for theological reflection. What do shepherds actually mean when they e.g. say "assaulted by demons", "seized by demons", or "demoniac"? Only a few of their expressions are taken from a biblical vocabulary. How may the shepherds be able to legitimise theologically this terminology and how do they deduce practical consequences from this? A second problem emerges when the different words are translated e.g. into English. If the English translation is unable to render the Malagasy shepherds' connotations with the various concepts, it follows that our understanding of the practice based on this terminology also will be incomplete, which again advises Western researchers to be careful in evaluating the practice.

Sin is the fundamental human problem according to the Bible. Sin is also a main focus in the shepherds' work, but is there a danger that the borders between human sinfulness and demonic involvement in human life may be blurred in the shepherds' thinking, due to their rather elaborate demonology?

5.2.2 If it is not God, it is a demon

Whatever does not stem from God has to stem from the devil. To the shepherds, there seems to be no other possibility. At least some of my informants emphasise the dualism between God and Satan to such a degree that humans are in danger of becoming helpless victims in a cosmic battle. I consider this trait to be part of the shepherds' worldview and to a large extent unconscious. In my opinion, a deeper understanding of anthropology in a biblical perspective seems imperative. The synoptic Gospels portrays two kingdoms in opposition to each other, but when the Bible talks about rebellion and sin, humans are in focus. Humans are also responsible for their sin and its consequences. Are these aspects sufficiently taken into account in the shepherds' understanding, or have Satan and demons occupied too much space at the price of humans? This is not to say that humans are absent in the shepherds' thinking. A certain anthropocentrism can be traced and humans have a responsibility to strengthen their shield against demonic assaults. At the same time, however, an externalisation of evil takes place, which paves the way for shepherds to cast out sins and worries. My point is that the place of humans and human responsibility in the shepherds' understanding of spiritual encounter is in need of further and deeper theological investigation, both by researchers and by the shepherds themselves.[1552]

5.2.3 The appropriateness of exorcism for people with a wide range of problems

The shepherds' demonology and understanding of demons' involvement in human life somehow causes their practice of exorcism to include people with varied difficulties. The great majority of people treated with exorcism show no observable reactions and the shepherds do not seem to consider an identification of demons' work in a person as decisive before exorcism. Their practice seems rather consistent when evaluated from their underlying premises, but is exorcism unproblematic as a treatment for all these people, even if they are not "assaulted by demons", as some of my informants maintain? Seen in light of Jesus' exorcisms, is it possible to maintain that exorcism is what all these people need? How is it possible to argue for this extension of exorcism, seen in a biblical perspective? The two kinds of mighty acts in the Gospels, healing and exorcism are a challenge to a deepened investigation of relevant alternative treatment for some of these people.

It may further be asked how we are to evaluate the significance of exorcism in the healing process compared to the benefits of *toby* community, treatment with love and compassion and Western medicine? Does the comprehensiveness of exorcism indicate that the practice is in the process of being widened and extended, especially in the high plateaux and is about to become a liturgical ceremony in principle open for all? What will be the eventual consequences of such an extension?

The questions seem of special importance when we see that Christians are treated with exorcism and in some churches exorcism has even become part of the Sunday morning service. Although there seems

---

[1552] It has to be mentioned, however, that some of my informants distinguish between God, the human and the demonic realm. I believe that some of the controversy in my material can be more properly interpreted if the differences in opinion are traced back to this division of reality, on which the shepherds disagree.

to be certain unease among some of my informants about this, it may exemplify the need for a more thorough theological reflection on this point. According to the biblical message when people are baptised, they enter a new sphere of life where evil powers do not rule. Believers are summoned to live in correspondence with their baptism, renounce sin and resist the devil. In spite of this, do they still need exorcism?

5.2.4 Expulsion of sickness, sin and a variety of evils

Some shepherds expel undesirable human attitudes and conditions, like unbelief, temptations, pretence, weakness, envy etc, while others rather expel the spirits behind these things. The shepherds' purpose when casting out this variety of evils is to lead people to salvation and make their faith firm. The basis for this practice may be found in the shepherds' understanding of demonic assaults and of the conditions where demons are active, probably combined with some shepherds' thinking that all things either stem from God or from the devil.

The shepherds' expulsion of a variety of evils causes questions in relation to the biblical message and may need more theological reflection, especially on hamartiology but also, as already indicated, on anthropology. How are the shepherds to legitimise their expulsion of human conditions and attitudes as if sin and sinful desires come from outside the human? Human sin is a fundamental problem throughout the Bible and victory over sin is a main theme in the New Testament. The cross of Jesus shows that human sin is central in the fight between God and Satan and Satan looses his power over humans through the gift of forgiveness, obtained through Jesus' sacrificial death. How is the shepherds' expulsion of human sin to be understood in relation to this NT message? What is the relation between expulsion of sins and confession of sins? Is it possible that this practice may lead people to think that evil spirits are the real agents of their sin and give them hope to obtain a kind of sinlessness, as some non-shepherds indicate?

5.2.5 The position of shepherds

To become a shepherd is equalled with taking the Christian faith seriously and shepherds have a high self-awareness because of their calling and consecration. They assist people with special needs, resist the devil on behalf of people and increase people's ability to "cast out demons from themselves". They tear down the kingdom of Satan through expulsion of demons and establish the kingdom of God through prayer with the laying on of hands and they distribute forgiveness of sins and give the Holy Spirit.

This is an impressive list of responsibilities and theological reflection is needed on the position of shepherds in the church and the significance of their service. If exorcism develops into a practice intending to embrace as many people as possible, what are the theological consequences? What then is the place of exorcism in relation to absolution and the sacraments? How important are the shepherds for the people they serve? What are the relations between shepherds and other church workers, especially pastors, a relationship which at present is somewhat tense? What about the controversy concerning shepherds who receive "strengthening" publicly and possible theological consequences of the different views?

On an even more detailed level, several questions may be raised: Should an oral confession of sins be a theological condition for the shepherds' declaration of forgiveness? What are the theological implications of the shepherds' saying "Receive the Holy Spirit"? What kind of pneumatology do the shepherds advocate with such a saying?

5.2.6 Exorcism—faith—salvation: closing remarks

An outstanding feature in my investigation is the shepherds' focus on a distinct theological perspective. Exorcism aims at conversion and healing, where healing is interpreted spiritually and to a large degree understood as synonymous with faith in Jesus. The shepherds' main goal is salvation, i.e. restoration of fellowship with the living God through forgiveness of sins. The shepherds follow the example of Jesus in Mk 2: forgiveness of sins precedes healing and is therefore understood as more fundamental. As the whole of Jesus' ministry is seen in the perspective of salvation in the NT, so also the shepherds see their service in this perspective. Shepherds in my material do not emphasise salvation only as a means in order to obtain healing from sicknesses. They seem to have a holistic view of people and believe firmly in God's power to answer prayers concerning bodily and mental sickness. The biblical framework genuinely influences them. I find the Malagasy shepherds' distinct focus on salvation and their ability to orient all their practice and understanding around this perspective challenging.

The shepherds take seriously the NT teaching about Satan and demons. The kingdom of God conquering the kingdom of Satan is a vital part of Jesus' proclaiming of the kingdom and Jesus' exorcisms in the synoptic Gospels are seen as a demonstration of the presence and power of the kingdom of God. My investigation contributes to a deeper insight into the way the shepherds contextualise the NT teaching about Satan and demons and how influence from the traditional cultural context can be traced in their understanding. One may ask, however, if there is a possibility that the traditional context has led the shepherds to over-emphasise the NT theme of Satan and demons, but this question is not for me to answer as I have not entered into a normative evaluation of the validity of the shepherds' approach. Such an evaluation should not take place unless further research has tried to address the questions here mentioned. My conviction is that through further research both African and Western churches may learn from the Malagasy shepherds and the revival movement itself will benefit from a deepened investigation of its own practice and understanding of exorcism.

Appendices

Appendix 1: Questionnaire shepherds

QUESTIONNAIRE (mpianatra STPL)	Questionnaire (students STPL)
confidentiel - tsy avoaka misy anarana izay soratanao	confidential—what you write will not be referred to by name
MPIANDRY	Shepherds
1 ANARANA:	1 Name
2 TOERANA NIAVIANA:	2 Place of origin
3 FIRY TAONA IANAO REHEFA NATOKANA HO MPIANDRY?	3 At what age were you consecrated as a shepherd?
4 INONA NO NAHATONGA ANAO HO MPIANDRY (ataovy feno araka izay azao atao ny tantara!)? (Ataovy ao ambadika na amin'ny takelaka hafa)	4 What caused you to become a shepherd? (make the story as full as possible!) (use the reverse side or another sheet)
5 INONA NO MAHATONGA NY OLONA HO VOAN'NY DEMONIA?	5 What causes people to become "assaulted by demons"?
6 INONA NO MARIKA AHAFANTARANAO FA VOAN'NY DEMONIA NY OLONA IRAY?	6 What are the signs by which you know that a person is "assaulted by demons"?
7 INONA NO MARIKA AHAFANTARANAO FA NIVOAKA NY DEMONIA?	7 What are the signs by which you know that the demons have left?
8 RAHA NAHITA OLONA VOAN'NY DEMONIA MAHATSIRAVINA IANAO, DIA TANTERAO AN-TSIPORIHANY NY AMIN'IZANY (fotoana, toerana, fiainan'ilay olona, marika ahafantarana fa voan'ny demonia izy, fitsaboana/famoahana demonia, ny fahasalamany). Tantara iray ihany no ataovy! (Ataovy ao amin'ny takelaka manokana ny tantara)	8 If you have seen a person who is seriously "assaulted by demons", then tell about it in detail (time, place, the person's life, marks by which to know that he/she is "assaulted by demons", treatment/expulsion of demons, his/her health). Only tell one story! (Write the story on a separate sheet)
9 MOA MISY FITSABOANA HAFA AFA-TSY NY FAMOAHANA DEMONIA	9 Is there any treatment other than expulsion of demons that may be

VE IZAY METY MAHOMBY AMIN'IREO VOAN'NY DEMONIA? INONA?	successful for those who are "assaulted by demons"? Which?
10 MOA MISY OLONA IVELAN'NY FIANGONANA/MPIANDRY (tsi-kristiana izany) IZAY MAMOAKA DEMONIA? MOA EFA NAHITA ZAVATRA TAHAKA IZANY VE IANAO? INONA NO ZAVATRA NISEHO?	10 Are there people outside the church/shepherds (i.e. non-Christians) who expel demons? Have you seen this? What happened?
11 INONA NO VOTOATIN'NY VAVAKA MISY FAMETRAHAN-TANANA AORIAN'NY FAMOAHANA DEMONIA?	11 What is the content of the prayer with the laying on of hands after the expulsion of demons?
12 LAZAO NY HIRA 10 AMPIASAINA INDRINDRA AMIN'NY FOTOAM-PIFOHAZANA (No ao amin'ny Fihirana FFPM):	12 Record the 10 most used hymns in healing services (numbers in the Protestant hymnbook)
13 AHOANA NY FIFANDRAISANA AMIN'NY MAHA-MPIANDRY SY MAHA-PASTORA ANAO? (valian'ny ho pastora ihany!)	13 What is the relation between you as a shepherd and you as a pastor? (to be answered only by those who are going to become pastors)

Appendix 2: Questionnaire non-shepherds

QUESTIONNAIRE (mpianatra STPL) confidentiel - tsy avoaka misy anarana izay soratanao TSY MPIANDRY 1 Anarana: 2 Toerana niaviana: 3 Nahoana no tsy mpiandry ianao? 4 Ahoana ny fiheveran'ny olona momba an'i satana sy ny demonia (ny fandraisany izao tontolo izao manodidina azy)? 5 Inona no mahatonga ny olona ho voan'ny demonia? 6 Inona no marika ahafantaranao fa voan'ny demonia ny olona iray? 7 Inona ny fanasitranana mety mahomby amin'ireny olona ireny? 8 Moa misy olona ivelan'ny fiangonana/mpiandry (tsi-kristiana izany) izay mamoaka demonia? 9 Mety misy fifandraisany ve amin'ny famoahana demonia ataon'ny fiangonana sy	**Questionnaire (students STPL)** confidential—what you write will not be referred to by name Non-shepherds 1 Name 2 Place of origin 3 Why are you not a shepherd? 4 What do people think about Satan and the demons? (the opinions of this world [non-Christians] about these things) 5 What causes people to become "assaulted by demons"? 6 What are the marks by which you know that a person is "assaulted by demons"? 7 What treatment may be successful for these people? 8 Are there people outside the church/shepherds (i.e. non-Christians) who expel demons? 9 Is there a resemblance between the demon-expulsion done by the church and

ny famoahana demonia ataon'ny tsi-kristiana (fomban-drazana)?
10 Inona no tsy mety amin'ny fiheveran'ny fifohazana na pratikany momba ny famoahana demonia?

(soratana ao ambadika na amin'ny taratasy manokana izay tsy omby eto!)

the demon-expulsion done by non-Christians (ancestral practices)?
10 What is not appropriate regarding the thinking and practice of the revival movement concerning expulsion of demons?

(use the reverse side or a separate sheet if there is not enough space here!)

Appendix 3: Observation of healing services

ASA SY FAMPAHEREZANA	Work and strengthening
*TOERANA (fileovana/synoda):	*Place (district/synod)
*DATY:	*Date
*ISAN'NY OLONA AO:	*Number of people present
*ISAN'NY OLONA MANATONA HAMOAHANA DEMONIA	*Number of people moving forward for demon-expulsion
LAHY	Men
VAVY	Women
ZAZA	Children
*INFORMATIONS MOMBA IZANY	*Information about the following
TAONANY	Their age
FIHETSIKA MANOKANA	Special movements
ZAV. MISEHO	Things that happen
*ISAN'NY OLONA MITADY FAMETRAHAN-TANANA:	*Number of people asking for the laying on of hands
*ISAN'NY MPIANDRY MITONDRA AKANJO:	*Number of shepherds wearing their dress
*TORITENY	*Sermon
TEKSTA	Text
VOTOATINY	Content
*HIRA:	*Hymns
*OBSERVATIONS MANOKANA:	*Special observations
*NY PROGRAMAN'NY FOTOANA (en detail) (ao ambadika)	*The program of the service (in detail) (on the reverse side)

Appendix 4: Interview guide case histories

NY TANTARAN'IREO VOAN'NY DEMONIA	The story of the "assaulted by demons"
"Observations détaillées" momba ny cas tsirairay	"Detailed observations" about each case

1 Ny tantaram-piainany hatramin'ny fahazazana... Fitaizana kristiana? Moa nifandray tamin'ny ombiasa ve izy na ny ray aman-dreniny? Misy olon-kafa ao amin'ny fianakaviany izay voa?	1 His/her life-story from childhood... A Christian upbringing? Has he/she or the parents been in contact with a traditional healer? Are there other persons in his/her family who are "assaulted"?
2 Nahoana no voan'ny demonia izy? Inona no nahatonga izany?	2 Why is he/she "assaulted by demons"? What has caused this?
3 Inona no nahafantarana fa voan'ny demonia izy?	3 How is it possible to know that he/she is "assaulted by demons"?
4 Inona no fomba nahatongavany tao amin'ny toby? Naterin'iza? Izy tenany ve no nanatona?	4 How did he/she come to the *toby*? Who brought him/her? Did he/she come by himself/herself?
5 Ahoana no fisehoan'ny aretiny izao? (raha mbola tsy afaka izy)	5 How is his/her sickness now? (if he/she is not free yet)
6 Inona avy no miseho rehefa avoaka ny demonia? (manana anarana ve ny demona? miteny ve izy? mihetsika ve ny marary? "réactions" hafa...?) ITY FAHA-6 ITY NO ZAVA-DEHIBE!	6 What happens when the demons are cast out? (do the demons have names? do they speak? does the sick shake his/her body back and forth? other "reactions"?) This number 6 is very important!
7 Impiry no misy famoahana demonia amin'ny olona iray? Averina isaky ny oviana? Inona koa no atao aminy an-koatran'ny famoahana demonia (fandroana, fampianarana samy hafa sns.)?	7 How many times are demons expelled from one person? How often is it repeated? What is done with him/her in addition to demon-expulsion (bathing in water, different kinds of teaching etc.)?
8 Inona no nahafaka ny voan'ny demonia? Inona no ahafantarana fa afaka izy?	8 What made the "assaulted by demons" to become free? How is it possible to know that he/she is free?
9 Naharitra fotoana firy ny aretiny? (Hatramin'ny nahatsapany azy voalohany indrindra ka hatramin'ny fahasitranany tanteraka. Hazavao ny zavatra niseho!).	9 How long has he/she had the sickness? (From the first time he/she became aware of it until his/her complete healing. Describe what happened!)
10 Inona no tantarain'ny marary momba ny aretiny sy ny fampijalian'ny demona azy ary ny nahafaka azy? Ny fahatsapany tao anaty... Ny zavatra reny na hitany na nofy izay nananany na zavatra hafa... Nanahoana ny fisehoan'ny "krizy" tao aminy? ZAVA-DEHIBE ITY TANTARA ITY! Raha afaka manoratra ny tantarany ny voan'ny demonia, dia tsara indrindra izany! (Omeo taratasy izy!!). Mbola hataonao feno ihany anefa ny "interview"!	10 What does the sick tell about his/her sickness and the suffering caused by the demons and the way he/she became free? What did he/she feel inside...? What did he/she hear or see or what dreams did he/she have or other things...? What did his/her "crisis" look like? This story is very important! If the "assaulted by demons" is able to write his/her story, this is the best! (Give him/her a sheet!!). You should still do the "interview" in full, however!

Hatao araka ny zava-misy hatrany ny "observations" (ny fanoratana). Izay niseho ihany no soratana! Ianao dia "neutre" (= tsy manapaka-kevitra mialoha) eo anatrehan'ny cas dinihinao!	The "observations" (the writing) have to be according to what happens. Only write what happens! You are "neutral" (= you do not make up your mind beforehand) in relation to the case you study!
Raha tianao dia azonao aroso ny hevitrao rehefa vita tanteraka ny fanoratana ny "observations". Lazao mazava anefa rehefa ny hevitrao no aroso!	If you want, you are able to give your opinion when you have completely ended the writing of your "observations". Tell plainly, however, when you come with your own opinion.
Raha olona marary tezaina amin'izao no anaovanao fikarohana, dia ataovy karazana diary: soratana tsara izay miseho isan'andro (avy eo dia lasa "dossiers"). Hans Austnaberg, Mpamp. STPL Atsimoniavoko, B.P.49, Antsirabe 110	If you do your investigation with a sick person under treatment, then make a daily journal: write what happens each day (then this will become a "file"). Hans Austnaberg, teacher at STPL Atsimoniavoko, B.P. 49, Antsirabe 110

Glossary

The following are major reoccurring Malagasy words and expressions. It is not a complete glossary.

adala	mad
ambalavelona	sickness considered to be caused by sorcery
andriamanitra	name of god/God
androbe	epileptic
aretina	illness, sickness
asa	work
asa sy fampaherezana	work and strengthening. The most common way for the shepherds to denote exorcism
azon'ny demonia/devoly	seized by demons/devils
dada	dad, father
dadatoa	uncle
demonia	demon
demoniaka	demoniac
devoly	devil
fametrahan-tanana	imposition of hands
famoahana demonia	expulsion of demons
fampaherezana	strengthening
fanafody	medicine
fanahy ratsy	evil spirit
fanokanana	consecration. Mostly used regarding consecration of shepherds but can also be used regarding ordination of pastors
fifohazana	The Malagasy revival movement. Literally: revival, awakening.
fihirana	song
hasina	holiness, sacred power
iraka	itinerant shepherd. Literally: messenger
kalanoro	name of a nature spirit
kasoa	a sort of madness connected to love affairs
katekista	local church worker/church leader
lahatra	order, organisation, arrangement
lolo	name of a nature spirit. Literally: butterfly

mama	mother, mam
mamaoaka	expel, cast out
mandroaka	expel, cast out
marary	to be ill/sick
miasa	to work. Often used about the first part of exorcism, the expulsion of demons
mihetsika	move, sway the upper part of the body
mivavaka	to pray (to pray to God or to attend a church service)
mpanandro	traditional Malagasy healer, diviner, specialist in determining destinies
mpiandry	shepherd
mpimasy	traditional Malagasy healer
mpiomana	novice, a person following the instruction program to become a shepherd
neny	mama, mother
njarinintsy	name of an evil spirit
ody	charm, amulet
ombiasa/ombiasy	traditional Malagasy healer
ratsy	bad, evil
razana	ancestor
sampy	idol
toby	revival centre, camp
tody	retaliation
tromba	a distinct group of spirit possession
tsiny	blame, name of a nature spirit
vazimba	original inhabitant, spirit of original inhabitants
very saina	"lost mind", a mentally ill person
vintana	destiny
voa	assaulted, hurt, wounded
voan'ny demonia	assaulted by demons
zanahary	name of god/God

Field material

When I conducted the fieldwork in Madagascar, I made an agreement with my informants only to cite them in public by anonymising their sayings. This is the reason for my consistent use of identification numbers.

The variation in numbers is due to computer processing of greater amount of material than I have used in the investigation. The list below does not indicate, however, that all this material is specifally referred to in the text/footnotes. The function of the digits is only to identify and be able to verify my sources. The same number across categories of material refers to the same person.

I have chosen to sort the lists according to numbers in ascending order.

A. Interviews

A.1 With shepherds

Identification[1553]	Date	Place	Person
IS 76	June 1998	Antsirabe	Shepherd/pastor[1554]
IS 200	Mey 1993	Antsirabe	Pastor/shepherd
IS 201	June 1993	Fianarantsoa	Pastor/shepherd
	Mars 2001	Stavanger	
IS 202	June 1993	Fianarantsoa	Pastor (practising exorcism)
IS 205	August 1993	Antsirabe	Pastor (practising exorcism)
IS 206	September 1993	Antsirabe	Shepherd leader
	June 1998	Antsirabe	
IS 210	October 1993	Antsirabe	Shepherd/pastor/*toby*-leader

[1553] IS = Interview with shepherd.

[1554] The labels "shepherd/pastor" and "pastor/shepherd" mean that the person is both consecrated as a shepherd and ordained as a pastor. When it is said that the person was consecrated as a shepherd before ordination, I write "shepherd/pastor". The ordination gives the full right to work as a shepherd, according to the teaching in the church and the revival movement, so I am counting all the pastors, who are performing exorcism, at the same level as the consecrated shepherds. All pastors referred to in this category perform exorcism regularly.

	November 1993	Antsirabe	
	June 1998	Antsirabe	
IS 212	December 1993	Antsirabe	Pastor (practising exorcism)
IS 213	March 1994	Antsirabe	Pastor (practising exorcism)
IS 214	June 1994	Antsirabe	Pastor (practising exorcism)
IS 217	April 1994	Antananarivo	Pastor (practising exorcism)
IS 218	April 1994	Antananarivo	Pastor (practising exorcism)/*toby*-leader
IS 310	June 1998	Antsirabe	Shepherd/pastor
IS 311	June 1998	Antsirabe	Pastor (practising exorcism)
IS 312	June 1998	Antsirabe	Shepherd/pastor
IS 314	June 1998	Antsirabe	Shepherd
IS 315	June 1998	Antsirabe	Pastor (practising exorcism in a Reformed church)[1555]
IS 316	June 1998	Antsirabe	Shepherd leader
IS 318	June 1998	Antsirabe	Pastor (practising exorcism)
IS 320	July 1998	Antananarivo	Pastor (practising exorcism)
IS 321	July 1998	Antananarivo	Pastor (practising exorcism)
IS 322	July 1998	Antananarivo	Shepherd leader
IS 323	July 1998	Antananarivo	Shepherd leader
IS 325	November 2000	Stavanger	Pastor (practising exorcism)
IS 328	June 1998	Antsirabe	Shepherd

A.2 With non-shepherds

Identification[1556]	Date	Place	Person
IN 207	September 1993	Antsirabe	Patient at a *toby*
IN 208	September 1993	Antsirabe	Patient at a *toby*
IN 313	June 1998	Antsirabe	Pastor
IN 317	June 1998	Antsirabe	Pastor
IN 324	July 1998	Antananarivo	An experienced Lutheran Christian
IN 329	June 1998	Antsirabe	Theological student, STPL Atsimoniavoko

A.3 Group interviews

Identification[1557]	Date	Place	Person
IG 330	June 1998	Antsirabe	Novices[1558]
IG 331	June 1998	Antsirabe	Congregation leaders[1559] (shepherds

---

[1555] This informant only figures in footnotes.

[1556] IN = Interview with non-shepherd.

[1557] IG = Interview with a group of people.

[1558] They were interviewed a week before their consecration.

FIELD MATERIAL

IG 332	May 1993	Antsirabe	and non-shepherds) A class of theological students working on Synoptic biblical theology: evil spirits[1560]

B. Selected case histories[1561]

B.1 Interviewed by me

Identification[1562]	Date	Place	Person
CHIS 8	December 1993	Antsirabe	Novice.[1563] Formerly "assaulted by demons"
CHIS 12	May 1994	Antsirabe	Shepherd. Formerly "assaulted by demons"
CHIN 31	September 1993 April 1994	Antsirabe Antsirabe	Patient at the *toby*. In treatment.[1564]
CHIS 130	March 1994	Antsirabe	Shepherd. Formerly "assaulted by demons"
CHIN 171	June 1994	Antsirabe	Young boy in treatment.[1565]

[1559] Mal: *katekista*. These people take care of the congregation when the pastor is absent. They lead the service and often they preach.

[1560] Written contributions from five groups and discussion in the class, shepherds and non-shepherds.

[1561] I have selected these histories of people who have been "assaulted by demons" from a larger material because they shed light on my topic. Some of the histories are rather short, while others are detailed and extensive. Some have the form of interviews, others are taken from the questionnaires. For the sake of clarity I have chosen to present these histories in a separate category.

[1562] CHIS = Case history interview with shepherd. CHIN = Case history interview with non-shepherd.

[1563] It is most accurate to label this interview as a shepherd interview (IS) although the person is not formally consecrated. He has been in the instruction program to become a shepherd for one year, he occasionally brings his testimony at healing services and he reports to have expelled demons outside healing services.

[1564] The parents are telling his story.

[1565] His father (IS 214) tells the story.

B.2 From interviews by field assistants

Identification[1566]	Date	Place	Person[1567]
CHINA 27	1993/1994	Antsirabe district	A man
CHISA 81	December 1993	Antsirabe	A married man
CHISA 100	January 1994	Antananarivo	A young man
CHISA 104	1993/1994	Antsirabe district	A man
CHISA 114	December 1993	Antananarivo district	A woman
CHINA 116	1993/1994	Antsirabe district	A 20 year old unmarried woman
CHISA 117	December 1993	Antsirabe district	A 24 year old married woman
CHISA 130	January 1994	Antsirabe	A 25 year old woman
CHISA 156	April 1994	Antsirabe district	A 25 year old man

B.3 From the questionnaires[1568]

Identification[1569]	Date[1570]	Place[1571]	Person
CHQ 3	1989	Betafo	Young woman
CHQ 6			Young woman
CHQ 12			20 year old woman
CHQ 41	1992		22 year old man
CHQ 42			Woman
CHQ 54			Man

[1566] The identification number refers to the field assistant interviewing the patient. CHINA = Case history from interview by non-shepherd field assistant. CHISA = Case history from interview by shepherd field assistant.

[1567] All these people are either formerly "assaulted by demons" or in treatment at the time of the interview.

[1568] These histories were told from memory and they vary much in length and content. The informants were not asked to present data about date, place etc., so this lacks to a certain extent.

[1569] CHQ = Case histories from the questionnaires. The identification numbers refer to the informant, who told the story in the questionnaire. This fieldwork material was produced between September 1992 and June 1994. All the informants were shepherds.

[1570] Refers to when the person was "assaulted by demons", if indicated.

[1571] Refers to where my informant encountered this case.

CHQ 57	1993	Antsirabe district	Young married woman with one child
CHQ 64	1992	Antanifotsy	Man
CHQ 68		Betafo	Young man
CHQ 69	1991		91 year old man
CHQ 79		In a *toby*	
CHQ 81	1992	Ambohimahazo	Young man
CHQ 84		Antanifotsy	Woman
CHQ 84		Antanifotsy	Man about 50 years old
CHQ 84	1992?	Antsirabe district	Woman, student
CHQ 101	1984–1986	Antananarivo	Man
CHQ 104			Old man
CHQ 110	1982	Ambohimahazo	Man, unmarried student
CHQ 112			
CHQ 117	1982		Woman
CHQ 133		In a ceremony of turning the corpse[1572]	Pregnant woman
CHQ 135	1992	At a church festival[1573]	Man
CHQ 142			A boy less than 12 years
CHQ 145	1991	Betafo district	Man
CHQ 156	1983		Young woman
CHQ 161			20 year old woman, student
CHQ 166	1983	Antananarivo	Man
CHQ 167	1987	Ambatolampy	Young woman

[1572] Mal: *famadihana*.
[1573] Mal: *Isan-telo volana*.

388 FIELD MATERIAL

C. Questionnaires[1574]

C.1 From shepherds[1575]

Identification[1576]	Man/ Woman	Theology class/ Women's class	Year of study[1577]
QS 2	W	W	4
QS 3	M	T	4
QS 6	M	T	2
QS 12	W	W	2
QS 21	M	T	4
QS 41	M	T	4
QS 54	M	T	2
QS 57	M	T	2
QS 64	M	T	1
QS 68	M	T	2
QS 69	M	T	3
QS 76	M	T	1
QS 79	M	T	4
QS 81	M	T	1
QS 84	M	T	2
QS 87	M	T	2
QS 88	W	W	4
QS 97	M	T	2
QS 100	M	T	1
QS 101	M	T	2
QS 103	M	T	3
QS 104	M	T	2
QS 105	M	T	4
QS 110	M	T	4
QS 112	M	T	1
QS 114	M	T	1
QS 117	M	T	4
QS 125	M	T	4

[1574] These questionnaires with open-ended questions (see Appendices 1, 2), which resemble structured interviews, were distributed to students at the STPL Atsimoniavoko. The period of this fieldwork was between 1992 and 1994. The contributions are in writing and they vary in length from 1 to 5 pages.

[1575] I have not distinguished the novices (*mpiomana*) from the shepherds in this material since the novices are in the middle of formation and thus updated on the "theology" of the revival movement. What they lack is experience. There are 7 novices in the QS-material.

[1576] QS = Questionnaire from a shepherd.

[1577] Total length of the study at the seminary was four years. I mark which year of study the student attended at the time of the interview (i.e. 4 = he/she is in his last year of study).

FIELD MATERIAL

QS 127	W	T	4
QS 130	M	T	1
QS 133	W	W	4
QS 135	W	W	2
QS 142	M	T	4
QS 144	W	W	4
QS 145	W	W	3
QS 150	W	W	1
QS 153	M	T	2
QS 156	M	T	1
QS 160	W	W	4
QS 161	W	W	4
QS 163	M	T	3
QS 166	W	W	2
QS 167	W	W	4
QS 181		T	4

C.2 From non-shepherds

Identification[1578]	Man/ Woman	Theology class/ Women's class	Year of study
QN 7	M	T	1
QN 11	M	T	1
QN 27	M	T	1
QN 38	M	T	1
QN 60	M	T	4
QN 62	M	T	4
QN 72	M	T	3
QN 78	M	T	3
QN 82	M	T	4
QN 103	M	T	1
QN 108	M	T	4
QN 109	M	T	2
QN 111	M	T	1
QN 113	M	T	3
QN 116	M	T	1
QN 119	M	T	2
QN 121	M	T	1
QN 124	M	T	2
QN 131	W	W	3
QN 136	M	T	2
QN 138	W	W	3
QN 139	M	T	4
QN 143	M	T	1
QN 147	W	W	3

[1578] QN = Questionnaire from a non-shepherd.

| QN 151 | W | W | 1 |
| QN 162 | W | W | 4 |

D. Healing services:

STPL Atsimoniavoko	08 November 1992
Ambohimahazo *toby*	08 March 1993
Ambohimahazo *toby*	15 March 1993
Ivohibe, Antaolanomby	21 March 1993
Ambohimahazo *toby*	22 March 1993
Antananarivo, Log 238, 67 Ha[1579]	07 April 1993
67 Ha-church[1580]	10 April 1993
Ambohimahazo *toby*	10 May 1993
Ambohimahazo *toby*	24 May 1993
Ambohimahazo *toby*	02 August 1993
Ambohimahazo *toby*	23 August 1993
Isan-taona[1581] Loharano	09 September 1993
Ambohimahazo *toby*	13 September 1993
Ambohimahazo *toby*	04 October 1993
Ambohimahazo *toby*	29 November 1993
Ambohimahazo *toby*	06 December 1993
Antananarivo, Log 238, 67 Ha	30 December 1993
Ambohimahazo *toby*	03 January 1994
STPL Atsimoniavoko	10 April 1994
Ambohimahazo *toby*	06 June 1994
Ambohimahazo *toby*	14 June 1998
Ambohimahazo *toby*	16 June 1998
Ambohimahazo *toby*	17 June 1998
Ambohimahazo *toby*	18 June 1998
Ambohimahazo *toby*	25 June 1998
Antananarivo, Log 238, 67 Ha	01 July 1998
Antananarivo, Log 238, 67 Ha	02 July 1998

[1579] This refers to the house where *Mama* Nenilava used to live and where there were healing services regularly. Log 238, 67 Ha refers to the apartment number (Logement 238) and the section in the city (67 hectare).

[1580] This refers to the main Lutheran church in this section of Antananarivo called "67 hectares".

[1581] This refers to the annual church meeting for the Avaratrimania church synod of FLM.

FIELD MATERIAL

E. Observation material[1582]

Identification	Date	Place	Event
O 340	1992–1994	Antsirabe Antananarivo	Diverse observations. Short conversations.
O 341	September 1993	Ambohimahazo	Visiting the patients at the *toby*
O 342	June–July 1998	Antsirabe. Antananarivo	Diverse observations. Short conversations.
O 343	19 June 1998	Ambohimahazo	Consecration of shepherds
O 344	June 1998	Vatotsara	Visit at the Vatotsara *toby*

F. Information in letters etc.

Identification	Date	Sender	Subject
L 210	09 May 2001	Pastor/toby-leader	The life in a *toby*
L 322	08 March 2000 18 May 2000	Shepherd leader	Statutes, liturgy Statutes
L 335	01 February 1996	Norvegian missionary	Statistics on the revival movement
L 336	07 November 1994	Shepherd	Exorcism and people "assaulted by demons"
L 337	30 August 2001	Rakotomaro Jean-Baptiste (General secretary FLM) and Rabenorolahy Benjamin (President FLM)	Diverse themes on the *Fifohazana* (an open meeting at the NMS-building in Stavanger)
Radio	31 May 1994	Malagasy radio (Radio Coreille)	The story of a young woman who became a spirit-medium

---

[1582] This material exists in notes, written shortly after the observation/incident.

Bibliography

A.M.M.T. 1999A. "Ny devoly sy ny asany ary ny fandroahana azy." *Ny Mpamangy*. Taona 117, Laharana 1412, Aogisitra, 5–8.
———. 1999S. "Ny devoly sy ny asany ary ny fandroahana azy." *Ny Mpamangy*. Taona 117, Laharana 1413, Septambra, 7–10.
Abijole, Bayo. 1988. "St. Paul's Concept of Principalities and Powers in African Context." *Africa Theological Journal* 17, no. 2, 118–129.
Abinal and Malzac. 1930. *Dictionnaire Malgache-Français*. Quatrième édition. Tananarive: Imprimerie de la Mission Catholique.
Alasuutari, Pertti. 1996. *Researching Culture. Qualitative Method and Cultural Studies*. London, Thousand Oaks, New Dehli: SAGE Publications.
Althabe, Gérard. 1984. "Schema pour une Anthropologie de la Vallée Antemoro de la Mananano." In *Ny Razana tsy mba maty. Cultures Traditionelles Malgaches*, ed. Jean-Pierre Domenichini, Jean Poirier and Daniel Raherisoanjato, 143–204. Antananarivo: Editions de la Librairie de Madagascar.
Andrianjafy, Michel. 1985. *Firy no efa nifanena tamin'ny mpamosavy*: Fo. Fi. Pa.
Ankaramalaza, Ny Komity Lehibe. 1997. *Fivorian'ny Mpiandry sy ny Mpiomana. Fanontaniana-Valiny*: Fifohazana Tobilehibe Ankaramalaza.
Ankaramalaza, Tobilehibe. Undated. *Tantara sy fijoroana ho vavolombelona. Jobily faha-50 taona Tobilehibe Ankaramalaza*. Antananarivo: Edisiona FLL, TPFLM.
Appiah-Kubi, Kofi. 1981. *Man Cures, God heals. Religion and Medical Practice among the Akans of Ghana*. Totova, NJ: Allanheld, Osmun.
Austnaberg, Hans. 1996. "Fifohazana. Skisse av ei aktuell rørsle i madagassisk kyrkjeliv." *Tidsskrift for Teologi og Kirke*, Vol. 50, no. 2, 131–143.
———. 1997. "Evangelium og kultur i madagassisk erfaring. Eit autentisk vitnemål om frigjering i evangeliet." *Norsk Tidsskrift for Misjon*, Vol 51, no. 3, 139–155.
Barrett, David B. 1968. *Schism and Renewal in Africa. An analysis of six thousand contemporary religious movements*. Nairobi, Addis Ababa, Lusaka: Oxford University Press.
Bassler, Jouette M. 1992. "God in the NT." In *The Anchor Bible Dictionary*, ed. David Noel Freedman, 1, 1049–1055. New York, London, Toronto, Sydney, Auckland: Doubleday.
Bauckham, Richard J. 1983. *Jude, 2 Peter*. Vol. 1 Word Biblical Commentary, ed. David A. Hubbard and Glenn W. Barker. Waco: Word Books.
Berentsen, Jan-Martin, Tormod Engelsviken and Knud Jørgensen (red). 1994. *Missiologi i dag*. Oslo: Universitetsforlaget.

BIBLIOGRAPHY

Birkeli, Emil. 1944. *Forelesninger over Madagassisk Religion*. Stavanger.

Bloch, Maurice. 1971. *Placing the Dead. Tombs, Ancestral Villages, and Kinship Organization in Madagascar*. London: Seminar Press.

———. 1986. *From Blessing to Violence. History and Ideology in the Circumcision Ritual of the Merina of Madagascar*, ed. Cambridge studies in social anthropology. Cambridge, London, New York, New Rochelle, Melbourne, Sydney: Cambridge University Press.

———. 1994. "The Slaves, the King, and Mary in the Slums of Antananarivo." In *Shamanism, history, and the state*, 133–145. Ann Arbor: Univ of Michigan Pr.

Botofotsy, Georges. Undated. *Ny Fifohazana ao Ankaramalaza*: Unpublished. Misjonsselskapets Arkiv: Madagascar AVD, Boks nr. 58, Legg nr.3.

Bruce, F. F. 1964. *The Epistle to the Hebrews*. Vol. 1. The New International Commentary on the New Testament, ed. F. F. Bruce. Grand Rapids: William B. Eerdmans Publishing Company.

———. 1984. *The Epistles to the Colossians, to Philemon and to the Ephesians*. Vol. 1. The New International Commentary on the New Testament, ed. F. F. Bruce. Grand Rapids: William B. Eerdmans Publishing Company.

Bruknapp, Bjørg. 1979. "Ankaramalazavekkelsen og vekkelsene i dag." A paper delivered at the annual missionary meeting, Antsirabe, Madagascar.

Brunstad, Paul Otto. 1998. *Ungdom og livstolkning. En studie av unge menneskers tro og fremtidsforventninger*. KIFO perspektiv; nr 3. Trondheim: Tapir.

Cabanes, R. 1972. "Cultes de possession dans la plaine de Tananarive." *Cahiers du Centre d'Etudes des Coutumes, Université de Madagascar, Antananarivo* IX, 33–66.

Chapus, G.S. and Bøthun. 1951. *Au souffle de L'Esprit. La vie consacrée du pasteur Daniel Rakotozandry et l'Historique du Réveil de Farihimena*. Tananarive: Imprimerie Luthérienne.

Childs, Brevard S. 1992. *Biblical Theology of the Old and New Testaments. Theological Reflections on the Christian Bible*. London: SCM Press Ltd.

Cover, Robin C. 1992. "Sin, sinners." In *The Anchor Bible Dictionary*, ed. David Noel Freedman, VI, 31–47. New York, London, Toronto, Sydney, Auckland: Doubleday.

Dahl, Øyvind. 1993. "Malagasy Meanings. An interpretive approach to Intercultural Communication in Madagascar." School for Mission and Theology.

———. 1999. *Meanings in Madagascar. Cases of Intercultural Communication*. 1 vols. Westport, London: Bergin & Garvey.

Daneel, M.L. 1987. *Quest for belonging. Introduction to a study of African Independent Churches*. Gweru, Zimbabwe: Mambo Press.

———. 1990. "Exorcism as a means of combating wizardry: liberation or enslavement?" *Missionalia* 18, no. 1, 220–247.

Danielli, Mary. 1947. "The witches of Madagascar; A Theory of the Function of Witches and of their Organisation Based on Observations of an Existing Cult." *Folk-Lore*. Volume LVIII, June, 261–276.

Dubourdieu-Jacquier, Lucile. 1996. "Représentation de l'esclavage et conversion: un aspect du mouvement du réveil à Madagascar." *Cahiers Sciences Humaines* 32, no. 3, 597–610.

———. 1999. *Soatanàna, une Nouvelle Jérusalem en pays betsileo (Madagascar). Mise en espace d'un nouvel ordre politique et religieux*. Stavanger: Arkiv NMS.

BIBLIOGRAPHY 395

Dunn, James D. G. and Graham H. Twelftree. 1980. "Demon-Possession and Exorcism in The New Testament." *Churchman: a quarterly Journal of Anglican Theology* 94, no. 3, 210–225.

Edwards, Felicity S. 1989. "Amafufunyana Spirit Possession: Treatment and Interpretation." In *Afro-Christian Religion and Healing in South Africa*, ed. G. Oosthuizen, 207–225.

Ejizu, Christopher I. 1991. "Cosmological perspective on Exorcism and prayer-healing in contemporary Nigeria." *Mission Studies* 8, no. 2, 165–176.

Engelsviken, Tormod. 1978. *Besettelse og åndsutdrivelse i Bibelen, historien og vår egen tid*. Oslo: Lunde forlag i samarbeid med Credo forlag.

Estrade, Jean-Marie. 1985. *Une culte de possession à Madagascar: le tromba*. Paris: Editions L'Harmattan.

Ferdinando, Keith. 1999. *The Triumph of Christ in African Perspective. A Study of Demonology and Redemption in the African Context*. Paternoster Biblical and Theological Monographs. Carlisle: Paternoster Press.

Ferguson, Everett. 1984. *Demonology of the Early Christian World*. Vol. 1. Symposium Series. New York and Toronto: The Edwin Mellen press.

Fiangonana Loterana Malagasy. 1984. *Ny Lalam-panorenana sy ny Fitsipika ary ny Toro-hevitra*. Antananarivo: Trano Printy Fiangonana Loterana Malagasy.

———. 2001. *Lalam-panorenana sy Fitsipika ary Toro-hevitra*. Antananarivo: T. P. F. L. M.

Fifohazana FFPM. 1980. *Fitsipika (statut) itondrana ny fifohazana ao amin'ny FFPM*. Antsirabe.

Fifohazana miray ao amin'ny FFPM. 2000. *Fitsipika anaty. Fandaharam-pampianarana ho an'ny mpiomana ho mpiandry*, ed. Soatanana-Manolotrony-Ankaramalaza-Farihimena: TPFLM.

Fihirana. 1982. Fiombonana'ny Fiangonana Protestanta eto Madagasikara (F.F.P.M.). Ed. fahatelo. Antananarivo.

Fikambanana Toby Lehibe Ankaramalaza, Birao Foibe. 1990. "Volavolam-pitsipika anaty. Tananan'ny Toby Lehibe Ankaramalaza." A paper delivered at the Fivorian'ny Komity Foibe Mpanorina, Ambohibao, Antananarivo, 30 Janoary–01 Febroary.

FJKM, Sampana Fifohazana. 1997. *Boky fampianarana. Fitsipika fototra. Fitsipika anatiny*. Edisiona fahatelo, Antananarivo: T.P.F.L.M.

Foerster, Werner. 1979a. "δαίμων." In *Theological Dictionary of the New Testament*, ed. Gerhard Kittel, II, 1–20. Grand Rapids: Wm. B. Eerdmans Publishing Company.

———. 1979b. "διάβολος." In *Theological Dictionary of the New Testament*, ed. Gerhard Kittel, II, 71–73, 75–81. Grand Rapids: Wm. B. Eerdmans Publishing Company.

Fossåskaret, Erik, Otto Laurits Fuglestad and Tor Halfdan Aase. 1997. *Metodisk Feltarbeid. Produksjon og tolking av kvalitative data*. Oslo: Universitetsforlaget.

Fridrichsen, Anton. 1929. "Jesu kamp mot de urene ånder." *Svensk Teologisk Kvartalskrift* 5, no. 4, 299–314.

Gonia, James. 1993. "Mpiandry. The healing shepherds of Madagascar." *Areopagus*, 24–26.

Graeber, David. 1997. "Painful Memories." *Journal of Religion in Africa*, Vol 27, Fasc. 4, November, 374–400.

BIBLIOGRAPHY

Hafner, H. 1989. "Schöpfung." In *Das Grosse Bibellexikon*, ed. Dr. H. Burkhardt, 3, 1384–1387. Wuppertal und Zürich: R. Brockhaus Verlag.

Hamilton, Victor P. 1992. "Satan." In *The Anchor Bible Dictionary*, ed. David Noel Freedman, V, 985–989. New York, London, Toronto, Sydney, Auckland: Doubleday.

Hammersley, Martyn and Paul Atkinson. 1995. *Ethnography: Principles in Practice*. 2nd ed. London: Routledge.

Hardyman, Marjorie. 1971. "The church and sorcery in Madagascar." In *African Initiatives in Religion*, ed. by D.B. Barrett, 208–221. Nairobi: East African Publishing House.

Haus, Grete. 2000. ""I Jesu Kristi navn befaler jeg ...". En analyse av gassiske hyrders tolkning av fenomenene "besettelse" og "utdrivelse"." Hovedfagsoppgave, Det Teologiske Menighetsfakultetet, Oslo.

Hegstad, Harald. 2002. "Hvordan er *empiriens* status og funksjon innenfor aktuell teologi?" A paper delivered at a seminar on Grunnlagsproblemer og forskningshverdag. Hvor viktig er debatten om metodespørsmål i hverdagen? Oslo, 12th November.

Hiebert, Paul G. 1985. *Anthropological Insights for Missionaries*. Grand Rapids, Michigan: Baker Book House.

———. 1994. *Anthropological Reflections on Missiological Issues*. Grand Rapids, Michigan: Baker Books.

———. 2000. "Spiritual Warfare and Worldview." *Evangelical Review of Theology* 24, no. 3, 240–256.

Hill, Harriet. 1996. "Witchcraft and the Gospel: Insights from Africa." *Missiology: An International Review*. Vol. 24, no.3, 323–344.

Holme, Idar Magne and Bernt Krohn Solvang. 1991. *Metodevalg og metodebruk*: Tano.

Holy Bible. Revised Standard Version. 1952. Reference Edition. Thomas Nelson & Sons. New York

Hovland, Halvor. Undated. *Misjon og vekkelse. Et bidrag til belysning av Soatananabevegelsens historie med særlig henblikk på de forhold som førte til skisma mellom misjon og kirke*: Unpublished manuscript.

Hummelvoll, Jan Kåre and António Barbosa da Silva. 1998. "The Use of the Qualitative Reseach Interview to Uncover the Essence of Community Psychiatric Nursing. Methodological Reflections." *Journal of Holistic Nursing* 16, no. 4, December, 453–478.

Hwa, Yung. 2000. "Some Issues in a Systematic Theology That Takes Seriously the Demonic." A paper delivered at the Deliver Us from Evil Consultation, Nairobi.

Igenoza, Andrew Olu. 1985. "African Weltanschauung and exorcism: the quest for the contextualization of the kerygma." *Africa Theological Journal* 14, no. 3, 179–193.

———. 1986. "Christian Theology and the Belief in Evil Spirits: An African Perspective." *Scottish Bulletin of Evangelical Theology* 4, Spring, 39–48.

———. 1999. "Medicine And Healing In African Christianity: A Biblical Critique." *AFER* 41, no. 2&3, 145–163.

Jaovelo-Dzao, Robert. 1992. "Ireo harem-panahy fonosin'ny kolontsaina sy ny lovantsofina (Zanahary, Sampy, Razana, Fivavahana silamo)." In *I Madagasikara sy ny Fivavahana Kristianina. Tantara iraisan'ny Fiangonana*, 67–94. Antananarivo: Editions Ambozontany.

BIBLIOGRAPHY 397

Johnson, Johs. 1914. *Det første Hundredaar av Madagaskars Kirkehistorie*. Stavanger: Det Norske Misjonsselskaps Boktrykkeri.

Kitshoff, M C. *Exorcism as Healing Ministry in the African Independent/Indigenous Churches*. http://www.uzulu.ac.za/the/bibs/sys-kit3, 1997. Accessed 17 June 1997. Website.

Kraft, Charles H. 1996. *Anthropology for Christian Witness*. Maryknoll, New York: Orbis Books.

Kratz, Reinhard G. and Herman Spieckermann. 1999. "Schöpfung, Altes Testament." In *Theologische Realenzyclopädie*, XXX, 258–283. Berlin, New York: Walter de Gruyter.

Krogseth, Otto. 1991. "Kulturanalyse – forholdet mellom det fremmede og det fortrolige." A paper delivered at a seminar: Veiledningsseminar for forskerrekrutter i teologi/kristendomskunnskap, Aurland, Bergen.

Kuemmerlin-McLean, Joanne K. 1992. "Demons, Old Testament." In *The Anchor Bible Dictionary*, ed. David Noel Freedman, 2, 138–140. New York, London, Toronto, Sydney, Auckland: Doubleday.

Kvale, Steinar. 1992. "The Qualitative Research Interview. A Phenomenological and a Hermeneutical Mode of Understanding." *Journal of Phenomenological Psychology* 14, no. 2, 171–196.

———. 1996. *InterViews. An Introduction to Qualitative Research Interviewing*. Thousand Oaks, London, New Dehli: SAGE Publications.

Ladd, George Eldon. 1975. *A Theology of the New Testament*. Vol. 1. Second ed. Grand Rapids: William B. Eerdmans Publishing Company.

Larson, Pier M. 1997. "A Cultural Politics of Bedchamber Construction and Progressive Dining in Antananarivo: ritual inversions during the Fandroana of 1817." *Journal of Religion in Africa*. Vol 27, no. 3, 239–269.

Laugerud, Tore. 1993. "Okkultismen og kirken. Kan vi lære noe av den afrikanske erfaring?" *Norsk Tidsskrift for Misjon*, Vol. 47, no. 2, 61–79.

Lie, Bjørn Sverre. 1981. "Misjonærene og vekkelsesbevegelsene." Oppgave på Praktikum, Menighetsfakultetet, Oslo.

Marshall, I. Howard. 1986. *The Gospel of Luke*. Vol. 1. Reprinted ed. The New International Greek Testament Commentary, ed. I. Howard Marshall and W. Ward Gasque. Grand Rapids: William B. Eerdmans Publishing Company.

McAlpine, Thomas H. 1991. *Facing the Powers. What are the Options?* Innovations in Mission. Monrovia: Marc.

Meling, G. Andreas. 1972. "Nenilava. En profetinne for sitt folk." In *Jeg glemmer dem aldri*, 51–70. Oslo: Lutherstiftelsen/Sambåndet.

Meyer, Birgit. 1992. "'If you are a Devil, you are a witch and if you are a witch, you are a Devil.' The integration of 'pagan' ideas into the conceptual universe of Ewe christians in southeastern Ghana." *Journal of Religion in Africa* 22, no. 2, 98–132.

Moreau, A. Scott. 1990. *The World of the Spirits. A Biblical Study in the African Context*. Nairobi, Kenya: Evangel Publishing House.

Mugabe, Henry J. 1999. "Salvation from an African Perspective." *Evangelical Review of Theology* 23, no. 3, 238–247.

Nel, P.J. 1987. "The Conception of Evil and Satan in Jewish Traditions in the Pre-Christian Period." In *Like a Roaring Lion. Essays on the Bible, the Church and*

Demonic Powers, 1; 1–21. Pretoria: C.B. Powell Bible Center, University of South Africa.

Newsom, Carol A. 1992. "Angels, Old Testament." In *The Anchor Bible Dictionary*, ed. David Noel Freedman, I, 248–253. New York, London, Toronto, Sydney, Auckland: Doubleday.

Nielssen, Hilde. 1995. "Manao tromba – en studie av åndekulten tromba blant betsimisaraka på Øst Madagaskar." Hovedfag, Universitetet i Bergen.

Nishioka, Yoshiyuki Billy. 1998. "Worldview Methodology in Mission Theology: A Comparison between Kraft's and Hiebert's Approaches." *Missiology: An International Review*. Vol XXVI, no. 4, 455–476.

Nyamiti, Dr. C. 1995. "The Problem of Evil in African Traditional Cultures and Today's African Inculturation and Liberation." *African Christian Studies*, no. 1, 39–75.

O'Brian, P.T. 1992. "Principalities and Powers: Opponents of the Church." *Evangelical Review of Theology*, no. 4, 353–384.

Olson, Duane A. 1970. *The Malagasy Ancestral Cult*: Unpublished paper.

Oosthuizen, George C. 1988. "Southern African Independent Churches Respond to Demonic Powers." *Missiology: An International Review* 16, no. 1, 414–433.

Pitaka, Daniel. 1999. "Ny fampianaran'i Mama Volahavana Germaine Nenilava ny amin'ny fitoriana ny tenin'Andriamanitra, ny asa sy fampaherezana ary ny fitaizana marary tao amin'ny toby Ankaramalaza." Maîtrise en theologie, Sekoly Ambony Loterana momba ny Teolojia.

Pobee, John S. and Gabriel Ositelu II. 1998. *African Initiatives in Christianity. The growth, gifts and diversities of indegenous African churches—a challenge to the ecumenical movement*. Risk Book Series. Geneva: WCC Publications.

Pretorius, H. L. et.al. 1987. *Reflecting on Mission in the African Context*. Bloemfontein: Pro Christian Publications.

Rabarihoela, Bruno. 1999. *Ny teny fito fanendrena ny asa. Jona 1974. Fanehoampanokanana an'i Mama Volahavana Germaine Nenilava, Raiamandreny Tobilehibe Ankaramalaza*. Antananarivo: Edisiona Tobilehibe Ankaramalaza.

Rabehatonina, James. 1991. *Tantaran'ny Fifohazana eto Madagasikara*. Antananarivo: Trano Printy FJKM.

Rabenandrasana. 1998. "Mama Volahavana Germaine." *Ny Mpamangy*, Marsa, 14–20.

Raison-Jourde, Françoise. 1991. *Bible et pouvoir à Madagascar au XIXe siècle. Invention d'une identité chrétienne et construction de l'État (1780–1880)*. Paris: Éditions Karthala.

Rajaonarison, Elie and Malanjaona Manoelina Rakotomalala. 1987. "Anthropologie Medicale et Developpement à Madagascar." A paper delivered at the Seminaire National de Reflexion sur la Politique et la Pratique de la Recherche en Sciences Sociales, Antananarivo, 23–28 février.

Rajemisa-Raolison, Régis. 1985. *Rakibolana malagasy*. Fianarantsoa: Ambozontany.

Rajoelisoa, Armandin. 1977–80. "Etude de quelques réveils à Madagascar." Mémoire de Maîtrise, Université des Sciences Humaines de Strasbourg.

Rajosefa, Danielson. Undated. *Fifohazam-panahy eto Madagasikara*: unpublished manuscript. Misjonsselskapets Arkiv, Madagascar AVD, Boks nr.56, Legg nr.2.

Rakotomalala, Malanjaona, Sophie Blanchy and Françoise Raison-Jourde. 2001. *Madagascar: Les Ancêtres au Quotidien. Usages sociaux du religieux sur les Hautes-Terres Malgaches*. Vol. 1. Paris: l'Harmattan.

BIBLIOGRAPHY 399

Rakotomamonjy. 1993. *Ny tantaran'ny Fifohazana Farihimena.* Antananarivo: TPFLM.
Rakotonaivo, François. 1997. *Ny Riba Malagasy eran'ny Nosy.* Fianarantsoa: Ambozontany.
Rakotondrasoa, Ralay Nakely Modeste. 1996. "Tromba and the lordship of Christ. A systematic Missiological Study of Christianity Encountering the "Tromba" Phenomenon in the Region of Morondava." Thesis [Master of Philosophy in Theology], School of Mission and Theology.
Rakotovao, Joseph. 1993. "Ny fombam-pisoronana merina sy ny litorjia Loterana momba ny fanasan'ny Tompo miatrika ny teolojian'i Paoly." Maîtrise en Théologie, Sekoly Ambony Loterana momba ny Teolojia, Ivory avaratra.
Ralisoa, Hélène. 1991. *Fahatsiarovana ny jobily faha-40 taonan'ny Fifohazana eto Farihimena. Taona: 1946–1986.* Antananarivo: TPFLM.
Ramambason, Laurent W. 1999. *Missiology: Its Subject-Matter and Method. A Study of Mission-Doers in Madagascar.* Frankfurt am-Main: Peter Lang.
Ramamonjisoa, Suzy. 1997. "Considérations sur quelques pratiques cultuelles. Guérison, possession, ..., dans les nouveaux groupes religieux à Madagascar." In *Madagascar, Eglises Instituées et Nouveax Groupements Religieux,* 67–82. Antananarivo: Collections ISTA No 7, Institut Catholique de Madagascar.
Ramampiandra, Solonjatovo Augustin. 1986. *Nenilava. Volahavana Germaine.* Antananarivo: T.P.F.L.M.
Randriakoto, Anselme William. 1982. "Deux exemples des initiatives des malgaches du Vakinankaratra: Le Toby d'Andemaka (1933–1960) et le Toby Ambohimahazo (1949–1960)." C.E. no 163-H, niv. D, Université d'Antananarivo.
Randriamalala, Augustin. 1998. "Mama Volahavana Germaine Nenilava." Baccalauréat en Theologie, STPL Atsimoniavoko.
Randrianarivelo, Joseph. 2000. "The Revival Movement in Ankaramalaza under the leadership of the priestess and prophetess Nenilava, from 1941 to 1998. Its rise and its relation to the Malagasy Lutheran Church." Master of Philosophy, School of Mission and Theology.
Randrianarivony. 1942. *Filazana tsotsotra momba ny fifohazana any Vangaindrano nanomboka tamin'ny 9 Juin 1938*: Handwritten manuscript.
Randriantsitohaina, Patrice Emmanuel. 1992. *Doany: Trafonomby sy Nanohazana. Fasana: Tsaramody.* Antsirabe: STPL Atsimnoniavoko. Fikarohana Fivavahana tera-tany tao Ambohibary Sambaina, Antsirabe.
Randriatsarafara, Jean Gaston. 1998. *Ny Fifohazana.* Handwritten manuscript. Antsirabe.
Rasolondraibe, Péri. 1994. *Fampianarana Mpiomana ho Mpiandry.* Antananarivo: Unpublished.
———. 1989. "Healing ministry in Madagascar." *Word & World: Theology for Christian Ministry* 9, no. 4, 344–350.
Ratongavao, Charles Raymond, et.al. 1997. "Madagascar, Eglises Instituées et Nouveax Groupements Religieux." A paper delivered at the Seminaire interdisciplinaire, Ambatoroka, Antananarivo.
Reese, David George. 1992. "Demons, New Testament." In *The Anchor Bible Dictionary*, ed. David Noel Freedman, II, 140–142. New York, London, Toronto, Sydney, Auckland: Doubleday.
Ruud, Jørgen. 1970. *Taboo, a Study of Malagasy Customs and Beliefs.* 2nd ed. Oslo /Tananarive: Oslo University Press/TPL.

Sangboken. Syng for Herren. 1983. 1st ed., ed. Det Norske Misjonsselskap, Det norske lutherske Indremisjonsselskap, Det Vestlandske Indremisjonsforbund and Norsk Luthersk Misjonssamband. Oslo: Lunde Forlag og Bokhandel A.S

Scherer, James A. 1987. "Missiology as a Discipline and What It Includes." *Missiology: An International Review* 15, no. 4, 507–522.

Scullion, John J. 1992. "God in the OT." In *The Anchor Bible Dictionary*, ed. David Noel Freedman, 1, 1041–1048. New York, London, Toronto, Sydney, Auckland: Doubleday.

Sharp, Lesley A. 1990. "Possessed and dispossessed youth: spirit possession of school children in northwest Madagascar." *Culture, Medicine and Psychiatry* 14, 339–364.

———. 1993. "The Possessed and the Dispossessed. Spirits, Identity, and Power in a Madagascar Migrant Town." Doctoral dissertation, University of California Press.

———. 1994. "Exorcists, psychiatrists, and the problems of possession in northwest Madagascar." *Social science and medicine: an international journal* 38, no. 4, 525–542.

Shorter, Aylward. 1985. *Jesus and the Witchdoctor. An Approach to Healing and Wholeness.* London, New York: Orbis Books.

Simensen, Jarle. 1996. "Kristendommen i Afrika. Forskningsutvikling og forskningsoppgaver." *Norsk Tidsskrift for Misjon*, Vol. 50, no. 2–3, 157–166.

Skarsaune, Oscar. 1997. "Besettelse og demonutdrivelse i den oldkirkelige og nytestamentlige litteratur." *Norsk Tidsskrift for Misjon*, Vol. 51, no. 3, 157–171.

Skeie, Karina H. 1994. "Religious and Cultural Identity in Times of Change. Beliefs and Rituals Around Death Among the Merina of Madagascar 1866–1895." Hovedfag, Oslo University.

Spradley, James P. 1979. *The Ethnographic Interview.* New York: Holt, Rinehart and Winston.

Stene Dehlin, Harald. 1985. *Madagaskar i sikte.* Oslo: Luther Forlag.

Stieglitz, Gilbert L. 1991. "Breaking Satanic Bondage." Doctor of Ministry, Biola University.

Sundkler, Bengt G. M. 1961. *Bantu Prophets in South Africa.* Second ed. London, New York, Toronto: Oxford University Press.

Syvertsen, Aage J. 1983. "Besettelse og demonutdrivelse i den gassisk lutherske kirke. Foredrag holdt på misjonærmøtet Antsirabe, 1.3.1982." *Norsk Tidsskrift for Misjon*, Vol. 37, no. 3, 161–181.

Saayman, Willem. 1992. "Concepts of sickness and health in intercultural communication in South Africa. A semiotic approach." *Journal for the Study of Religion* 5, no. 2, 31–46.

Taylor, Walter F. Jr. 1992. "NT view of Humanity." In *The Anchor Bible Dictionary*, ed. David Noel Freedman, III, 321–325. New York, London, Toronto, Sydney, Auckland: Doubleday.

Thatcher, Virginia S. and Alexander McQueen. 1980 Edition. *The New Webster Encyclopedic Dictionary of The English Language.* Chicago: Consolidated Book Publishers.

Thomas, John Christopher. 2000. "Spiritual Conflict in Biblical Perspective 1." A paper delivered at the Deliver Us From Evil Consultation, Nairobi.

BIBLIOGRAPHY

Thunem, A and Joela Rasamoela. 1972. "Ny tantaran'ny Fifohazana Soatanana." In *Ny tantaran'ny Fifohazana eto Madagasikara. Soatanana. Farihimena. Ankaramalaza*, 1–84. Tananarive: Trano Printy Loterana.

Tobilehibe, Ankaramalaza. 1997. *Ny fifohazana, ny toby, ny mpiandry, ny asa sy fampaherezana. Foto-pampianarana momba ny asan'ny mpiandry*. Edisiona faharoa: Fifohazana Tobilehibe Ankaramalaza.

Tobilehibe, efatra. 1995. *Fihaonamben'ny mpiandry sy ny mpiomana FFPM. Fehin-kevitra*. Antsirabe-Antananarivo: Tobilehibe Efatra: Soatanana-Manolotrony-Ankaramalaza-Farihimena. Sampana Fifohazana FJKM - Firaisan'ny Fifohazana Loterana.

TPFLM. 1998. *Ny Diary Malagasy*. Antananarivo: TPFLM.

Tsivoery, Zakaria. 1972/1991. "Ny tantaran'ny Fifohazana Ankaramalaza." In *Tantara sy Fijoroana ho Vavolombelona*, 1–65. Antananarivo: TPFLM.

Twelftree, Graham H. 1993. *Jesus the Exorcist. A Contribution to the Study of the Historical Jesus*. Vol. 54 Wissenschaftliche Untersuchungen zum Neuen Testament: 2. Reihe, ed. Martin Hengel and Otfried Hofius. Tübingen: J. C. B. Mohr.

Unidentified. Undated. *Foto-mpampianarana momba ny Asan'ny Mpiandry. Asa sy Fampaherezana*: Fifohazana Tobilehibe Ankaramalaza.

———. 1966(?). *Fitsipika Fitondrana ny Sampan'Asam-Piangonana atao hoe Ny Fifohazana*: Fiangonana Loterana Synoda Rezionaly Andrefana.

———. 1972. *Ny Fon-janak'olombelona*. Translated by Razanajohary, Professeur. 7th ed. Antananarivo: Trano Printy Loterana.

———. 1989. "Sünde." In *Das Grosse Bibellexikon*, ed. Dr. Helmut Burkhardt, 3, 1500–1502. Wuppertal und Zürich: R. Brockhaus Verlag.

van der Ven, Johannes A. 1993. *Practical theology: an empirical approach*. Kampen: Pharos.

Virkler, Henry A. and Mary B. Virkler. 1977. "Demonic Involvement in Human Life and Illness." *Journal of Psychology and Theology* 5, 95–102.

von Rad, Gerhard. 1979. "The OT view of Satan." In *Theological Dictionary of the New Testament*, ed. Gerhard Kittel, II, 73–75. Grand Rapids: Wm. B. Eerdmans Publishing Company.

Walls, Andrew F. 1996. "Introduction: African Christianity in the History of Religions." In *Christianity in Africa in the 1990s*, ed. Christopher Fyfe and Andrew Walls. Edinburgh: University of Edinburgh. Centre of African Studies.

Watson, Duane F. 1992. "Evil." In *The Anchor Bible Dictionary*, ed. David Noel Freedman, II, 678–679. New York, London, Toronto, Sydney, Auckland: Doubleday.

Yates, Roy. 1980. "The Powers of Evil in the New Testament." *The Evangelical Quarterly* 52, April–June, 97–111.

Yin, Robert K. 1994. *Case Study Research. Design and Methods*. Vol. 5. Applied Social Research Methods Series. Thousand Oaks, London, New Delhi: Sage Publications.

Østberg, Sissel. 1998. "Pakistani Children in Oslo: Islamic nurture in a Secular Context." Doctor of Philosophy, University of Warwick.

Aano, Kjetil. 1984. *Mellom kors og fedregrav. Portrett av Den gassisk lutherske kyrkja*. Oslo: Luther Forlag.

Aase, Tor Halfdan. 1997. "Tolking av kategorier. Observasjon, begrep og kategori." In *Metodisk Feltarbeid. Produksjon og tolking av kvalitative data*, 143–166. Oslo: Universitetsforlaget.

Index of Authors

A
Abijole, B.: 13, 29, 177, 186, 189
Abinal & Malzac.: 66, 68, 74, 88, 89, 152, 164, 193, 201
Alasuutari, P.: 15, 31
Althabe, G.: 27, 334
Andrianjafy, M.: 162
Appiah-Kubi, K.: 29, 168, 169, 292, 302, 303, 354
Austnaberg, H.: 28, 57, 306

B
Barrett, D.B.: 7, 9, 29
Bassler, J.M.: 176
Bauckham, R.J.: 177
Berentsen, J.-M., Engelsviken T. & Jørgensen K.: 29
Birkeli, E.: 152, 154
Bloch, M.: 29, 153, 156, 157
Botofotsy, G.: 50
Bruce, F. F.: 186, 188
Bruknapp, B.: 53
Brunstad, P.O.: 14, 16, 31

C
Cabanes, R.: 29, 156, 157
Chapus, G.S. & Bøthun.: 28, 44
Childs, B.S.: 34, 175, 176, 177, 178
Cover, R.C.: 176, 177

D
Dahl, Ø.: 16, 24, 26, 28, 34, 148, 150, 162, 163, 164
Daneel, M.L.: 10, 14, 29, 258, 269, 314
Danielli, M.: 162

Dubourdieu-Jacquier, L.: 3, 8, 28, 42
Dunn, J.D.G. & Twelftree G.H.: 29, 178, 180, 182, 185

E
Edwards, F.S.: 206
Ejizu, C.I.: 10
Engelsviken, T.: 206, 207
Estrade, J.-M.: 3, 27, 29, 152, 153, 155, 157, 159, 160, 171, 249, 341, 343, 355, 357

F
Ferdinando, K.: 336
Ferguson, E.: 29, 180, 181, 184, 187, 188, 189
Foerster, W.: 178, 179, 180, 182, 186
Fossåskaret, E., Fuglestad O.L. & Aase T.H..: 16, 22
Fridrichsen, A.: 188

G
Gonia, J.: 26, 121
Graeber, D.: 156, 161

H
Hafner, H.: 176
Hamilton, V.P.: 177, 179, 189
Hammersley, M. & Atkinson P.: 23
Hardyman, M.: 167, 233
Haus, G.: 5, 16, 26, 68, 87, 94, 195, 200, 213, 216, 220, 222, 227, 239, 263, 266, 272, 274, 275, 279, 281, 283, 287, 291, 300, 303, 304, 317,

321, 322, 325, 327, 341, 343, 345, 347, 349, 356, 358
Hegstad, H.: 14
Hiebert, P.G.: 5, 29, 33, 82, 147, 172, 173, 182, 183, 187, 189, 331
Hill, H.: 162
Holme, I.M. & Krohn Solvang B.: 15, 16
Hovland, H.: 7
Hummelvoll, J.K. & da Silva A.B..: 4, 15, 19, 22, 30, 332
Hwa, Y.: 29, 174, 177, 178, 179, 183, 186, 188

I

Igenoza, A.O.: 9, 10, 13, 29, 292, 308, 352

J

Jaovelo-Dzao, R.: 148, 150, 151
Johnson, J.: 58, 151, 154

K

Kitshoff, M C.: 10, 269, 314, 321
Kraft, C.H.: 29, 173
Kratz, R.G. & Spieckermann H.: 176
Krogseth, O.: 5
Kuemmerlin-McLean, J.K.: 180
Kvale, S.: 17, 23, 24, 30, 31, 36

L

Ladd, G.E.: 29, 177, 178, 179, 180, 181, 182, 183, 184, 185, 187, 189
Larson, P.M.: 154
Laugerud, T.: 297, 307
Lie, B.S.: 59, 61, 63, 65, 66, 67, 68, 72, 194, 224, 262, 280, 320, 325

M

Marshall, I.H.: 177
McAlpine, T.H.: 10
Meling, G.A.: 52, 53
Meyer, B.: 239, 249
Moreau, A.S.: 10, 186
Mugabe, H.J.: 292

N

Nel, P.J.: 179, 182, 183
Newsom, C.A.: 182
Nielssen, H.: 160, 161, 164, 166, 168
Nishioka, Y.B.: 33
Nyamiti, Dr.C.: 148

O

O'Brian, P.T.: 177, 183, 184
Olson, D.A.: 150
Oosthuizen, G.C.: 9, 10

P

Pitaka, D.: 26, 50, 116, 117, 119, 121, 123, 125, 136, 138, 194, 201, 214, 215, 246, 256, 285, 286, 287, 288, 296, 297, 318
Pobee, J.S. & Ositelu II G.: 4, 9
Pretorius, H.L. et.al.: 9

R

Rabarihoela, B.: 28
Rabehatonina, J: 42, 43, 44
Rabenandrasana.: 54, 55
Raison-Jourde, F.: 29, 149, 150, 151, 152, 153, 155
Rajaonarison, E. & Rakotomalala M.M.: 27, 165, 166, 168, 169, 301
Rajemisa-Raolison, R.: 207, 213
Rajoelisoa, A.: 28, 42, 44, 46, 47, 50, 57, 111, 199
Rajosefa, D.: 53
Rakotomalala, M., Blanchy S. & Raison-Jourde F.: 334, 341
Rakotomamonjy: 28
Rakotonaivo, F.: 151, 154
Rakotondrasoa, R.N.M.: 26, 306, 313
Rakotovao, J.: 152, 170
Ralisoa, H.: 295
Ramambason, L.W.: 1, 9, 28, 29, 44, 49, 54, 58, 63
Ramamonjisoa, S.: 148, 155, 156, 157, 160
Ramampiandra, S. A.: 28, 50
Randriakoto, A.W.: 54, 292, 293
Randriamalala, A.: 50

Index of Authors

Randrianarivelo, J.: 1, 26, 50, 54, 59, 62, 63, 64, 66, 67, 68, 72, 219, 267, 356
Randrianarivony: 43
Randriantsitohaina, P.E.: 170
Randriatsarafara, J.G.: 107
Rasolondraibe, P.: 1, 25, 26, 29, 59, 62, 100, 111, 116, 120, 138, 162, 163, 164, 166, 167, 168, 169, 171, 205, 233, 247, 274, 286, 289, 291, 292, 295, 307, 317, 354, 355
Ratongavao, C.R. et.al.: 317
Reese, D.G.: 180, 181, 185
Ruud, J.: 167, 170, 171

S

Scherer, J.A.: 5, 29
Scullion, J.J.: 175, 182
Sharp, LA.: 3, 27, 28, 98, 116, 121, 122, 124, 126, 128, 131, 135, 155, 157, 158, 159, 160, 161, 164, 166, 167, 168, 169, 170, 171, 206, 231, 234, 249, 292, 293, 307, 334, 341, 352, 356
Shorter, A.: 10, 353
Simensen, J.: 4, 5
Skarsaune, O.: 185
Skeie, K.H.: 29, 150, 153, 154, 155, 166
Spradley, J.P.: 5, 15, 18, 24
Stene Dehlin, H.: 128
Stieglitz, G.L.: 10

Sundkler, B.G.M.: 10, 267
Syvertsen, Aa.J.: 26, 105, 107, 122, 131, 141, 230, 249
Saayman, W.: 292, 308

T

Taylor, W.F.Jr.: 184
Thatcher, V.S. & McQueen A.: 151
Thomas, J.C.: 185
Thunem, A. & Rasamoela J.: 42
Tsivoery, Z.: 28, 49, 296, 297
Twelftree, G.H.: 185

V

van der Ven, J.A.: 16
Virkler, H.A. & Virkler M.B.: 215
von Rad, G.: 179

W

Walls, A.: 4
Watson, D.: 182

Y

Yates, R.: 178, 179, 180, 183, 184, 187
Yin, R.: 22

Ø

Østberg, S.: 5

Aa

Aano, K.: 35, 43
Aase, T.H.: 92

Index of Biblical References

Genesis
    1:1   176
    3   176, 275
    3:7–17   177
    3:17–18   203
    6:1–4   177

Exodus
    3:15   175
    20:3   175

1 Kings
    19:11–13   48

2 Kings
    5   270

Job
    1–2   78

Psalms
    46:5   266
    68:5   139
    84:11   110
    89:10   178
    104   176

Isaiah
    14:4–23   78
    27:1   182
    40:19–20   175
    41:9   265
    45:7   182
    45:14–25   176
    53:4   271
    59:16–19   178

Jeremiah
    1:10   349

Ezekiel
    28:1–19   78
    37:28   266

Daniel
    1:8–16   203

Amos
    4:13b   114

Zechariah
    3:4   265

Matthew
    4:24   185
    5:6   114
    7:11   184
    8:3   257, 318
    8:14–15   282
    8:15   318
    8:16   258
    8:28   180
    9   356
    9:1–8   356
    9:2   277
    9:32   185
    9:33–34   79
    10:16   243
    10:30   337

12	201, 203, 344	16:16–18	198
12:22	185	16:17–18	115, 356
12:22–29	185	16:18	257, 318
12:24–29	180	16:20	266
12:26	179		
12:28–29	181	Luke	
12:43–45	83, 85, 187, 193, 245, 344	4:1–12	185
		4:5–6	179
13:36–43	180	4:38–39	282
13:41	182	4:40	318
15:19	180	8:27	93
17	277	9:37–43	207
17:15	207, 277	10:10–21	111
17:15–18	185	10:18	78
17:18	125, 258, 277	11:20	257
18:18–20	98, 116, 117	13:6–9	110
25:41	180	13:11–13	283
26:41	245	15:5	184
26:53	182	15:10	182
28:18–20	270	15:22	265
28:20	139	22:3	183
		22:51	257

Mark

1:15	181	John	
1:23–26	180	1:12	316
1:24	180	3:19	184
1:25	258	5	203
2	203, 300, 372	8:31	61
5	200, 239	8:34	186
5:1–20	176	8:44	337
5:2	93	9	201, 311
5:24–34	358	9:1–3	310
5:28	284	9:2	310
5:34	318	12:31	179
6:5	318	14:12–17	98, 116
7:33	257	14:13	204
9	200	16:11	179
9:14–29	202, 207, 358	17:3	302
9:29	48	20:21	255
12:24	179	20:21–23	98, 116, 117, 192
14:36	187		
16:14–20	111, 116	Acts	
16:15–16	356	13:6–11	217
16:15–17	200	16	203, 222
16:15–18	99, 116	16:16	277
16:15–20	98, 116, 344, 364	16:31	192, 202
16:16	350	19:12	119

26:18	179	Philippians	
28:8	318	2:4–7	184
		3:2	266
Romans		3:13	61
1:18–3:20	184		
4:17	176	Colossians	
5:12	177	1:13	184
6:3–11	186	1:20	189
6:23	281	2:13	188
7:15–20	184	2:14	188
8	187	2:15	186, 188
8:28	280		
8:38–39	184	1 Timothy	
13	184	1:20	179
14:9	109	3:6	60
16:19–20	186	4:1	180
1 Corinthians		Hebrews	
2:8	183	2:14	188
7:31	184	12:1	322
10:20–21	180		
11	264	James	
11:7	264	1:14–15	263
15:24	186	1:22	201
		5:16	195
2 Corinthians			
4:4	179	1 Peter	
5:3	265	4:11	125
		5:8	266
Galatians		5:8–9	186
1:4	181		
5	187	1 John	
5:17	187	1:8–2:2	109
		3:8	116
Ephesians		3:10	187
1:21	79	4:1	60
2:2	79, 179	4:3	216
3:10	79	5:4	304
4:1–6	68		
4:11	68	Revelation	
4:27	179, 186, 304	3:18	265
5:13	221	7:15	265
6	263	10:1–7	182
6:11–12	178	12	178
6:11–13	186	12:7–9	182
6:12	79, 183, 200, 252	12:9–12	79
6:16	301	13	184

13:3 189
16:13–14 180
19:8 265
19:14 182
20:9–10 179

Bible & Theology in Africa

The twentieth century made sub-Saharan Africa a Christian continent. This formidable church growth is reflected in a wide range of attempts at contextualizing Christian theology and biblical interpretation in Africa. At a grassroots level ordinary Christians express their faith and read the bible in ways reflecting their daily situation; at an academic level, theologians and biblical scholars relate the historical traditions and sources of Christianity to the socio- and religio-cultural context of Africa. In response to this, the Bible and Theology in Africa series aims at making African theology and biblical interpretation its subject as well as object, as the concerns of African theologians and biblical interpreters will be voiced and critically analyzed. Both Africans and Western authors are encouraged to consider this series.

Inquiries and manuscripts should be directed to:

>Associate Professor Knut Holter
>School of Mission and Theology
>Misjonsvegen 34
>N-4024 Stavanger
>Norway
>*e-mail*: knut.holter@mhs.no

To order other books in this series, please contact our Customer Service Department:

>(800) 770-LANG (within the U.S.)
>(212) 647-7706 (outside the U.S.)
>(212) 647-7707 FAX

Or browse online by series:

>www.peterlang.com